MY DESCENT
FROM
Colonel William Randolph
OF VIRGINIA

CHARLES   MONCURE   FRANCES   NATHALIE
my mother, m. Algernon Sydney Biddle

FRANCIS BIDDLE (1886-)   SYDNEY GEOFFREY BIDDLE (1889-1954)
m. Katherine Garrison Chapin

EDMUND RANDOLPH BIDDLE (1921-)   GARRISON CHAPIN BIDDLE
m. Frances Disner   (1923-1930)

STEPHEN GARRISON BIDDLE (1952-)   DANIEL ROBINSON BIDDLE
(1953-)

❧ IN BRIEF
AUTHORITY

❧ IN BRIEF AUTHORITY

Francis Biddle

Doubleday & Company, Inc.
Garden City, New York

To the memory of
Franklin Delano Roosevelt

Give therefore thy servant an understanding
heart to judge thy people, that I may discern
between good and bad; for who is able to judge
this thy so great a people.

I Kings 3:9

340.092
B584

CONTENTS

Book Four THE NÜRNBERG TRIAL

But man, proud man,
Drest in a little brief authority,
Most ignorant of what he's most assured,
His glassy essence, like an angry ape,
Plays such fantastic tricks before high heaven
As make the angels weep.

MEASURE FOR MEASURE
Act II, scene ii.

ACKNOWLEDGMENTS

Again I record my gratitude to Bernice Kenyon and my wife, Katherine Garrison Chapin, for helping me with the whole manuscript; and to James H. Rowe, Herbert Wechsler, Edward J. Ennis, Lloyd K. Garrison, Ugo Carusi, Telford Taylor, Thurman Arnold, James V. Bennett, Hugh Cox, Robert Marques, David E. Lilienthal, and Stetson Conn for reviewing and criticizing substantial parts of it.

MY SECOND VOLUME

In the first volume of my reminiscences, published last year by Doubleday & Company, Inc., I tried to bring alive some of the odd, lovable, and often eccentric individuals who peopled my background and youth—the Virginia Randolphs and Robinsons, on my mother's side; and the Biddles, on my father's; and a few of my teachers at Groton School and Harvard University. I described my year with Justice Oliver Wendell Holmes in Washington in 1911–12 when the Progressive movement was forming that would soon culminate in the nomination of Theodore Roosevelt for President. I ended with several chapters dealing with my law practice in Philadelphia. The political and public world that I was about to know would be based on more stimulating relationships and more human values. I added that I would find it a deeply satisfying way of life.

But not all of my readers took the hint that another volume was to follow. A few looked forward to a second book, more were annoyed that I was apparently avoiding my New Deal adventures, and one reviewer remarked indignantly that in a biographical book by a man who held high office in an epochal period like the New Deal and knew everybody of importance in such a period, one would expect observations and reflections of historical significance. Whether my observations will have historical value I do not know, but perhaps they can serve as footnotes on the history of those fermenting years. I have tried to keep the characters in this other half of my career in the same human scale as those who inhabited *A Casual Past*. Much of the public work which I describe was in association with Franklin Roosevelt. He appointed me Chairman of the Labor Board, a judge on the bench of the Third Circuit, Solicitor General, and, finally, Attorney General.

Not wishing to perpetuate the Roosevelt myth, from which he sometimes is transformed into a superman, I have tried to see him as he was—an intensely human man, with his faults as well as his strength. This was no easy task, to be objective about a man whom I loved and admired, although we were friendly rather than intimate. As I thought about him and remembered our association I came to believe that the central quality of his leadership was that he gave the people a vision of what their country could be, of what their government could mean to them. They realized that life might be adventurous as well as secure; and others throughout the world caught the same faith. That was the effect he had on a whole generation.

THE LABOR BOARD, THE TENNESSEE VALLEY AUTHORITY INVESTI- GATION, THE CIRCUIT COURT OF APPEALS

❧ *Book One*

*Who will change old lamps for new
ones? . . . new lamps for old ones.*

ARABIAN NIGHTS

THE LABOR BOARD
—TRYING
TO ENFORCE THE LAW
(1934–1935)

❧ ❧ Chapter One

I have never felt that life was preordained, that I was "destined" to take part in public work, or destined to do anything in particular. In the autumn of 1934, when I had my first taste of the New Deal in a fairly important job, I was forty-eight, a successful lawyer engaged in trial work and corporate practice in Philadelphia, making substantially more money than I spent (and thirty years ago one could still save), with three partners with whom I was congenial, a wife whom I loved, and a fifteen-year-old son who had been named after Edmund Randolph, my mother's great-grandfather, the first Attorney General of the United States. My boy was at Millbrook School, a boarding school in a rolling hunting country in Dutchess County, New York. I was not fond of Philadelphia—this was fifteen years before Joseph S. Clark, now the Democratic senator from Pennsylvania, Richard Dilworth, later mayor of Philadelphia, Edmund N. Bacon, the executive director of the City Planning Commission, and many others, whose imaginations had been stirred and whose wills were persistent, had been able to breathe new life into the city, so long "corrupt and contented," and to bring about a renaissance that is still in flower.

When I went to Washington to work with Franklin Roosevelt I had not very much altered my view of him, gleaned during the 1932 campaign. The miraculous "hundred days" of his first year had impressed me; but somehow I had not yet been drawn into his camp. Once before, in the disillusioning adventure of Theodore Roosevelt's Progressive Party, I had had my fingers scorched; and I wanted to be doubly sure next time that this was my game, even if a side show. I suppose the unconscious tug toward public work set up a conscious pull in the other direction—I would not admit to myself that I should like to be a part of the new movement because my experience warned me against embracing too easily another such enthusiasm. Since my first few years of practice in Philadelphia I had not touched the political world. But I was growing a little restive.

Also the schoolboy relationship to F.D.R. persisted . . . I had been a shy new boy at Groton, thirty years before, when he was a sixth former, a magnificent but distant deity, whose splendor added to my shyness. In some hidden depth of me that early link, undefined yet unbroken, existed below the normal external successes which had, rather late, brought me to maturity; and I was still faintly conscious of it as I came to know him well during my various adventures in Washington. That he was aware of it was a mark of that subtle sense of relationships which gave him understanding of men—I doubt whether he had the same understanding of women—coupled with so sure an instinct of how to frame his particular purpose within the outline of a human equation. All this sounds as if he was calculating and a little inhuman. I do not at all mean that. The man was far too complex for such easy characterization, too complex indeed for denying that carefully balanced calculations did very often enter into the picture. There was another, simpler explanation of this intuitive grasp of a man's weaknesses. He loved to tease you. It was a show of affection, or sometimes a way of seducing a senator who was against what F.D.R. for the moment sought by this sharing of intimacy which could be so flattering. It was not devoid of cruelty. And part of the man's refreshing difference from all the rest of us was an edged and acid weapon, never far from his hand, though sparingly used. The providence he so firmly believed in, *his* Providence, has given him this defense against even intimate friends, and particularly against the men he had to see constantly. He could use it to block bores, and to save him from the horrible *ennui* of the impersonal life of politics. He was a Christian, but an Old Testament Christian, who believed, like Jehovah, that his friends should be rewarded and retribution visited on his enemies, for, like most great statesmen, once his will was marshaled behind a defined and felt vision it became sinful for others to interfere with its fruition.

However genial his teasing, it was often, when he felt in that particular mood, pointed with a prick of torment, and went to the essence of a man, pierced him between the ribs into the heart of his weakness, which might be an unreasonable affection for his chief, as it was in the case of Harold Ickes. Never come too close to a prince, says Machiavelli—and some sense of that more appropriate relationship guided me. I admired him enormously. Often I felt he was my friend. But I believed that if we came too close I might suffer from his capacity to wound those who loved him. Occasionally he could not resist yielding to such an impulse when he knew that the other was emotionally defenseless. And in the subsequent years in Washington I saw him wound members of his entourage who were more sensitive or had allowed themselves to become more personally involved than I. What an attraction the man had for the innocent and loving flies that walked about that intricate web!

Henry Morgenthau, for instance, was probably more consistently devoted than the rest of us to his chief and to the philosophy of the New Deal—if the pragmatic steps to bring into balance conflicting powers which had got greatly out of balance can be gathered under the loose description of such a phrase. But while Morgenthau was more devoted, more loyal, and more all-out than the other members of the Cabinet, those qualities did not prevent his chief from pricking him occasionally at a Cabinet meeting into a mute unhappiness which his lack of humor was powerless to conceal. The President was fond of the Secretary of the Treasury and appreciated his courage and capacity to surround himself with men of ability without regard to political consequences, in a world in which political consequences were his chief's primary consideration, as they had to be if he was to achieve something of his purposes. The President never over-looked the value of any quality which might bring strength to his vital center. But there was a limit to balancing one consider-ation by another, just as there was a limit to a selfless devotion that sometimes became a bore. One had to dissipate the irri-tation—the mild irritation—by stroking Henry's fur the wrong way in public now and then. There was no fun teasing a man in private.

The President responded to charm. I remember his speaking more than once of the impression made on him by Jack Kelly, Grace's father—his physical beauty, his straightness and hardness, the clean balance of his square shoulders and lean thighs, the erect beauty of a great athlete. Archibald MacLeish represented charm of a different sort—the grace and ease of his way of moving, something luminous about his youthfulness, a quick responsive-ness if he liked you. And he liked the President very much. But he was without defenses, had not learned the discomfort of too great intimacy with a prince. A nod from the lord—as the an-cient proverb goes—is the breakfast of a fool. Archie was as alertly sensitive to praise—or absence of it—as he was to criti-cism. So that when the President "discovered" him and for a brief period asked him constantly to the White House, and as suddenly dropped him out of an atmosphere that was rare and inhabited by few—by no other for the brief moment of its exaltation— Archie was profoundly hurt, as his friends could tell not so much by what he hinted as by a look about the jaw as if to say he could take anything.

One must not underscore a single characteristic. The President was not one-sided. Like most great men he was full of contra-dictions. If he could hurt his friends he also went out of his way to help them, even if he made little distinction between friends and men to whom he owed some political debt, often very moderate, sometimes more fancied than real. He hated to hurt people except when the temptation to "tease" was too strong, but he was not conscious of hurting them when they stood in the actual relationship of friends. F.D.R. was himself strong-willed.

He had got on top of life. Nothing could touch him. He did not worry—a quality which made the people count on him, for he took the burdens of worry from their narrower backs, and adjusted them with a grin.

I think that if he had read this page he would have called it nonsense. Hurt Henry Morgenthau, Archie MacLeish, Tom Corcoran—ah! but Tom was different, he would have added thoughtfully, grinding the cigarette stub in an ash tray as he thought about Tom, that was a different story. Archie? He was sorry if he had ever hurt him. He didn't believe he had. He had never thought about it . . . the President distrusted intellectual subtleties. Himself infinitely subtle in understanding people, he believed that brain-trusters should be kept in their place. A look at the clouds was all right, it reminded us that the sky was there. But you must live firmly planted on the earth.

He sometimes teased me, and I liked it. When Madame Chiang Kai-Shek was in Washington in 1943, he asked a few of us to meet her. She sat on a sofa, next to him, while we trooped by, pausing for a moment to sit down facing them. She was very tired. And it could not have been much fun to go through the meaningless little gestures of official politeness. "I was a sixth former at school," said the President as he introduced me, "when the Attorney General was a second former." He looked at me. "He hasn't forgotten it," he added, and he smiled, with a little tightening of the lips, to make sure that I should get the point of reference.

My appointment as chairman of the National Labor Relations Board was in no sense "personal." Nor was it political. I had not at that time been active in Democratic politics, had not registered as a Democrat until 1932, although I had voted for Al Smith and done some work in his support in 1928. Lloyd K. Garrison was resigning as chairman of the Board. He suggested to the President and to Frances Perkins, the Secretary of Labor, that I should succeed him. Miss Perkins liked the idea chiefly because I was "respectable." Our firm represented solid interests, and the country would have a feeling that the appointment was that of a man who had dealt with the practical affairs of business, an experience generally believed to make him "safe," particularly in a position where the diverging conflict between labor and industry was at white heat. Doubtless, for the same consideration, William Green, president of the American Federation of Labor, mildly opposed the appointment.

But I doubt whether I would have been considered had not Garrison thought of me as the result of one of those chance meetings which so affect the course of one's life. It was the beginning of my public career.

For four years we had rented a summer house at Black Point, near New London. I saw Garrison there occasionally. And when, after two years at Fisher's Island, we went back to spend a night with Mr. Harry Platt at Black Point, I saw him again. We lay on the sand for nearly an hour before swimming—it must have been in August—and he told me about the Labor Board and its problems. I was at once interested. I had been vaguely intrigued by the New Deal during those first eighteen months of its existence, but had not seen any of its aspects at first hand. Lloyd must have talked well, for I can still remember my excitement as I asked him questions. This was something new. He had been pioneering in a field where there was little experience and no body of clearly developed doctrine to guide him. The fight was on not only for recognition of the function of organized labor but also for its role in American society. Soon afterward Lloyd wrote to the President recommending me to take his place, and sent me a copy of the letter. Mr. Platt, who was Boss (Senator) Platt's son, an amusing, benign, dyed-in-the-wool Republican, gave us a cocktail party at which Lloyd turned up, and later insisted with a chuckle that pretended to be sardonic that the horrid plot had been hatched in his respectable house!

My law firm in Philadelphia, particularly Jack Barnes, the senior, to whom I was devoted, were uncompromisingly opposed to my accepting. The Railroad (there was but one railroad to Pennsylvanians) liked my work. I was bound to lose clients if I deserted their interests for such a doubtful cause, even if it turned out that I expressed, or at least respected, their points of view in my official pronouncements. What was it all about anyway? What was I to do? My answers were a bit vague, even after my talk with Lloyd and a visit to Washington to look over the field. The few friends to whom I talked shared in general the point of view of the members of my firm. There was one exception.

Roland Morris had taken an active part in Democratic politics. With Vance McCormick and Mitchell Palmer, before the latter had become notorious for the alien raids in 1920 when he was Attorney General, he had reorganized and liberalized the Democratic party in Pennsylvania. He served as President Wilson's ambassador to Japan from 1917 to 1921. He was progressive for his day.

He heard me patiently—it was natural that I should overemphasize the argument against my going—then urged me to go if I were tempted; it could not possibly hurt my practice, it would bring me new clients, it would add growth and experience, which would some day prove invaluable. He had been through the same choice, had listened to the same arguments, and had left his city, and come back and prospered.

Charles Wyzanski, who later was appointed to the U. S. District Court of Massachusetts on my recommendation when I was Attorney General, was counsel for the Labor Department, and Miss Perkins deputized him to talk to me. I suppose this was more or less *pro forma;* but it was essential from their point of view that the new chairman should agree with the Board's interpretation of the principle of majority rule, which had lately been formulated with care and precision, and about which violently differing positions were already developing. Section 7-a of the National Recovery Act, under which the Board was functioning, had been held by the Board to require that where a majority of employees chose a union to represent it the company must bargain exclusively with that union as representing *all* the employees. This was the chief issue around which the future battles would revolve, both within and without the administration, and the clans were gathering, each side grimly determined to put teeth in the enforcement of the rights of the laboring man, or to extract them, depending on the point of view.

Even before I was sworn in about the middle of November, 1934, I became conscious of the impending conflicts. Knowing no one in Washington, I called on my old friend Morris Llewellyn Cooke, who was living in a sunny apartment in the Hay Adams

House looking across Lafayette Square to the White House. Cooke had had his cake and had eaten it (an adventure that made me turn to him to find out how that feat could be managed), had represented the great corporations as one of the leading consulting engineers of the country, but had served even more often the public, a breadth of viewpoint which made him suspect to many private clients. He was American to the core—friendly, generous, idealistic; sensitively receptive to new ideas, and therefore unusually effective in getting them started, more effective there than as an administrator. Cooke was one of the leaders of the successful revolt against the Republican machine in Philadelphia in 1911, and Mayor Blankenberg appointed him director of Public Works. Just now he was director of the water resources section of the National Resources Board.

"What is the first thing I do?" I asked him.

I think he half expected my visit. He was close to many labor leaders, and knew what was brewing.

"Before you do anything else, talk to the three newspaper correspondents who know more about labor problems, particularly the way those problems are developing at this moment, than anyone else in town: Louis Stark, of the New York *Times;* Paul Ward, of the Baltimore *Sun;* Bob Allen, of the Philadelphia *Record.* Ask them to stand by you, and to let you know what's going on. They'll keep you straight."

I talked to each of them within the next few days. All three were liberal, as most newspaper reporters are. Louis Stark was born in Hungary, had begun teaching at the public schools in New York, was older than the other two, more of a specialist in the labor field, cautious and wise, overtired usually, like so many men in his profession, not passionate or extreme like the two younger men. He was awarded the Pulitzer prize for journalism in 1942.

Bob Allen, whom I did not then know well but with whom I later became intimate, was without fear of anyone on earth, picturesquely profane, tending to think that what he didn't agree with was "baloney"; a man who loved a fight for the sake of a fight—moral, intellectual, or physical. Once I asked Ruth Finney, his clever, modest wife, who for years has been on the Scripps-Howard *Washington News,* why she married Bob. She was interested, knitting her brows over the question. "I think," she finally answered as if she had been making a discovery, "because of his lovely exaggerations." I knew exactly what she meant. Bob was tough, American tough, and extreme; Bob was the American West, not yet gone, with its undefined and undefinable immensities; he was the American weather, with its absurd and explosive changes; he shared the American dislike of subtleties, which never interfered, however, with his shrewd appraisals.

Paul Ward, like Bob, took his politics seriously. But he was more suspicious, more *farouche*. Where Bob expressed his dislike and contempt of other men in language which convinced one that this undiscovered world was peopled by strange and scabrous monsters passing as human beings, Paul really hated. At that time he was particularly down on Frances Perkins, and suffered from the frustration of so many flaming young liberals whose disappointment with the New Deal had already begun to show. They could not be patient; they wanted instant action; they would not admit that compromises on "matters of principle" were necessary to President Roosevelt's leadership. If he would only rely on the people, they said, but did not seem to realize that reliance on the people was an emergency measure— F.D.R. knew that—to be used sparingly. It did not solve everyday situations. The people came in every four years. But in-between it was the leaders of the people who counted, the industrialists, the labor leaders, the newspaper publishers, and particularly the congressmen, so often touchy and provincial, so adept at blocking and slowing, so quick to jealousy, and yet so effective when they lined up on your side! So Paul Ward wrote of the "hope-sodden liberals," seeking to bolster their dwindling faith in the New Deal; suspected it of being fascist (in the labor field); found that Miss Perkins with her "ramrod back," her almost pathological abhorrence of publicity, and her "middle-class mind," could talk endlessly with professors and social workers about the "inevitability of gradualism"; but had little to say in the policy decisions shaped by the President himself in the application of his "Boy Scout technique" to the class struggle. Miss Perkins held her ground and did her job, and carried out what she believed the President wanted, selflessly, courageously, and loyally.

I was to go to Washington on a Monday to see the Secretary
and be sworn in. On the preceding Saturday I got a telegram
from Harry Millis and Ed Smith, the two other members of the
Board, asking me to be sure to talk to them first. They were very
disturbed, were ready to resign—a suggestion not very encourag-
ing to a new chairman just as he was taking over. Had I seen the
order appointing me? I had not. The second section, they told
me, stripped me of the power of appointment and of budget
control, and placed the Board under the Secretary of Labor.
Hitherto the Board had been independent, and Millis and Smith
were fiercely jealous of their freedom, which Garrison had been
able to sustain in spite of occasional differences between him
and the Secretary.

Miss Perkins talked to me for half an hour when I called on
her the next day, a copy of the order in my pocket, before asking
me whether I was ready to be sworn in? I was not, I told her,
producing the order. There had evidently been a misunderstanding. Lloyd Garrison, telling me about my work, has assured
me that part of its attraction was that I should run my own
show, reporting to no one but the President, working of course
in close co-operation with her—a co-operation from which he had
greatly profited—but that I should in fact be my own master in
matters of policy and personnel. I was sorry. I had come assum-
ing that such would be the case. Since it was not the case I
could not accept the appointment. I stood up and held out my
hand.

Miss Perkins, taken by surprise, was angry. I couldn't do that,
she said, the appointment had been given wide publicity. I
must not do that to the President . . . I was sorry, I had not
been shown the order, and up until now the Labor Board had
been independent. She was vexed, but saw I was determined,
and believed that I would go home, which I was determined to
do. The only thing was to take the matter up with the President,
who had already signed the order, which had not, however,
been entered in the Congressional Register. What made it
awkward was that the President was cruising in the Caribbean.
The Secretary managed to reach him on the telephone.

The "compromise" that was finally arranged was that all my
appointments were to be submitted to Miss Perkins for her con-

sideration, but that I was to have the final say—there was to be no veto. Nor was there to be any interference with budget or policy, although I do not think that the Secretary cared much for anything except the appointments. The budget was pretty well fixed by our limited needs, and there was no question of policy for a quasi-judicial body set up to arbitrate and, arbitration failing, to decide cases. But appointments, although there were few, did count. For instance I had received from the Labor Department a colorless public relations man, appointed by the Secretary, who was convinced that in this instance, as in most, the least publicity was the best. I soon replaced him by Malcolm Ross, who knew the field, knew something of the art of congressional relationships, and could find his way about Washington. Miss Perkins was against him; but there was no veto.

Mike Ross—as he was everywhere affectionately called—had the kind of richly colorful temperament which, aside from anything more specific, might have accounted for the instinctive recoil of Miss Perkins' cautious New England temperament. After serving in the Air Service in the First World War he had been a reporter for the Dallas *News,* the Louisville *Courier-Journal,* and the New York *Morning World*—and had gathered no moss in the process. He was six feet two, with curly brown hair seldom cut, and the face of a Mantegna. Women found him agreeably difficult to resist. He put the shyest child immediately at ease, and touched the exact spot in the range of his humor. He was a Renaissance man, talented in many fields: he wrote fluently and freshly—he had published three novels and two other books before I knew him—he cooked with taste and dash, and sang a great variety of ballads to the guitar, including those which he composed about the New Deal.

Frances Perkins and I talked to the President when he came back, but there was no change in the arrangement, an arrangement which was typical of his skill in holding together the organization of administration, keeping conflicts below the surface, even when they were not settled and at times erupted again to trouble the apparently smooth surface. That after all was one way of exercising his own ultimate control. Throughout that year in Washington I was to have constant evidence of this basic genius for compromise, so typically characteristic of Amer-

ican political leadership as displayed by such Presidents as
Lincoln and Franklin Roosevelt. This particular compromise was
an abandonment of principle, which the Secretary had on her
side. She argued persuasively to the President, who kept nodding
as he listened to her with his usual patience. He was rarely
impatient with Miss Perkins, of whom he was very fond. The
pattern of the New Deal, she insisted, was spreading irresponsibility over the earth, with no co-ordination or shape. Proper
organization meant lines of responsibility running up and down,
not sideways. If the Board reported directly to the President it
would mean that it would in fact be responsible to no one; or,
worse yet, he would have another burden, comparatively unimportant, on his overburdened back, a responsibility the intricacies of which, she hinted, he knew little about and cared
for not much more so long as there was sufficient peace to allow
due progress for the flight of the Blue Eagle under the National
Recovery Act.

I said nothing more about going home, which would merely
have irritated him, although I was determined not to serve unless
I had a free hand. I knew already that it was too new and
difficult a task for us to be tied down by the traditional routine of
an established department. I suggested to the President that the
Board could be given status as a quasi-judicial body only if it
were independent. We had been working together for several
weeks under this loose arrangement—why not try it a little
longer, he said. He hated to make sharp decisions between conflicting claims for power among his subordinates, and usually
decided them like an arbitration: each side should have a slice.
Now run away, both of you, and be happy, and don't bother
me any more. . . .

So the loose arrangement went along, confirmed by an exchange of letters, and the Secretary opposed many of the few
appointments I made, but it was never suggested that we should
go back to the President. Other members of the Cabinet might
have appealed to him, probably separately, each insisting on his
"rights," arguing that the particular exercise of power came "nat-
urally" under *his* jurisdiction—Harold Ickes and Henry Wallace
for instance, fighting violently over whether the public grazing
lands should belong to the Interior or to Agriculture, Harold with

sharper tools, Henry with an impenetrable armor of obstinate righteousness. But Miss Perkins loved her old friend Franklin Roosevelt, and was loyal to him not only in act and word, but in the whole purpose and each part of her work; loyal in her heart as well as her mind, in the selflessness of her being, behind the clear-eyed view she had of him, far clearer than most of us; so that when Paul Ward suggested that her motto was "see what the boss in the back room will have," he was right, though the implication was twisted, for she stood up to the boss, but *inside* the circle of his policies. It is so easy to destroy a policy, to inhibit it on the second level, the operating level, just below policy, but the level on which, in practice, policy is defined and created over the long run.

I was amused, occasionally flattered, and more often irritated by the newspaper comments on my appointment, background, and appearance. For years I had felt handicapped under their insistence that all Biddles were wealthy society playboys, with an exciting, adventurous, and not unimportant past, but apparently a pretty thin present and rather mild future.

The Daily Worker assured its readers that I was a member of the family "dominating J. P. Morgan's Philadelphia affiliate." The affiliate was of course Drexel & Co., and the "domination" was based on the fact that some fifty years before, Edward Biddle, Major "Tony" Biddle's father, had married a daughter of Mr. George W. Childs Drexel. His father-in-law gave the young man an opportunity to work in the great banking firm. After two or three years—so the story ran—Edward had a falling-out with another young clerk, Edward T. Stotesbury, and announced to his father-in-law that one of them would have to leave the firm. "I guess it will have to be you, Edward," Mr. Drexel replied, and Edward accordingly departed, and never again ventured into any occupation which yielded him financial reward. He became a gentlemanly expert on the Biddle family history, and on eighteenth-century American portraiture, writing occasionally a brochure on some little-known or altogether forgotten painter in a journal devoted to that subject; a not unpleasant if slightly pedantic and innocently snobbish old boy when I knew him, with carefully trimmed side whiskers, living with pretty decent chairs and silver around him in West Philadelphia in respectable but not extreme reduction of circumstances; playing tennis when he was over seventy; kindly, cautious, never having outgrown the adolescent pride of the clerk whom Stotesbury had once offended. His first wife died when the children were small, and they were brought up by the Drexels, and inherited substantial fortunes, and moved among the smartest and the richest, playboys and athletes, devoting themselves exclusively and happily to the social game, eschewing business, making the headlines—so that the Biddles, generically speaking, who up until then had been generally and accurately regarded as hard-working if slightly unimaginative professional and business men, recently Quakers, now became the symbols of the successful leisure class.

It was suggested that the wealthy young Biddle who would preside over the destinies of labor would bring to his task the same kind of background as the President's. His father, a teacher and artist, had gone to live in Paris. He was descended said the Omaha *Bee News* from "that suave old Nicholas Biddle who stood at the head of the United States Bank when Andrew Jackson humbled it to the dust, and who went down to oblivion with it." I was not "wealthy"—my father was not an artist and never lived in Paris, nor was I descended from Nicholas Biddle.

There was apt to be a note of malevolence in the attacks on New Dealers and liberals in general, as if there were something inherently shameful about being a liberal, even before Fulton Lewis, Jr., and George Sokolsky, and Westbrook Pegler. Liberals were referred to as "so-called liberals," as if the true spirit of liberalism resided in those who were invariably opposed to the rather moderate reforms they were advocating. I never heard any allusion to "so-called conservatives"—I wonder why. Liberals were disliked from one approach because they were amateurs and professors, eggheads more recently; from another because they had seized power and were conspiring to turn America into a socialized society, regimented and enslaved. One would have thought that the wide and often bitter difference in outlook among New Dealers themselves, so eagerly seized upon by the gentlemen of the press, might have contradicted the conspiratorial theory.

I find in my scrapbook an example of this muffled repugnance to "liberalism," the word dipped in quotation marks to show that not true liberalism but the pseudo, modern kind was meant. The *Awakener* said: "It is possible that contact with the hard realities of the labor struggle will soon soften Mr. Biddle's present asperities. Such disillusionment usually comes when enchanting theory hurls itself against the hopeless irrationalities of social life. But for the present Mr. Biddle is still in the land of his abstractions. He will make furious debating gestures against the oppressive master class. He will arouse eager and impossible hopes in an organized labor movement which dreams of itself as the destined ruler of America. And then, after a few months of fits and starts he will return to Philadelphia, as Garrison has returned to Madison, wiser in the knowledge that 'Liberalism' may win an argument in the Philadelphia Foreign Policy Association, but that it cannot make the lion of our industrial system lie down together in an AF of L closed shop." Rather neat. But I wish that he had been more specific about which was the lion, and which the wolf.

George Creel, writing in Washington for *Collier's Weekly,* and I became friends; and how much that relationship tends to modify an objective approach! Not that Creel ever was objective. He was well-disposed to our work, and often came to see me to find out what was going on. He had been in charge of propaganda as chairman of the Committee on Public Information (his account, *How We Advertised America,* bore a more accurate title), during the First World War. President Wilson, when Creel first called on him, said, "Mr. Creel, when a man comes to Washington, one of two things happens to him. He either grows or swells. I hope you will grow."

Creel had recently been badly defeated in the Democratic primary for governor by Upton Sinclair, with his End Poverty in California League. He was strange-looking, his teeth suggesting fangs, strong, slightly twisted hands, a not unpleasant violence of expression, a power of droll and telling mimicry, and a flair for shrewd journalism. He wrote an article in *Collier's* at about that time called "Team-Play," dealing with the "team" around F.D.R. There were twelve of us. Of Secretary Perkins, Creel

said that she was "trained in a school that regards the home as a
subject for social study rather than habitation." Donald Richberg,
once a lawyer for the railroad brotherhoods, was now anathema
to labor by reason of his stand on the automobile code. About
me he wrote: "Lean, youngish, precise, a Harvard man and bred
in the purple, but a valiant and unchanging champion of the
rights of the worker." Jesse Jones was "a lumber man and banker
originally, smelling money even when the wind was against
him." This view of Jones I came to share when, seven years
later, I knew him in the President's cabinet.

Creel's publisher, William Ludlow Chenery, editor of *Collier's*,
gave a stag luncheon at the Mayflower Hotel in honor of H. G.
Wells, who was interested in the New Deal and doing a piece
on it for the magazine. There were about a dozen of us. Creel,
who was in charge of the arrangements, and was fond of good
food and good wine, had ordered carefully, and the menu included an excellent Liebfraumilch, which had slept untouched
through fifteen dreary years of Prohibition. I remember that
Henry Wallace, who sat next to me, turned his glass down with
a gesture that irritated me. Over coffee and cigars, Chenery
suggested that Mr. Wells would like to hear our points of view
about this interesting new experiment. . . . We looked solemnly and silently at each other. Finally Wells broke the ice.
What were we doing about the trusts, the giant corporations,
monopoly? Were we for the big boys or the little fellows? Again
we glanced doubtfully around. Arthur Morgan, the recently appointed chairman of the Tennessee Valley Authority, took it on
himself to answer, with a tone that suggested by its rounded
seriousness that the question had been a little flippant: America,
Mr. Wells, was a democracy—growing, experimental, with room
for everyone to live, with space for competing ideas, where both
the big and the little had a chance. . . . We looked at Wells. "I
see," he piped in that queer, shrill, emasculated voice. "I see.
Muddling along, just like us! . . . I have heard that in the visitors'
book of the Tavern Club of Boston there appear these two signa-
tures, with the following observations:

Jack London   I'm all for the Revolution!
H. G. Wells   There ain't going to be none.

I liked the other two members of the Board, particularly Dr. Harry A. Millis, who was on leave of absence as chairman of the department of economics of the University of Chicago. He was cautious, thoughtful, patient; profoundly conscious of the injustices that had been done labor's attempt to organize, although at the same time aware of the dangerous weaknesses in a good deal of labor leadership: not only the racketeering and the feather-bedding, but the lack of imagination, the insistence on improved wages and hours as the sole end, the petty jurisdictional jealousies and squabbles. He had not only a theoretic knowledge of our problems, but, what was far more important, a long and varied experience in arbitration work. He was fair, honest, and objective. During the eight months that I was on the Board he educated me in the background and history of the labor movement, and made me realize the changes that were taking place in its present evolution. We would always have bitter and violent strikes as long as management resisted the right of workmen to organize, and refused to deal with unions. It was a fight necessary for union survival, and inevitably developed labor leaders chosen for their capacity to use tooth and claw, and often little else. Few Sidney Hillmans grew out of the industrial jungle. The system produced men who were not affected by economic arguments and pressures, and would listen to them without consideration of the employer's loss or gain. If the employer, with a hand around the union's throat, insisted that the union take it or leave it, strikes or lockouts followed as the only means of deciding the question. Such training didn't breed gentlemen with kid gloves in either camp. And if management hired thugs disguised as deputy sheriffs, the strikers could not be expected to sit by and obey antistrike injunctions, but were more prone to turn over automobiles, or beat up the scabs, or use a stick of dynamite now and then in the coal-mine wars.

No, without the recognition of organized labor there was no good talking about collective bargaining, Millis continued. Of course collective bargaining was not in the free tradition of Ernest T. Weir, of the Weirton Steel Co. His economic theology forbade you to interfere with the sacrosanct workings of supply and demand, a providential as well as natural law. True supply and demand would have meant hiring the workman as cheaply as you could get him—there was usually a substantial supply of workmen, so you got them pretty cheaply, particularly before the wide-open immigration policy was modified in 1924, when the supply of good, cheap, raw, unorganized labor was cut down. And, continued Millis, collective bargaining tends, if you look at it fairly, to interfere with competition, as its results are not based on demand and supply in the market, but on a balance of power, on what the union will take as well as on your competitor's costs, on many imponderables, hardly economic, largely psychological. But, he would add, many other generally accepted phenomena in the free economy are anticompetitive, and check and interfere with competitive forces, such as the rigidity that comes from underwriting indebtedness by long-term bond issues instead of by getting your money by issuing stock, a method far more flexible than freezing your costs—in this case cost of money, but no different from cost of labor—for thirty, for sixty years ahead, irrespective of changing and often suddenly fluctuating prices. If you want proof, look at railroad financing over the past fifty years. Practically every railroad has been through the wringer, often two or three times; and that is not altogether accounted for by the antics of the railroad gamblers.

Thus he would talk, with his feet up on his desk, puffing away at his pipe; an endless worker, doing a lot of dull reading of reports and statistics and articles, with a certain dour satisfaction that to get anywhere you had to drudge; wise, cheerful, courteous; old-fashioned, correct, a little formal in personal relationships—it was almost always "Biddle" and Millis"; serene enough if he could have the feeling of too much work—and play nine holes of golf every other week.

The other member of the Board, Edwin S. Smith, was very different in outlook and temperament. Bred in the bone New England, he had a hard gizzard of obstinacy, touched with an unwavering fanaticism, not the fanaticism which Santayana once defined as redoubling your effort when you had forgotten your aim, but a kind that enlarged its aim as means opened new vistas; kindly, but seeing more of the evil than good in the society which had constituted his particular experience; dissenting constantly in spirit with the judgment of the other two members of the Board, even if he dissented on paper only on rare occasions—his "mission" to change and alter society, a conscious and steadily held effort, a vision which explained his thinking in terms of the mass rather than of the individual. Smith had been employment manager of William Filene Sons Co. in Boston, and for three years had been commissioner of Labor and Industries in Massachusetts, so that he came trained in the field in which we were dealing. The chairman, indeed, was the only member of the Board who could lay no claim to any technical competence or experience in labor relations.

As I look back, writing twenty-five years after the events, the little strip of history that I saw unfold during those brief months is framed for me now in the faded mood of a play that had seemed very stirring and dramatic when first seen, but when revived, dated. The dramatic element in Washington in 1934 lay in the struggle between men who wielded power not only to hold and to increase their influence, but to achieve ends in which they believed. These ends would shape the future of American life. Our consciousness of that fact cast the players in moral roles —or immoral ones—depending on whether you saw them from the admiring approval of your side, or scanned the indefensible activities of the other. The newspapers, as was their immemorial role, deepened and broadened the conflict, and apportioned virtue and guilt according to the views of their respective editors or publishers.

The issues were of ideas rather than of personalities. Public opinion was at the moment little interested in foreign affairs compared to domestic problems. Among the chief of these was the relation of industry to labor, and the bearing of that status on the recovery program. There were the long- and the short-term problems, the desirability of establishing large-scale collective bargaining, and, for a briefer view, the consideration that production would get ahead faster if you deferred such a very important decision a little longer, until businessmen got back on their feet again.

The short-term view was more pressing on the President than any temptation to take a longer look in determining just what should be done. He was bent on getting the economy once more in high gear, rather than on building a more permanently satisfactory society. He was not much interested in the problems of labor. His sympathies were directed toward concrete individuals, men and women whom he knew, talked to, heard about; and whose needs and aspirations and ways of life he could project to include a nation. He was concerned with human beings, not with humanity. He was not an economist, was not partial to any particular formula, but was troubled by human suffering and alive to human needs; optimistic and serene, experimental, yet cautious; determined to do something about it all.

The long-term problem of the particular segment of the economy with which I was dealing interested me more.

The National Recovery Act was one of the less fortunate efforts of the Roosevelt administration to stimulate production and end the disheartening depression that had settled on the country before the President was inaugurated, and lingered on through most of the 1930s. The act, adopted in the spring of 1933, sought reform as well as recovery in industry. The reform was directed at the elimination of child labor and the establishment of a minimum wage (forty cents an hour). Recovery, it was hoped, would spring from the abolition of "unfair" trade practices—i.e. slashing prices—and the adoption of "fair rules" that would be promulgated and enforced by industry and labor under the benevolent eye of a government interested in everyone. But it was soon apparent that the lion and the lamb would not work together to achieve this desirable result. It was not the nature of the lion to forgo any profit with which he might feed his lean ribs, even temporarily, in order to allow the lamb a rise in wages. By the time I arrived in Washington it had become pretty evident that big business, which in the short run knew what it was about, would write its own codes, and choose the personnel who would administer them. This gigantic attempt to create an industrial self-government, based on a romantic trust in human nature, so typically American, shared apparently by a President whose faith was able to live beside his more realistic sense of how men in fact behaved, was deemed workable in these bad times, which, it was supposed, would draw men together. That the Congress and the country should have accepted so queer an adventure in unity bore evidence of the magic of his wand. He had done so much already in so short a time that

Americans were still breathless with the accomplishments of the "hundred days," and ready to accept new experiments. But by the time five hundred codes had been adopted in the first year, enforcement began to break down; small business distrusted and feared its fellow giants; labor and industry were openly in conflict; and the huge, complex, confused recovery mechanism was everywhere creaking at the joints, under "the cascading energies of the national administrator, General Hugh Johnson," to use a happy phrase of Morison and Commager.

Section 7-a of the National Recovery Act provided that employees should have "the right to organize and bargain collectively, through representatives of their own choosing," free from interference by employers. Shortly after it was adopted, the President, on August 5, 1933, appointed the National Labor Board, which preceded our Board, composed of representatives of industry and of labor, with Senator Robert F. Wagner of New York as impartial chairman.

When my appointment was announced I made clear my position on the highly controversial question of representation: where a majority of workmen chose a union to represent them that union was entitled to represent not only the men who had voted for it but *all* the workmen in the given plant or industry. Any other construction would have been unrealistic, although nothing in Section 7-a threw much light on the problem. This did not mean that any individual or group should be denied free access to the employer to discuss and settle grievances and complaints. But these were not matters for collective bargaining, which deals with wages and hours, and basic conditions of work. Such things must be identical through the plant. This was a highly practical consideration, which could not be solved on a theoretical and basically misleading plane of the "rights of the minority"—a plane upon which employers argued for the "rights" of men whom they did not represent and whose interests they liked to reduce to the manageable proportions of complacent company unions formed and dominated by management.

It was interesting to note the rapid growth, and brief vitality of this device to meet the threat of genuine collective bargaining. Company unions sprang up in steel, in rubber, in automobiles, in the great unorganized or partly organized industries, claiming that they fought for "freedom" against the new oppression. They were seldom supported by a majority of the employees; and when occasionally they succeeded in winning the majority support, it was almost invariably as the result of the aid or coercion of management. "I am tired of hearing theoretical arguments about the rights of the minority," wrote Lloyd Garrison. "I have never yet seen a case in which these arguments were advanced by a *bona fide* minority group genuinely concerned with negotiating a collective agreement applying to all." To recognize several bargaining units—several unions—would have been endlessly confusing, a set of different agreements in the same shop. This would have broken down collective bargaining altogether. If an employer, opposed to collective bargaining, could choose with whom he should bargain, he could play one group against another and bargain with none.

But this point of view was not shared by many influential members of the administration, particularly Donald R. Richberg, general counsel for the NRA; and I suspect that the President would have preferred "muddling along" if that had been possible, and thus avoiding a clean-cut decision. The day I was appointed I announced my belief in the majority-rule principle. Three days after I had been sworn in Richberg told a meeting of the Associated Grocery Manufacturers that it was a mistake to say that "representatives selected by a majority . . . must be accepted as the exclusive representative of all employees— The right of self-organization certainly included the right of each man to decide for himself with what man he desires to be associated." No one had ever been authorized to herd employees into a voting unit and compel them to select their representatives by a majority vote. He doubted whether, legally, anyone could be given such authority. This was an interpretation flatly in contradiction with the *Houde* case, and the often repeated views of Garrison. The battle was on, one of those fierce internecine struggles which, to the special joy of newspapermen in particular and the public generally, broke out so frequently in the undisciplined ranks of the New Deal.

I went immediately to see the Attorney General, Homer S. Cummings. Was the *Houde* case ready to take to court? Yes, he thought so, but of course he didn't know the details. Mr. Golden

Woolfolk Bell had been assigned to handle it. Would I see him? Mr. Bell, a day or two later, agreed it was at last ripe for action. He was cordial and friendly, as we walked out of his office in the Department and ran into a small group of reporters who had smelled a story and followed us. Paul Ward was there, the light of battle in his eye. Would the law be enforced? he demanded. I told him that the Department of Justice was going to take "speedy action." The reporters insisted on a flat commitment—they had heard this kind of talk before. "Speedy action," I repeated, "isn't that so, Mr. Bell?" He nodded, not altogether happily—no lawyer likes to face speedy action on anything.

The Attorney General filed a bill of complaint a week later, asking the court to direct the company to bargain collectively with the union that had been selected at an election by the employees. The forces of labor, who had been pushed around a good deal, hailed the announcement enthusiastically; and the forces on the other side girded their loins for further battle. After all, this was but the first round, and the court had not yet spoken. Finally the court spoke—the ruling of the board was illegal, unconstitutional, un-American, invalid. That of course was but a lesser tribunal, and the ultimate test was yet to come. But it was not to come in this particular case, and meanwhile a good many minor skirmishes and major conflicts occurred along the extensive line of struggle.

There were two methods of enforcing decisions of the Board, neither of which the Board itself could exercise. It could ask the National Recovery Board to remove the Blue Eagle—the mark of patriotic compliance—or, as in the *Houde* case, send the record to the Attorney General with the request that he file a bill in equity in a United States District Court praying for an injunction directing the employer to obey the order of the Board. But we could only request; and the Attorney General could always refuse to go into court on the ground that the case was not a strong one. The Department of Justice was, not unnaturally, cautious and slow to move. No statute authorized the procedure. If the District Court found for the employer, a reversal would be difficult to obtain, since an Appellate Court will not usually reverse a trial court on a finding of fact. The District judges were at that time for the most part conservative. They watched with skeptical and jaundiced eyes the vast jumble of executive orders, issued under this New Deal law. They noted the thin and ambiguous declaration of principle in Section 7-a. And they were usually disinclined to enjoin employers whose acts they instinctively approved.

If the attempt to enforce the law in the courts was burdened with difficulties, the alternative was hardly more inviting. Blue Eagles were given under the act to "good" employers, and withdrawn from "bad" ones—that is those who would not comply. But this manner of punishment was either totally ineffective, or destructively successful. If the firm held a government contract it was theoretically canceled after the Blue Eagle was removed. If its business was chiefly with the government, the employer ran the risk of being ruined; whereas a corporation without government orders was not affected. In several cases where large companies were concerned the government could not get along without them, and restored their eagle after removing it.

An interested spectator of these difficulties from the removed heights of the Supreme Court was Justice Benjamin Nathan Cardozo, who had been sitting for two years. He asked me to have tea with him in his chambers. Something I had said about him in some speech or paper touching on his detachment, and his unceasing sense of the flux and change of life, pleased him. We were alone. He said, almost as soon as I sat down: "Mr. Biddle, I envy you—developing, creating the common law of labor, case by case—while we spend at least a third of our time construing tax statutes, trying to guess what Congress meant— and then as like as not Congress amends the law, showing that it had not at all meant what we thought but something entirely different."

In an article about Cardozo, Judge Learned Hand observed that the wise man was the detached man. This wisdom of detachment gave Justice Cardozo's judgment an objectivity that was impersonal because it was pure. His face was without a trace of the sensual, as finely cut as an eighteenth-century cameo, under a shock of white hair, splendid burning eyes, more the look of a scholar than a saint, a blend of prophet and intellectual.

I saw him a few months later, March 8, 1935, walking with

the other justices of the Supreme Court behind the coffin of Mr. Justice Holmes, at All Soul's Church, the Unitarian Church in Washington at Sixteenth Street and Harvard Avenue, moving alone behind the six others, who went up the aisle two by two; bowed in his sorrow, a steady radiance about his face and head, his spirit brooding on the past, remembering how much the older man, whose place he had taken on the Court, had meant to him. I had a sense then of something of a god about him—old Whitman must have had that look. I felt at the time that Cardozo did not have long to live. He died in three years.

Our work in mediation deserves a word. That it was tied in with the more formal adjudication functions of the Board had advantages and drawbacks. Not being an enthusiastic proponent of the doctrine of complete separation of powers—legislative, judicial, administrative—I was less impressed by the theory that a *quasi* court should never drag its dignified robes in the rough and tumble of trading to reach some sort of acceptable compromise, than by the actual results which such a course of mixed activities brought about. Negotiation is a slow and time-consuming process, and time is of the essence where the question involved is the discharge of a workman and his demand that he be reinstated. Negotiation delays action, and is usually abandoned when formal rights are asserted. But of course there was nothing to prevent settling a case in the midst of the controversy, which often happened.

I remember one interesting adjustment. The clothing plant involved was not a large one, but because it was the opening wedge in unionizing some small Southern town, Sidney Hillman, president of the Amalgamated Clothing Workers of America, came down to the formal hearing before the Board. The evidence on each side was unusually acrimonious. By the mill owner we were told that a happy family of father and children, master and men, had been torn apart by lies and foul propaganda, erupting in occasional violence, caused by the onslaught of Yankee thugs on this little self-respecting Southern community. The union claimed that the employer had ruthlessly discharged every man who showed independence by asserting his inalienable right

to join a union of his own choosing. Recrimination and bitterness
zigzagged through the charged air.

Thus it stood when we were about to adjourn for lunch. Hillman (with the lawyer for the company, who expressed no objection) came forward to make a suggestion. Would we be willing to take a little longer for recess than usual, say two hours?
He thought he could settle the case. When we reconvened he
came up for a private word, looking pleased. It was all worked
out—the Amalgamated was to be recognized as the sole unit for
bargaining, the discharged employees reinstated with back pay,
the strike called off at once, they were members of a happy
family again. . . . When I asked him later how he had managed,
he told me that he had been studying the company's tax problems for some time, had seen ways of saving substantial federal
income taxes through certain structural reorganizations, a rather
complicated matter; and the president of the company, whom
Hillman had known when he was a Yiddish cutter on the East
Side years before, jumped at the suggestion. They didn't need
lawyers, they understood each other, they talked the same language.

Our mediation work was carried on by the twenty-four regional labor boards scattered through the country. Each local
board had a small staff, which investigated and passed on
complaints before they were brought to us by appeal. But outside
of this more formal work the regional board, through a panel of
industrialists and recognized labor spokesmen, with an "impartial" chairman who represented the public, settled an immense
number of cases, usually before they got into the strike state.
When it "settled" a case no formal charge was filed, and no
decision was rendered. The conferences were private and unre-
ported, no record was made, and an air of informality prevailed.
The problems were local, not national. The regional board determined no questions of policy or principle, and therefore
handed down no "precedents" to plague the future.

The Philadelphia board was the outstanding example of this
type of informal community work. Jacob Billikopf, its impartial
chairman, had dealt with labor problems most of his life. Born
in Wilna, Russia, and coming to America as a child, he had
lectured on sociology and economics, served as impartial chair-

man of the Men's Clothing Industry in New York City, and of the Ladies' Garment Industry in Philadelphia—this catalogue but hints at his manifold activities, which made his reminiscent talk sometimes tiresome. He got along with everyone, flattered and liked to be flattered, was not so much vain as eager for the approval which would never come to him fast enough. He was a devoted and effective community worker.

And he was able to persuade representatives of industry, among them Lessing J. Rosenwald, chairman of the board of Sears Roebuck and Co., and Morris E. Leeds, one of Philadelphia's leading manufacturers and philanthropists, to work on the board with the enthusiasm that characterized his own efforts— and even that generous contributor to the Republican party, John C. Pew of Sun Oil. Here were centers of power—and of course their work was successful. Emil Rieve, head of the Hosiery Workers, and James L. McDevitt, president of the Pennsylvania State Federation of Labor, were typical of the eight labor representatives. George W. Taylor, who taught labor relations at the Wharton School and was impartial chairman of the hosiery industry, with years of experience in arbitration, was vice chairman of the board. It was a group of successful men, working together easily and directly—no representatives, alternates, substitutes, or lawyers at the meeting—working hard, proud of its work. And no wonder—715 disputes involving 600,000 employees were handled and 85 per cent settled. The approach was preventive and prophylactic—amicable settlements behind the scenes by men who knew and trusted each other. Billy used to like to quote a line from Isaiah: "Come let us reason together." The moment trouble began to brew—it mattered not how small, for trouble has a way of spreading quickly in these delicate human relationships —the board got both sides together "around a big table," and gave them all the time they wanted.

Of course getting people around the table was no panacea. It worked well with local and relatively small-scale businesses, in a union town where for generations labor unions had been established, and knew how to get along with employers. Such a simple technique could not have avoided the strife that broke out in the basic manufacturing industries, such as steel, textiles, and automobiles, and in the whole range of metal working industries, where the employers were determined to "slug it out" with the unions and cared nothing for federal mediators, or even the courts, until the United States Supreme Court had finally validated the National Labor Relations Act.

Occasionally I took a personal part in helping to avert a strike, and those brief incursions into the mediation field made me realize something of the skills needed for successful negotiation. I would consult Edward F. McGrady, the Assistant Secretary of Labor, a shrewd Irishman, before offering the Board's assistance to bring about peace. It was not unusual to find that the lawyers, once they got into the situation, made it difficult for their principals to get together—one meets the type frequently; aggressive, obstinate, inflexible, high priests who whisper to their clients that if they surrender to that particular demand the door will be open to far more unreasonable requests, and where will it end? They talk much about principles; they glower across the table; humor, that most reliable solvent for bringing snarling opponents together, deserts them, and stiffness and stuffiness settle.

Early in February a walkout of building-service workers, including elevator operators, in the garment and fur district of New York, was about to break. Every effort had been made to avert it. Mayor La Guardia had appointed an arbitration committee, which was holding daily—and nightly—conferences to try to avert the suspension of service. Jeremiah T. Mahoney, chairman of our regional board, an attractive Tammany politician and lawyer, called me. The walkout had been ordered for the next day. He thought the union might postpone it a little longer if I would come over at once to see what could be done. This was arranged; and I spent a long evening with Mahoney and Samuel Lamport, another member of the regional board, a successful and influential Jewish exporter. Apparently the landlords and the union were not far apart. The union was asking for a minimum wage of twenty-two dollars. The landlords had about agreed to that. What was holding them apart, then, I asked. The lawyers, said Mahoney, particularly Walter Gordon Merritt, who represented one of the large building associations—a very eminent lawyer, a very stupid man, a very obstinate man. . . .

We finally concocted a scheme and sent for the lawyer for the union. He agreed that Merritt was not very co-operative. Did he think things might move along if Merritt was out of the picture? Sure did. Would he move out, too? What did we mean, he asked suspiciously. This was the plot, we told him. La Guardia would call a special meeting tomorrow, in his office, personally presiding. Then it was up to the union lawyer, he must get ornery, must do a bit of shouting, must just be impossible, you know, you're an Irishman, you'll know how to behave . . . He grinned. Then, we explained, the mayor would toss you out, probably losing his temper; and if you were out Merritt couldn't very well stay in, that wouldn't be fair, and the principals would get together. Might he call his chief? No, get him over, and we'll settle it here and now. And settle it we did, and got La Guardia out of bed; and he agreed at once, was keen about the idea, as he was keen about any plan where he could play a part, if it was not a minor part. He called the meeting. Not only the labor lawyer but his opposite numbers (Merritt had associates) proved really impossible. La Guardia lost his temper beautifully. The lawyers were told to leave; then, said the mayor, "this case is now going to be settled"; and he kept half a dozen "principals," and two of our negotiators. At 4 A.M. the next morning these gentlemen announced that the elevator strike was over, and the *World-Telegram* editorially praised "the timely and effective intervention of the National Labor Relations Board," which had "averted a paralyzing tie-up," and gave due credit to the union leadership, which had decided "to seek its further objects by peaceful parleying instead of by a strike that would have meant great public suffering."

The most widely advertised decision of the Board was the famous *Jennings* case. Dean Jennings was the chief rewrite man on the *Call-Bulletin*, a Hearst newspaper in San Francisco. He charged the paper with firing him on account of his activities in organizing the Newspaper Guild, which was then considered radical and dangerous by most publishers. Eventually the Guild revolutionized the conditions under which reporters worked, and

was instrumental in bringing about long overdue reforms in
wages and security of tenure. But at that time hands were raised
in horror by the publishers and the more conservative members
of the public at the idea that newspapermen could sell their
freedom by joining together in a union. Writers were artists,
individuals. Such combined action would turn them into robots,
incapable of original work. What was to happen to the freedom
of the press? It was all very well for bricklayers to join up, but
reporters! . . . Jennings took his case to our local board in San
Francisco, which filed a complaint based on the alleged discrimination. The newspaper refused to appear, claiming that the
board had no jurisdiction, since a special board had been set up
by the Newspaper Code Authority of the NRA to handle such
cases, which excluded any interference on our part. Pretty soon
the case came up to us. Should we affirm the trial board's
decision in favor of Jennings, or dismiss the case?

The newspaper code had been drafted by the publishers, without the co-operation of labor, presumably because the guild was
not yet strong enough to be consulted. The Newspaper Industrial
Board, which had been established under the code, was biparti-
san, with four labor members and four publishers. In case of a
tie, provision was made for the appointment of an impartial
chairman; but such a reference seldom occurred, as the members
could not agree on a chairman considered sufficiently impartial.
Of the thirty-five cases coming before the Board, action had been
taken only in five. If we determined that Jennings should have
been relegated to the code board that would have been an end
of the case. It would have slept there peacefully while Jennings
was out of a job.

Millis was worried, saw a row coming, and would have
avoided the decision if possible. He was liberal and progressive
in point of view, but cautious in approach. I agreed there would
be a row, but rather relished the idea. I felt the weakness of our
setup, and thought that a showdown would clear the air, emphasize the inconsistencies, the contradictions, the wearying
slowness and vagueness of the way labor disputes were being
handled. We decided to take the case. The newspaper, given
another opportunity to present its side of the dispute, again refused to introduce evidence, claiming that we had no jurisdic-

tion. It argued that we should not hear newspaper cases because if the executive order, from which we drew our authority, were applied to newspapers it would modify the newspaper code without the publishers' consent; and, even more shocking, that Jennings' actions involved a violation of the freedom of the press guaranteed by the First Amendment. How could a reporter who was a member of a union write independently? . . . We ordered the *Call-Bulletin* to reinstate Jennings in ten days or be cited for removal of its Blue Eagle, and the case sent for enforcement to the Department of Justice. There had been no agreement in the code to keep newspapers out of the Board's jurisdiction. The Constitution did not grant the newspaper business immunity from regulation—as to that, it was like any other business. What Congress could not do was to pass any law abridging the freedom of the press. That freedom had not been affected.

The publisher's argument had sounded too thin to hold any ring of honest belief. Yet, when the Board's decision was announced, almost the entire press of the United States echoed the line. Unhallowed hands had been laid on the ark of the covenant. This was the beginning of the end—the press would be free no more. The publishers to a large degree believed that they were writing—I don't mean only the Hearst press, which talked about our "Communistic dictation," and whose counsel announced that our decision was designed "to seize the overlordship of the press of the United States for three obscure appointed politicians." Even the New York *Times,* seldom unduly excited, ventured to think that the freedom of the press had been put in jeopardy.

Donald Richberg, even more excited than the press itself, rushed over to see us. He hinted at a secret "understanding" with the newspapers—an understanding reaching very high up indeed. We thought if there had been a deal we had better bring it to the surface. We'd reopen the case, but we wanted to hear facts. Blackwell Smith had succeeded Richberg as counsel for the NRA, and Richberg had taken on the job of co-ordinator (in this instance, I suppose, he was trying to "co-ordinate" the Board with the press). We announced two days after our decision that we had reopened the case to afford the NRA an opportunity to "present the circumstances connected with the adoption of the newspaper code"—in a word to prove any special agreement, if there was one.

Smith reargued the case and added nothing. He suggested that our Board should have brought the complaint to the attention of the newspaper board, and acted only if, after a reasonable time, no action was taken. But obviously that did not challenge our jurisdiction, but only the wisdom of exercising it. There had never been any agreement that all cases would go to the code board. Richberg's activity in trying at all costs to get us to drop the case was perhaps accounted for by the fact that, with or without the nod of his chief, he had induced the newspapers to come into the code by assuring them that complaints from the Guild would go to the code board. If the President had dropped such an assuring word, obviously that could not be revealed; and perhaps Richberg was merely taking the rap, as all of us were glad to take it from time to time, if we weren't rapped too hard, merely made to look like fools. But Richberg did not take any rap, and he did not appear before us. His case would have been greatly strengthened if he had publicly testified that he had assured the newspapers that their own board would be exclusive. He made the extraordinary suggestion that under the executive order creating our Board the provision that it *might* refer cases to code industrial boards meant that it *must* do so. I suppose if he had testified to an "understanding" it would have further separated labor from NRA. These special boards in most cases were distrusted. That the administration had made a deal with the publishers would not have looked very nice.

"Big, baggy Heywood Broun," writing his indomitable column in the New York *World*, was president of the Newspaper Guild, and greeted the first decision of this "brash young Biddle"—a year before him at Harvard—with enthusiasm tinged with skepticism. Biddle was either without fear or "exceedingly naïve" to proceed on the assumption that Section 7-a meant precisely what it said. "Hold 'em Harvard!" . . . When the case was reopened, unhappy and chaotic Broun led the representatives of the Guild out of a code hearing called to consider wages and hours, in protest against the "terrorization" of the NRA by the publishers. The Guild had come prepared to show that American newspapermen must work for twenty years before achieving a

salary of forty dollars a week. Broun, who had tried in vain to
see us before the decision, intimated that there was something
evil and surreptitious about our conferring privately with Richberg—whom did he consult, what was said, what did he tell
NLRB? Richberg complained to the President that he had been
"viciously" libeled by Broun, accused the Labor Board of
"arrogant self-assertion," and asked that its power for mischief be
curbed. "So Biddle," Arthur Schlesinger, Jr., commented, "the
former counsel for the Pennsylvania Railroad, contended for
labor organizations against Richberg, the former counsel for the
railroad brotherhoods."[1]

Richberg exercised this brief authority as the President's right
bower during the NRA days. I think he was loyal to the President; but he showed his loyalty by improvising a sort of back-
stairs activity, an *éminence grise* whose manipulative skill
suited the President's own inclination to complicate issues by
balancing the forces of political power. The President had deep
if simple convictions; I doubt whether Donald Richberg had
any. Like a number of Americans who seem at a certain age to
lose the direction of their lives and make a complete circle from
left to right, he changed, when ambition touched him, from a
supporter of liberal labor policies to an instrument to prevent
their success. I could not trust him, and I do not think that his
influence on the President was healthy. But it was brief.

In a week we handed down our second decision, affirming
our previous position. There was, indeed, nothing new to consider. No fresh evidence had been presented, no new argument
submitted, no gentlemen's agreement unearthed.

Immediately, to put it mildly, hell broke loose.

A convention of the 1200 newspapers that had joined the code
was called to meet on January 28 to consider "the gravest
problem with which the press of this country has yet been confronted"—with a strong intimation that they would resign from
the code. The publishers would not, they said, permit the future of the press of America to be compromised and endangered.

[1] *The Coming of the New Deal,* (New York: Houghton Mifflin Co.,
1959), p. 399.

They had felt from the beginning that the code system could not safely be applied to a free press. It had taken centuries to end government licensing of the press.

When the period for reinstating Jennings elapsed we sent the case, in accordance with the current practice, to the National Recovery Administration for enforcement. Under an agreement between it and our Board, action was taken on our recommendation automatically in ordinary instances, but NRA retained "ultimate discretion" in exceptional cases—and obviously it considered the *Jennings* case exceptional. It referred the case—a good way of marking time—to the Newspaper Industrial Board for its "opinion on the merits," an opinion which was never forthcoming.

But the great newspaper convention called to protest against the attack on free speech (in reality what was being protested was union organization of reporters) never came off. A week before it was to take place the President stepped in on the side of the newspapers against the Board. His letter to me was in the form of an informal "request." A few codes, wrote the President, probably less than five, contained provisions for final adjudication of labor complaints. These had been inserted in the early days, and were not found in later codes. Nevertheless the government must live up to the letter of its agreement. The National Labor Relations Board was therefore requested to conform to certain "principles": keep out of cases where the codes contain such a provision, unless complaint is made that the appeal tribunal (code board) had not been properly set up, or its decisions were contrary to existing interpretations of Section 7-a; then report to the President.

It was a curious document, half casual, half peremptory. It had the earmarks of having been written hastily to avoid a crisis. It was clumsy and lacked frankness. The stated facts were wrong —there were not less than five, but twenty-seven special boards, twelve of them under codes. The letter did not touch the issues that were involved—whether there had been any agreement with the publishers, and whether the language in the Newspaper Code intended that its board should alone have jurisdiction. The President was definite in specifying the limits of the Labor Board's jurisdiction, wholly vague as to what he was to do if an appeal were made to him (which it never was). Would he then refer the matter to some special *ad hoc* board for a sort of arbitration? He could hardly be expected to decide it himself.

The way the incident had been handled bore the marks of Richberg's uninspired manipulation. When he called me to announce the President's decision—about which we had not been consulted—and I reported it to the other two members, they both said at once that they could not stay on after such treatment. The President had appointed the National Labor Relations Board with complete powers in all cases, had given us explicit and unlimited jurisdiction. We were to be the final voice in labor disputes, a labor court. And now without consulting us he had overruled us, and pinned back our ears because we had stood up against Mr. Richberg and the newspapers.

But I was against resigning. Perhaps it would have cleared the air. And then? The action would not have led anywhere. Labor was weak, was badly organized in the great industries like steel and rubber and automobiles. NRA was breaking down. Section 7-a was but an affirmation of a right, something would have to take its place if the right was to be protected by law. And the statute had been drafted, was almost ready. Bob Wagner, with whom I had been working on the draft, begged me to stay, to hold the Board together. A new fight was on the horizon. Let us keep what we had, as we affirmed our position. Labor would back us unanimously, there was a chance to win . . . Hesitatingly my associates agreed to reconsider their decision.

We saw the President. I did not think that his blandishments would carry much weight with Millis and Smith, who were by then inclined to stay if he was moderately sympathetic—and he was more than that, stroking down their angry feathers, showing sympathy, exhibiting almost an understanding of the difficulties, at his best, as he always was when he had to smooth over a prickly situation—and was having his way.

In a conciliatory note to me, a few days later, he scribbled after his signature: "You and I have had enough publicity."

Perhaps his sense of timing was wisely exercised, his instinct, too, to choose the right issue. If a showdown was coming there was no use lining up the press against you before the time came.

Not that he was ever enthusiastic about majority representation. But if there was to be a real issue he *had* to be on the side of labor. All his instincts and ideology made that inevitable. But in the little fights around the great ones, leading up to them, there was room for compromise, particularly if you didn't want to marshal your forces on a battlefield in which the country might be persuaded that freedom of the press was involved.

Heywood Broun told reporters that the newspaper publishers had cracked down on the President of the United States and Franklin D. Roosevelt had cracked up—while the *Jennings* case becomes "a pressed flower for our memory book." The more strident of the liberal voices urged the members of NLRB to resign. They must not connive with the President in stripping labor of the rights which it had been guaranteed by law, must not acquiesce in a practice leading to compulsory arbitration, and should dramatically protest against the President's constituting himself the final judge on questions of law. *The Nation* said that the President's letter was deceptive, petty and mean— we had been asked in effect to reduce our own jurisdiction. We should not do so.

In the chaos and confusion, the rushing forth and then walking backward; the enthusiasm channeled in a direction too soon embarked on—then frustration; the hope and the disillusion; the tug and pull of the theorists in power against the firmer hold of the practical men of business, and the conflict between those who thought economic health could be restored by cutting wages so as to give the ailing patient a chance at the decent nourishment of modest profits, and those who maintained that without living wages there would be no one to buy the goods that business wanted to sell and the country longed once more to enjoy; the pressure of different theories as to how and when and how fast to stimulate the listless economy of the nation—in all this humming activity it was natural that mistakes should have been made. It was not that the New Deal, as its critics insisted, was planning the future economy of the nation. On the contrary the immediate experiments were not co-ordinated into any national plan. Our Board was but a small wheel in the complicated NRA machinery, yet our consistency was doubtless irritating to the President. There were doubtless more fundamental considerations affecting the President's decision to clip our activities than merely a desire to conciliate the newspapers. F.D.R. had a sturdy contempt for newspaper publishers and a genuine respect for the men who wrote the news, and who were more often than not on his side of a controversy. That he was not afraid of the publishers was evidenced by his approval of my filing an antitrust suit as Attorney General a few years later against the Associated Press. But in the *Jennings* case more than the press was involved.

The reporters asked me at my press conference a day or two after the Board's second decision whether it would intervene in labor troubles in the automobile industry, and I answered, a little too impulsively, that we would if circumstances made it seem advisable, and that I would not stand on technicalities.

I had touched a particularly sensitive spot. Leo Woolman, an active economist, particularly in the field of production, unemployment, and labor problems, was chairman of the Automobile Labor Board (he had also been chairman of the Labor Advisory Board of NRA), which had been set up by mutual agreement in the industry the preceding March. He did not believe in majority rule, which was cardinal to our view. His board had established a form of proportional representation—the employers had to recognize whatever union was elected, but only as representing the men who had voted for it. Needless to say the employers went along with enthusiastic co-operation, but not the men. There were a good many unions in the automobile industry, craft as well as industrial, and under Woolman's plan the employer could "bargain" with competing groups of union representatives, frequently at cross purposes with each other. The American Federation of Labor had recently organized the workers under the United Automobile Workers Union. The members of the union and the leaders of the AF of L felt bitterly about Woolman's arrangement, and repudiated it before the year was over. In setting up this special Board, the President, who had a strong sense of the incidence of power, knew that the balance of power in this industry lay with management, and not with organized labor. He was, I think, conscious of an ambiguity in the language of his executive order with respect to majority rule. That did not mean that he would condemn majority rule. One need not be too explicit. The law of politics is not consistency or logic.

In steel somewhat the same situation prevailed. The American Federation of Labor steel union—this was before the founding of the Committee on Industrial Organization a few years later— had rejected several offers of the steel industry made through Myron Taylor (he was during the war to be Mr. Roosevelt's unofficial ambassador to the Vatican), the most recent of which, said to be backed by Miss Perkins and therefore by the President, was the recognition of the union, but only as to the employees whom the union represented. Management would not stand for majority rule. The steel workers' union was not strong in those days, but William Green stuck to his guns in face of administration pressure, and turned down Taylor's overtures. Labor could hardly be expected to give up its right to strike for the duration of NRA under such a one-sided bargain. As had happened so often before, the workers had their cake on paper but the employers ate it. Bill Green made a counterproposal, which was rejected: that steel accept the Board's construction of collective bargaining—the right to hold elections and majority rule. The workers were growing restless, and the first antiadministration strike under the New Deal was in the making.

THE LABOR BOARD—A
FRESH START

By now it had become apparent that the paragraph of the National Recovery Act safeguarding unions could not and would not be enforced. This was a bitter conclusion to the representatives of labor who, like most Americans, prone to pin great faith in paper rights, believed that the brief declaration of the freedom of workmen to join unions without the risk of being fired, now written into the law, would be self-enforcing, and new members would freely stream into their organizations (pushed a little by union leaders). To realize failure was particularly galling because they had stood by, agreeing to keep the men from striking for the glory of the Blue Eagle, while the employers did the planning, fixed the prices, held down the wages, and sat on the lid. I was convinced that the present law was unclear and imprecise; that it could not be enforced; that a new law was needed with enforceable remedies; and that, given this opportunity and some protection, the strength of organized labor and its effectiveness to meet the corresponding power of organized capital would be greatly enhanced.

The second part of my brief term as chairman found me, therefore, involved in a different preoccupation. We had, as Cardozo suggested, been pioneering in the field of labor law under the wing of a very loose definition of congressional policy, which, against the raw and immediate facts of the labor market, had to be practically and realistically interpreted. This we had done; but there had been no enforcement and no results. It seemed to me that the country must be told this—must be told that strife between the two factions would inevitably and before very long increase if a fair mechanism for peaceful adjustment was not found; must be persuaded that organized labor had come to stay and management should accept that disagreeable fact and deal with it; and finally must be given a true picture of what the new labor bill might be expected to accomplish. The new law should be given a chance. It was but the culmination of experiments in the field of collective bargaining. The techniques for enforcing the findings of the Board had successfully been used in other fields. All this must be said.

On February 1, 1935, Senator Wagner introduced his National Labor Relations Board bill. For a month, in speeches in industrial centers in the East and Middle West, I had been insisting that enforcement of judgments of the Board had broken down. With the necessity of accepting the principle of collective bargaining and majority rule I emphasized the concomitant duty of union responsibility, which should go with union power. Speaking before groups of businessmen and union representatives, usually brought together by the regional boards, before chambers of commerce and economic forums—in Cincinnati, Cleveland, Columbus, St. Louis, Detroit, Pittsburgh, Akron, Philadelphia—I outlined what from our experience seemed to be the necessary features of any new legislation: majority rule should be clearly defined; the board should be given powers of vigorous and prompt enforcement; its finding of facts if supported by the evidence should be final, and any appeal based only on errors of law. The widest scope should be allowed to the new board in order to permit it to build up a constructive body of labor law. For this purpose rigid definitions to cover every contingency must be avoided, and the approach should be empirical and realistic rather than formal. Decisions must be prompt. Men out of a job could not wait indefinitely to be reinstated. In my formal report of the Board's activities, reviewing our work for the six-months period, I had written: "Court enforcement under the present machinery is slow, uncertain and cumbersome."

On February 27, 1935, John P. Nields, a United States District Judge in Delaware, held Section 7-a unconstitutional in the suit which the government had brought against the Weirton Steel Co. to enjoin it from dealing with an employer-organized and -financed company union. The decision was an important test case. The court disregarded the findings of fact of the Board with respect to the company union, which had been built on a pattern which Eugene G. Grace, president of Bethlehem Steel, and Walter C. Teagle, president of the Standard Oil Company of New Jersey, testifying as experts at the trial, characterized as adequate for the interests of employees. The court also brushed aside the whole government machinery for settling labor disputes by holding that the federal government had no jurisdiction over the relation of company and employees, which in Judge Nields' view was *purely a local affair.*

A week after the Weirton decision a statement of a witness before the Senate Interstate Commerce Committee that NRA was "a failure and a flop" was sympathetically endorsed by four Democratic senators on the committee. It was pretty evident by then to most of us that not only was the famous section unenforceable, but that the National Recovery Act, in which it had found lodgment, would be toppled over either by the Congress or by the courts.

Hearings on Senator Wagner's bill began two weeks after Judge Nields' opinion had thus sharpened the issue. The senator explained his bill to the Senate Education and Labor Committee in great detail. William Green, president of the American Federation of Labor, was to testify before the committee the next day. The chief difference of opinion among those who favored the bill was whether the Board should be independent of the Labor Department. Senator Wagner, Green, and most labor leaders wanted an independent board, an opinion which I shared—a quasi court passing on facts and developing labor law should be free of executive control; and in view of the serious constitutional and practical difficulties that it would confront, it was essential to achieve for it the vitality of a young and unabashed bureaucratic entity (to use an awkward but

exact term) for the coming struggle with the most powerful
forces in America. A David was needed to meet Goliath.

At about five o'clock on the day before I was to appear before the committee, Paul Ward called me on the telephone. Had
I heard about the deal between Secretary Perkins and Mr. William Green that the Board should be placed under the Department of Labor? I had not—when did that happen? Oh, about
fifteen minutes ago. But I thought Bill Green had previously
come out in favor of an independent board? Sure, but that was
before Miss Perkins talked to him. Better get busy. I got busy.

Yes, Mr. Green said, when I called on him a few minutes
later, certainly at one time—very recently in fact—he had been
all for an independent board; our Board had shown what could
be done when we were let alone. But the Secretary had been
to see him, had indicated that she would not support the new
bill if the Board were not within the Labor Department. She
had never been a champion of majority rule. The Board, she
felt, should be attached to a department whose head reported
directly to the President. You couldn't have the chairman dealing
directly with the President when the Secretary was charged
with the duty of formulating the government's labor policy. The
New Deal was already proliferating into a tangled wilderness
without paths leading anywhere. . . . But I don't think Bill
Green was so much impressed with this by no means uncon-
vincing argument as by Miss Perkins' vigorous and persuasive
personality. He didn't say she had hypnotized him, but there was
a suggestion of that, covered half-humorously by a masculine
deference to the mightier power of the female of the species. He
was a lovable, courageous, rather stupid man.

"She kept fixing me with her eye," he said. . . . I asked him
if his testimony had been written. Yes, Miss Thorne had it, I
could see it, but he wouldn't change his position; he had given
the Secretary his word.

"But she has to support the bill," I urged. "You didn't get
anything by shifting your position."

"She kept fixing me with her eye," he repeated.

Back at the office I called Bob Wagner and told him the situation. He was not the least upset. "Leave him to me," he said.

The next day at the hearing Mr. Green testified at length

in favor of the bill. Toward the end of his statement he said, rather casually, that the Board should be "lodged in the Department of Labor." He concurred with the Secretary that it should be "connected" with the Department, but also was convinced that it should be "absolutely independent." It should have a close "relation" with the Department, so it would be free to utilize the Department's machinery for research and mediation. But it should be separate and not subject to review. Senator Wagner, in an attempt to clarify this muddled viewpoint, asked Mr. Green whether the Secretary should have control over personnel, or should have a right to veto appointments by the Board— a power which her testimony indicated she desired to exercise. Mr. Green answered that he had not taken the veto suggestion into account, but gallantly refrained from expressing his own opinion. The other senators, who had sympathy with his dilemma, left it at that, to his obvious relief.

Miss Perkins had urged an amendment subordinating the Board to the Department, and giving the Department control over personnel and expenditures. This arrangement, I told the committee when it came my turn, would not make the Board independent and impartial, attached to a Department whose function in fact and in the public view was to look after the interests of labor. To succeed in the long run the Board must have the confidence of industry as well as labor, and of the country at large.

I added that Section 7-a was nothing more than an "innocuous moral shibboleth"; that re-enacting it without definite clarification or adequate enforcement machinery would be writing on the statute books the emptiness of a law which everyone knew could not be enforced, and would perpetuate the existing ambiguities and uncertainties. A labor court, I concluded, to have dignity and usefulness should be permanent, and not subject to any control, even that of the Chief Executive—a reflection on the administration's labor policy as I had seen it for the last five months, a policy of drift and manipulation. Important labor policies and decisions should not be handled by temporary bodies hastily summoned to placate a particular demand or to ease an uncomfortable situation.

On April 26, Louis Stark reported in the New York *Times* that the "battle of the century" was being waged around the Wagner bill. Chambers of commerce, manufacturers' associations, and representatives of company unions were drowning legislators with appeals to head off the bill, prophesying darkly that it would foment industrial strife. Spokesmen for organized labor, on the other hand, assured the Congress that without the provisions of the bill there could be no enforcement of labor's rights, and chaos would indubitably result. As usual, the public, confused by these extremes, reacted more or less as individual temperament or economic conditioning suggested. The President in this gathering storm had given no hint of his views.

On May 3, 1935, the Labor Committee reported the bill favorably, saying that the "time had come for a clean decision" either to withdraw the government guarantee of collective bargaining or to implement it by effective legislation.

Everyone thought the vote would be close; but on May 15 the Senate passed the bill by a vote of sixty-three to twelve. Four Democrats and eight Republicans voted against it. On May 27 the Supreme Court held the National Recovery Act unconstitutional in the famous *Schecter* decision, the "sick chicken case." No one knew what would happen to Section 7-a, shivering in a twilight of lonely uncertainty. The decision brought closer to the Congress the necessity of immediate action. On June 19 the House enacted the bill without a record vote, giving the new board independent status, as had the Senate, but adding a rider that no bargaining unit "should include the employees of more than one employer." This amendment would have excluded mass bargaining and crippled the power of the great international unions. It was struck out in conference, and the bill was passed substantially in the form in which it had been originally introduced. President Roosevelt signed it on July 5.

It was to be expected that the New York *Times* and David Lawrence in the U. S. *News* should have had qualms about this new piece of legislation, which, though not without precedent, carried a disquieting sense of power and determination, as if it was actually meant to be enforced. The New York *Times* was concerned with the scope and cost of the effort to regulate a vast network of industrial relations from Washington, and thought the law unconstitutional and biased, and that it would create confusion and controversy rather than industrial peace. Walter Lippmann's discomfort was even greater. Emphasizing his liberal sympathy with the statute's aims, he thought that labor had won a Pyrrhic victory by granting a government board power to allow skilled labor to be superseded by unskilled labor, and putting its neck in the federal yoke, which would inevitably lead to compulsory arbitration, and thus defeat the whole purpose of free collective bargaining. Lippmann dreaded labor monopolies in a world in which industrial monopolies had for a good many years been firmly entrenched. The single ray of light was, he declared, that the Wagner bill was "obviously unconstitutional."

Sometime that spring I decided to resign after the bill had been disposed of. The time had not yet come when I was ready to cut my links with my own past and the future that normally would grow out of it. Very definitely Jack Barnes had written me that I must come back now or else make some other arrangement. I loved practice and had no idea of giving it up for a life of public work, even if I had been able to afford it—that is afford living without having to worry about money. I did not realize, would not realize for another four or five years, how much the satisfaction that comes from public service had begun to tug at my moorings. It is hard to define what makes up that satisfaction. I suspect a number of imponderables—the almost physical invigoration that springs from wielding power; the comfort of security, though not in my case—I was not interested in a career in the government. Largely it is the steady well-being flowing from absorption in work that seems to be worth while. But fundamentally the gratification of working for the government derives from the experience of giving and sharing below any surface pleasure in work well done. It is rooted in the relief of escaping the loneliness and boredom of oneself, and the unreality of personal ambition. The individual effort is merged into the community itself, the common goal and the common end. This is no escape from self; it is the most profound realization of personality.

When I told Harry Millis of my decision to resign, he shrugged, smiled, got up, and shook hands with me rather formally. "You've steered us through the first struggle," he said. When I informed

Ed Smith he stared at me glassily, and said merely, "My God!" He didn't remonstrate, realized it was my choice, saw that it was hard for me to leave. He doubted whether he'd go on without me—the chances were too uncertain . . . but the hardest to tell was Senator Wagner, who expected me to stay on, and his assumption of my willingness to do so embarrassed me.

Soon after he had got his bill through the Senate I asked him to dine with me, softening what I knew would be his disappointment over my decision by a bottle of Burgundy which I knew he liked. He took it hard. It threw everything back into the hands of the Secretary, he said, made quick action uncertain, might disrupt the small admirable staff, most of whom I had inherited from Lloyd Garrison. Couldn't I stay on for a year to get it going? It would be an exciting year; and then perhaps, not much later, I could argue the test case in the Supreme Court. Why did I want to go back to practice? . . . He paused, and looked at me. "Gee," he added, "I wouldn't have pushed the bill if I'd known that. I counted on you. You made it possible."

"Do you think I'm a quitter?" I asked.

He grinned. "Pretty much." Then he talked about the new America. "Roosevelt can never be defeated . . . you'll come out all right. You'll hate trying cases, and thinking about us down here . . . I don't know how I can tell Leon." Leon Keyserling, a brilliant young economist, was his secretary and legislative assistant, and ten years later was to become chairman of President Truman's Council of Economic Advisers.

Bob Wagner was nine years older than I. He was born in Germany and had come to the United States in childhood. One of the striking group of New York politicians with an imaginative and generous outlook, he had, like his old friend Alfred E. Smith, come up through the ranks of Tammany Hall. Also like Smith, although always a Tammany man, he was independent in his social outlook, if not in his recommendations for appointments. Wagner had been hurt, a little wryly amused, and not altogether surprised when Al joined the Liberty League, made up of the country's leading millionaires.

Wagner was in his full power at that time, the darling of the liberals and of labor groups, next in popularity only to Franklin Roosevelt; affable, shrewd, the best-dressed man in the Senate, if one did not count James Hamilton Lewis with his curled pink whiskers and suggestion of eau de cologne on a gentleman's thin linen handkerchief. Bob Wagner had great influence with his associates, less on account of his speeches—they never got very far off solid ground—but by reason of his very considerable knowledge of economic issues, which he marshaled with skill and effectiveness, and his transparent goodness. He sponsored much of the New Deal legislation—the National Industrial Recovery Act, the Social Security Act, the Railway Pension Law, the Housing Act of 1937.

After about seven weeks' delay, Warren Madden, whom I had come to know well when we both were members of Governor Pinchot's committee which investigated the Pennsylvania Coal and Iron Police, was appointed chairman of the new statutory board, and my two associates were designated to serve with him. Under his skillful leadership and with the wise advice of the Board's chief counsel, Charles Fahy, who would be Solicitor General when I was Attorney General, the statute was declared constitutional by the United States Supreme Court in a series of test cases, one of which Fahy argued.

Looking back over the work of the Labor Board twenty-five years later I find it possible to estimate its value. Although ambiguously expressed and given an inadequate basis of implementation, Section 7-a profoundly affected the development of collective bargaining. The National Labor Relations Act supplied the deficiencies. In spite of claims to the contrary, the law did not require recognition of any particular existing trade union (unless it had a majority); or outlaw a company union (unless dominated by the employer, as was usually the case); or compel men to join unions, or invalidate closed-shop contracts, or limit the right to strike, or require compulsory arbitration. And the statute was neither novel nor revolutionary. The right to organize and to bargain collectively, recognized by the government during the First World War, though not expressed in the Transportation Act of 1920, was specifically accepted by the Railroad Labor Board, operating under the act, which also adopted the principle of majority rule. Free organization of employees and collective bargaining were expressly guaranteed by the Norris-LaGuardia Act of 1932, in President Hoover's administration; and the central core of Section 7-a and of the Wagner Act was taken from the declaration of policy in that law. This historical continuity has been little noted by critics of these New Deal labor policies, who damned them as socialist innovations, when they were nothing of the sort. The feature of the act attacked as the most radical was in fact the least novel—the provision authorizing the Board to request a court to enforce its orders, which derived from the Federal Trade Commission Act of 1914.

Our Board, although it was unable to enforce its decisions, gave reasonable content and construction to the meaning of the section, which in effect, as Justice Cardozo had suggested to me, was a development of the common law of labor. The broad definition of the right to bargain, found in the section and repeated in the National Labor Relations Act, gave room for an empirical development of this common law over the years, so that the change, even if it had come about by legislative fiat, was gradual, and pragmatically applied.

The chief effect of the new law was that, by legalizing collective bargaining and coupling it with majority rule, a more even balance of power between employers and organized workers was made possible. And the shift took place in a handful of years. In 1935, when the act was adopted, there were hardly five million workers in the labor unions. Ten years later there were fifteen million. This meant a new freedom for working men when the imbalance had been readjusted. They could vote at national and local elections at the steel mills in Pennsylvania without fear or intimidation, and could organize and strike without having their meetings and picket lines broken up by deputy sheriffs—an essential development of American industrial democracy.

My distrust of theories of political science and of generalities makes me cautious and doubtful. No one likes government interference. Yet situations arise where it becomes advisable. Such a situation existed in 1935. The legislation that resulted was an attempt, largely successful, to allow men to organize when they wanted to. It represented a point of view common to much of the New Deal philosophy—that a free people should not hesitate to use their government to protect them from the unregulated energies which threaten that freedom.

THE TENNESSEE VALLEY
AUTHORITY
INVESTIGATION

※〔〕※ *Chapter Three*

   The Tennessee Valley Authority had been approved on May 18, 1933, one of the earliest and perhaps the
greatest achievement of Franklin Roosevelt. This experiment in
living, with its triple purposes of flood control, navigation, and
the production of cheap electric power, was in full swing by the
time the committee began its investigation. Two new dams had
been completed, and electricity was being supplied to municipalities and co-operatives.

  Roosevelt had been thinking for years about multiple-purpose dams, and the reclamation of entire regions by the co-
ordination of their resources. The use of the Tennessee River
and the rebuilding of its valley, cruelly eroded and despoiled,
transcended power development, and spread to the broad
problems of preventing soil erosion, reforestation, and the elimination of marginal lands. This he told the Congress in a brief
message suggesting legislation to create the Authority. The way
led to national planning for a complete river watershed "involving many States and the future lives and welfare of millions.
It touches and gives life to all forms of human concern." Until he

died he continued to dream of other river authorities that would do with the great streams of America what was being done with the Tennessee. Several times he talked to me about them, and drew little maps with his big clumsy hands, showing how they would operate through the country—the Columbia, the Sacramento, the Colorado, the Missouri, the Ohio, even the Connecticut if the New Englanders would ever stand for it.

The act embodied his recommendations, and created a corporation clothed with the authority of government but possessing flexibility and the opportunity for initiative. The Authority was to be free of the timid controls of civil service, and divorced from the nagging interference of the General Accounting Office. There would be a broad fertilizer program and the regulation of stream flow, primarily to promote navigation and control floods. The law was an expression of the faith of the people in their own institutions, and of the belief that their government should perform a needed service on a national scale, which no private enterprise could undertake.

The Tennessee River basin makes a great curving loop through seven states—Virginia, North Carolina, Tennessee, Georgia, Alabama, Mississippi, and Kentucky. It is difficult to describe its course by reference to the points of the compass, as rivers in the area flow north in order to run south, and at times seem to turn east in order to go west more comfortably. In its course first south, then west, and finally north, the Tennessee meets the Ohio at Paducah, and the enlarged river turns to join the Mississippi. The Tennessee has countless tributaries, which are themselves fed by smaller streams—the Cumberland and the Clinch, the Hiwassee, the Nolinacky, the Powell, the Duck. . . . In the past, with a fifty-two-inch rainfall, the floods were disastrous, and the land, stripped of its timber after the Civil War, lost its fertility in the unchecked erosion. Poverty spread and stayed; tuberculosis and malaria followed. In the year that TVA began to operate, over half the families in the highland counties were on relief. The valley was rich in resources, but there was no access to the transportation system of the Mississippi.

On the Tennessee the most severe floods occurred at Chattanooga. The flood of March, 1936, which without control would have reach forty-one feet, was held at a thirty-seven-foot level by impounding water at the Norris Dam, the only dam in operation above the city. When completed, the system of dams was expected to reduce floods at Chattanooga by about seven or eight feet. In 1937, during a great rush of water on the Ohio, the river crest at Cairo was reduced six inches, and the city probably saved from destruction by the operation of the three or four dams then completed.

Somewhere President Roosevelt had read an article by Dr. Arthur E. Morgan, dealing with unified river development. Dr. Morgan was then president of Antioch College. He had built reclamation works, designed "conservancies" to prevent floods, rewritten several state drainage-control laws; and, at a telling moment of history, he put into words the vision of the use of rivers on a grand scale for the American people, which had plucked so long at the President's heart and mind. Arthur Morgan seemed to be just the man. Roosevelt sent for him, talked to him, and appointed him chairman of the new Authority.

The two other members were David Lilienthal and Harcourt Morgan. Lilienthal was thirty-four. He had left a lucrative practice with Donald Richberg in Chicago to serve briefly but with marked success on the Wisconsin Public Service Commission before joining TVA. His dedication to public service was as real as Arthur Morgan's, but Lilienthal was precise and realistic in his outlook, where Arthur Morgan was loose-minded and touched with mysticism. Once Lilienthal came to see me to ask my opinion as to whether it would be a mistake for him to sue Arthur Morgan for libel—his charges had been grossly libelous, and Lilienthal felt them deeply under his cool and disciplined behavior. I advised him against bringing any action, at least until the investigation had been completed. I hardly knew him then, but much later, when I was vice chairman of the Twentieth Century Fund and he was a director, we grew to be friends. He had a genuinely Christian outlook—perhaps a curious word to apply to a Jew, but one that fits exactly his compassionate sensitiveness.

The third member, Harcourt A. Morgan, was almost twice Lilienthal's age. A former president of the University of Tennessee, he was trusted by the people of the valley, and was responsible for helping to build the great program on existing local institutions. This was what Lilienthal meant by his frequent references to "grass roots"—the power of the federal government decentralized in local administration, what F.D.R. was always harping on, that national power could be used locally.

During the investigation we saw little of the three directors— Arthur Morgan avoided us, showing by his aloofness that he was convinced that we were prejudiced against him; and we made a point of seeing as little as possible of the other two. Neither of them made a good witness—Lilienthal, who must have been under a great strain, had a trick of smiling slightly before answering a question, which gave him a suggestion of the supercilious—he was quite unconscious of it; and Harcourt Morgan seemed to know very little about his own work. I was told afterward that he was alive to the constitutional doubt as to whether the federal government could undertake broad-scale agricultural experiments that had nothing to do with control of navigable streams.

The arrangement in the statute of a three-man board might have been administratively feasible to run this ambitious undertaking if the three directors had confined their work to over-all direction and planning, keeping it within the limits of an active board of directors of a private corporation, and placing the operation in the hands of a single executive responsible to the board. But from the beginning the board—whose functions were not defined by the act with sufficient clearness—assumed executive powers and divided them: Arthur Morgan took construction, education, and land planning; Harcourt Morgan would deal with agriculture and fertilizers; and David Lilienthal had power and transportation, and (being a lawyer) legal relations. Obviously someone had to pull all this together, and in true New Deal fashion John B. Blandford, an experienced expert in public administration, was appointed "co-ordinator" after five months of experimental unco-ordination, and finally general manager. By then the row among the board members was in full swing, reaching down into all levels of administration. Within a year Blandford, with the help and advice of some of the best men in the country, had reorganized the setup, and clarified the lines of responsibility.

A natural feature of the new organization was a policy under which board members had access to the staff only through the general manager, so that they might be relieved from attention to administrative detail, which in the past had made smooth operation impossible. But Arthur Morgan did not want to be relieved of detail. Suspicious and jealous, he insisted on knowing everything that was going on. He found it galling to turn to the general manager instead of to one of his own engineers, and refused to recognize the new arrangement. He was unhappy, felt out of things, his life dream was slipping away from him. . . .

Arthur Morgan had the strength and the smaller weaknesses of the American zealot. Born in 1878 in Cincinnati, his career as a consulting and government engineer had taken him into Colorado, Minnesota, and the Southern states. He distrusted and disliked the more complex culture of the East. He was a man with a mission, deeply apprehended, yet largely inarticulate, so intensely nursed in the passionate depths of his personality that it came to rule his life and undermine his judgment. He would have expressed the mission in terms of public service; and he had the destructive egotism of a human being who believed that he had been chosen to reshape the world, so that disagreement with him, or with some cherished policy that he held, seemed to him blasphemous. At the very time when the Tennessee Valley Authority, attacked on all sides, most needed his strength, he turned on it and did his best to destroy it, joining with those forces that saw a chance to render it impotent.

To understand this complete about-face and the baseless accusations with which he charged his associates, it is essential to realize this strange delusion of certainty that at times attacks the vicar of God on earth. We find this self-delusion in other great Americans—and Morgan had a touch of greatness about him—in Woodrow Wilson, for instance, who would not compromise about *his* League of Nations. Arthur Morgan confused policies with principles; and when he reiterated that he would never compromise with principle he meant that he would not yield to someone who disagreed with him on policy. Related to such Messianic temperaments is lack of humor, humor in the broadest sense that tempers opinion with a feeling for relative values. The men who knew Dr. Arthur Morgan well felt that he was without that healthy and saving grace.

This moralistic obstinacy appeared again and again in his statements to the press and in his testimony before the Congressional investigating committee. On March 3, 1938, before the President discharged him, Arthur Morgan announced to the press in words that were given wide publicity "that to fight for certain decencies and proprieties in public life was more important to good government than any particular government program"; and cited the Berry marble claim as an example of what he meant.

United States Senator George L. Berry, beginning in 1932, had leased lands containing marble deposits that were flooded by the erection of one of the dams, and made claim for the resulting damages. Dr. Arthur Morgan made no charges at the time, but when the breach became public announced that he had been contending with conspiracy, secretiveness, and bureaucratic manipulation, whereas the public had been led to believe that the difficulties within the Board were due to differences as to policy. Finally he became more specific: the Berry marble claim was an effort at a "deliberate, bare-faced steal." He suggested a congressional investigation. It would be pleasanter to resign, but that would be to "surrender the chance to make some contribution to decency and effectiveness in government."

Dr. Morgan had been making these charges widely before President Roosevelt took action, in an unprecedented hearing. He summoned the three directors to his office. Harcourt Morgan and Lilienthal were prepared to meet their associate's accusations. Arthur Morgan was asked to present the evidence behind them. But he refused to specify—he would give the evidence only to a congressional committee. Every word was taken down, and the record was made available so that the public could grasp the degree of his willfulness. The President understood him—he understood most men—and the great strain he was laboring under, and was patient and gentle, but had no choice except to dismiss him for cause, and this he did on the ground of "contumacy"—pertinacious resistance to authority.

Morgan's action was violative of every principle of administrative decency and loyalty to his superior. He would spread his accusations before reporters, but would not discuss them with the President, who had appointed him. Already he had given the Tennessee Valley Authority—*his* Authority—a black eye. People got the idea that Lilienthal and Harcourt Morgan were corrupt and incompetent, and that Arthur Morgan had stepped in just in time to prevent their approval of an agreement under which Senator Berry would have exploited the government.

After Dr. Morgan's dismissal Congress authorized the investigation, and the first task of the joint committee was to hear the evidence, which he had refused to give to the President. When the time finally came for him to testify before the committee, and before the press of the country jammed into the courtroom in Knoxville, and eager to spread the news of another Teapot Dome scandal—this time at the very heart of the New Deal—when the time came the whole tissue of suspicions and inferences, born and bred of jealousy and of a deepening sense of his own diminishing importance, collapsed. Before he left the stand he had withdrawn or explained away his charges. He had not intended, he testified, to accuse his colleagues of corruption in the sense of taking bribes or profiting financially. The differences of opinion on the Board, the committee concluded, were exaggerated out of all proportion because of the chairman's unfortunate propensity for attributing moral delinquencies to anyone who opposed him.

This propensity was demonstrated in his charges about the way his two associates on the Board had handled the Berry claim. They had agreed with Senator Berry to "negotiate"—in substance to discuss—a settlement with the Senator, and this action Morgan thought "unspeakable"; not that he meant by this (he said under cross-examination) that there was any intent to pay Berry more than the value of his claim. But what then was the objection? It was that one should not even negotiate with a person believed to be acting in bad faith, even if he had an enforceable legal right. He thought that if it were proved that Berry's leases on the marble lands had been acquired for the purpose of unloading them on the government, they should be declared void by the judges. He admitted under questioning that he had been mistaken on the law—the leases could not be voided.

Yet nothing had come of the effort to settle with Senator Berry. Unable to agree with him on a figure, the Board condemned the land. There was no question that the marble deposits existed. The sole issue was whether they could be commercially operated, a matter of judgment for the experts. During the trial Dr. Morgan did everything he could to harass Evans Dunn, the lawyer in charge of the case for the Authority. The condemnation commissioners disallowed the claim.

Arthur Morgan's capacity for harmful meddling, and his tendency to characterize disagreement with his own views as something highly improper, were even more apparent in the *18-Power Companies* case, as it was called. Suit had been brought by a group of private utilities to enjoin the TVA from producing and distributing electricity. The litigation, when it got to the Supreme Court, was expected to test the constitutionality of the Authority's powers. John Lord O'Brian, one of the leading lawyers of the United States, was taken into the litigation by TVA. The case was complex and highly technical. Mr. O'Brian gave us a vivid account (in his testimony at an early meeting of the committee) of Dr. Morgan's eccentric behavior at the trial in the U. S. District Court.

One did not immediately get the full effect of O'Brian's quiet power. He was not particularly impressive-looking—short, bald-headed, and nearsighted. He spoke quietly and with conviction. But when he had been testifying for a while his fairness of appraisal became persuasive. As a witness he was cool, clear, and exact, and very definite in his recollection of what took place. He told his story reluctantly and with the evident distaste of a man who disliked to fan the fire of personal recrimination, but felt it his duty to make the committee see Dr. Morgan's charges in their proper setting. He was without trace of vindictiveness or partisanship. He had excellent manners, but was unshakable. An eminent Republican himself, the Republican members of the committee, who usually did their best to destroy the testimony of any witness who favored TVA, did not press him.

The case before the District Court, which was tried in the autumn of 1937, had been prepared, Mr. O'Brian said, for a year and a half. Over a hundred witnesses, most of them engineers, were ready to testify. Their statements and the possible line of cross-examination had to be carefully gone over. Few of them were ultimately called, but the complaints in the bill of equity were so broad that the defense had to be ready on many different fronts. A great many theoretical studies were made. The hydraulic engineers themselves often disagreed; and when it came to the problems of measuring the stream flow, cutting the crests of floods, computing the volume of water released, the engineers were leading and educating the lawyers.

The trial was to begin on November 15. In the midst of the strain that preceded it, Arthur Morgan started to make trouble.

O'Brian, looking back, was sorry for the chairman. Dr. Morgan came to see him and James Lawrence Fly, chief counsel for the Authority, with whom O'Brian was associated, a week before the trial opened. They talked for two hours. Dr. Morgan read aloud a long and discursive memorandum, interrupting the reading to refer to other complaints: the lawyers had not consulted him, engineers under his supervision had been talked to without his permission, he had been ignored and humiliated. He was resentful—not just angry but deeply moved, O'Brian said. He was overwrought and distrustful of everyone, the attorneys were in conspiracy to keep him out of the case. He wanted to know what kind of "policies" Fly and O'Brian were evolving. He added that "so far as the hydraulic work was concerned [his work] there was no better in the country—so far as the other engineering work went it was rotten."

Without saying a word to O'Brian, three days before the trial started Dr. Morgan warned one of the most important engineer witnesses about the effect of "misleading testimony"—he must not permit himself to be misled by the lawyers. Whether Dr. Morgan realized it or not, he was making a direct charge that false testimony was being intentionally suggested by the lawyers, for which there was absolutely no basis in fact. Mr. O'Brian wrote Dr. Morgan of his concern, and for answer there came another memorandum to the effect that other engineers were complaining of the way the trial was being prepared. No names were given and no facts to support the charge. The trial staff was thrown into a state of alarm. They were in the last two weeks of the trial. Fly thought that Dr. Morgan would make an open complaint in court, and O'Brian was fearful that the trial might blow up under their feet. But it did not, and the case finally came to a close.

Dr. Morgan later recommended to our committee—a recommendation that would be adopted by the three Republican members in a minority report—that TVA's agricultural activities be transferred to the Department of Agriculture; its river control responsibilities to the War Department; and that only its power operations be retained. In short, he hoped it would be dismembered. He was tearing down the temple of his dreams to satisfy an overpowering hate for the men who had helped him to build it. The personal tragedy of it all was that Dr. Morgan might have gone down to posterity as a great man.

After Dr. Morgan's charges collapsed, newspaper interest in the case, disappointed at having the promise of a scandal snatched from the headlines, largely evaporated. As David Cushman Coyle put it, there were "mighty few lice on such a big dog." At Knoxville the committee settled down to the real question: was TVA doing a competent job, and would its operation afford the "yardstick" to test the reasonableness of electric rates charged by private utilities?

We started our investigation with a trip through the Valley to survey the dams and talk to farmers who had benefited by cheap TVA power. It was by now terribly hot, and poor Fred Brown, a Democratic senator member of the committee from New Hampshire—where he had seen eye to eye on many progressive policies with Gil Winant when Winant was governor—short and squat, dripped with sweat as he toiled up the scaffoldings, his shirt sleeves rolled up, a quid of tobacco in his jaw. He had been a professional baseball player, and discovered in Knoxville a cool stadium where baseball was played at night, and he went there whenever he could. He said little during the hearings; but after them he would come into my office, where he could "chaw" without concealment, spit freely, and curse the Republican members of the committee. I liked Brown. He was without frills of language or behavior, and he thought straight.

Senator Vic Donahey, the chairman, leaned over backward to be fair, and particularly to give the appearance of fairness. He had a great reputation for honesty, having, as auditor of the State of Ohio, once refused an expense account on the ground that it contained an item of thirty-five cents for one baked potato—and he was thereafter known as "Honest Vic," was promptly elected governor by a huge margin, and twice re-elected. He was tall, and swayed a little on his heels when standing. He was nearsighted and, like so many American politicians, suffered from active indigestion, so that between sessions he would lie down in acute discomfort, or now and then adjourn the hearing for a few minutes. He chewed gum incessantly, and dozed as he presided, waking up to rule on the admission of disputed evidence, when he would strike the desk lightly with his gavel, and say "so ordered" before closing his eyes again. He thought of me as young and impetuous—I was his junior by only a few years—but gave me a pretty free hand. He hated to spend money—that was his "line" and he stuck to it. When, for instance, I suggested that the committee retain Leonard D. White to make a detailed report on the TVA personnel, the senator agreed enthusiastically, provided I could find the money from one of the foundations.

This was accomplished, and Dr. White, who was ideally suited for the job, as a former member of the United States Civil Service Commission, and a Republican—and might therefore be expected not to be oversympathetic to this Democratic experiment —reported that in the personnel work new and significant improvements had been introduced. He found the quality of the personnel high; yet, having been a civil service man, recommended that the Authority be brought under Federal Civil Service procedure. But the committee did not follow this suggestion, believing that the success of the Authority's merit system—based largely on past record and oral interviews rather than standardized written examinations—was resulting in the flexibility and promptness of action characteristic of business organizations.

A section of the TVA act provided that the selection and

promotion of employees should be made on the basis of merit; that no political qualification should be permitted; and that any member of the Board found by the President to be guilty of a violation of this provision should be removed from office. Dr. White found that there was no evidence that appointments had been made as a result of political influence. The provision— a tribute to President Roosevelt's leadership in those early shining days of the New Deal—was a continuing source of irritation to Senator Kenneth McKellar, who had never been able to get his claws on appointments in TVA that by immemorial right should have been his in his own state of Tennessee. When David Lilienthal's name came before the Joint Congressional Committee on Atomic Energy in 1947 for appointment by President Truman as chairman of the Atomic Energy Commission, the Senator abused and vilified him recklessly in an attempt to establish his "convictions on communist doctrine."

But there was more than an effective merit system under a statute that outlawed politics. We found the sustained enthusiasm that goes only with work performed for an impersonal end. There was a strong community sense, and a profound conviction that the work was creative in human terms. The stretch of an enterprise that was to raise the level of a whole region stimulated the social imagination latent in the average American. And this enthusiasm was kept going not by the passing exhortation of improving talk, but by the concrete visible reality of building things that the inhabitants of the Valley needed and came to enjoy—cheap electricity, better fields and farms, the spreading of new young forests, and the splendid lakes formed by the dams, where wild life was carefully preserved.

The questioning by the Republican minority was left to the two members from the House, Charles A. Wolverton of New Jersey, a former assistant prosecutor for Camden County, and Thomas A. Jenkins of Ironton, Ohio.

Wolverton was affable, soft-spoken, shrewd, and hard-working. He had been told to take over the cross-examination of TVA witnesses and turn up what he could—he was considered the perfect man for the job. His technique was effective, not so much to find out the truth as to create an impression that facts were being concealed from the committee and the public. He liked to introduce slanted questions with such phrases as "for my information" or "I am simply interested in getting at the facts." He would constantly recall TVA officials to leave the suggestion that he was not satisfied with their evidence, or repeat a question with the implication that he was on the track of something, or that the witness was trying to cover up.

Jenkins, who tried to take an equally active part in the cross-examination, but soon ran out of questions, was neither shrewd nor polite. Wolverton knew how to handle witnesses. Jenkins did not. If he did not get the answer he wanted—and he seldom waited for it—he began to shout. He had once been a football player. He was "tough," but not very bright. Every now and then he would run into a witness who was skillful in rejoinder and unafraid, as when George Fort Milton, president of the Chattanooga *News*, was on the stand. We had gone to Chattanooga to investigate the subsidies in advertising paid to certain newspapers by the Tennessee Electric Power Company in an effort to block their support of public power. Milton's paper was in favor of TVA, and as a result had lost a substantial amount of advertising. Jenkins, now openly defending the utilities under attack, insisted that Milton be called.

Milton's appearance was misleadingly mild. He was not impressive. A short fat man with wide-open, watery blue eyes, he constantly fidgeted in the witness chair. He was gently ironic— which confused the Ohio congressman—and venomously polite. Jenkins, as one reporter described it, launched his attack with the swift directness of a falling stepladder. Milton, a distinguished historian, had for a year been a special assistant to Secretary of State Cordell Hull. Jenkins kept calling him "Mr. Special Assistant"; and finally said sententiously: "I am just a common congressman," upon which, Milton, to the delight of the spectators, addressed him as Mr. Common Congressman. . . . Jenkins was not very mature. But as a local columnist, Alfred Mynders, remarked, he must have been an extremely clever man in Ironton, Ohio, as he was a member of the U.C.T., the Masons, Odd Fellows, K.P., Red Men, and was past Supreme Master of the Knights of the Golden Eagle.

Quite early in the investigation General Hugh S. Johnson attacked me as timidly supporting the TVA witnesses and "bulldozing" those who knew the truth. Stripped of his once magnificent role of directing the National Recovery Act, he had turned, like other public men before and after him, to the lesser satisfaction of writing a syndicated column. He asked whether this vast experiment tended to prove that it would be better to scrap the capitalist system and local self-government in favor of the systems of Germany, Italy, and Russia.

My wife (Katherine Garrison Chapin) stirred to the depths, said nothing to me, but consulted Mike Ross, who had been my public relations officer when I was chairman of the Labor Board, and had come out to see what was going on, whether there was any reason why she should not answer the general. Mike was horrified at the idea. Whereupon Katherine, unable to hold in her mounting irritation any longer—there had been several other similar outbursts from the conservative press—sat down and wrote a letter to the general, signing herself Mrs. C. Kingsland Garrison, her great-grandmother's name. "As an old reader of your column," she told him, "may I express my criticism of what you said about the TVA probe?" She hoped in the interest of fair play he would come to Knoxville, and not be satisfied with newspaper reports. If he had sat in the court room, she continued, and watched, as she had, the slow unfolding of testimony day by day, the courtesy and fairness with which Dr. A. E. Morgan and other witnesses had been treated, and the deft, determined penetration of the cross-examination of all witnesses by Francis Biddle, the general would not have made his distinctly prejudiced and very misleading statement—"quite unlike what we count on from you." The general, confessing to a flood of other protests, published Katherine's whole letter, *"in the interest of fairness."* He thought that something might be said for TVA, but could not resist repeating a few more platitudes about earnest planners in Washington and the value of state institutions, however inefficient, slow and expensive.

Katherine did not reveal to me the authorship of the letter, which I had read with a glow of pride, until the investigation was over.

The most troublesome problem facing the committee—and the most controversial—was whether the Authority provided a "yardstick" on which to test the rates charged the public by private utilities. By many it was believed that these rates were far too high; and that the valuations of the utilities' property on which the rates were based included huge write-ups, characteristic of the twenties and early thirties when holding companies were buying stock of the operating companies. A holding company often not only wrote up the value of a stock when acquired, but would continue to "milk" the operating company by charging large management fees, in many instances uncalled for.

Specifically, Wendell Willkie's extensive holding company, the Commonwealth & Southern, owned the Tennessee Electric Company, operating in the Tennessee Valley in competition with the Authority, whose retail rates it claimed to be unfairly low because subsidized by the government. To what extent was this charge justified?

Confusion as to what the yardstick meant had been increased by the loose ways in which the phrase had been used first by President Roosevelt, and later by David Lilienthal and others. Was the cost of the manufacture of power by TVA to be compared to what it cost a private company, operating under similar conditions? If that was the test, government subsidies must be considered. But was not the true comparison between retail rates—those charged on the one hand by the utilities and on the other by the co-operatives and municipalities to which the TVA sold power?

More than two years before the investigation began, Walter Lippmann sensed this confusion and ventured an accurate definition of the yardstick, and of the issue between the Authority and the private utilities. The experiment, he thought, was by far the most interesting of the New Deal undertakings, and destined to exercise the largest and longest influence. The war between the Authority and the utilities over rates was really an insubstantial matter, because the TVA wholesale rates (not cost of production) for electricity varied very little per kilowatt hour from the wholesale rates generally charged in the area by the private companies. But TVA consumers paid only two fifths as much for electricity as the national average. The saving was found in the local retail system of distribution. It was not the power at the dam that was cheaper than private power. It was the power at the little town of Tupelo, Mississippi.

The witnesses for the private utilities did not appear to understand this conception, and devoted much of their elaborate technical evidence to proving that the TVA could not produce hydroelectric power at as low a cost as it could be produced by steam. This testimony of course concerned the problem of allocation of construction costs between the three uses of the dams—navigation, flood control, and power, but did not touch the yardstick.

I developed the yardstick largely through the mouths of the experts called on behalf of Commonwealth & Southern, under cross-examination. Mr. C. W. Kellogg was president of the Edison Electric Institute, the trade association of the electric light and power industry. It had succeeded the notorious National Electric Light Association following evidence brought out in the investigation of the industry by the Federal Trade Commission that the public schools had been flooded by "educational" material protesting against public power, prepared by professors paid by the industry. The present trade body, in the early days of TVA, had published a legal opinion, signed by Wendell Willkie, among others, that TVA was "palpably unconstitutional." More recently it distributed a booklet, *The Case for Private Ownership of the Electric Utilities,* to high schools all over the country, which the witness called the brief of the utilities, in the same breath insisting that it was not propaganda.

It was clear that neither Mr. Kellogg nor his institute understood the nature of the yardstick. Answering my questions, he readily agreed that the cost of production of the Tennessee Electric Power Company (with which the TVA wholesale rate could be compared) represented a proper charge for power at the dam in the Valley, about 4.18 mills per kilowatt hour, which included a return of 6 per cent on the investment. He kept emphasizing that this was less than it could possibly be produced by water, and that TVA must be subsidized. But that was not the point. If the wholesale charge for TVA power at the dam was not below that of the private utility, all distributors started at scratch. Actually TVA showed that its average charge to the municipalities and co-operatives was 5.6 mills. If anything, therefore, the private distributor, who paid 4.18 mills, started a little ahead.

Nor was the choice between steam and electricity. Most of the values to be obtained from the use of a river system are outside the field of private business. A power company cannot collect on any benefits to navigation or flood control produced by its dams; and even less on the diffused benefits of conservation of forest and soil. If such a unified river control is to be brought about, it must be financed and operated by the federal government. Hydroelectric power generation, often uneconomic when standing alone, becomes economically sound in combination with other public services.

As the committee said in its report, the Authority was a river control project, not only in theory but in practice, to which power generation was an incident. Therefore in order to justify the cost of generating hydroelectric power it was necessary only to show that the added cost of power would be repaid from the revenues from power. The use of power was not intended to pay the construction costs, but to reduce them.

The extent to which the various uses of the water would conflict was an engineering problem. In general, navigation, flood control, and power generation all called for producing as nearly a constant flow of water as possible, although at times it would be necessary to release water that in a purely power-generating system would be held. Under a unified management of a series of dams it was possible to manipulate the flow of water, so that water released for navigation at one point might be held or released further down as various uses of the river might require. Power production was secondary in the sense that the schedule for firm power had to be planned *after* allowing for the other uses of the water.

In the autumn of 1938 the investigation moved to Washington. Although the newspapers had long since lost interest in Dr. Arthur Morgan's charges, there was new excitement in Washington when Wendell Willkie took the stand.

This "barefoot boy from Wall Street"—as Harold Ickes called

him—knew thoroughly the fine art of publicity. On the stand he could be modest—or moral. He became indignant—and his indignation was that of a plain American attacked by the "interests"; he could be simple, talking the language of the man on the street—the little, average, everyday man who stood up for his rights, and brushed away the pettifogging of the lawyers (government lawyers), and got down to ordinary decency. When I asked him whether it was not true that values fixed by condemnation commissions usually ran 15 per cent higher than market values, Mr. Willkie replied: "No, I always assume that the courts of America are fair . . ." He could be a gentle witness, but he was more apt to be aggressive, shaking his fist and shouting at his questioner. He never descended to discussing details, but referred me to the little group of Commonwealth & Southern executives who had marched into the big Senate caucus room, where the hearings were being held, followed by two workmen carrying a trunk presumably full of reference material. I do not remember any other witness being called, and the trunk was never opened; but it stood there impressively, ready for instant action.

The press tables were filled, eight or ten photographers snapping the great man. He reminded me of the quality I had found twenty-five years before in Theodore Roosevelt, a vividness that lifted the spirits of everyone in the room when he came in, and communicated excitement, *joie de vivre*, and an intense consciousness of the moment. This capacity to stimulate his hearers made Willkie, when he ran for the Presidency the next year, an admirable campaigner for the first few months of the long effort *somehow* to win. But in the last weeks the public grew a little tired of excitement and variety. He failed to impress them with a steady and considered approach, and seemed to be performing a brilliant *tour de force* to amuse rather than to convince.

I asked Mr. Willkie if the municipalities selling TVA power were making or losing money. He answered that they were operating at a loss if you took into account "the true wholesale cost of power." He admitted that the books did show a profit for most of them. He had fallen into the yardstick error.

Events moved fast after Willkie had testified.

On December 31 the Authority announced in its annual report

an increase of 37 per cent in its revenues from the sale of power.
On January 30, 1939, the Supreme Court rejected in a five to
two decision the attack on the Authority by the private utility
companies in the *18-Power Companies* case (in which Dr. Arthur Morgan had been such a dangerous nuisance) on the
ground that they had no standing to challenge the validity of its
activities. Competition by the government was not a wrong
against which the Constitution granted immunity. It is no ex-
aggeration to say that John Lord O'Brian, who argued the case
for TVA, was responsible for saving it from legal destruction—a
fate which such eminent legal lights as Mr. John W. Davis had
prophesied was undoubtedly coming to it.

A few days later the TVA and Wendell Willkie's Commonwealth & Southern announced they had agreed on an amount to
be paid for the acquisition of the properties of Tennessee Electric
Power Company by TVA, nearly eighty million dollars, a sum
sufficient to pay not only the bondholders and preferred stock-
holders, but also a substantial equity in the common stock.
Payment of the common stock had been resisted during the negotiations on the ground that it was heavily watered. The compromise was greeted as a victory for Mr. Willkie. General
gratification exuded from the conservative press, from which
came no suggestion that the government had been overgenerous.
Finally the committee on April 1, 1939, submitted its report
and minority report, almost exactly a year after President Roosevelt had discharged Arthur Morgan from his post as chairman
of the board.

The majority report was signed by the six Democratic members of the committee, and by Senator Lynn J. Frazier, of North
Dakota, an independent Republican. The Republican press attacked the Democratic members of the committee for acting
politically, and in the same breath criticized Senator Frazier's
independence for not joining the three Republican dissenters.
The task of writing the report of a congressional committee falls
on its counsel. In this case I had excellent assistance from my
staff, and David Cushman Coyle, whom I arranged to have
transferred from another branch of the government where he
was working, put our loose-jointed narrative into readable and
lucid prose.

Regional planning, the report pointed out, was largely new in the United States. Our culture patterns were too tenacious to yield to regimentation. The Authority had wisely recognized that its planning could only suggest, and that any development was in the hands of the local communities. The presence of this regional planning agency, *decentralized from Washington,* had stimulated in the region a desire to solve its own problems.

The committee credited Dr. Arthur Morgan with the efficient and economical construction of the dams, and for the Authority's enlightened labor policy. Since only four of the eleven dams that were contemplated had been built, and the Authority was still operating at a loss, largely on account of the litigation instituted by the private utilities that had tied up operation with one court injunction after another—twenty-six injunctions had been granted—the report was necessarily prophetic. After discussing the costs and estimated revenues the committee concluded that the power revenues on the eleven-dam system with a 60 per cent load factor would be $22,925,000 annually, with operating total costs of $20,103,000, leaving a profit of $2,822,000. According to our engineers this profit should eventually be increased to $6,985,767. On this basis the expected revenues would pay for all power costs, cover the annual expenses of navigation and flood control, and finally, in about fifty years, return the total investment. Although the costs included an allowance for replacement of the dams, the engineers did not believe that these mammoth concrete structures would depreciate to any substantial degree over the period.

An ultimate value of the TVA experiment in the production and sale of electricity was suggested by Harlow S. Person, an expert on conservation of natural resources, water planning, and rural electrification, in an article in *The New Republic* two months after the report was filed. Its far-reaching significance, not yet appreciated he believed, was incalculable. If expansion of our economy depended on breaking monopoly and quasi-monopoly influence on the price structure, this instrument was at hand—injecting a public enterprise into any industry, and by yardstick measurement establishing prices that would ward off overinvestment, squeeze the water out of overcapitalization, prevent excess profits under the guise of "earnings," and yet leave a reward for everyone in the industry, private as well as public. By this device the Swedish Government had assured its people low-cost electric energy.

Such discourse was nicely calculated to make the normal businessman shudder; but normal businessmen do not read *The New Republic*.

The TVA program was not limited to the production of power, the control of floods, and the creation of a navigation channel. National in a larger sense, the agricultural program was particularly directed to a region of the South at that time substandard. Soil exhaustion, said the committee, had been disastrous in the South on account of dependence on cash crops. Crop rotation and use of cover crops were little practiced. It was estimated that a million and a half tons of phosphorous were annually lost to the soil by the removal of cover crops and grazing of animals. Two thirds of the fertilizer sold in the United States went to thirteen states in the South. It was primarily nitrogenous with very small amounts of phosphate in the mixture. A large proportion of waste material was found in the commercial fertilizers at that time in use, and resulted in heavy freight charges. A highly concentrated phosphate was required, and was not available at any price prior to TVA. The Authority developed a process for the manufacture of high-grade phosphates, which it did not sell commercially, but, in co-operation with land-grant colleges, tested in agricultural experiment stations and on demonstration farms selected by the farmers. Already about 23,000 of these farms were active in the demonstration program.

The committee found that the main purposes of the act had been honestly and efficiently performed. The control of the river in the public interest had been well designed. The Authority had passed through the period of legal obstruction and of the preliminary lean years characteristic of the construction phrase of any large enterprise. It should now be regarded as a settled institution in the Valley, which had already demonstrated the value of unified river control under public management.

The minority report, written by Mr. Wolverton and concurred in by Senator Davis, was in the nature of a political speech or party platform. It talked about dissension on the board, but did not mention Dr. Morgan's charges of corruption—which had brought about the investigation. It expressed regret that the committee had not investigated losses to the private utilities— although the resolution authorizing the investigation did not suggest such a line of inquiry. Mr. Jenkins, evidently thinking that his colleagues had not been sufficiently bloodthirsty in their attack on the TVA, added an "Individual Minority View" of his own. TVA would, he prophesied, continue its arrogance, bold tactics, and extravagant program with little regard for the law. He characterized me, the general counsel of the committee—a New Dealer "with a well-known propensity for the New Deal philosophy of government."

The public must have been thoroughly confused when the newspapers began to run their editorials. Few of them understood the measure of the yardstick. The New York *Times* thought that an objective reader of both reports would conclude that the engineering work had been well performed, and that TVA, cooperating with other agencies, had done much to stop soil erosion, improve agricultural practices, and promote the use of electricity in the area; and noted that the effective competition with private enterprise was less in the wholesale rates for power charged at the dams than in the retail rates charged by municipalities and co-operatives—a cautious step in the direction of understanding.

What really interested the press was the political issue, and on that most papers took clear-cut if unenlightening positions. The Columbus *Dispatch*, for instance, announced that *from its inception the TVA power project had its base in socialistic and undemocratic principles*, and was *a major New Deal effort to gain its ends by subterfuge*—the most extravagant, wasteful, and needless of all the Roosevelt administration's costly experiments.

But all of the Republican press were not so frankly partisan. It warmed my heart, after such a deluge of vilification and misunderstanding, to have the sturdy *Springfield Republican* say in an editorial that the TVA had been "morally vindicated" by the entire committee. The demand for the investigation had been by Senators like Styles Bridges, who looked forward to another Teapot Dome exposure—"rather hopefully, indeed, if the truth must be set down." The complete failure of the charges of corruption—the editorial added with a touch of irony—should be immensely gratifying to everyone who wished to think well of his country and of democratic processes of government. Underlying the long warfare on the TVA had been the private utilities' hostility to the development of hydraulic power as a by-product of government enterprise. TVA, the editorial concluded, had withstood the formidable legal assault up to the "last word" of the United States Supreme Court. It had now repelled the moral assault implicit in the congressional inquiry. "It has earned the privilege of settling down to business as an established agency and showing what it can do without being harried forever by enemies."

In May 1958 TVA celebrated its twenty-fifth anniversary. Its accomplishments in a short generation have been spectacular. The floods of 1946, 1947, and 1948 were the fifth, sixth, and seventh largest on record. From ten to twelve and a half feet were clipped from their crest. In the 1948 flood the reservoirs at Norris, and at Cherokee, Douglas, and Fontana on the tributary streams took and held the rush of water, and had room to spare. At Chattanooga the estimated saving of property loss was six million dollars. In 1950 TVA reduced the Mississippi at Cairo by two feet, rescuing about 2000 square miles of farmland. Four years later the multiple purpose of the dam system prevented the destruction of seven and a half million dollars worth of property at Chattanooga. In 1957—one of the worst floods on record—it was estimated that sixty-six million dollars of damage was prevented. The average annual benefit from flood protection was put at eleven million dollars.

It is a fascinating process, this control of a great river system. When to hold and when to release water often involves a nice judgment. Water flow must be maintained if the generators along the main stream are to be kept running; yet enough room must be left in the reservoirs to take care of a sudden or prolonged rain. When there is a flood on the Ohio or upper Mississippi, as much water as possible must be kept out of the Tennessee. In general the reservoirs are operated on an annual cycle. From

December through March, when the major floods occur, water is maintained at a low level. As the floods recede and the danger passes, the reservoirs are filled gradually, reaching their highest point about July 1. During the last half of the year, the dry season, water is released gradually to supplement the natural stream flow and keep the main channel filled for navigation. By January 1 the reservoirs are at their lowest level.

Malaria, once the worst scourge of the Valley, has disappeared. By fluctuating the water levels at the dams in early summer the larvae of the dreaded Anopheles mosquito is left on the shore to die. In 1934 TVA made an effort to determine the incidence of malaria among the population in the danger zone. More than 6000 blood tests were made. Of these about 30 per cent showed the presence of malaria. In 1941 there was none.

The program of testing TVA fertilizers is being carried through on 71,000 farms in thirty-eight states; the valley forests, a generation ago cut over and depleted, have been replanted, and forest products are now valued at four hundred and fifty million dollars a year. The timber is protected from fire by the states and counties, which, before the advent of TVA, afforded virtually no protection to the dreary and decimated land. Forty-five thousand valley landowners have, over this quarter century, planted over three hundred and sixty million seedlings.

But of these dry if satisfactory statistics the most human are found in the recreation activities. Hiding places for fish were provided deep in the reservoirs when the land was being cleared before flooding by fastening trees and brush to the ground. The fish multiplied so fast in the new lakes that stocking was unnecessary, and year-round fishing, even during the spawning season, was finally permitted. Now and then TVA would take a chance, as when in 1936 it stocked what is now the Central Peninsula game-management area between two parts of the Norris Reservoir with thirteen deer. Today the best deer hunting in the state, and perhaps the best in the South, is in that section. In 1956 hunters killed 1026 deer in the area, descendants of the original thirteen.

Of all these services there is but one that is considered "creeping socialism," a phenomenon which President Eisenhower discovered shortly after his first election—the supply of cheap electricity. It is not suggested that government should not supply other needed services—highways, schools, parks, the control of floods—or that it should stop selling cheap power to the utilities. Critics of the TVA have no objection to the government's undertaking nonprofitable services—but electricity is a different matter!

And the profits on TVA's books are by no means negligible. During the first five years its power revenues exceeded all out-of-pocket costs but were insufficient to cover depreciation charges. In the next fiscal year (1939) earnings also covered depreciation charges for the six-year period. As of June 30, 1961, the total net income, after operating and maintenance expenses, provisions for depreciation, and payments to states and counties in lieu of taxes amounted to $622,000,000!

"Megalopolis" has almost obliterated municipal boundaries in our country, and the problems of sewage disposal, of traffic control, of sanitation, of housing and parks cannot be solved by the cumbersome method of attempting to persuade local minicipalities to agree on what should be done and who should do it. Greater resort must be made to regional agencies like the Tennessee Valley Authority, and the New York Port Authority, the jurisdiction of which will be defined by the nature and extent of the needs of these new sprawling communities.

Senator Lister Hill, of Alabama, believes that the unified plan of TVA has promoted the prosperity of the people, added to their security, and multiplied their sources of enjoyment, besides bringing strength to the nation. Fifteen years ago Julian Huxley said that everywhere the initials TVA stood for multiple use of a single river to meet all the needs of man. John Gunther remarked that TVA might be called the greatest single American invention of the century.

The private utilities were desperately afraid that the TVA idea would catch fire, but it did not; and this extraordinary example of what the government could do to help the people develop their river resources to serve their needs was not followed in the United States. A bill was occasionally introduced for unified treatment of some great river valley, particularly in the West; but little has been accomplished, and the fight for public control of suitable sites for multiple-purpose dams still continues. It could hardly be expected that under a conservative Republican administration, such as that in power from 1953 to 1960, such a program would have spread. But it is more surprising that similar valley developments did not spring up during the two years, before our entry into the war, that followed the political and judicial approval of the TVA, in 1939; or under President Truman when the war was over. The failure to follow through is somewhat accounted for by the intense rivalries between state and government authorities, and between the departments of the federal government. A co-operation which was momentarily achieved at the birth of TVA could not be recaptured.

This failure was in interesting contrast to what has been undertaken in other countries. The Authority's structure and techniques have been studied and applied to control the terrible floods on the Damodar River in India. When David Lilienthal was still chairman of TVA the idea of a unified development for the Damodar Valley so attracted the Indian authorities that they "borrowed" William L. Voorduin, the TVA chief design engineer, who guided the form of legislation resulting in the Damodar Valley Corporation and the planning of the system. The sixth dam on that great river has been completed. Like TVA this project is a comprehensive, long-term plan of which dams are but a part.

Lilienthal and Gordon R. Clapp (who for fifteen years served TVA as general manager and chairman of the board), through their Development and Resources Corporation, are transplanting in Iran the basic TVA idea on a large scale. A series of fourteen dams on the rivers of the Khuzestan region has been projected, and the Dez Dam, the highest in the Middle East, will be completed in 1962. Irrigation, industrial development, and land reform are under way. There is restoration of sugar cane after 2400 years. As I write this the first crop of eight square miles has been harvested, and a sugar mill refinery is now (1962) in operation. There is electricity in the villages, which are mostly mud houses in a desert. Colombia in South America has adopted Lilienthal's proposed version of a TVA in the Cauca Valley, and after seven years it is a going concern run by Colombians along TVA lines, region-wide and decentralized.[1]

Nor is Russia neglecting the use of her great rivers. The Columbia, which carries 40 per cent of America's hydroelectric capacity, is the only river which, according to General Emerson C. Itschner, until recently chief of the Corps of Army Engineers, "begins to compare with the four major rivers in Siberia." In the U.S.S.R. more than forty river projects are under construction. Four of them will contain the most powerful electric plants ever built: the Krasnoyarsk Dam on the Yenisei River will have a capacity of 4,404,000 kilowatts. Our largest, the Grand Coulee on the Columbia, has a capacity of 1,944,000 kilowatts. General Itschner testified before the Senate Interior and Insular Affairs Committee that Russia now approaches us in total installed hydroelectric capacity, and that its projects under construction far exceed ours. The United States knows what Russia is doing, but takes no steps for further river development in America: but it must not be forgotten that we are avoiding "creeping socialism."

[1] See David E. Lilienthal's *TVA: Democracy on the March*, New York, Harper's, 1953 revision, for a list of countries that have followed the TVA lead.

THE CIRCUIT COURT
OF APPEALS
(1939–1940)

≈≋ *Chapter Four*

While I was finishing up the TVA report in Washington, Frank Murphy, then Attorney General, asked me to come
to see him. He told me that he wanted me to agree to go on the
Circuit Court for the Third Circuit—Pennsylvania, New Jersey,
Delaware, and the Virgin Islands. Murphy was trying to get
better men on the courts—he had spoken to the President about
it, and the President had approved. It was my duty to accept,
I owed it to the country, to my profession, to myself. I said no, I
did not want to be a judge. I loved practice, and did not wish
to give it up. Think it over, he pleaded. There was no good
thinking it over, I answered, I knew my own mind. I owed nothing to anyone. I was sorry but I could not agree. That was that.

A day or two later Senator Joseph Guffey, of Pennsylvania,
called me up to say that he heard I was being proposed for
this vacancy, did I want it? If I did he would not stand in my
way; he did have a candidate of his own, however, in case I
was not interested. I assured him that I would not accept the
offer under any circumstances. He seemed relieved, and
thanked me rather profusely.

I was exhausted after the long stretch of concentrated work, much of it at night, and contracted a bad cold, which kept me in bed for several days. Katherine and I decided to go down to Key West for a holiday. We had left Washington and were spending a few days at our School House Lane house in Philadelphia, before leaving. About six o'clock on the evening of February 5, 1939, the telephone in our library rang. I did not hurry to answer it—we were dining with Hugh Hamilton and his wife at their pleasant old farm in the White Marsh Valley, and were already late in starting. When I picked up the receiver President Roosevelt was on the wire.

"Francis, I want you to do something for me." It was the rich, friendly, seductive voice, which anyone sitting near me could hear as it rolled through the room.

"Yes, Mr. President?" I said a little nervously.

"I want you to be a judge. I want you to go on the Third Circuit Court."

"But I don't want to be a judge, Mr. President. It's like retiring. It's like becoming a priest, taking the veil."

I could hear him chuckling at the other end, leisurely, amused, sounding as if he were repeating what I had said to someone else. "But it won't be for long," he continued. "Frank Murphy wants to be Secretary of War, why God only knows. But it will take a little time to persuade Harry Woodring [who was then Secretary of War] to resign, perhaps five or six months. When he does go I'll put Frank in his place, make Bob Jackson Attorney General, and you Solicitor General. What do you say? Bob Jackson and Felix Frankfurter are sitting here next to me and they are witnesses to the plot."

I told him I should like to think it over. Of course every lawyer would like to be Solicitor General—did he have to know at once? Yes he did, he might announce my appointment the next day, he was moving up Robert Patterson from the District Court in New York to the Second Circuit, and making John Cahill U. S. Attorney in New York City. I'd be in good company. He would like to know in an hour—that ought to be time enough for anyone to make up his mind . . . I knew then that I would agree. Very well, I said, I'll call Mac (Marvin McIntyre, his secretary) in an hour. His response was typical. "No, don't call Mac, *call me.*" And he rang off.

Katherine is more cautious than I, weighing possibilities, seeing both sides. "Do you want to be a judge?" she asked me. I told her I did not, and we agreed that I would be taking a chance, not so much because Woodring perhaps could not be got out—I don't think that possibility occurred to us—but because F.D.R. might change his mind. One has to take a chance in life, I said, and we discussed every angle of it, driving out to Hugh's place, soon losing our way, until I looked at my watch—the hour was up. We went to the nearest house and rang the bell. Chalk answered, Chalk the renowned Philadelphia caterer—he "did" for us at the Hand-in-Hand dinners after the directors' meetings. I shook hands with him, and said that I had to call the President at once, he was expecting my call—could I use his telephone? Chalk looked as if he thought I was slightly deranged, but took me to the telephone, and the President was almost at once on the line. I told him he could send in my name, but would he do one thing first: I had only a few days before told Senator Guffey that under no circumstances would I go on the court. Would he please call Guffey himself, and get everything straightened out? He promised, but forgot; and the next morning my appointment was announced in the newspapers. The Senator had been urging the appointment of Michael Angelo Musmanno, a picturesque Pittsburgh judge, who, with the endorsement of the Pennsylvania labor leaders, got himself elected to the Pennsylvania Supreme Court a dozen years later. When the Senator came out for a candidate he announced his selection and stuck. He believed in the right of senators to name federal judges in their own states, and had recently said so in public. The papers seized upon my appointment as a rebuff by the President to Guffey. The Newark *Evening News* ran a cartoon of F.D.R. with a broad grin handing me to the Senator, sitting with a blue ribbon around my neck on a copy of *The Constitution According to F.D.R.*—"Song without Words." The Democratic representatives met to discuss the adoption of a resolution repudiating Guffey's leadership.

Senator Guffey got on our train in the Union Station in Washington, on our way to Florida, hurt by the White House "repudiation," and furious with me for "deceiving" him—particularly after he had told me that he would not have opposed me had he known that I wanted to be a judge. I could not blame him—after all was not Senator Guffey the only 100 per cent Simon-pure supporter of the New Deal and all its ways, voting for every measure sponsored by the administration? I explained to him my sudden shift as best I could; but I don't think he believed a word—it must have sounded lame. He never trusted me after that, and always opposed the appointment of any Pennsylvanian whom I suggested when I was Attorney General.

Senator Styles Bridges called my selection a reward for my "one-sided" service in the TVA investigation. The Senate confirmed me promptly without a record vote, and I was sworn in at the end of March.

The newspapers reacted to my appointment with friendly approval. Arthur Krock, of the New York *Times* (in spite of my New Deal record on the Labor Board and in connection with the TVA investigation), called my qualifications outstanding, and added that I owed nothing to politicians, and would elevate the level of the bench in Pennsylvania. I felt respectable again.

Judge J. Warren Davis was the senior judge of our court. A few weeks after I had been sworn in he announced that he was retiring as presiding judge at seventy-two, after nineteen years on the court. Frank Murphy, who had an unfortunate habit of commenting on matters pending before him, was asked at a press conference whether Davis had not been under investigation—for years the Philadelphia bar had suspected that he was crooked, but had hardly imagined the extent of his corruption. Frank bridled with indignation, saying that he was confident that Judge Davis's record was clear. In less than two years Davis was indicted and tried under Robert Jackson as Attorney General; and a second time when I succeeded Jackson, the jury disagreeing each time.

Warren Davis was a smooth, sanctimonious old rascal, who had taught Greek, Sanskrit, and Latin at the Crozer Theological Seminary at Upland, Pennsylvania, instructed at Sunday school, entered the ministry, and accepted a call from the Baptist Church at Pedricktown, New Jersey. Finally he caught Woodrow

Wilson's coattails, and landed on the District Court, and the Circuit Court in 1920.

Davis was tried with William Fox, the movie magnate, and Fox's lawyer, Morgan S. Kaufman of Philadelphia, on charges of conspiracy to obstruct justice. Fox, who pleaded guilty and turned state's evidence, testified that he had loaned Judge Davis $27,000 through his lawyer in an effort to get favorable decisions in litigation then pending before Davis's court. Three judges had sat in the cases, among them old Buffington, almost completely deaf, suffering from defective eyesight, his senility ending a long career of ineptitude. Judge Davis wrote the opinions, all favorable to Fox, and persuaded Buffington to sign them —with the third judge, Whitaker Thompson, dissenting. The government traced five thousand-dollar bills to Belle Fox, who testified that she had given them to her father; and in turn they were traced to Judge Davis's daughter. I do not know why the jury did not convict. He was a gentle-spoken, persuasive scoundrel, and knew how to act the "ceremony of innocence." He took the stand, testifying that the money was in repayment of a loan by a person since deceased. But he admitted that he met Fox in New York after he knew that his affairs were being investigated, and registered at a hotel in Hoboken, New Jersey, as Herman Goldberg.

One of the first decisions I had to make as Attorney General was whether I should ask for a third trial. In determining not to do so I was not so much guided by Davis's condition—he was old and infirm; nor did I think that a conviction would be impossible. But by tradition the government does not take three bites at the apple. Davis was still on the bench, having retired but not resigned, and drawing a full salary of $12,500. I wrote to Representative Hatton Sumner of Texas, chairman of the House Judiciary Committee, suggesting that impeachment proceedings be started promptly. Then Davis resigned, and impeachment would no longer lie—but that was the end of his retirement pay.

My associates on the bench were all Roosevelt appointments. John Biggs, Jr., the senior judge, Albert Maris, William Clark (a Republican), and Charles Alvin Jones were all men of unusual ability; and, with the exception of "Willy" Clark—who had the instability of an advanced egocentric—exhibited careful judgment and common sense. I don't think we ever measured up to the Second Circuit, illuminated by those two brilliant cousins, Learned Hand and Augustus Hand. But after the Second, many members of the bar put the Third Circuit next.

Biggs was an excellent judge and administrator, who kept us abreast of the work, all except Willy Clark, who was always four or five months behind, spending his time in the highways and byways of little-known legal precedents, upstream and cantankerous by nature, suspicious and therefore often suspected. Biggs had left a successful practice in Delaware to go on the court. At Princeton he had been an intimate friend of Edmund Wilson and Scott Fitzgerald (he was Fitzgerald's literary executor). He had contributed stories to *Scribner's Magazine* and written novels. He had been active in Delaware politics as Democratic state chairman, doubtless inheriting his taste for politics from his father, who had been attorney general of Delaware, and his grandfather who had been governor.

I grew to delight in his companionship. He was a man to whom strange and lurid adventures were always happening. He had, for instance, a run-in with a ubiquitous poltergeist who inhabited the body of a Newfoundland dog which mounted the stairs in the cottage that the Biggses had taken in Bermuda (the rent had been suspiciously low), and disappeared when it had reached the top. But the nimble little spirit remained to plague John by whisking his black bow tie across the room . . . There was that unnerving dream about the funeral of John's mother, a week before she died; and, detail by detail, the funeral when it came re-enacted the dream. What made these wonderful tales taller was that John was himself skeptical about such incarnate mysteries, touching them up like most good talkers with a stroke of the brush here and there, but essentially factual. We became close friends, and when he is in Washington working indefatigably for some administrative judicial committee appointed by the Chief Justice, he stays with us, and again I share the sense of fresh life and adventure that stirs in him.

Albert Maris I knew only when I was on the court. A long-standing Democrat, his appointment was strictly political—he had been the Democratic committeeman for Delaware County,

Pennsylvania, through the slow, lean years before 1933—resulting from an endorsement by Senator Guffey, not because Maris was a good lawyer but because he was a good Democrat. And it was a first-rate appointment. During the Second World War he served with admirable common sense on the United States Emergency Court of Appeals (he was designated Chief Judge in 1943), which heard appeals from price-fixing. Maris, now retired, has devoted his life to the law, modestly and successfully, and is a lawyers' judge, knowing the technical side of his profession thoroughly, but also conscious of the law's scope and limitations.

I saw less of Charley Jones, who was appointed in August, 1939. He had been the unsuccessful Democratic candidate for governor the preceding fall. I grew to like him and to admire his liberal outlook held in proportion by experience in practice and a cool judgment. He ran for the Pennsylvania Supreme Court and was elected in 1944.

The members of our court were, comparatively speaking, young men. When Biggs went on the court in 1937 he was forty-two; Maris, joining the next year, was forty-five; Jones and I came on the following year, Jones at fifty-two and I at fifty-three. What a contrast this was to the old court. In 1937, Buffington, who had been a Republican delegate at the convention of 1880 that refused to nominate General Grant for a third term to the presidency, was eighty-two. He was led by the nose by Davis, who was seventy, for his own crooked ends. The other two members, Woolley and Thompson, were upright and competent men; but Woolley entrenched in conservatism, was a sick man at eighty-two; and Whitaker Thompson was seventy-eight.

In spite of my cordial relation with my associates I was not happy as a judge. Sometimes the arguments were alive and interesting, but most of them were platitudinous and without style or sharpness. I had been very active at the bar, and had the sense that now I was removed from that goodly fellowship. Old professional friends treated me with too much deference, too little informality. Perhaps that feeling on my part would have worn off as time went on; but my judicial career was to be brief. As month followed month, and I was still a judge, I was worried that the President's neat arrangement, like the fitting of the final pieces in a picture puzzle, might never come off, the pieces refusing to slide into the few spaces that were left. It was expected that the shift would take place in the summer. July went by and August, and I grew restless. There was no hint from Washington. Would I be condemned to the distasteful choice of being chained to the bench, or resigning after a few years, my practice gone, my future uncertain?

I went down to Washington to see Bob Jackson. Woodring, he told me, refused to budge. He had declined to be shifted into diplomacy—the embassy to Canada had been offered him—and his part in the reshuffling of the pack had leaked into a column, so that his back was stiff and his legs firmly planted behind the desk. Should I see the President? Bob thought that would be appropriate, but I should go not to ask him to fulfill a promise, but to seek his advice.

I got an appointment promptly. The President had an air of being busy, of having little time at his disposal, he was stiff, and I could sense a covert irritation. But when I said that I had come to ask his advice on a personal problem, I knew how right Bob had been. F.D.R. leaned back, relaxed and intimate after he had lit his cigarette—"What do you think I ought to do, Mr. President?" He assured me that everything would work out if I would be a little patient—these things take time. The old school relationship having been re-established, the third former to the sixth, we both felt better. I left with a sense of renewed loyalty. . . . Two months later on November 16, when I was in Cambridge to sit on a moot argument at one of the law clubs of the Harvard Law School, passing the *Lampoon* building I saw on the news bulletin in the window the announcement of the death of Pierce Butler of the United States Supreme Court. Of the "four horsemen," as they were known, the four ultra-conservatives, McReynolds alone remained, and he would retire in 1941. I knew instantly that the shift would take place—Frank Murphy, a Roman Catholic, would be a natural to follow the only other Roman Catholic on the Court, an arrangement sanctified by tradition. I had a tremendous sense of relief when I saw the news. I suspect that the President, too, was pleased by the change in his plan that the vacancy created, for he must have known after Frank Murphy had been a year in office as Attorney General how incompetent a Secretary of War he would have made.

Early in December 1939 newspapers were speculating on the shift. On January 4, the official announcement was given out. I had already recommended to the President, Herbert Goodrich, dean of the University of Pennsylvania Law School, to take my place. And when, just a little too late, Senator Guffey hurried over to the White House to obtain the judgeship for a certain John McCann, a Common Pleas judge in Cambria County, and old-line Democratic wheel horse, who, it was rumored, might oppose the Senator who was running for re-election that autumn, he was told that the vacancy had been promised. But he did not oppose Goodrich, who made an excellent judge. I am sure that the Senator smelled my hand in the matter, and scored another black mark against my name. And when a year or two later, after I had become Attorney General, there was a vacancy on the District Court in Philadelphia—indubitably in Joe's baili-wick—and I persuaded Jack Kelly, the Philadelphia Democratic leader, to back Shippen Lewis, who would have made a good judge, Guffey called me on the telephone, outraged at my "in-terference." Did I know that he had publicly come out for Cullen Ganey? Did I know that Jack Kelly had been opposing his re-nomination for the Senate? I would not block him again, he shouted, the way I had on the CCA—it was none of my business —he would see the President. This time the Senator got his man. The President telephoned me please to convey to Jack Kelly, firmly but discreetly, that the administration would be pleased if Joe Guffey were renominated. I relayed the message to Kelly's secretary, Lucy Duval. The next day the newspapers carried the surprised news that the Democratic organization in Philadelphia had shifted its support to Senator Guffey. There was no hint of "undue pressure." The Senator was renominated and re-elected. But our disagreements were not yet over.

SOLICITOR GENERAL

1940-1941

❧ *Book Two*

The people ought to fight in defense of the law as they do of their city wall.

HERODOTUS

ARGUING CASES

⋙{}⋘ *Chapter Five*

The Washington of 1940, the year that I was appointed Solicitor General of the United States, was very different from the hectic days of the Labor Board, five years before, when the ardent if often confused gusto of the New Deal was at its height, and young men, unwilling to accept the tried formula of their elders that as things had been so they should be, found endless opportunities to express their restless dissatisfaction with the universe, and, their feet on the desk, told the particular elder who ventured to register objection just where to get off. . . . The stages of the New Deal's advance could now be ticked off—it had arrived, had seen, had succeeded in making the social and economic changes so long overdue, and now there was less grist for the mills. President Roosevelt had got about everything he wanted. He had not succeeded in packing the Supreme Court. But though the Senate prevented this particular experiment, apparently so dear to his obstinate heart, Nature quietly removed the aging gentlemen who stood in the path of his will. Now he would have a certain majority, men he had himself appointed: Black (1937), Reed (1938), Frankfurter (1939), Douglas (1939), and Murphy (1940). Of the four horsemen who had so consistently opposed any significant social change, because change was not contemplated by the Constitution of the American democracy, Van Devanter and Sutherland had retired; Pierce Butler had died; and only McReynolds was left, sour rather than bitter, lonely on the changed bench without the sense of effective negation so relished by men of his cantankerous temperament. He thought of Holmes—as the latter wrote Laski— as a bird who had befouled his own nest. . . . McReynolds, after serving for twenty-seven years, was to retire in 1941, remembered as the Attorney General who had been kicked upstairs by President Wilson, and as a justice whose language had been picturesquely impolite in the *Gold Clause* case.

Frank Murphy's appointment is revealing of the way President Roosevelt handled men. Murphy had not abandoned his ambition to be Secretary of War. He did not, I am tempted to believe, if he ever thought about that aspect of the appointment, consider that his qualifications entitled him to sit on the exalted bench. He had taught law at a night school in Detroit, while clerking in the firm of Monaghan & Monaghan, had been the chief assistant U. S. Attorney for the Eastern District of Michigan, and filled the position of a judge of the Recorder's Court in Detroit from 1923 to 1930, before his political career advanced as mayor of Detroit. That trenchant aphorist, the late Thomas Reed Powell, Story professor of law at the Harvard Law School, suggested when he heard of the appointment that thereafter justice would be tempered with Murphy.

He was a "lame duck," having been defeated in 1938 for governor of Michigan, with little prospect of settling to a lucrative lobbying practice in Washington, the normal anticlimax of successful political activity. He would not have liked such a practice, or any practice for that matter. His year as Attorney General had built a bridge in the direction of the Court, and his incapacity as an administrator had suggested a change. War was on the horizon, and F.D.R. must have by then abandoned any idea of putting Murphy at the head of the War Department. Henry L. Stimson was soon to fill that office. The President wanted to make a shift, and there was nowhere else to put Frank Murphy except on the Court. Like most vigorous Presidents, Roosevelt was not very much concerned with the Court, as long as it did not interfere with his plans. He had never had sufficient training as a lawyer to understand that the art of judging required skill, although he must have appreciated that the quality of judges had some relation to the country's direction.

The irony of the situation was that Frank Murphy, who as Attorney General insisted with a good deal of zeal that only first-rate men should be appointed to the federal courts, even persuading his chief to act on his advice, finally accepted an appointment that could by no stretch of sympathy with the President's problems be called first-rate. It was a bad appointment, and Murphy knew it, and everyone knew it. I suspect that he might have resisted and argued had he been consulted. But he was not consulted, and woke up one morning to find himself thrown at the bench, part of a shuffle that put Jackson in his place, and Biddle in Jackson's. Murphy told the incredulous newspapermen that he had not made up his mind whether to accept—he did not tell them that he had not been asked—he might still turn it down. He may even have remonstrated with his chief, with a humorless glow in his mildly mystical eye, and said that he wanted to be Secretary of War, why could he not be Secretary of War? Of course he would rather be on the Supreme Court than have nothing, and be left out in the cold.

The President by then must have become persuaded that his Attorney General was not functioning as he should. Complaints had come in. F.D.R., who never paid much attention to administrative etiquette, as he might have called it, was consulting Bob Jackson, his Solicitor General, over the head of his Attorney General. Bad blood had arisen between the two men, and things were not flourishing in the Department of Justice. Murphy had no administrative competence. He was vain, self-conscious, and avid for publicity. I have no idea why the President liked Frank Murphy, but he did. Frank had no humor, he preached at you, he must have been a bore as a companion. He was like a ham actor, beating his chest, stepping aside, throwing his head up, darting a piercing look. Perhaps all this amused the President; it might even have impressed him a little. Murphy believed in his God, in his country, in himself, a trinity that fused and merged, spiraling ever upwards and outwards above that dreaming horizon on which his spirit vaguely yet triumphantly appeared to float. When the news of his elevation to the bench was announced, an item that must have been confided by him to the press stated that: "a bachelor, Murphy never smokes nor drinks"; and that in the past twenty-eight years he has read the Bible fifteen times. He was a man I thoroughly disliked.

Let me add at once that Frank Murphy was unfaltering in his support of civil liberties and individual rights. His opinions evinced moral conviction on a high level of indignation. But the man saw always in values of black and white, knew no intervening shades, disentangled none of those perplexities and balanced values the discovery of which distinguishes the searching mind of a useful judge.

That wise and witty American judge, Learned Hand, did see the perplexities; and, when we were fellow passengers on the *Exochorda* from Naples to New York in 1951, discussed them with me as we walked the decks. The nub of the difficulty lay in the Constitution itself, he said, which forced you to decide issues that were essentially moral and political. He wanted to act like a judge, grinding no ax, carrying no banner, caught in no net of prejudice, whether of habit or of conviction, neither to the right nor to the left. It was in that sense, he added, that Holmes had insisted that law did not concern itself with morals, and that when you decided on the basis of a moral standard you exercised the influence of partisanship. The tests should be discernible, and a judge should not have to exercise political and social judgments.

Precedents don't help much, Hand continued, for on almost any broad issue that has once burned and will burn again, such as free speech versus control, the road is littered with precedents on both sides. He did not believe in the attempts to meet the threat of communism embodied in the Smith Act of 1940, under which the first eleven Communists were convicted for preaching and preparing conspiratorially for the "day of revolution." That was not the way to handle the matter. But Congress thought otherwise, and he sustained the constitutionality of the act, disappointing many of his liberal admirers. If the United States determined that her protection involved trying to stop this kind of business by a criminal statute, why should a judge stand in the way, no matter how dearly he held to the freedoms, not only as a way to an end, but as a good way of life?

But, I would say to him, the system *has* worked over the years.

It has not, he replied. You New Dealers were the first to say so. For a long half-century after the Civil War the Supreme Court knocked out one attempt after another to regulate, in rather mild and tentative ways, the injustices and cruelties of the industrial system—and it became virtually impossible to get any normal reform through. It was precisely that which made F.D.R., in despair, try to pack the court. Now the pendulum has swung in the other direction, and some of your New Deal judges write their prejudices into their opinions precisely as Van Devanter and Sutherland and Pierce Butler did before them.

Learned Hand was endowed with so many talents of heart and mind that it was difficult to choose those which were most characteristically his. He was thoroughly normal in his gusto for living, and excellently balanced. As a skeptic he discarded the comforting magic of absolutes, and stood alone facing the adventure of life, while he felt its mysticism and asserted its values. Like Justice Oliver Wendell Holmes, whom he greatly admired, he was not cynical, because life without values seemed to him intolerable. He did not believe that his values were eternal, but they were his—courage, a sense of humor that kept things relative, the spirit of liberty which "is not sure that it is right," and seeks to understand the minds of others. Above all he was tolerant. Yet his tolerance never touched indifference, and he was passionate in his beliefs as well as his feelings. I shall never forget what he said at a meeting of the Law Institute in Washington in May of 1941, putting aside his prepared address, trying to make us realize what the fall of France meant to civilization with an eloquence that made us ashamed that we had not felt as deeply about it as he felt.

Murphy, Jackson, and I were to be sworn in together in the Oval Room of the White House, which the President used for his study. I delayed, however, taking my oath of office until my wife and son could join me, but came down to witness the ceremony for the other two men. Murphy was given the oath by Justice Stanley Reed, the strange oath prescribed by statute that he had not paid any money to obtain the appointment, his hand

on a battered Bible, presented to him by his mother when he
graduated from high school. Ever since then, he informed reporters, he had read it daily.

When it came my turn the following Monday, more humbly
in the Department of Justice, Murphy asked me to lunch with
him after the ceremony. I thought that he might give me a few
hints on how to carry on. He did. What was my religion? I was
born an Episcopalian. He said he hoped I read the Bible every
day. I let that pass. He told me one thing that did interest me.
When Secretary of War Harry Woodring would not resign, the
President asked Murphy whether he should make me an Assistant Secretary of the Treasury—there was a vacancy. According
to Frank's account he had sternly rebuked his chief, reminded
him of his promise, said he must keep it. "It would not be right,
Mr. President . . ." He kept emphasizing the part he had
played in my appointment, expecting some expression of gratitude, suggesting that without his intervention I would never have
been where I now was. I did not believe him and said nothing.

Jackson told me that there had been general relief in the
Department when Murphy left.

As was the custom I called on the members of the Supreme
Court. The Chief Justice could not understand why I had resigned from the Circuit Court. He embarrassed me by asking
whether perhaps the action came from a reluctant sense of
obligation to serve, as Frankfurter had hinted. He would not
have understood if I had said flatly that the court work bored
me. But McReynolds, who was not without a certain cunning
insight, understood—being a judge had always bored him, he
said; and added that lawyers, not judges, make the law.

Frankfurter told me to know thoroughly the records in the
cases I argued—an admirable counsel; and to keep out of politics—not a difficult suggestion for a Solicitor General to follow.
He hoped that I would pass on some advice to my assistants
when they argued cases: X to keep his voice up at the end of
sentences; Y to be less discursive; and Z—well Z was hopelessly
dull, keep him away from the Court. Never he said—and here
again he was right—never pad your briefs with makeweights,

which but dissipate your argument, pick a single issue and stake everything you have on it.

On the whole the newspapers were pretty decent about my appointment. *Life* posed and photographed me under my brother George's mural on the fifth floor of the Department of Justice building, standing on the steps immediately below my own likeness in the panel depicting "ordered plenty." The St. Louis *Post-Dispatch* confessed to an "inescapable feeling" that I had made the sacrifice out of personal loyalty to the President.

The letters of congratulation from lawyers were divided between those who thought it a sacrifice to give up a lifetime judgeship for such a temporary office, and the advocates—the true lawyers—who had no doubt that being Solicitor General was the ultimate professional satisfaction. To John G. Buchanan, of Pittsburgh, it was the one office he ever had any ambition to occupy; and he was reminded of what Job Hedges had said at a Princeton alumni luncheon twenty-five years ago in honor of Henry Van Dyke, who had just been appointed minister to the Netherlands: "We are for you Mr. Van Dyke. We want you to have anything we can't get for ourselves." Charles C. Burlingham, the dean of the New York bar, a very old friend, understood perfectly that "having tasted the bench" I preferred the bar, where the air was freer, and this for a lawyer was the most satisfying post in the United States.

The reasons that lawyers consider the office of Solicitor General so satisfying are not hard to find. His job is to represent the United States—his only client—in arguments before the Supreme Court of the United States. The work combines the best of private practice and of government service. He determines what cases to appeal, and the client has no say in the matter, he does what his lawyer tells him, the lawyer stands in his client's shoes, for the client is but an abstraction. He is responsible neither to the man who appointed him nor to his immediate superior in the hierarchy of administration. The total responsibility is his, and his guide is only the ethic of his own profession framed in the ambience of his experience and judgment. And he represents the most powerful client in the world.

Nor are there any of the drawbacks that usually go with public work, no political compromises, no shifts and substitutes, no cunning deviations, no considerations of expediency. The Solicitor General has no master to serve except his country. Patronage is outside his ken, and administration usually reduced to a minimum.

The Solicitor General's office was small, compact, and easily managed, with a tradition that excluded hacks and enlisted men of marked ability, all of them young. They were not particularly well-paid, but were not tempted by the fleshpots of private practice if they could get into court now and then, and run their own show with their chief without too many encroachments from outside departments. They loved their work and they believed in it. They wrote or rewrote most of the briefs that came up from other divisions of the Justice Department, or from other departments, in the immense litigation in which the government was engaged in the Circuit Courts as well as the Supreme Court—about a third of all the cases in the United States Supreme Court at that time involved the government. My assistants could draw rings around most of their contemporaries in private practice.

On the average I argued a case every two weeks. I had to work through long evenings to master the records, to be ready to answer Mr. Justice Frankfurter's questions—he had the ability to swallow records like oysters, to parody an expression of Justice Holmes in a letter to Harold Laski when the younger man had boasted about the books he had been consuming. Frankfurter liked to pick out some obscure morsel not referred to in the briefs—which became horribly relevant if the Solicitor General missed it—darting down into the record apparently at random and pulling out and holding up the telling bit. A suspended and involuted question would then emerge, as if Henry James had been dictating *The Wings of the Dove* to a new amanuensis. Do you see what I mean, Mr. Solicitor? The answer need not be simple, he seemed to indicate, sitting back to watch the government lawyer's reaction.

Occasionally it was hard to state the facts, if it was your appeal, when the questions came from several members of the Court at once; hard to channel your argument when the stream of your thought was constantly interrupted; but what a stimulus, what fun to find and feel the intellectual resistance, to argue to a *live* Court, instead of washing up against an ominous and uninterested silence. . . . I had fortunately been trained in this sort of thing, for the Pennsylvania Supreme Court had the same habit, and once or twice Chief Justice von Moschiszker had extended the half-hour rule when his talkative brethren had left but little of it to a struggling lawyer, eager to argue his point if he could find a little space of silence. Justice Brandeis once said to me that Pennsylvanians presented their arguments better than lawyers from any other state, and thought the reason for their admirable concision lay in the rules of their Supreme Court: the question involved must be stated in not more than a page of the brief, under penalty of having it suppressed; and the argument, except by special permission of the court, could not take more than half an hour.

Jackson was not happy as Attorney General. He disliked the daily grind of administrative work, and remembered the charmed days when he was arguing cases before the Court that he was soon destined to enrich, instead of trying to persuade Mr. Edward J. Flynn, chairman of the National Democratic Committee, to withdraw his resolute opposition to the appointment of a moderately competent man for a judgeship in New York; or to convince Senator George W. Norris that the Director of the Federal Bureau of Investigation had not been guilty of fascist methods when he arrested the American Spanish loyalists—a statute had made it a crime to enlist in the army of a foreign country—in the early hours of the morning, and had handcuffed them in accordance with the usual practice of the Bureau to prevent armed resistance.

The first two cases that I argued were neither complicated nor important. They both involved the right to counterclaim against the United States, and were listed to be argued in succession. A week before the day they had been set for argument I developed a nasty attack of flu. I could readily have had them postponed or arranged to have someone else argue them. But having done the work I wanted to make the argument. And there was a reason against asking for a postponement. On the day after the date set for argument a dinner in my honor in Philadelphia had long been scheduled, and I could not very well go to it if the Court were informed that I was too ill to appear the day before. I decided to take a chance, swallowed a Benzedrine pill early in the morning of the argument, and turned up in Court a bit shaky.

The cases were to be argued separately as they involved different claims. As we had lost both in the courts below, I opened for the United States. I got through the first pretty well. But when the second was called, and I rose to open, everything went black, and my memory became a blank filled only with a sense of shame. I hesitated. Justice Owen Roberts, a Philadelphian whom I had known well before he went on the bench and greatly liked, sensing the situation, leaned forward. "Mr. Solicitor General," he said, "I have read the briefs, but I am not sure that I have the facts accurately. Will you correct me if I am wrong? It would appear that . . ." and he proceeded to state the facts in his admirably lucid style. The blank vanished, the case came back, shame evaporated, the law of the case was easy to present. Roberts did not have to prompt me again, but the faint trace of a friendly smile was there, as if he were saying "It's all right, Francis, it's all right . . ." Many years later I taxed him with it. He said yes, you did look pretty white, and you kept mopping your forehead. He didn't think the brethren had noticed particularly, though he did not remember any very favorable comments on the first appearance of the new Solicitor. . . . How could you help loving a man who did that sort of thing for you?

George Stuart Patterson, a former president of the Union League, spoke at the dinner with the casual wit that always characterized what he said—with his slow friendly Philadelphia drawl—about the confusing rapidity with which I seemed to be turning over jobs. George Wharton Pepper recalled the days when he had been a law student in the office of the Solicitor General's grandfather, George W. Biddle; and reminded his audience that although of twenty-five former Solicitors General only one had been elevated to the presidency (William Howard Taft), there were those present "who thought that the record in this respect should be amplified." The Attorney General, as chief speaker at the banquet, said he thought it was some indication of the revolutionary character of the New Deal when the Jacksons welcomed the Biddles to Washington and the Biddles welcomed the Jacksons to Philadelphia.

What could one say in responding to such a warm group of friends—harder to speak to than an audience at arm's length? I talked of the balance that a civilized man might achieve between change, which is the law of life, and a longing for the illusive sense of permanence, a permanence which one found in Philadelphia, returning home to enjoy one's slice of the fatted calf. . . . I had no creed to deliver, I concluded, no faith to expound. But I would remember this evening, where we broke bread together, and a friendly spirit brooded over us.

Most of the cases testing the constitutionality of the New Deal legislation had been argued by Stanley Reed or Robert Jackson, my two predecessors, but there were still a few undetermined issues, which fell to my lot to present. Since the shift on the Court had taken place my task was less hard than that of the other two men.

The argument I felt a certain historical pride in winning was *U.S.* v. *Darby Lumber Co.*, which overruled *Hammer* v. *Dagenhart*, decided twenty-two years earlier when the Supreme Court had held that Congress was powerless to exclude products of child labor from interstate commerce. Under this decision there was no way in which a state could be protected from having its factories threatened by the competition of cheap goods produced by child labor in other states. They could not be excluded by a state—an obvious interference with interstate commerce; and *Hammer* v. *Dagenhart* held that the United States could not regulate practices which affected this commerce. The decision was an extreme example of the application by the Court of the dogma of *laissez faire* run rampant. "I should have thought," Justice Holmes, dissenting, remarked caustically, "that if we were to introduce our own moral conceptions where in my opinion they do not belong, this was pre-eminently a case for upholding the exercise of all its powers by the United States . . . It is not for this Court to . . . say that [prohibition] is permissible as against strong drink but not as against the product of ruined lives."

The *Darby* case did not directly involve child labor regulation, but dealt with the same constitutional question, the regulation of interstate commerce by a law which affected manufacturing. The Federal Wage and Hour Law forbade shipment in interstate commerce of materials produced by employees receiving less or working longer than the standards set in the act—twenty-five cents an hour for cotton textile workers in the South, and time and a half for more than forty-four hours a week. The times demanded the result. As in *Hammer v. Dagenhart*, state controls had proved inadequate since the unorganized Southern mills could undercut their organized rivals in the North, where the unions had brought about better wages and shorter hours. The power granted was in substance without limit—"the power of Congress under the commerce clause . . . to exclude any article from interstate commerce"—and thus establish national standards for the whole country.

Chief Justice Stone, speaking for a unanimous Court—Justice McReynolds had retired—referred to the "powerful and now classic dissent" of his old friend and former associate. Tom Corcoran, who shared my admiration of the insights that Holmes had afforded us both as his secretaries, suggested that together we place a nosegay on the great man's grave at Arlington to celebrate the Court's adoption of his views. He would have liked that. But the impulse was frustrated when one of the newspapers picked up the story with the suggestion that the Solicitor General was considering thus crowning his victory.

The decisions at that time were broadening the scope of the federal government. Thus in the suit of the Federal Power Commission against the Appalachian Power Company a divided Court gave the government sweeping control over water power, expanding the former test that the particular stream must in fact be navigable to include waters that could be made so. The Court, in line with cases that had sustained the power activities of the Tennessee Valley Authority, upheld the constitutionality of the provisions of the Federal Power Act of 1920, which authorized licensing and control of water power development by the federal government. The government's authority was "as broad," said the Court, "as the needs of commerce." The ruling affirmed the entire New Deal water power program. I had my moment of triumph.

Justice Reed wrote the opinion for the majority; McReynolds joined in a dissent by Justice Roberts. Historically it was interesting and indicative of the political change of the times that Justice Reed, a Democrat, expounded an unusually broad view of federal authority; while Justice Roberts, a Republican, held closely to the limited definition of Jefferson's narrower theory of constitutional interpretation.

If the river were not navigable, the Court ruled, it could be made navigable by reasonable improvement. The underlying touchstone of the federal power was not control of navigable streams; and the test of navigability in such cases has since then been abandoned. The real test was whether commerce in the broadest sense was affected so that Congress was warranted in acting under the Commerce clause. Put in another way it was whether the government had adequate power to govern the country—a proposition which was the broad legal basis that we advanced to support the administration's program. The decision implemented and enlarged a philosophy of the government of which I was a part, and with which I was on most issues in active sympathy. Seeing what the government could do to raise the standard of life for a large community in the Tennessee Valley by an imaginative and resourceful development of a great river had been to me pragmatically convincing. The Constitution should be read as the effective charter of governmental power and organization that it was intended to be.

I had my first taste of administrative work when the Attorney General motored to Florida to spend two weeks finishing his admirable study of the change that had come over the Court of which he was about to become a member, *The Struggle for Judicial Supremacy*. Returning brown, relaxed, and energetic, he summoned his executive assistant, Ugo Carusi, and me—I had been acting in his stead—to breakfast in his office to bring him up to date. Carusi was one of those rare figures who survived changes in administration, and continued to act for each succeeding Attorney General since John Garibaldi Sargent had brought him to Washington from Vermont in 1925, when Coolidge was

President. Jackson inherited him from Murphy, Murphy from Cummings, Cummings from Mitchell. That he should have gone on in such a highly personal key position under Republicans and Democrats alike was evidence of that need for continuity felt by each new incumbent, and testified to Carusi's ability and discretion. He knew the department inside out. He was cautious, modest, and good-mannered. He knew the Hill, and the Hill liked him. He never proffered advice to his Attorney General, but gave it when asked. He had at one time done a vaudeville turn, could sing funny songs, imitate "personalities," had a deadpan quality about him. He was greatly loyal to his chief.

"Mr. Attorney General," said Carusi, when we had filled our second cups of coffee and were lighting cigarettes, "before I take up the routine business, I think I should mention that last week you had a visit from two ladies."

Our chief's face brightened. "Yes?"

"I didn't think I should disturb the Acting Attorney General," Carusi continued. "He was very busy at the time with an important elderly senator."

"What nonsense!" I remonstrated.

"Who were the gals?"

"Olivia de Havilland and Evie Robert." (Mrs. Lawrence Wood Robert, whose husband was a highly successful consulting engineer, and had been treasurer and secretary of the Democratic National Committee). "I said you were away, and suggested that the ladies might like to see your offices. They said they would. I showed them your reception room, your outer office, your office, your secretaries' rooms, your private elevator . . . 'Is that all?' asked Miss de Havilland. No, I said, that was not all. On the top floor, the next floor up, there was a small room under the eaves—the architect had to do something with the space—which was reserved for the Attorney General in case he was very tired, and felt like taking a few minutes' rest. But there was no elevator to that floor. The steps were steep. I did not think the ladies would wish to see it.

"'We want to see that room,' said Miss de Havilland very firmly. So I took them up, and unlocked the door. The room was dark. I pulled up the shade. I don't think you have ever seen it, Mr. Attorney General, have you? It's not much to see—a desk, two chairs, a horsehair sofa . . .

"'You see,' I explained 'there is no telephone. I suppose the architect thought that when the Attorney General was exhausted he could come up here without fear of interruption, and lie down for a few moments.' I pointed to the horsehair couch. 'But the Attorney General has never used it yet,' I announced. The two young ladies gazed at the sofa. Then Olivia wobbled up to it, you know, this way"—and Carusi illustrated what he meant, vibrating his own solid posterior as he walked across the room. "Then," he concluded, "she leaned over and delicately picked a bronze hairpin off the sofa. 'Ah,' she said, turning to me, 'dear, *dear*, Mr. Carusi, the Attorney General has *never* used it yet?'"

We both looked at the Attorney General, who exclaimed delightedly, "That's the nicest thing I've heard about Frank Murphy since I've been in Washington!"

REGISTERING ALIENS
AS WAR THREATENS

❧ Chapter Six

The life of a Solicitor General was, to my satisfaction, more variegated than I had supposed. The core of the
work was absorbing the records and arguing the questions of law
before the Court. But there were a good many "extracurricular"
activities, particularly after the Court adjourned in June and
until it sat again in early October, which the Attorney General
turned over to me. One of these involved the transfer of the
Immigration and Naturalization Service from the Department
of Labor to the Department of Justice.

In the spring of 1940 Jackson, after a Cabinet meeting, told
me that the President had decided on the transfer, and asked me
to take charge. The Secretary of Labor acquiesced readily, as she
had never relished its supervision. Miss Perkins had been neglecting the Service, and it had withered, as any human organization will, from lack of encouragement from the top. I cannot
now remember the immediate cause of the transfer—there was
something about the Secretary's failing to furnish the President
with information that he wanted urgently, the number of deportable aliens in the country—something of the sort. But that
was probably no more than the spark to action. The President
had, it soon became apparent, decided that immigration control
should be tightened.

The burden of co-ordinating this bureau with its four thousand employees into the Department was immediately made more difficult by the new requirement of Congress that the three and a half million aliens living in the country be registered and fingerprinted. The transfer of the bureau at the same time to the Department of Justice, which was thought of as prosecuting criminals, caused a stir of uneasiness among the resident aliens. Country after country, with little resistance, had swiftly fallen to the German invasion, culminating with France on June 16. A new expression, *fifth column*, was on everyone's lips. Something must be done. Fifth columnists in the popular mind came from the alien population—the very word *alien* suggested those who had been estranged and excluded. And in a tide of enthusiastic energy the beginning of a witch hunt was on.

The aliens, who had seen Hitler register the Jews as a preliminary to stripping them of their rights before they were tortured and burned in the concentration camps, were troubled when Senator Byrd suggested that they should be photographed and fingerprinted. The governor of Georgia, with its tiny proportion of foreign-born, by executive order decreed a burdensome form of registration. The Southern states, with the lowest proportion of aliens—a negligible number—were in the forefront of these repressive measures. Aliens were further terrified when the Senate, carried from its moorings in the flood of excitement and fear, passed the La Follette Civil Liberties Bill by a vote of forty-seven to twenty. This law was originally intended to outlaw labor spies and professional strikebreakers, but had been amended by Senator Reynolds of North Carolina, a thorough-going isolationist, to make it a criminal offense, subject to a $10,000 fine and five years imprisonment, for employers in interstate commerce to give more than one job in ten to aliens. Sugar beet and other vegetable and fruit growers were exempted so that they could go on using cheap Mexican labor—senators liked to eat some of their cake as well as have it. Chairman Martin Dies of the Un-American Activities Committee, which had not yet become notorious but soon would, was crusading for more money to carry on the investigation; and the Hoboes of America proudly pledged themselves to be on the lookout for "fifth column stuff."

All this could not have come at a worse time. Immigrants from war-torn Europe were pouring into the United States, particularly Jewish refugees from Hitler's unceasing and increasingly savage persecutions. Here, I felt, would be a test of American democracy, an opportunity to show that we believed what we said. We must give them shelter; but more than shelter. We must show a frightened world that we could share our country with the exiled and the oppressed, as we had done before.

The particular brand of "toughness," which had moved the President to transfer the Immigration Service to the Department of Justice, was to influence him again as the shadows of the war deepened over the country. It was all very well, he believed, to be liberal, but you must not be soft.

But Jackson could not forget his experience in the last war. As a young man he learned to hate the German baiting, which he saw run through the little town he lived in—the busybody snooping and spying, the rash of cruel meddling, suspicion of everyone who was not a native son and 100 per cent American. He saw the rise of the American Volunteers and other zealous vigilantes. He remembered the Palmer raids in 1920, and the prairie fire of federal and state indictments for sedition, when men were prosecuted for uttering language critical of the war effort. As the attorney for the city of Jamestown in New York, Jackson twenty-two years before, stood with his back against the flood of hysteria, and refused to be carried off his feet. But in that earlier war he was not confronted by the dilemma which now faced him as Attorney General of the United States. The American people had to be reassured. The appearance was as important as the reality. This the President knew well; and his Attorney General must appear to be tough, even though he was not temperamentally inclined to such a role. He must make the people feel secure against these new totalitarian threats.

Jackson, remembering the earlier war, vowed that he would protect the foreigners who were living here, a hundred thousand of them illegally, chiefly for technical reasons. They had deserted their vessels and come ashore, without papers, or had overstayed their passport time, many of them settling years ago, marrying Americans, becoming parents of American children.

He requested citizens to report evidence of sabotage, espionage, or other disloyal activities to the FBI, thus displaying the appropriate toughness; and at the same time asked everyone to keep cool and not get frightened. The response to his first plea was prompt and enthusiastic. The New York office of the FBI was flooded with complaints, and vigilante groups, including volunteer firemen and female rifle clubs, sprang up overnight. Before long, requests for investigation of aliens for espionage activities were coming into the Department of Justice at the rate of 3000 a day. The tough program did not seem to be calming the country.

Typical of the manner in which the President liked to handle difficulties was the way in which the Immigration Service was "co-ordinated" into the Department. James Lawrence Houghteling, who had married the President's first cousin, Laura Delano, had been commissioner of immigration since 1937. A former vice president of the Chicago *Daily News,* he had shown his enthusiasm for the New Deal by working in the public works program, and had been a loyal supporter of the President and his policies. Humane and progressive, Houghteling, from the point of view of preserving civil liberties, was an ideal commissioner. His administrative qualifications were less pronounced, but had not been allowed much scope for broadly effective work. He did not present the harsh façade which the President considered at the time to be desirable. But the President would not fire him. He hated to dismiss anyone, let alone a man who was part of his clan, and of whom he was fond.

Therefore he directed a thoroughly Rooseveltian compromise. Houghteling would continue as commissioner, but he would in the future work under a new Special Assistant Attorney General who would have charge of administrative control of the Service. Major Lemuel Bradford Schofield, of Philadelphia, was, said the Attorney General when he told me about the arrangement, ideally suited for the job. Jackson had known him as a neighbor in Warren, Pennsylvania, across the New York border. Schofield was really tough, a characteristic exhibited when an assistant district attorney in 1928 he had conducted an investigation into police corruption, and had later served as director of

public safety (police commissioner) in Philadelphia. His fearless-
ness—stepping on toes irrespective in enforcing the law—had
been shown when he raided the Union League Club during one
of his spectacular attempts to enforce Prohibition. He was as
thick as he was square, with a chest like a hogshead, and huge
chin below enormous spectacles. He was a sadistic cross-ex-
aminer when the temptation was afforded. It was of course an
impossible arrangement, and lasted for a little over a month,
when Houghteling resigned, and after a brief period was made
assistant to the Secretary of the Treasury.

At the end of June, 1940, the President signed the Alien
Registration Act, issuing at the same time a statement, prepared
by Jackson and myself: the program was designed to protect the
country and the loyal aliens who were its guests; no stigma was
carried with the requirement of registration, most aliens were
loyal, and were entitled to receive full protection of the law,
without harassment. Since Congress had now provided a single
uniform method of handling this difficult problem, any attempts
of the states or municipalities to deal with it would result in undesirable confusion and duplication.

The statement reflected our concern over state and local "war"
activities. Increasingly the states, counties, and cities were
adopting measures to force foreigners to register. Occasionally
an individual had to register under two or three overlapping
regulations. We did our best to persuade municipalities not to
try local experiments to control aliens now that the national
government had taken over the job.

The question was settled by *Hines* v. *Davidowitz* in January,
1941, when the Supreme Court decided in favor of the government, holding that the Pennsylvania law requiring registration
had been superseded by federal act. The issue was narrow,
it involved no constitutional difficulty of conflicting state and
federal powers, but only the meaning of the act. It was conceded
that federal and state powers existed concurrently, but that the
state power to control aliens was subordinate to the national
law. Had Congress intended the statute to assume exclusive control, thus ousting state authority? Black, writing the majority
opinion, held that when Congress passed the act it manifested

a purpose to protect the personal liberties of law-abiding aliens through a uniform national system. I argued the case, and was of course gratified by the result. I was surprised that Stone and Chief Justice Hughes (joined by McReynolds) should dissent.

I heard later that Justice Stone had been annoyed at the careless drafting of the statute. There was a note of irritation in the dissenting language. Congress could have set up an exclusive registration system but it had not, and "it is not the province of the courts to do that which Congress has failed to do." Then came the slap: "At a time when the exercise of the federal power is being rapidly expanded through Congressional action, it is difficult to overstate the importance of safeguarding against such diminution of state power by vague inference as to what Congress might have intended." In this instance the Attorney General had sent me to give his views informally to the members of the Senate committee who were considering the bill, and I had been able to persuade them to modify certain highly dubious criminal provisions which dealt with organizations advocating the violent overthrow of the government. But it had not occurred to me that the bill was silent on the important question of state power to exercise the functions that in public I was constantly suggesting should be left to the national government. No wonder Stone was irritated—competent technicians do not like sloppy work. I was relieved by the result, but it had been a close shave.

The effort to co-ordinate state and federal legislation dealing with national defense, and then with the war effort, was successful largely owing to the effectiveness of the federal-state meetings, initiated by Jackson and continued by me during the war years, under the highly competent direction of Lawrence M. C. Smith of Philadelphia. I was anxious to avoid the hasty and harmful state legislation which had broken out like a rash when the United States entered the First World War. To a meeting in August of the state attorneys general the President sent a letter (which I prepared) suggesting that the common defense should be through normal channels of local, state, and national law enforcement. "The untrained policeman," he wrote, "is as ineffective as the untrained soldier. The amateur detective soon becomes a fussy and malicious busybody." The conference recommended that in view of the national character of sedition, with which the Alien Registration Act of 1940 dealt, no state sedition laws be adopted.

The statute for registering the aliens gave me only two months to get ready the machinery to register and fingerprint them. I was encouraged by the friendliness and intelligent help in and out of government. At the beginning I was solaced by a New York *Times* editorial. The registration was to be directed, said the *Times*, "temporarily at least, and, one hopes, permanently," by the Solicitor General. "Of Mr. Biddle it may be said," the editorial continued, "that he is a fine and generous liberal, who has never forgotten the lessons he learned as law clerk for Justice Holmes. The rights and liberties of the humblest stranger will be sacred to him." Language like this was not easy to live up to; and at night, worrying about the countless details—what had I overlooked?—I would wonder whether I had acted in the spirit of Holmes: not in making a speech here, uttering some beautiful platitude before a women's club or civic association, but in the daily dedication of work, in the anonymous, telling details, which would carry the plan through and kill the hysteria, so that we could act once more like free Americans. The idea of this broad "protection" by registration might be vindicated against the doubts and criticisms of the professional libertarians who had begun to shake their heads and prophesy that the persecution was beginning . . .

During the spring and early summer I devoted most of my time to registration problems. I persuaded Earl G. Harrison, a rising Philadelphia lawyer, to take the job. At that time he had not had much administrative experience, but he was conscientious, had a social outlook unusual among most successful lawyers, and, like many other men of the younger generation, was eager to perform his share of public work, particularly as war approached.

When Harrison resigned as director of alien registration, completing the job between July and mid-January, the *Survey Mid-Monthly* wrote that he had carried through the program in such a way that anxieties were allayed, and what might have been a witch hunt became an orderly experience "in sound public administration and compliance with the law." I wrote Harrison in accepting his resignation: "I hope that the temptation towards public work will keep simmering in you. Once you have yielded to it, nothing else can be as good."

When I became Attorney General, and it seemed desirable to fill the vacancy, I recommended to the President that he appoint Harrison Commissioner of Immigration, which he did without much enthusiasm—the President knew nothing about him except that he was an independent Republican, and carried no political weight. But F.D.R. was usually willing to follow the Attorney General's recommendations as to vacancies within his department, particularly if there was no political opposition from a Senator. But in this case there was, as soon as the appointment was announced. I had thought it wise to clear with Senator Guffey just before I sent the nomination over to the White House. The position was a national one, not like a Pennsylvania United States attorney or judge, so that it was not Pennsylvanian patronage. He not only did not approve but resisted the appointment, telling me that he would claim senatorial privilege. He sent in a "blue slip" to the Senate Committee on Immigration and Naturalization, which showed his opposition to the nomination, and the fight was on.

Neither the President, nor Senator Richard B. Russell of Georgia, chairman of the committee, wished a showdown. The Senator from Pennsylvania was not in the full flower of his political strength, as he had been in 1935 when, without consulting him, I had appointed Clinton S. Golden Pittsburgh regional director of the Labor Board. It had never occurred to me to defer to the Senator until his assistant, Mr. Bailey, over the telephone immediately after the appointment had been announced, wanted to know just what my relation to the Senator was going to be. . . . Clinton Golden, it appeared, had enthusiastically joined an immense group of miners—he had been an officer of the Brotherhood of Locomotive Firemen and Enginemen, and later became a distinguished labor economist—who, led by Gifford Pinchot, in opposing Guffey for the Senate in 1934, sang with delighted enthusiasm the refrain: "We don't want Guffey, we don't want Guffey!" Then there was the little misunderstanding over the federal judgeship in 1939. No wonder the Senator did not trust me.

Joe Guffey was a tireless, not highly intelligent, old-line Democrat, who had always voted the way the President wanted him to vote, and in the early days enjoyed more patronage than any other Senator in Washington. He was an interesting example of the combination of the "liberal" and politician occasionally found in the ranks of the New Dealers. He outdid his associates in saluting "The People," and in attacking "The Powers," expressions which dated him a little. He managed to stuff the federal agencies, particularly the Coal Board, with unusually incompetent camp followers who had trooped behind his oriflamme for many years.

The appointment was held up for six months, Harrison still on ice. I begged the President to push it through, and finally he wrote a letter which did the trick:

> Dear Jo: As one old friend to another I want to ask you to forego your fight on the Harrison appointment. I know how deeply you feel about it, but I do not believe that the matter is one of sufficient importance to make an issue out of it that is bound to embarrass a lot of your and my good friends.
>
> Will you do this for me.
>
> F.D.R.

The next day F.D.R. sent me this "private and confidential" memorandum:

> I think it would be good politics if you could call on Jo Guffey just to pass the time of day and sweeten him up.

We arranged to have the registration done by the post offices instead of the FBI, from August to December, and a great deal of advance publicity in many languages told the "American aliens," as I liked to call them, exactly what we were doing, why we were doing it, and when and where. The questions that the alien was asked to answer were not particularly complicated— how he entered the country, the means of transportation and name of the vessel, the length of time he had been here and expected to stay, his military or naval service. He was required to list the name of any club or other organization to which he belonged, and to say whether the organization furthered the interests of a foreign government. This was intended to find out as much as possible about German-Americans, as the Bund was active at that time in furthering German war aims.

The press backed our efforts to concentrate all control of aliens in the United States Government, to block hysterical outbursts, and to bring about orderly registration. The foreign-language newspapers were commendatory. A newspaper in New York, published in English and Hungarian, ran a leader thanking the Solicitor General by name—Hungarians knew that the Department of Justice "would protect rather than prosecute, shield rather than expose, harbor rather than deport those . . . loyal . . . aliens who came to the United States to salvage sunken hopes and gain new aspirations."

I made a number of radio speeches emphasizing what foreigners had given to the United States. I was stirred with the theme—out of the dreams of these refugees from intolerance and oppression in the old world had come the strength, the imaginative energy, the freedom of the new. I remembered that two years before our entry into the First World War—it was on the night of the torpedoing by the Germans of the Lusitania, May 7, 1915—I had heard President Woodrow Wilson develop this theme in Philadelphia before a group of 5000 newly created citizens. What he said moved me. He did not lecture them, like the usual pedantic patrioteer telling them what they ought to do and be. He said that to the immigrants America had looked and would look for the strength and the freshness of its inspiration. "This is the only country in the world [he told them] which experiences this repeated rebirth. This country is constantly drinking strength out of new sources by the voluntary association with it of great bodies of strong men . . . out of other lands. And so by the gift of the free will of independent people it is constantly being renewed from generation to generation, by the same process from which it was orginally created."

Speaking constantly about the registration program, I emphasized the importance of treating loyal "noncitizens" as we did citizens. All Americans were descended from those who were once aliens, and immigrant families were soon absorbed. Ellis Island—as one writer put it—was beginning to share honors with

Plymouth Rock. The old people might speak the language of their fatherland, but they felt and dreamed American aspirations: the Slavic-American, who created our empire of iron and steel, rail and bridge and skyscraper; the Scandanavian-American, who built the Northwest; the German-American, whose ancient culture was still preserved here on our shores; the Italian-American, stonemason, skilled artisan, artist.

This theme I kept emphasizing throughout those spring and summer days of 1940, when one could almost hear the tramp of the German soldiers' boots across the conquered countries—Greece, Yugoslavia, Norway, and Denmark in April; the Netherlands, Belgium, Luxembourg, France in May—nine countries of Europe in thirty days. Now was the time, I insisted, to educate aliens in our ways—not by hatred and oppression, but in the generous light of shared knowledge—knowledge of our struggle for independence, of our tradition of free speech and equality under the law, of the history of our achievements—and of our failures, too, so that the sum and substance of the American adventure, struggling, failing, but achieving and growing steadily, could be set against the deeds of the Germans as they conquered and enslaved.

Aliens came to realize they were to be treated like human beings, and that this measure was not, as so many of them had at first feared, preparatory to a pogrom. The post-office officials, training the clerks who were to handle enrollment, emphasized politeness and patience. In Philadelphia, Postmaster Joseph Gallagher's last minute instructions to the clerks, before the first day of registration of 80,000 foreigners, were that they should be courteous, and must keep all information revealed by the questionnaires confidential: "No matter how they act," he said, "no matter how slow they are to understand or co-operate, you must at all times be nice to them. I know it will be hard sometimes to be patient, but you must . . . in Europe they may have learned to fear government officials. You must make them feel that this is their government and that you are simply trying to help them."

Mrs. Mary Giannini, of County Cork, Ireland, whose husband George, a longshoreman, was born here, declared that it was a good thing if the people understood it right—"the government must have a reason for it." Frank Di Lacqua, vice president of the Guilio Cesare Lodge, Sons of Italy, arrived at a branch post office with sixty-seven lodge members who were unable to speak or understand English, and in many cases incapable of reading or writing, but who could make crosses under their leader's stern dictation. Language was seldom a bar. Post-office employees spoke at least a score of tongues from Gaelic, Syrian, and Serbian to Russian, Turkish, and Portuguese. If a rarer language like Lithuanian turned up the applicant was asked to wait until the mail carrier who spoke it fluently could be taken off his beat to act as an interpreter. Natives of conquered countries—Poland for instance—were allowed to name the country of their birth. Nineteen men and eleven women were registered at Moyamensing Prison in Philadelphia. Agents were sent to industrial plants, to cause as little work interruption as possible. Seamen were "printed" on their ships as they docked by representatives of the Immigration Service.

The director of registration and I received many letters—inquiring, uncertain, frightened, and, toward the end, enthusiastic. One registrant turned up five hours before the registration began so as to have the honor of being the first to join. A woman living in Berkley, Michigan, had married an American, and had five children born in America. She wrote to her father, an Englishman, asking for a birth certificate, only to discover that she was an adopted child. In the *Titanic* shipwreck in 1912, when she was three years old, she had been handed to her foster parent by another passenger, from Pennsylvania. With the child in his arms the Englishman had been hustled into a lifeboat, then rescued by the *Carpathia*. She had tried to trace her father, without success. What should she do? "Please, sir, because I said so many times I was an alien, should I register? . . . Please, sir, believe me, I hate taking up your time but if anyone can tell me anything you are that person."

"I'm happy," wrote another applicant, "to live in a country where letters from the authorities read like letters from friends." We were proud of the Service. . . .

Soon after war broke out, enemy aliens—Germans, Japanese, Italians, of whom there were about 1,100,000—were required to register again. After explaining this additional wartime precaution in a radio talk, I received a letter from Beatrice H. David, a Radcliffe student and evidently a refugee from Nazi persecution, which moved me. She wrote: "I don't need to tell you that we—perhaps even more than you 'real' Americans—wandering, uprooted and haunted, as we have been for the last eight years, need your United States: not just as a piece of land, a material living space; for much more than that. We need America to regain our faith in living and dying: human beings, and above all young people, do not live off of bread alone; we have the urge of being loyal to something on this earth, of pledging our allegiance to some Flag; we crave to be let to love, and be at least accepted in return. We want to know why we breathe, and eat, and study; why we should work, get married and have children. We need America to give us the answer."

An Americanization program, which included a series of broadcasts by famous naturalized Americans, was arranged by the Immigration Service. *I Am an American*—telling what America promises—included Ludwig Bemelmans, born in Meran, the Tyrol; Thomas Mann, Lubeck; Albert Einstein, Ulm; William Knudsen, Denmark; Ferdinand Pecora, Nicosia; Robert F. Wagner, Herse-Nassau; Tony Sarg, Guatemala; Claudette Colbert, Paris; Walter Damrosch, Breslau; Gaetano Salvemini, Molfetta; Elissa Landi, Venice. "I like America," said Bemelmans, "because it's so different from any other place. You couldn't take your dog into the Army with you in Austria where I was born, for instance. But when I joined the United States Army in 1917 I told the Major that I had a dog, and the Major said to his Adjutant, 'Say, Charlie, he has a dog—can we use a dog?' and Charlie hollered back, 'It's all right with me,' and the Major said, 'All right, son, bring your dog.' The Adjutant had his legs on the Major's desk, and the Major told me how much he had enjoyed a trip down the Rhine, and that's one of the reasons I like America."

We persuaded the President to designate "I Am an American Day" to be observed as an occasion to welcome those who had become citizens by majority or naturalization, and to urge the holding of patriotic exercises "to impress upon all our citizens, both native-born and naturalized, the special significance of citizenship in this Nation." As a member of the Philadelphia Board of Education I had come to realize how much school exercises meant to children and parents alike—the welcome of adolescents to their adventure in the world, a pause for the beginning of a larger identification. We were bare of traditions, we did not appreciate the value of symbols and ceremonies in our American culture, with its noisy foreground and thin colorless background. But the Germans did. If symbols and exercises could be used to stimulate imperialism and race hatred, why not to further the ends of the democratic state? Such outward signs seemed to me as I thought about it, watching the world fall to the German *putsch,* to be particularly needed in our democracy—easygoing, careless, repudiating discipline, free (thank heaven) from the Messianic complex, yet longing for some visible sign to which could be attached the inward meanings that in a democracy were so difficult to put into words. I talked to United States judges and attorneys about the value of rendering naturalization ceremonies moving and significant—now was the time if ever to teach democracy—not by orations on the Fourth, which when we were children had left us bored and drowsy, but by something stirring and actual, filled with the meaning of the contemporary world, *our* world. The idea took, and the ceremonies became more alive, joined in by veterans' organizations, with music and singing, and brightened by the color and variety of almost-forgotten folk songs and folk dances.

Now and then I made the address: Tyranny, I would tell them, was very old; democracy was as young as our national life. In the past the melting pot process had sometimes seemed to melt out all that was individual and therefore valuable into a thin and tasteless brew. Roots could not be cut with impunity. Large segments of our population were German and Italian, with ancient cultures. They should not be made to feel that we had turned against those cultures, but rather that we cherished them as part of the heritage of all free men, and that we too knew them to be profoundly threatened.

Up to Pearl Harbor the isolationists did their best to break down the close sympathy which most of the country felt for the cause of the allies. I was drawn into indignation by a speech of that once popular hero, Charles Lindbergh, in Madison Square

Garden on May 23, 1940, in which he said that if America went
to war to preserve democracy abroad we were likely to end by
losing it at home. He was convinced that the United States was
powerless against this German "wave of the future," that we
must accept it, and that we must not fight. The speech was rank
defeatism, and I was worried about the immense crowd at the
Garden who wildly applauded Lindbergh's exhortations. I
thought that the time had come to hit back at this noisy rabble
who sought to divide the country—Lindbergh was their bell-
wether: the pro-Nazis, the anti-Semites, the isolationists, Father
Charles E. Coughlin, attacking the Jews in his radio talks from
his Church of the Little Flower in Detroit, much in the manner of
Julius Streicher in Germany in *Der Stürmer;* George E. Deatherage, Hon. Grand Commander of the Knights of the White
Camellia, who wished to unite all Christians under the emblem
of a fiery swastika: William Dudley Pelley, whose Silver Shirt
Legion of America had been launched the day Hitler took
power, January 31, 1933; the Rev. Gerald B. Winrod, who published the *Defender Magazine* and the *Revealer,* viciously anti-
Semitic.

If our democracy was profoundly threatened, I said, as I
believed it to be, let us not say as Lindbergh had said that we
should not fight to save it, if fight we must, because in doing so
we could not help but lose our rights. Did we care less for our
independence than Washington and Samuel Adams and the
Minute Men, who did not discuss the loss of civil liberties when
they chose to fight? We must not yield to those sterile doubts and
fears with which the isolationists were summoning the liberals to
share their distorted point of view.

Congress had caught the fever, was leading the country to
discard American traditions to satisfy the sweep of hatred based
on fear that must have quick relief in violent action. Representative Sam Hobbs of Alabama introduced a bill to incarcerate
aliens who, on account of their criminal record, had been ordered
deported, and who could not be sent back to the countries of
their origin. The House, by a vote of 330 to 45, passed a measure
directing the Attorney General to deport Harry Bridges, the West
Coast radical labor leader after the Secretary of Labor, with
her usual courage and independence, had refused to deport him.

Her action was based on a report of James M. Landis, dean of the Harvard Law School, acting as a special commissioner, that the deportation statute did not apply to persons who had become Communists after their arrival in the United States, and that there was no evidence that Bridges had been a Communist when he entered the country.

At a meeting of the Pennsylvania Bar Association at Bedford Springs, I voiced as strongly as I could my opposition to the bill. I had no sympathy with Bridges and, as Attorney General, in less than two years I would order his deportation under circumstances which will later be recounted. But I thought this act of Congress was an outrage—it ordered the Attorney General to "take into custody forthwith and deport forthwith to Australia, the country of which he is a citizen or subject, the alien, Harry Renton Bridges, whose presence in this country the Congress deems hurtful." That was all—no investigation, no determination of illegality, no chance for Bridges to speak in his own behalf. It was not suggested that he was here illegally; it could not be, for the official constituted by the Congress to make this determination had said that his presence was lawful. This was, I told the Pennsylvania lawyers, a star-chamber proceeding directed against a single individual, amounting to a bill of attainder, which the Constitution expressly forbade. And yet, I continued, I had heard no leader of the bar protest. I read to them the Attorney General's letter to Senator Cooper, of Tennessee, who had asked him what he thought of the bill. It would be the first time, the Attorney General wrote, that an act of Congress had singled out a named individual for deportation, and the first deportation in which the alien was not even accused of unlawful entry or unlawful conduct while here. Congress, without changing the general law, was simply suspending all laws protecting individuals, and directing the Attorney General to disregard them, and to deport "notwithstanding any other provision of law." There was not the slightest pretense of due process.

It was hard, I said, to have to sit still, with hands folded, while the Paris that we loved was dark under the swastika, and the beautiful, proud, reasonable French spirit was flickering in the night. But as lawyers, trained to leadership in our communities, and following the tradition of the rule of law, we must voice our opposition to the surrender of that tradition, and protest against the Bridges bill.

During the two years preceding the Second World War, a hysterically restrictive impulse was in the air, but never carried the country with it, as it had in the earlier war. The Bridges bill was canned in the Senate. Another bill, which got through the House, introduced by Representative John J. Dempsey of New Mexico, who was later to be governor and senator, which provided for the deportation of any alien who believed in or advocated "making any change in the Government of the United States of America," received a similar fate.

It is worth noting, I came later to reflect, that the legislative mind, reflecting the attitude of the conservative bar, considered the protection of property more important than that of individual rights. Although Congress, in the Administrative Procedure Act of 1946, provided for the agencies of the government a set of procedural rules, calculated to ensure, so far as possible, fairness in the activities of federal administrative bodies, no comparable effort was made to protect government employees suspected of disloyalty. President Truman's loyalty program was adopted a year after the Procedure Act became law. The chief attack on government procedure before the passage of the act was that the same body was allowed to act as prosecutor and judge, and yet this dualism of function was permitted under the loyalty program when the loyalty of employees was being questioned, and to the public disloyalty meant treason. Under the administrative statute, public hearings were mandatory; in the loyalty program the employee had no right to insist that his trial should be public. By the statute the right to cross-examine was absolute; but employees were not permitted to cross-examine informants —the chief source of the charges brought against them. The right to a subpoena under the Procedure Act was granted; an employee had no such right. Although there is a difference between the nature and purpose of the two procedures, both are administrative. The meticulous protection thrown around property in the statute is in sharp contrast to the shadowy safeguards given by executive order to the employee.

WASHINGTON NOTABLES

❦ *Chapter Seven*

During the summer of 1940 we had our first taste of the horrible Washington heat; worse, said Sir Girja Shankar Bajpai, the envoy from India to the United States, than anything in India. The saturated air would settle over the long days and nights, without relief—breathless, enfeebling. After my court engagements were over we went to Saunderstown for a few days to stay with my first cousin, Constance Biddle. There I was happy, facing a quiet ocean, the satisfying sea smell in my nostrils, under a mild sun, Katherine in a tomato colored tweed at my elbow, scribbling notes. I turned my happiness over in my mind and through my senses, so much stronger and deeper than when we had spent a week on our honeymoon in the same house twenty-two years before . . . We drove over to see Leonard Bacon at Peacedale. He had given up teaching at thirty-six, and at fifty-three had a substantial shelf of books to his credit, half a dozen slim volumes of verse and some scholarly translations. But he was lonely, like so many American men of letters, without real recognition, lacking the appreciation of his own "group"—there was no group, they were scattered individuals, some on New England farms to "get away from New York," some in New York under the wings of the publishers, but without the sense of an inherited culture, of a frame of reference, of a national will and common purpose. Writers and artists were isolated, many of them grubbing away at teaching in sprawling universities that

they detested, drinking too much, the better to make terms with
the neglect that they could not forget. Leonard had begun to
suspect that his creative impulse had burnt out—had it ever
existed, he may have wondered. He was a rewarding companion,
with a broad, discriminating culture. He liked to relate his life
to the great past. He told us that his grandfather had gone for
a boat ride on Lake Geneva in 1849, and the boatman had
said to him that thirty years before he had taken out two Englishmen, one with a club foot, to see the Chateau of Chillon. That
took you back; and Bacon had known an old Frenchman who
had fought at Waterloo . . .

In the early autumn of 1940, James Boyd, with whom a
dozen years before I had hunted foxes at Southern Pines, came
to see me. He and his wife had been my hosts there when my
horse—hired for the day's drag—had missed his takeoff in the
sand and smashed into a fence and landed on me, breaking my
right collarbone rather badly. While I was having it X-rayed she
had moved my clothes from my hotel to their house, so that, as
she said with a grin as I walked out of the doctor's office, there
was no good arguing about it, and I was soon as comfortable as
the circumstances permitted.

Jim had come to enlist my support for a series of short plays
given by The Free Company, to be broadcast over a Columbia
nationwide hookup. Authors and actors, all top drawer, volunteered their services: William Saroyan, Marc Connelly, Robert
Sherwood, Sherwood Anderson, Orson Welles, Archibald Mac-
Leish, Burgess Meredith, Melvyn Douglas, Franchot Tone,
Margot and Betty Field. Jim's novels, which Scribner's had published from 1925 to 1939—*Drums* and *Marching Along*—were
still popular. His enthusiasm made him exactly the right man to
vitalize and hold together such a group.

The plays were to illustrate specifically what our freedoms
meant in the United States: free speech, a free press, the right
of assembly, trial by jury, religious and economic freedom, racial
equality and the right to vote, due process, the right of property,
freedom for thinkers, writers, and artists to express themselves,
freedom to teach the truth. Ten plays were produced, one or

two first-rate within the necessarily imposed limits of persuasion, most of them concrete, all of them giving the radio audience the cue. The first by Saroyan, bearing the alluring title of *The People with the Light Coming Out of Them*, was just that—how well he could do it in those days—their friendliness, their optimism, their good nature—Italians and Japanese and children and an artist who lived in one block. Marc Connelly wrote *The Mole on Lincoln's Chin*—you must teach the truth about history, not prune it to the 100 per cent shape, and fight the Veterans' League when it protested to the Board of Education that this particular textbook was un-American. Archie MacLeish's play was in verse—state calling to state, struggling to say what these freedoms meant. Robert Sherwood dramatized Owen Lovejoy's protesting death, which so few Americans remembered after a hundred years—Lovejoy, shot at Alton, Illinois, by ruffians because he would not stop printing articles advocating the abolition of slavery.

On April 6, Orson Welles' play was presented. *His Honor the Mayor* posed the problem of whether a mayor should permit The White Crusaders, an alleged Communist group, to meet in the town. The program, according to the chairman of the American Legion's National Americanism Commission, was "cleverly designed to poison the minds of young Americans." Perhaps the state legion in California would not have jumped in so blantantly had not William Randolph Hearst started the ball rolling by calling certain members of the *Free Company* "Communistic." Orson Welles—he was then only twenty-five—from Kenosha, Wisconsin, had recently written, directed, and produced *Citizen Kane*, a film about the career of a journalistic empire built on lies and corruption. Ever since then Hearst had been "after" Welles. The executive committee of the legion reported that the play advocated violence, "pitted class against class" and labor against capital, and would never have been endorsed by the two high government officials involved had they known what it was about. Hearst's New York *Journal American* demanded editorially that the Federal Communications Commission keep these subversives and un-American programs off the air—"you can do your part in *making* radio serve the cause of good citizenship . . . write to your Senators and House members."

The Columbia Broadcasting System, buckling down under the attack of the Hearst press, announced that the series would be discontinued shortly.

On our arrival in Washington in February, 1940, we took an apartment at 2101 Connecticut Avenue—our stay might be cut short by the November election. President Roosevelt was elected for the third time, and we rented for four years a pleasant house in Georgetown on the top of the hill that runs up Thirty-first Street from Q to R, unfurnished, for what now seems a modest sum, $250 a month, until the next election; and brought our effects from School House Lane, in Philadelphia. When Franklin Roosevelt was again re-elected in 1944, our landlord would not continue to lease; and Katherine bought the house that we had learned to love—so much had happened in it—and ever since then we have continued to live there. There was something gay and fresh about the place, with its little overshaded intimate garden in the back. Like so many Georgetown houses, under a great maple, it was a part of a small friendly world, breathing the air of a village, linked to a more serene century of a hundred and fifty years ago, tidy, informal.

We were growing nearer to the war, yet the sense of a slower pace that one found in Georgetown persisted, and all that winter and summer social amenities continued much as they had before. Washington for those brief months was more like the city that I had known for the first time as a young man when I was Justice Holmes's secretary thirty years before. After Pearl Harbor the city was bursting at the seams, overcrowded, overworked, and that sense of energetic confusion was to persist continuously— except in Georgetown. There was always a rational peace in Georgetown, a little down at the heel in summer, when the "cave dwellers" went away to escape the heat, and houses were boarded up, and copies of the *Post* or *Star* accumulated on the front steps, or blew untidily along the block, and everywhere— only interrupted by the war years—there were building and repairs and alterations which never altogether stopped, but advanced in a leisurely way like the rest of the town, the neat brick houses gradually taking the place of the brightly painted wooden shacks of the Negroes, green and red and yellow, assertive untidy spots, like straggling zinnias, among the graver, gentlemanly structures, which for a while they so gaily elbowed. . . . One Sunday afternoon in February, when yellow jasmine lay along the warm brick of Dunbarton Oaks, and here and there a yellow or purple crocus spoke, we saw a parrot staggering slowly down Wyoming Avenue singing "Rock-a-by Baby" in a cracked falsetto like some roguish old prima donna, following a Japanese butler who walked backward as he led him line by line. . . .

If the wife of the Dutch Ambassador, "Betty" Louden, an American, was the most beautiful woman in Washington walking "in beauty like the night"—the Richard Caseys were the most popular of the foreigners. Australian soldier and diplomat, he served as minister to Washington from 1940 to 1942, and was successively British Minister of State in the Middle East, governor of Bengal, and foreign minister. He was handsome, with a mobile, slightly strained expression; and his wife had a quick perception, and was friendly and generous. She was interested in paintings, and we asked them to dinner the night the National Gallery of Art was formally opened. Sitting on my right (protocol was never disregarded), she said, with the faintest of burrs, that the Anzacs were "such simple dears." When they surrounded and captured the Italians in Northern Africa there was no hard feeling—"poor bloody wops" the Anzacs called them.

We lunched at Eugene Meyer's cabin, which hung over a splendid reach of the Potomac, above Great Falls, to meet Thomas Mann, who was a friend of his wife's. At the time Meyer was publisher and editor of the Washington *Post*. Agnes Meyer believed that Mann had rescued Germany's cultural traditions from the moral collapse under the Nazis by a humanism that sought a balance between spontaneity and responsibility, between freedom and self-discipline—a dichotomy which, one felt, listening to her interpretation, had forever plagued that strange, clouded irrational substance, the German soul. Paul Claudel, Mrs. Meyer remarked, had learned to live with himself, but Mann had learned to live with all mankind. Erika Mann, who had married Auden, the poet, to get out of Germany, sat next to Senator Taft, whose face loomed, expressionless but friendly, like a rising moon. They did not seem to have much to exchange. It was a large luncheon, four or five Supreme Court justices and their wives; Adolf Berle, the Assistant Secretary of State, and his wife, who had rented Henry Stimson's beautiful old house "Woodley"; Henry F. Grady, of the Foreign Service—"every inch a politician," someone muttered; Felix Frankfurter's law clerk, Edward Prichard, from Paris, Kentucky, who could be funnier than anyone else; Mr. Justice Murphy, sitting as if he expected to be photographed; the Brazilian Ambassador, Carlos Martins, a plump, jovial, friendly *bon vivant*, and his raven-haired wife, who had a look of a half-tamed Indian about her.

The rigid Washington protocol decreed that in the presence of so many public officials, Mann, the guest of honor, should sit not on Agnes Meyer's right but below the salt, and Katherine to her delight found herself between him and Archibald MacLeish, who was then Librarian of Congress, and who introduced Mann with a boyish reverence and charm that struck exactly the right note.

That year we saw a good deal of the Frankfurters, Dean Achesons, Archibald MacLeishes, Robert Jacksons—all close friends. There were others on the edge of this tight little group: Harold Ickes, who was a friend of Jackson, but whom Acheson disliked, and William C. Bullitt, recently back from Paris. Frankfurter felt the war deeply—was his beloved England to go? MacLeish, of the four friends, was closest to his point of view, both frustrated that they could do so little about it, longing for our country to give greater help than the fifty old destroyers that the Attorney General had blessed with his famous opinion. Frankfurter was disturbed into angry vehemence by what he thought of as the indifference around him, an indifference to moral values, to our common culture that was being trampled in the mud of Belgium and Holland and France. Of course British imperialism still existed, he would admit, but it was receding while German imperialism was expanding.

MacLeish, equally unhappy, felt the special failure of his profession, and spoke of it in public more than once—the failure of American writers of our generation to rouse the country against the Nazi barbarism. In *The Irresponsibles* (1940) he attacked intellectuals for not taking sides in this cultural crisis. They had freed themselves from "subjective passions" to emerge in the "antiseptic air of objectivity." Like Frankfurter, but for a different reason, he could not bear the indifference, the cautious timidity, the lack of moral indignation, and, Scotch to the bone, his instinctive reaction was to preach and to exhort. But to me, intellectual objectivity was a part of the tolerance that our culture had achieved, now threatened by the Nazi revolt against the democratic outlook. We needed not be timid to remain tolerant, or tolerant of evil to keep an open mind. Yet the poet stirred in him, more in his talk than in writing; for the form of his attack, with its lyrical phrasing—"the writer . . . leaves the past to rot in its own rubbish"—"laboratory words"—"the man of letters of other countries domesticated the past within the rustling of the present"—assaulted and seduced the ear, but tended to evaporate under the colder scrutiny of the eye, so that the drift and shape of his thought seemed beautiful but opaque, like some uncertain cloud of which the curving outlines muted the angles of reality over which it hovered. He believed mystically in the power of the word, touched on the prophetic, but found only uncertain vehicles with which to convey the burden of his prophecy—as in *J.B.*, written twenty years later.

Jackson's mind was centered on the monstrosity of war rather than on the importance of saving England. He was no Anglophile, he was small-town American, definite, at core isolationist in the best sense, like Bob La Follette, holding hard to the old, simple American values, worried lest, as we did more for England we should stumble into war as we had in 1917. He never could forget the cruel vigilantism of that war—one could imagine how narrow and mean it must have been in the unrelieved concentration of a little place like Jamestown, New York. Once, in a moment of harsh argument, he said to Frankfurter, "But you have no son," and the remark, one could see, hurt the older man. Acheson was cool and wise and could disentangle the issue, and present it more clearly than his three friends. I was closer to Frankfurter's view than to those of the others, but doubted the value of war, and something in Felix's idolatrous worship of the British irritated me, just as the British themselves irritated me at times. But we were not yet at war. Bullitt had already begun to criticize the President. He was to continue increasingly to do so. The President, he told me once—and I suspect he had told many others—had promised to make him Secretary of the Navy, and had not done so. The period of long disappointment turning to frustration, ending in hate, had begun in Bullitt's heart. He was certain war was coming. He wanted to be in the eye of the hurricane when it came.

Washington conversation was better than other talk. If it had less of the local flavor of Boston or Philadelphia it had a range and speculation that is the essence of all good talk. The women— so Katherine said—did not after dinner invariably fall back on babies and household cares. There were fewer bores about, or perhaps I saw less of them than when I had been in private practice. The "cave dwellers" were the same in prejudice and outlook as they had been (once upon a time) on Beacon Street or Washington Square or Rittenhouse Square. But they gave one a pleasant, half-worldly sense of overlapping the past, and were more firmly rooted than the rest of the Washington world. They stood on the shore and watched the passengers move along the gangplank, coming for their temporary adventure, or walking to the vessel that was to take them home again. The cave dwellers afforded the town the only feeling of stability that it knew. Half the army of clerks who stayed on increased the illusion, savoring the pleasant mediocrity of their uneventful lives, while the other half created the vast turnover, the disappointed girls who thought that Washington would be glamorous and found it lonely, and went back to Kansas or Alabama.

And sooner or later everyone came to Washington. Alexander Woollcott came, staying with his friend Joseph Alsop, the columnist who should have been a historian, just turned thirty, shortly to enter the Navy, then resign and join General Chenault as an aide in the Volunteers Force, where he was captured by the Japanese at Hong Kong and held prisoner until 1942 to be exchanged and returned to the United States. John Foster made the fourth at dinner, to which Alsop invited me. Foster was an English barrister, later in Parliament, an uncertain drawing of a handsome man, with his long nose, dark curly hair, great height. Foster and Woollcott exchanged curious now forgotten murder cases, swapping them like stamp collectors, the stories spilling out so breathlessly they could not be seized long enough for me to remember. . . . Woollcott asked me where in Philadelphia he could get a comfortable flat, completely furnished; and a few days later sent me a "utilitarian whimsy," which he was having inserted in the Philadelphia *Bulletin:*

WANTED: a Philadelphia family living in an apartment or house with at least four bedrooms, who, for a reasonable financial consideration, will be willing to depart for Bermuda or somewhere on March 9 and stay away for three weeks, subletting their quarters, staff and all. The prospective tenant is guaranteed to be housebroken. All answers should be addressed to Alexander Woollcott.

There were occasional stag dinners, which I particularly enjoyed, for general conversation was almost never broken. At Bob La Follette's the talk was economic (the kind of talk women never like, Barbara Ward the only exception I can think of). Marriner Eccles, chairman of the Board of Governors of the Federal Reserve System, gave his opinion (he was seldom hesitant) that we were in for a serious depression, that the industrial index might soon plunge downward, and then the President would have very little chance of re-election. La Follette thought that might be a good thing—F.D.R. always backed down when it came to a test, as in 1937; he was too conservative and had to be pushed into action. The others agreed that bad times were coming: Paul Appleby, the Undersecretary of Agriculture, an unusually competent public servant, who, when he resigned from the department in 1950 became dean of the Maxwell School of Citizenship and Public Affairs at Syracuse University, and in 1955 Governor Averell Harriman's budget director; Philip La Follette, Bob's older brother, something of a Boy Scout out of uniform; Lowell Mellett, for years editor of the Washington *Daily News* (Scripps-Howard), which was lively and liberal when I was in Washington in 1934–35, and a close friend and administrative assistant of the President.

I saw a good deal of Mellett in the war years, and later even more intimately, and learned to admire his fairness, his warmth and loyalty to his friends and to his ideals. His Indiana drawl was like Elmer Davis's, and I think of them together—the dry humor, the balance, the courage and sanity, a mixture coming down from a less complicated America, an America that was more leisurely, more thoughtful, nearer to roots of the pioneers, lingering still in a half dozen of the Midwestern agricultural states. Bob La Follette had something of that quality, but was more dedicated than the other two men. He had been elected to the Senate at the age of thirty to succeed his father, who had been independent, like George W. Norris and Hiram Johnson of California, and the group of Republican congressmen who had ended "Canonism" in 1910. Young Bob was popular in the Senate. It was natural that he should support the New Deal, as his father had co-operated with Woodrow Wilson in sponsoring progressive measures of the New Freedom almost thirty years before. I had voted for the elder La Follette in 1924 when the other alternatives had been Calvin Coolidge with his lackluster dryness, and John W. Davis for the Democrats—correct and conservative, his personal charm exclusive and withdrawn as he campaigned.

When I suggested to young Bob, soon after our first meeting, that I should like to call him by his first name (I have always been old-fashioned about an indiscriminate use of first names), he said, flatly enough, "Sure can. Everyone in Wisconsin calls me Bob, or that son of a bitch!" He told me a good deal about his father, whom he admired without stint, and what I chiefly remember was his description of his father's intimacy with Senator Boies Penrose of Philadelphia. They were very close friends, about contemporaries, although no two men in the Senate were completely opposed politically—La Follette, by five years the Pennsylvanian's senior, a Wisconsin progressive, spending his life fighting the "interests" in his own state when he was governor and later in the Senate, making the "Wisconsin idea" of scientific public service a watchword throughout the country, hating Wall Street; and Penrose, of a cultivated Philadelphia family, a *magna cum* at Harvard, his earliest interest an essay on reform politics ("The City Government of Philadelphia"), but soon turning cynical, buying legislatures, picking off promising reformers by giving them jobs, serving power and wielding power—as when in 1920 he chose Warren Harding to run for President, dictating his will from a sickbed in Philadelphia to the delegates in Chicago—Penrose sneering at everything La Follette valued, and La Follette despising what Penrose admired: yet these two men were close personal friends in the Senate for nearly fifteen years. They liked each other.

Young Bob's last years were sad, for they did not bear out his brilliant promise, I think because he was split about the war, seeing with his mind that an America free from the entanglement of Europe could no longer exist, yet still nostalgic for the America of his youth, the America of his father, incapable of replacing the simpler vision by a new one, and therefore unable to continue his natural role of leadership. A few years after the war he committed suicide. He was very normal. He had not been sick so far as the world knew. He was the least introverted, the least depressed man I knew. But one never knows.

In June we went to New York for the first performance of Katherine's ballad poem *And They Lynched Him on a Tree,* which had been set to music by the Negro composer, William Grant Still, for chorus, contralto solo, narrator, and full orchestra. It was given out of doors in the Lewisohn Stadium by the Philharmonic Orchestra, with Artur Rodzinski conducting. The chorus was from the Scuola Cantorum and the Wenn Talbert Negro Choir. Katherine had been told that no production with such a theme could be given with whites and Negroes on the stage. But there was no "incident," indeed no criticism on that score.

As the program notes suggested, the work was conceived as a poem of protest, a human document to be "sung in the rhythmic expression of poetry through music and thence to the hearts of the people."

The introduction was starkly dramatic. It is night. "In a clearing by the roadside among the turpentine pines, lit by the headlights of parked cars, a Negro has just been lynched." The white crowd has done its business and is going home. The Negroes come out from hiding. The boy's mother sings her dirge:

Oh sorrow, of sorrow,
    You've taken my hand.
I must walk with you
    To the Promised Land.

Oh sorrow, oh sorrow,
    Oh my son!
Oh Jesus, my Jesus,
    What have they done!

The chorus of Negro men and women join her and retell the
story of the murdered boy's life:

He was a man, quick with a gun, he fell on evil days
Trouble was after him, trouble followed his ways . . .

The mother's final lament, had a simple colloquial line:

He did wrong—
    But couldn't they let him be?
Not die like this
    On a roadside tree?

Louise Burge, a young contralto at Howard University, who
later became head of the music department there, created with
a deep natural voice a moving song out of these passages, words
completely welded with the quality of the Negro spirituals suggested by the music. The final chorus, white and Negro singers
joining together, protests against the lawless mob violence—"the
long dark shadow . . . that falls across the land."

It was New York at its best—Rodzinski, a Pole, conducting
the orchestra; Hugh Ross, an Englishman, leading the Scuola
chorus; Mrs. Gugenheimer, the Jewish producer; Negroes everywhere in the audience of fourteen thousand, Italians everywhere.
The *Times*, vaguely lyrical, said that the concert—which also
included Earl Robinson, Paul Robeson, and Jerome Kern—had
democracy as its theme, and showed that "music could come to
grips with this tremendous subject." *Time*, with its typical knack
for too pat a phrase, reported that the words were by "Lincoln,
Jefferson and Mrs. Biddle."

Before the concert a personal drama behind the scenes heightened for a few of us the dramatic impact of the singing. Rodzinski, as the time approached, was in an agony of uncertainty
and anxiety. His wife had been prevented by the Gestapo from
sailing from France. Refugees, he reminded Katherine, looked
to the Solicitor General—could he do nothing? Katherine called
me from her hotel bedroom in New York; Dorle Jarmel, who was

doing the successful publicity work for the Stadium concerts, by her side; Rodzinski sitting in a corner of the room, his tense hands folded, whispering a quiet prayer. After first clearing with Adolf Berle in the State Department I cabled William C. Bullitt, our ambassador to France, who had not yet left Paris. He got Mrs. Rodzinski on the *Ile de France*, and she arrived just in time for the concert. There were tears, and kissing of hands, and gratitude, and overflowing Polish happiness. . . .

A little later Leopold Stokowski spent a night with us to discuss with Katherine rendering her ballad with the Youth Orchestra, which he had just organized. Actually, this never came off, but he played it the next winter with the NBC orchestra, which he was then conducting. There were a hundred instruments in the Youth Orchestra, he said—no manager, no assistants, no offices, no committees, simply wonderful youngsters. But no Negroes. They do not fit into a single unity, their art is different, they cannot be disciplined in a group. After only two weeks of rehearsals the orchestra could play *Tristan* so that it became orgiastic. . . .

One morning Marguerite Le Hand, "Missy" as she was affectionately known to all of us, the President's secretary, called up to know if we would join the President for a two-day cruise on the *Mayflower* down the Chesapeake Bay. The only other guests would be Jesse Jones and his wife. We drove from the White House through the city in an open car to the dock. Word that the President was going out must have spread because I can remember Negro women here and there holding up their babies so they could see him. The Negro children were always the first, the President said, to recognize him. It was sultry . . . the President was restless and impatient with Missy when she tucked the rug about him as a fresher wind blew up in the afternoon. He asked me how well I knew Billy Bullitt and, without waiting for an answer, went on to say that Billy was all wet about Pétain, he had given out a statement when he got back from France that Pétain was a great national hero, which he was not. He was a shrewd old peasant who had decided to sell France to the Germans, and had been able to twist Bullitt around his finger. . . .

We fished. Katherine alone caught anything, a sizable eel, which the President christened "Wendell Willkie" and consumed the next morning for breakfast. Mrs. Jones was pleasant and easy. Jesse Jones was publisher and owner of the Houston *Chronicle*. For years he had been a powerful figure in Washington, chairman of the Reconstruction Finance Corporation from 1933 to 1939, and now administrator of the Federal Loan Agency and chairman of the executive committee of the Export-Import Bank. In the following September he was to join the Cabinet as Secretary of Commerce under the provisions of a special act of Congress giving him authority to hold more than one job at a time. Congress liked Jesse Jones, and thought of him as an American superman. He was Texas in the "giant" sense, conscious of his power, proud of his wealth, a pioneer who found no limits to his spirit in the acquisition of material possessions; hard, shrewd, ruthless, strong, conservative. He did not appear to be having much fun. The closest he came to enjoyment was a dour pleasure, which the misfortunes of his adversaries occasionally stirred around his eyes and mouth. He seemed a huge man. One had the impression that his mind never stopped circulating, never lay down or relaxed. There must be many such men in every land. I have never seen anyone quite like him, even in the United States.

Spending a few weeks to be near Eleonora Kissel in Taos, New Mexico, in the summer of 1939, I had been attracted by a smart-looking blue denim double-breasted coat with aluminum buttons, and being told by Eleonora that it had been made by a young Spanish-American dressmaker, I had her copy one of my coats in the same material. I wore the coat on our *Mayflower* cruise. The President liking it, I got Missy to "borrow" one of his, had the New Mexican copy it, and sent it to him. He took it to Hyde Park, and wrote me: "Tell Orcelia Archuleta that I am proud to wear her excellent coat." I wrote to her, and was informed a little later that the sign over her door, greatly enlarged, now read:

> Special Coat Maker to His Majesty
> President Franklin D. Roosevelt.

When we got back from our trip on the presidential yacht I found a letter from my brother George begging me to do something for his friend Maurice Sterne (George succeeded Sterne as a member of the Commission of Fine Arts). A distinguished sculptor and painter, Sterne was commissioned to execute twenty murals depicting "The Struggle for Justice," for the law library of the Department of Justice. He had completed them several months ago, but he was still paying a premium of $1500 a year on his completion bond because the government had not yet formally accepted the paintings. They were beautifully painted, but with a crude symbolism, which marred their effectiveness. An obvious Justice Holmes on a prancing white charger was piercing with his lance a cobweb of red tape—that sort of naïveté. George told me that they had been publicly exhibited in New York, and that one panel, a group of inquisitors with hard jowls and cruel hands, had caused unfavorable comment among Roman Catholics. One influential hierarch had expressed the opinion that the figure of Christ was made to look too much like a Jew. The Church, it would appear, had quietly arranged that they should not be hung. I said this was incredible, it sounded like nonsense. The Attorney General had no say in the matter, it was under the administrator of the Federal Works Agency, who had charge of public buildings, an independent establishment whose chief reported directly to the President. Would I go to the President, asked George. I would not, but I would talk to the administrator, John Michael Carmody, whom I had known in a friendly way since my Labor Board days, and who himself had served on the Board for a brief stretch a few years after me. But Carmody could not be reached—when I called him he was always busy; and my two letters elicited no response.

Justice Stone was ex officio chairman of the board of trustees of the National Gallery of Art, which had just been opened, and when I told him about the situation, he and Justice Frankfurter, who was a friend of Sterne's, agreed to lunch with Bob Jackson and me to meet Carmody, who had indicated that he would be delighted to join us. Mrs. Carmody telephoned my secretary five minutes before lunch that Mr. Carmody had sud-

denly become indisposed, and was threatened with intestinal
flu. . . . The next day she called to say that I would be relieved
to know that he was all right again. I felt nonplused and helpless.

I consulted Tom Corcoran, himself a Catholic, who knew his
way around in the hierarchy. As usual he at once suggested the
next step. Monsignor Michael Joseph Ready, the assistant
general secretary of the National Catholic Welfare Conference
in Washington, was the man. Highly intelligent, he knew the
ropes, and much to the point, was a friend of Tom's.

We three lunched together—I think Tom had deemed it wiser
to represent to him only that he could be of service to the A.G.
and the S.G., without mentioning details (that was my job), for
the Monsignor might easily have shied off. I found him chatty
and agreeable—not always the case with Tom's swans. That he
was a member of the President's Committee on Political Refugees
gave us a bridge of common interest. When lunch was over I
explained to him the situation. Did he know anything about it?
He did not. Would he help me? But how could he, it was
totally outside his bailiwick, he had absolutely no influence in
such a direction, he was a social worker, not a censor, he knew
John Carmody only slightly, in any event the story *was* incredible. . . . Not incredible but preposterous, I rejoined; it reflected
the stupid and provincial outlook of some myopic busybody. If
the right word were said in the appropriate quarters it would
avoid the possibility of a—misunderstanding. It was so much
better to sweep out these little difficulties before they swelled
into something that was worth printing, from the point of view
of a columnist—Maurice Sterne had so many friends. . . . But
what exactly did I want him to do? First take a look at the
murals, I suggested. All right, though it really was a waste of
time. When? Now, I said. I had arranged to have them on
display in the library. He shrugged, acquiesced, and we walked
over to the Department to see them. He looked at them carefully, not saying a word. What did he think of them, I asked,
when we had taken a turn around the room. Pretty awful, he
smiled back. He saw no objection to their being hung? Of course
he did not, why should there be any objection? Might I say that

in the proper quarter? I saw him hesitate. "It won't do any good," he replied, "but you can say just that if you want." I waited two days, and said just that to Carmody when, this time, he answered my call. The murals were immediately installed.

THE THIRD TERM
CONVENTION

≪{}≫ Chapter Eight

I was not a delegate to the Democratic Convention in Chicago, in July 1940, at which F.D.R. was to be nominated for his third term, but went out with Bob Jackson and our wives. It was pretty dull going, no one but F.D.R. could be nominated, and his blessing was assumed to have descended on Henry Agard Wallace, then Secretary of Agriculture, as his running mate. Wallace's strange letters to Dr. Nicholas Roerich, with their occult references to his fellow members in the Cabinet, did not come to the President's attention until a few weeks before the election.[1] Wallace had some political strength, particularly with the CIO, and he was a type—mystical, humorless, profoundly in earnest, indubitably American—and the President liked types, up to a point. F.D.R. was bored and tired and stale. There was a brief period, earlier in the spring, when he disliked the idea of a third term. He was not very much interested in his own nomination. It was as if he did not want to make the choice, and preferred to have someone else make it for him, an attitude which accounted for his behavior when the delegates met.

[1] For a brief description of the correspondence see Schlesinger, *The Coming of the New Deal,* pp. 31–32.

I did not feel critical of the President for allowing them to flounder around, uncertain of what the great man really did want. He dreaded another campaign, and would not raise a finger, or allow Harry Hopkins—his "messenger from the throne" as Harold Ickes called him in his *Secret Diary*—any leeway to influence the course of events, or interfere with the usual procedure. The spectacle was not edifying, partly because there was no one else in the field, no pressure and play of favorite sons; partly that the delegates showed sheeplike characteristics when they could not clearly hear their shepherd's voice; perhaps a little that Ed Kelly, the boss of the Chicago Democratic machine, tried to cook up enthusiasm to a noisy insistence—his henchmen screaming "we want Roosevelt" through the air vents from the cellar of the convention hall. The enthusiasm never jelled.

Yet even if it was a poor show, what difference did it make? Harold Ickes thought the convention was sordid, and was slipping away from the President, but it never did. No one doubted that he would take the nomination when it came. Even if he secretly longed for a stampede, he could not somehow get around to saying to Harry Hopkins over the telephone that a stampede would make acceptance of the unhallowed third term easier for him and more palatable to the people. Perhaps even, as Ickes imaginatively suggested, something in Roosevelt was allowing a situation to develop in which he could with good grace decline the nomination, and was forcing "the bitter pill of Wallace" with the hope that the convention would not swallow it, and thus give him a chance to say no. He sent word through Jimmy Byrnes, Ickes states, that he would decline if Wallace were not nominated. But I doubt if he would have; that would not have been like him. Ickes was himself longing to be nominated for vice president, and there was some talk of that, but the suggestion found little strength among the delegates.

A group of liberal newspapermen sat in the press gallery just below me: Herbert Agar, editor of the Louisville *Courier-Journal*, Ulric Bell, a correspondent of the same newspaper; Joseph Alsop; and Erwin Canham, news editor of the *Christian Science Monitor*. They were disillusioned by the way F.D.R. was treating the delegates. On the last day, while Wallace was being

nominated, they handed me up a note: "Are we right in thinking that the Administration is getting the proper kickback for
joking and farcing and doing the white-rabbit job instead of
saying 'here stand I: this is what I think; this is why I think it; if
you disagree with me, please don't nominate me; if you agree,
each vote you cast is an honest statement of your individual
choice.' The President could have had anything on God's earth
he wanted, if he had the guts to ask for it in the open. The people
trust him and the people want to follow him; nobody, no matter
how whole-souled, can follow a man who will not lead, who
will not stand up and be counted, who will not say openly what
we all know he thinks privately, who thinks you can substitute tricks for morals, smartness for passion, cunning for a soul.
. . . He'll get Wallace in the end, if he wants to stick it out.
He'll get Wallace. But he'll get him out of the gutter, which is an
insult to a President, to Mr. Wallace, to you, to me, and to the
American tradition which a few of us would still like to live and
die for, if we could only persuade some of you who think you
know all the answers that the way to defend democracy is to
persuade yourselves that the people like to hear the truth!"

Pretty strong language, particularly the suggestion that Wallace had to be got out of the gutter, which referred I think to
the fact that F.D.R. was forcing him down the throats of the
unwilling delegates, without ever coming out for him, so that both
nominations could appear to be their free and undictated choice.
It was an interesting example of how F.D.R. could infuriate
liberals who were on his side by refusing to fit into the moral
outline which they insisted should be his. He liked to pull out
white rabbits. He would never have asked for the presidency in
the open. He was not a knight in shining armor. He wore his
own rather complicated armor, and knew how to make it shine
before the faces of the people. They did not want to hear the
truth. They might suspect the complexities, sometimes devious,
that actually were his. But they felt his greatness. Though like
ordinary men, he was no ordinary man.

Ickes said that if, after all the glaring blunders he had made
at the convention, the President could retrieve the campaign,
then the god of elections was indeed on his side. But that god

was already there, and this the President knew. As soon as he got back to Washington he asked Ickes to lunch, told him that he had offered the vice presidency to Hull, who declined with tears in his eyes, added that the party leaders said Ickes could not be nominated but Wallace could. Governor Lloyd C. Stark of Missouri, (who was being talked about), the President thought, was really a conservative. "And besides," F.D.R. added in one of his typical and refreshing remarks, "he has no sense of humor and he bores me."[2]

To many people Henry Wallace was appealing and heroic. He could hold a vision before laboring men which stirred and moved them, and to not a few there was something attractive about the quality of his naïveté. He was a distinguished agronomist. But his political ideals had no solid or definite outline. His lack of humor prevented him from recognizing the relative significance of values. I remember dining with him one night at the British Embassy. Lord Halifax had just succeeded Lothian, and after dinner, among the men, the talk fell on conditions in England. Halifax, who was fond of fox hunting, spoke of the farmers in his region of Yorkshire—Garrowby Hall, Garrowby—voting to carry on the hunt and pay the expenses out of their pockets, in spite of the war; spoke of it in a casual tone, tinged with pride. As we went out Wallace murmured to me that the story showed what he had already suspected, that the English would not take the war as a serious business.

We saw a good deal of Lord and Lady Halifax. He was finishing his long and distinguished career of public service as ambassador to the United States from 1941 to 1946. When he first arrived Halifax was regarded with a distrust which associated him with the appeasement of the Cliveden set. Before he left he had become universally admired and liked.

He had succeeded Lord Reading as Governor General of India in 1926, inheriting the boycotts, riots, and strikes that had been plaguing the country for five years. He was not a brilliant man, but men trusted him. His high-church Christianity apparently made him blind to the necessity of arming England against the

[2] The Secret Diary of Harold Ickes.

threat of Hitler; but, with the exception of a few voices, he represented the point of view of the average Britisher of the unawakened prewar years. His continuation in high office by Churchill showed how the most ardent differences were forgotten and all men stood together when war came. He was not physically strong. With the war years in Washington, the vision faded of a pleasant and unperplexed life in Yorkshire when he was still young enough to hunt. Genuine, friendly, earnest, rather conventional, he took life as it came, holding his faith as simply as he did his work and met his fellows. Yet he was not innocent, and below the faith one suspected a layer of shrewd worldliness sometimes found in dedicated Anglicans. The German propaganda newspapers during the war always referred to him as the *heilige fuchs*—the "holy fox." His sorrow stamped him with a certain grimness and gauntness—one son had been killed in the war, another terribly wounded—but the faith shone through his endurance. Lady Halifax was always at his slightly bewildered right hand, suddenly gay and quick to laugh, altogether courageous, outgoing, and warm beside his more reticent good manners. She reminded me of Mrs. Endicott Peabody, whose friendly humorousness had made me, as a new boy at Groton School, feel less miserably homesick.

Soon after we came to know each other I said teasingly, but with a purpose, that he was not meeting the right people in Washington. The right people? he asked, looking down at me from his great height, puzzled. The congressmen, I said, not just the members of the Foreign Affairs Committee of the House, and the dining-out Senators, but the insiders, the chairmen of the committees that ran the show, the isolationists, the Irish, apt to be suspicious of a British gentleman. How well did he know John McCormack, the Democratic leader of the House? The upshot of it was as I had hoped—that I gave an informal stag supper in his honor at our house. There were fifty or sixty Senators and congressmen, who after bourbon whiskey, fried chicken, sweet potatoes, and apple pie, relaxing on a Saturday night, formed a ring about the ambassador, who talked to them of England and the war for twenty minutes, and then for an hour answered every conceivable question. He came out of it well, never saying that anything was off the record, and not evasive, so that they went out murmuring that he was not a bad guy. . . . An abstemious man, and modest, but now all shyness gone, mopping his brow in a relief that was not overemphasized, he asked if he could have a mild spot, with soda. "It really wasn't bad, Biddle . . . I had rather dreaded it, you know. But I really enjoyed it. Nice chaps, your congressmen. Don't forget to send me a list, and perhaps a little note on each. What was the name of the representative with red hair, who you said was a friend of Boss Hague? I liked him, though sometimes he was a bit hard to understand. Now what accent would you say that was?"

I remember on another occasion how shocked he was—shooked rather than indignant—when, accompanied by Adolf Berle, I reported to him the activities of one of the British secret service agents, which, unless stopped at once, would have got his government into the most serious kind of trouble. Edgar Hoover, in Jackson's absence, had reported to me that representatives of Scotland Yard had picked up at a bar in Baltimore two British sailors who had deserted their battleship, handcuffed them, thrown them into a car, and driven them back to their ship in New York. Nice story if it got out; and we would of course have to arrest His Majesty's agents, and indict them for kidnaping. There were the five state kidnaping laws, too. I could not remember which carried the death penalty, which only life imprisonment. I did not want any report, investigation, or apology. I wanted his immediate assurance that it would not happen again . . . He knew nothing about it. His government, he pointed out, never kept its representatives informed on secret service work. But he gave me his word.

I was not particularly active in the campaign. Realizing that the President expected members of the Cabinet to take some part in it, or at least that he was pleased if we did, I spoke a dozen times, beginning at the end of August at a Democratic rally in Seattle. In a state in which there was nearly a fifth of all the potential hydroelectric power in the United States, it was natural to devote a large part of my speech to public versus private power, always a burning issue in the Northwest. The people were being asked to vote on one of the current efforts to curb the spread of public power, backed by the private power interests, which had organized the Let the People Vote League, which was pushing a law that would have required a referendum before the creation of public utility districts. But the league was popularly regarded as a wolf clothed like a sheep.

The pattern of these rallies was much alike all over the country. You descended from the plane, "a member of a prominent Philadelphia family"—for years I had learned to dread this particular cliché —"unshaven from Cleveland," as in this case the Seattle *Times* was pleased to put it. You gave an interview to three or four reporters, usually callow, sleepy, half-baked youths; you conceded three states to the Republican candidate; and elicited and answered questions; you visited the local U. S. Attorney, the FBI office, the Immigration office; you lunched with the Chamber of Commerce, a city bar group, or sometimes the Kiwanians. It was always said that you conferred with the Democratic political leaders, and sometimes they were polite enough to come in and say "hello," and tell you what names to mention in your speech—this time it was Senator Bone, and Representative Mon C. Wallgren, later Senator, and my friend Representative Charles H. Levy, who was being "crucified" because he had voted against the bill to deport Bridges. I had the pleasure of nominating Levy for his United States district judgeship almost as soon as I became Attorney General.

You speak on the air. You sup at six o'clock and are expected to talk interestingly to prominent, uberous ladies, some great in their own right, others the wives of the great. You deliver the address, eleven o'clock by now, for others have performed; Lady Wilkie Mismas, whose subject is "Willkie, Wall Street and 1940"; and Mrs. Artemis Cornflit, introduced by the county chairman to introduce Biddle, after "specialties" by Cowboy Jones and Whistlin' Jack. Exhausted, you accept an invitation to have a quiet drink in a corner of the main entertainment room of the chief hotel with sixteen others who raise their voices and laughter to drown the jazz, to which, on a diminutive spot, businessmen, unable to look anything but respectable, push their spouses or an occasional younger girl friend forward and back,

back and forward, with unrhythmic formality, or gangling youths, not quite old enough to shave more than once a week, move cheek to cheek and loin to loin with their companions, devoid of all expression, gazing fixedly into space with the faraway look of constipated dogs. . . .

I liked all of it—well, almost all.

I do not think that all the oratory and radio broadcasts and rallies had much to do with the result. They seldom do. The President, toward the end, became worried and abandoned his aloof attitude for a few campaign speeches. Willkie was drawing immense crowds, but crowds do not mean votes, as Alfred Smith's campaign in 1928 proved. The voters not only liked F.D.R., they liked what he had done for them in his first two terms.

Fundamentally the Democrats are probably as much split as the Republicans except at a presidential election, when the Democrats seem to be able to unite more readily, and to drop for the time being the platitudes so dear to the hearts of their conservative opponents. The ideological issues that the Republicans advertised during this particular campaign were dictatorship, socialism and the third term—all of them allied, but the first two pretty shopworn, and the third too theoretic to be appealing.

Invoking the dictatorship issue on the edge of a war sounded hollow. A dictator suppresses free speech and a free press. Eighty-five per cent of the press were savagely criticizing the President—but there was no suggestion of censorship. Yet the spurious issue of dictatorship was constantly invoked. The ironic sadness of it all was that Franklin Roosevelt, who at this tense moment of history was the supreme symbol of the democratic ideal throughout the world, and the hope of a better life for millions of Europeans, should here at home be called "dictator" by his fellow Americans.

The Republican leaders, working themselves into a froth of fear, tried, with singular ineptness, to carry the people along in their awkward stride. Herbert Hoover, who to so many had become a symbol of defeat, solemnly announced a week before the election that "an economic system is being created which drifts steadily away from free men and free enterprise down the suicide road of national socialism." In Chicago the president of a bank added to the institution's financial statement a proud postscript to the effect that "in its last stand for democracy, every director and officer of this bank will cast his vote for Wendell Willkie." And doubtless they did, while the humbler and far more numerous employees of the same institution voted for Franklin Roosevelt. At the Philadelphia Club 90 per cent of the members were for Willkie, but all the waiters—so one of them, a Democratic division leader, informed me in a cautious but triumphant whisper as he handed me my lunch—the waiters to a man would vote for the President.

I tried to keep my audience straight on the third term issue. Almost everyone assumed that Washington had thrown the great weight of his authority against it. The exact contrary was the case. In a letter written to Lafayette on April 28, 1788, which was discovered by a research student less than a year before the election took place, Washington very clearly opposed any rigid traditional limit. "There cannot, in my judgment," he wrote, "be the least danger that the President will by any practicable intrigue ever be able to continue himself one moment in office, much less perpetuate himself in it . . . I can see no propriety in excluding ourselves from the services of any man, who on some great emergency, will be deemed universally most capable of serving the public." Prophetic and highly applicable words. And in like language James Buchanan, then a member of the Congress, speaking against a bill to limit the President's tenure to one term, said: "The day may come when dangers shall hover over us, and when we may have a President at the helm of State who possesses the confidence of the country, and is better able to weather the storm than any other pilot."

I believed that the tradition against more than two terms was unwise, and that our experience had not shown that we need fear but should welcome strong Presidents. The chief objection to a third term was not that the President might exhibit dictatorial proclivities, but that on the contrary he would more probably be far less potent, having by then exhausted his patronage and therefore his ability to get things done within the Congress. No President who had exercised leadership could hold it long in the tangled wilderness of senators and representatives. All Presidents must soon look to the public for strength, and this is what the politicians hated, and this is what President Roosevelt did.

DEFENDING CIVIL LIBERTIES

❈ *Chapter Nine*

I felt that war was coming to us, felt it in my bones during that spring and summer of 1940. Whenever the occasion seemed opportune, I said something to prepare the country when it did come. Public opinion was confused. How could the people understand, most of them still going about their business quietly, always skeptical of Jeremiahs? Until they became frightened, how could they take the meaning to them of this sudden obliteration in Europe of all basic decencies? A sound public point of view forms slowly, the people must guess and blunder, and be allowed mistakes, and must feel their way before they can decide and achieve. There was talk of using propaganda—we must do now in this uncertain peace what George Creel had done in the First World War through his Committee on Public Information, distributing seventy-five million copies of thirty-odd booklets in several languages, and 74,000 Four Minute Men making almost a million speeches. . . . But propaganda is a dangerous business—better let the people find their own way than whip them into the madness of war when the United States was not at war, not yet. But would there be time?

One decision I made as Solicitor General (for a few months I was Acting Attorney General, after Jackson resigned), after some uneasiness, may have been motivated by the instinct to display firmness on appropriate occasions. It is easier in the cooler breath of the passing years to disentangle the causes from the rationalizations which at the time I marshaled to support my action. I authorized criminal action against the Dunne brothers and others, under the Smith Act. I believed that under my direction the case could be tried fairly and would not result in a spate of prosecutions for sedition as in the twenties, immediately after the last war. The Smith Act, adopted in 1940, was the first peacetime sedition law since the notorious statute of 1798, which expired in two years and was not renewed, under which critics of the administration of John Adams, particularly newspaper editors, were sent to jail, sometimes for merely jeering at the President; and one outspoken Republican was fined for expressing a hope that the wad from the cannon to be fired in a presidential salute might hit President Adams on the seat of his pants! History showed that sedition statutes—laws addressed to what men said—invariably had been used to prevent and punish criticism of the government, particularly in time of war. I believed them to be unnecessary and harmful. This particular law made it criminal to advocate destruction of the government by force or violence. I doubted whether any speech or writing should be made criminal. I thought that this provision might be declared unconstitutional under the First Amendment of the Constitution, which protected freedom of utterance. And, with some reluctance, I authorized a prosecution so that the law would be tested at the threshold, and taken to the Supreme Court, where it would, I hoped and believed, be knocked out.

When the time came I sent Henry Schweinhaut to St. Paul to supervise the Dunne trial, to see that the United States Attorney did not let his patriotism run away with him, and to say quietly to the trial judge that the Attorney General was anxious that the trial be narrowed as much as possible. Schweinhaut had for several years been in charge of the Civil Liberties Unit of the Department, and shared my skepticism about sedition trials. He handled the situation well—the trial was fair, there were a number of acquittals, and although the Dunnes and several others were convicted, the sentences were comparatively light, running from a year and a day to sixteen months—a sentence of a year or less does not permit probation under federal law. The judgment was sustained on appeal to the Circuit Court of Appeals; but to my surprise the Supreme Court refused to review it. The victory for the government became a defeat for me. The law stood on the books. Uncomfortable about the result, I was not surprised when the American Civil Liberties Union and some of my liberal friends attacked me.

I have since come to regret that I authorized the prosecution. I should not have tried to test the criminal provisions of the statute in this particular case. The two Dunne brothers and their twenty-seven associates were the leaders of the Trotskyist Socialist Workers' Party, a little splinter group, which claimed 3000 members, and by no conceivable stretch of a liberal imagination could have been said to constitute any "clear and present danger" to the government, which, it was alleged, they were conspiring to overthrow. There had been no substantial overt act outside of talk and threats, openly expressed in the time-honored Marxist lingo.

The Supreme Court may have thought that the case did not present strong enough facts on which adequately to test the law. Eight years later it sustained the conviction of eleven leaders of the Communist Party and the constitutionality of the statute. In contrast to the trials during the First World War, Judge Medina tried the case with firmness and restraint, "sorely tried," as Judge Learned Hand remarked, in the opinion of the Second Circuit Court of Appeals approving the legality of the conviction—"for many months of turmoil, constantly provoked by useless bickering, exposed to offensive slights and insults, harried with interminable repetition."

The government, during the five and a half years when I was Solicitor General and Attorney General, occasionally intervened in the Supreme Court on behalf of an individual litigant to sustain his rights in furtherance of a policy against racial discrimination to which the Democratic administrations had long been committed on paper. The *Mitchell* case was an instance of this help, which presented an unusual example of conflict of interests. It was one of a series of decisions at that time which helped to bring about the striking change in our treatment of Negroes in the past fifteen or twenty years.

Arthur W. Mitchell, a Negro member of the House of Representatives, when his interstate train crossed into Arkansas, had been compelled under threat of arrest to move out of a Pullman car into a Jim Crow coach, in accordance with the provisions of the Separate Coach Law of that state. The Interstate Commerce Commission, six to five, dismissed his complaint. As Solicitor General it was my responsibility to represent the commission; but since I disagreed with its order, yet desired the questions of law which were not clear to be properly presented and argued, I authorized the commission to write its own brief and argue its position through its counsel, and with the permission of the Court filed a memorandum brief for the United States, in which I expressed sharp disagreement with the commission's decision.

In an opinion by Chief Justice Hughes the Court held that the discrimination shown was "palpably unjust," and was forbidden by the Constitution. The issue, the Court said, was equality of treatment. The denial of such equality because of Mr. Mitchell's race was an invasion of a "fundamental individual right which is guaranteed against State action by the Fourteenth Amendment." It was a simple and clear-cut issue, and the Chief Justice so treated it—"colored persons who buy first-class tickets must be furnished with accommodations equal in comforts and conveniences to those afforded to first-class white passengers." That Mitchell's ejection from the Pullman car and the requirement that he should continue his journey in a second-class car was "in accordance with custom," or that there was "comparatively little colored traffic," and few persons were therefore discriminated against—these considerations were irrelevant. The individual's right to the equal protection of the laws was at the essence.

As Katherine and I left the court after the argument a Southern lawyer, looking in my direction, muttered to a friend, "And now I suppose he's going over to have tea with the Japanese Ambassador!"

Most of these "civil liberty" cases resulted from the activities of the Civil Liberties Unit of the Department of Justice started by Frank Murphy in 1939.[1] The unit, with a handful of lawyers, carried on its highly effective and, in the South, thoroughly unpopular activities under a dedicated head, Victor W. Rotnem, with the assistance of Eleanor Bontecue, who had resigned as dean of Bryn Mawr College to enter the government service. Although most of the cases dealt with Negroes, the unit's work was not confined to any one racial group, and included Mexicans, Indians, and (in many instances) members of the sect known as Jehovah's Witnesses. The cases involved police brutality, and the related problem of lynching; election frauds and discrimination; and peonage and involuntary servitude in some of the Southern states.

The history of the long attempt to create and sustain these rights is an ironic chapter in the story of our slow and uneven effort to achieve equality under law. Perhaps if the Civil War could have been avoided; if, after it had been won and the slaves freed, the "rebels" had not been disfranchised; if the white Southerners had not tried to hold the Negroes virtually as agricultural slaves; if in retaliation federal troops had not been sent to the Southern states to enforce reconstruction, and kept there for a long generation; if Lincoln had lived, and a more sympathetic persuasion than force had been used toward the South; if cooler heads than Thaddeus Stevens of Pennsylvania and Charles Sumner of Massachusetts had been in command of Congress; then Negroes might have gradually received actual instead of paper rights. But the pendulum began to swing early, and in a handful of years the feeling behind the three Civil War amendments was being cooled by the breath of judicial construction and legislative indifference.

When the Civil Rights Unit began to work, only a few fragments of the Civil War statutes remained on the books, and the constitutionality of some of them was in doubt. No actions had been instituted for years, and most of them were dead-letter

[1] An excellent detailed discussion of the work of the Section is given in Professor Robert Carr's *Federal Protection of Civil Rights: Quest for a Sword*, published by the Cornell University Press in 1947.

laws. We determined to breathe new life in them, to see if we could not persuade the Court, now more sensitive to the values which they were adopted to achieve, to give them more humane interpretation. The law against peonage still stood, and two sections of the criminal code, 51 and 52, which soon became famous, dealt respectively with conspiracies to injure persons in the exercise of their constitutional rights, and the deprivation of those rights under color of state laws.

Peonage still persisted in a few plantations in the deep South. A typical case was that of Albert Sydney Johnson, who farmed about ten thousand acres in the rich black belt of Arkansas. He consistently terrorized both Negro and white laborers, threatening to kill them if they left, and lent color to the threat by carrying a gun, a revolver, and a pair of brass knuckles. He was so feared that his employees would slip away from his farm at night, leaving behind their possessions, even standing crops. Finally a deputy sheriff reported the case to the Department of Justice. An indictment was returned by a federal grand jury. The news spread and the news agencies sent reporters to cover the trial. Johnson tried to bluster his way out by intimidating and bribing witnesses. But the government's case was so strong that he pleaded guilty, was sentenced to two and a half years, and sent to prison.

Once the Unit was established complaints poured in, not only from the victims of the illegal acts but from their fellow townsmen, from whites as well as Negroes, often from local law-enforcement officials who found themselves powerless to deal with the situations they reported, and from groups organized to protect civil liberties. The denial of the rights—often merely of the right to live in peace—was tragic mockery after we had entered the war. A young Negro soldier wrote to the President, who forwarded the letter to me for investigation:

"I am a corporal in the U. S. Army. I have been in the Army for 17 months and in England for 11 months. I am a Negro with an American heart, and have been doing my duties as an American soldier. I consider myself as one of the best. I have never had a punishment. I have been awarded the 'Good Conduct Medal,' good driving medal, and sharpshooting with a 30-30 rifle and carbine, and a key man with a 50 calibre machine gun.

"I was sent some papers from the states a few days ago. And I read where colored people in my home, New Iberia, La., were being beaten up and chased out of town. Encluded in them was my sister's husband . . . They are being beaten up because they succeeded in getting a welding school for the colored, so they could build the tanks and ships we need so badly. They forced them to leave their homes, and also beat up the colored doctors and ran them out of town.

"I thought we were fighting to make this world a better place to live in . . . I am giving the USA all I got, and would even die, but I think my people should be protected. I am asking you, Sir, to do all in your power to bring these people to justice and punish the guilty ones."

Prosecutions were instituted against sheriffs, police officers, justices of the peace, and even judges who had misused the power of office under "color of law" to deprive individuals of their rights. Indictments were returned against a policeman for torturing a young Negro boy to force a confession of a theft of which he was later acquitted; against a sheriff, a jail "trusty," and a shyster lawyer for operating a notorious kangaroo court to extort money from prisoners in a county jail; and in a case involving members of that unpopular and masochistic sect known as Jehovah's Witnesses. One of the first cases brought under Section 52 was against a deputy sheriff and chief of police to whom a group of Witnesses had appealed for protection. The Witnesses were ushered into a police office, forced to swallow large quantities of castor oil while the police officer looked on, and then tied together and paraded through the streets of the town. The District Court decided that the two officers of the law were properly indicted for refusing to intervene to save the Witnesses from violence. Several convictions reached the Supreme Court; and Justice Frankfurter expressed his anxiety that "every illegal discrimination by a policeman on the beat would be State action for purposes of suit in a Federal court." In the *Screws* case that anxiety resulted in a severe check to the government's efforts.

Claude Screws was the sheriff of Baker County, Georgia, with a population of seven or eight hundred people, one of the very few counties in the United States where there was no railroad.

Bob Hall, a Negro, owned a pearl-handled automatic .45-caliber pistol, which he greatly treasured. Deputy Sheriff Jones wanted it, and took it. After a month Hall appealed to Sheriff Screws, and finally to the grand jury, who under instructions from the Solicitor of the Circuit ordered the pistol returned. The sheriff would not return it. On January 29, 1943, Hall's lawyer wrote to the sheriff demanding the return of the gun. Screws, Jones, and Kelley, the local police officer, under cover of a forged warrant charging theft of an automobile tire, arrested Hall the same day. The evidence showed that these officers of the law had been drunk for nearly six hours, boasted they were going to "get" a Negro who had "lived too long" and got too smart. They handcuffed Hall's hands behind his back, took him to the court house, and as he got out of the car beat him with their fists and a black jack until he was unconscious. They dragged him by the feet through the square into the jail, where he was thrown on the floor, dying. Fortunately he did not regain consciousness before he died.

The Department of Justice made every effort to persuade the State of Georgia to prosecute. The District Solicitor, whose duty it was to start criminal proceedings, was reported to have felt helpless in the matter, since having no investigative facilities he had to rely on the sheriffs and policemen of the various communities in his district for investigation—in this instance Screws, Jones, and Kelley. The United States finally brought action; and on October 7, 1943, a local jury in a United States Court, all of whom must have personally known the defendants, convicted all three. They received the maximum penalty—three years imprisonment, and a fine of $1000 each—not much for murder, but surely better than nothing. It was the first time a conviction of this kind had ever been obtained in Georgia. The members of the jury were not deflected from doing their sworn duty by the usual charge of "Yankee interference." They were enforcing *their* law in *their* court.

The Circuit Court of Appeals affirmed the judgment. The Supreme Court decided to review it, and after holding the case under advisement for nearly seven months, reversed the judgment.

There were four separate opinions. A majority of five sustained the constitutionality of Section 52, under which the indictment was returned, charging the defendants with depriving Hall of rights guaranteed by the Fourteenth Amendment under color of the law of Georgia by use of the warrant. Hall's constitutional right was the right to due process, for which the state officers had substituted murder. Justice Douglas, writing for the majority, said that the deprivation of a federal right must be willful—"a purpose to deprive a person of a specific constitutional right." Speaking for the Court he directed a retrial, since the trial judge had not specifically charged the jury to that effect.

It is difficult to follow Douglas's reasoning. If the defendants killed Hall "under pretense of law," to use his phrase, it would appear that the only intent involved was their intention to do what they did—deliberately assault and kill him. To charge the jury that the defendants to be guilty must have willfully intended to deprive Hall of his constitutional right was bound to confuse them—what did they know about constitutional rights? And it was inevitable that on a new trial the jury should acquit. If they didn't know about these federal rights that the judge was telling them about, how could Screws have been expected to know about them when he was beating Hall to death—Screws not being a lawyer, only a policeman? And he could not have intended to violate rights he had never heard of, so was not guilty . . . Thus they must have argued in the jury room, puzzled, uncertain, trying to do what the judge said they should do.

Two justices, Rutledge and Murphy, agreed with the majority that Section 52 was constitutional, but thought the conviction should have been sustained. Murphy filed a short and eloquent dissent, approving the action of the trial court in every particular. Roberts, Frankfurter, and Jackson also dissented but for reasons diametrically opposed to Murphy. They thought the section was too vague to be constitutional, and expressed their frank dislike of it—it was born of the "vengeful spirit" which "envenomed the Reconstruction era"; had "remained a dead letter for years"; it was "shapeless and all-embracing," and could be a dangerous instrument in the hands of politicians. The result of the decision was greatly to lessen the value of Section 52 in punishing atrocities of this character where the state refused to take action.

Under the law Negroes had the right to vote in general elections. But it was hardly worth voting since elections were in substance determined in the primaries, and the Supreme Court had decided that the Federal Corrupt Practices Act did not apply to primaries. We determined to try to persuade the Court to apply Section 52 to primaries—in effect to overrule the decision. We found a test case when Patrick Classic and other defendants, who were members of a "reform" faction fighting the Huey Long machine in a Louisiana primary, with overzealous enthusiasm stole a number of ballots and cast them in favor of their own candidate for a representative to Congress. No Negro was involved. They were convicted, and the Supreme Court agreed to review the judgment. I planned to argue the case, but I was sick at the time, and chose Herbert Wechsler in my place.

Wechsler was one of an exceptionally able group of young men who worked closely with me when I was Solicitor General and Attorney General. He had been editor of the Columbia Law Review, had clerked for Justice Stone in 1932–33, and went back to Columbia to teach law and in a few years became a leading authority in his fields—criminal law and federal jurisdiction. I liked the turn of his mind, and the sobriety of his measured judgment, not so much cautious as thoughtful, his humor warming his thought. He was cheerfully patient, a quality that calmed my own nervous restlessness. He was essentially happy, a virtue that I prize highly, happy largely because he possessed the quality of caring deeply for his friends, and of showing them that he cared.

It was argued by the defendants that federal law did not apply to primaries, because they were not in general use at the time the section was adopted. But the Court concluded that the primary was an "integral part" of the election procedure, and sustained the conviction, and the constitutionality of Section 52 as applied to elections. The vote stood four to three, and it is interesting to note that the three dissenters were Douglas, Black, and Murphy, who were usually the Court's most uncompromisingly "liberal" voices. They were apparently fearful of the extension of federal power to police state elections.

The importance of the *Classic* decision is realized when it is remembered that in the Southern states there is substantially but one party, and the primaries are therefore conclusive. At last the Negro could vote! And he did vote, in increasing numbers, all over the eleven Southern states where, before the decisions, he had been barred or frightened into abstaining.

I SUCCEED BOB JACKSON

․{}›› *Chapter Ten*

On June 2, 1941, Chief Justice Hughes retired, and I went to his chambers to pay my respects. I had not known him well. He was in a gay mood, like a boy just out of school, with summer ahead of him. At seventy-nine he was vigorous and happy. What would he do? I asked. Read the papers—he'd hardly had time to look at the *Times* for years—and go to a movie now and then. And perhaps write his memoirs, I suggested. No, that was not to his taste, he would rather have someone else do it, but he would see that his papers were put in order, so that if there were a biography the author would have it all there.

He reminisced. President Coolidge was a talkative man if he trusted you and no one was around. He trusted Hughes, and when Hughes would call on him after he resigned as Secretary of State, Coolidge would let go, after he had closed the door, so that it was hard to edge a word in. William Allen White's biography gave an exact picture. One never knew Coolidge well. We talked about Cardozo, such a different man, an incessant worker, who would plunge into his opinions immediately after the long Saturday conferences of the Court, which were tiring. Hughes spoke of some of his contemporaries at the New York bar. To a man they would show signs of restlessness when they had achieved the top in practice, and had everything that private work could offer, and began to look around for something else to do before the end. They grew lonely, he said, and added a little shyly that I had been wise to go into public work. There you found something that you never got in private practice.

I admired him without reservation. His rectitude, his courage, his learning, his insight made him a great man. To an unusual degree he was self-reliant and sure of himself, conscious of his power. Yet he was without vanity, reticent and modest. An observer once said he had a talent for minding his own business. The legend of his stiffness and coldness was apocryphal. The innate reserve accounted for an outward old-fashioned formality. His humor was human, and of a piece. "Don't you think, gentlemen," he once said to his associates after an unusually flat argument, "that we are entitled to a little more advocacy?" The Chief Justice was courtesy itself when one was arguing a case. He presided, as John Lord O'Brian remarked, with dignity amounting to a touch of majesty. It was impossible to tell what he was thinking, hard to find an opening to his point of view, for he asked few questions.

I like best to think of him in the *Mitchell* argument. It was an important case, and the Court swarmed with Negroes—friendly, hopeful, respectful, wonderfully attired—one of them beaming and immense, in a short-tailed cutaway with the sleeves just below his elbows. Thurgood Marshall, counsel for the National Association for the Advancement of Colored People, made an effective argument. He had occasion to introduce to the Court several of his associates who were on the brief. I was impressed with the bearing of the Chief Justice. He was grave, courteous, interested, but never gave an impression of going out of his way, of self-consciousness.

McReynolds had resigned in January 1941 so that the President had two vacancies to fill. A few weeks after Hughes retired, the President raised Stone to be Chief Justice and appointed Jackson and James F. Byrnes, who was to stay on the Court hardly more than a year before leaving to help the President with the war organization. Jackson told me that the President had indicated that he would have liked to make him Chief Justice immediately, but added that he was a little young (he was forty-nine), and that his time would come. Bob must have set his heart on it, for nothing but a deep disappointment could have motivated his bitter outburst at Nürnberg on June 20, 1946, when President Truman chose Frederick Vinson to take the place of Chief Justice Stone, after consulting among others Justice Owen Roberts, who had retired the year before, and told me later that he had recommended Vinson with several others to the President. Jackson could not resist striking out in public to relieve the bitterness of his heart. He was strained and over-worked in the trial of the German war criminals in Nürnberg, and a friend wrote him that Hugo Black, an associate justice of the Court, was opposing his nomination. Miserable with unhappiness he issued a three-page press release attacking Black in vehement language for not withdrawing from the argument of a case in which his former partner had appeared. There was no basis for the attack—and Jackson had not been sitting for a year. It was a foolish exhibition, and I felt sorry for him, stumbling like a child in pain. The British judges were profoundly shocked. They could not understand this washing of dirty linen in public, particularly by a judge.

I came to know Jimmy Byrnes well after we entered the war, and worked with him constantly during the war years. He was thoroughly loyal to President Roosevelt—his loyalty to President Truman was more doubtful—an uncannily skillful "operator" on the Hill. His judgment was excellent. He was friendly, quick, with a ready if not subtle sense of humor. Byrnes in the Senate and Fred Vinson in the House had probably more to do with getting Roosevelt's New Deal program through Congress than anyone else. Yet something was missing in the unusual gifts with which Byrnes was endowed, which made them seem, in the long run, turned to less worthy ends. Like Jackson he experienced a frustrating disappointment when his ambition to be nominated vice president in 1944 was thwarted. F.D.R., whom he had so faithfully served, had apparently encouraged him to believe that his nomination would please the President; and with this almost approval, as he arrived in Chicago, he must have held high expectations. Knowing his chief so well, he should have known, however, that those friendly and cordial words—repeated over the telephone from Washington to Chicago, and noted by Byrnes in shorthand—meant little more than that F.D.R. found it difficult not to give the appearance of yielding to any friend who asked for something. That he should have the best position that the new President, with a generous impulse, could give him—Secretary of State—was but a sop to his longing for power, and could not make him forget that by rights he should be in the place of the man who had appointed him, and to whom he felt superior.

In public life he has had everything—except the presidency: a representative from South Carolina for seven terms and Senator for two; resigning from the Supreme Court to become successively, director of Economic Stabilization, and director of War Mobilization; Secretary of State; and, finally, at seventy-one, welcomed back to his state as governor, to lead the extreme wing of Southern conservatives, who would not recognize the Negroes as equal citizens of the same country, in their hearts and sometimes openly secessionists, the last of the unreconstructed. To me it seemed tragic that James Francis Byrnes, the friend and admirer of Franklin Roosevelt, who had done so much to establish the principles of the New Deal, should end his extraordinary career in trying to solidify the racial prejudices from which, one would have supposed, his experience and association with Roosevelt might have freed him.

Byrnes and Robert Jackson sat together on the Court for about a year. The two men were not unalike in their native shrewdness. Byrnes, I suspect, never lived down his disappointment. Jackson, before he died, had achieved his full stride, moral and intellectual; and any bitterness for not being made Chief Justice had vanished.

When Jackson was told about his appointment on the Court in 1940, he said to the President that he hoped he would appoint his friend Biddle to take his place. The President was fond of Jackson, and talked freely to him. He asked him, "How does Francis get along with Hoover?" Murphy, it appeared, had hinted to the President that I could not get along with J. Edgar Hoover. The President asked Bob whether I would be tough enough; would I be too liberal, too conscientious? Frank Murphy, the President continued, was a tough guy; and Jackson got the impression, although the President did not precisely suggest it, that Murphy wanted to leave the Court, and might be eased off to be Attorney General for a brief space until he was sent back again to be governor general of the Philippines. Jackson told the President that he could not again appoint Murphy as Attorney General—it would acknowledge and underscore his failure as a judge. At about the same time there were suggestions by a columnist of a row between Hoover and me. A New York *Herald-Tribune* reporter was sent to ask me whether if I were made Attorney General I would fire the director of the Federal Bureau of Investigation. My denial was not published. Washington was like that.

The President must have known that Jackson would report the conversation back to me. He liked to "plant" an idea indirectly that way. He would never have said to me that he thought I might be too "soft"—that was not his way of doing things—and, knowing our dislike of Murphy, he probably relished keeping us worried by a scheme which he never seriously considered. Only a week before, he had sent for Senator Guffey and said to him, "Joe, I should like to appoint Francis Biddle Attorney General. What would your reaction be?" Joe answered that he would like to think it over. In Philadelphia, Al Greenfield, who had a good deal of influence in city politics, and some of the local Democratic leaders, getting wind of this, told the Senator that he would be crazy to try to block the first Cabinet appointment Pennsylvania had had for years. He must hurry back to Washington and get busy. He did. Was there anything, he asked me over the telephone, that he could do? Could he write to the President recommending the appointment? He could not have relished writing the letter.

The office of Attorney General was not filled for three months. The President never talked to me or to any of my friends except Bob, and I did nothing to further my chances. I never could do anything for myself in order to get a job. I do not cite this as a merit, but there it was. In this instance I don't think much pressure was exerted for anyone. There was talk about Thurman Arnold and Paul McNutt, and doubtless others whom I have forgotten. The members of the Tennessee delegation in the House led by Estes Kefauver, then a representative, urged my appointment, as did the Pennsylvania delegation, and a number of the congressmen individually. Representative Charles Leavy wrote the President that I had the confidence of every New Deal member of the House; and Graham H. Barden of North Carolina, who had been a member of the TVA Joint Committee, assured the President that a glance at the record made in that investigation would prove my ability. I was touched that a number of Negroes should have backed me, as "a friend of the colored people of America."

The appointment was announced on August 25, and on September 4 the Judiciary Committee met to hear objections from a few opposing witnesses connected with the Citizens Committee for Harry Bridges, who testified that they had watched FBI agents through binoculars from a neighboring building tap Bridges' telephone wire in New York City. They claimed that as Acting Attorney General I must have been responsible for this, that the practice was illegal, and that I should not be confirmed. There was no doubt that an FBI agent had applied the tap. Suddenly realizing that he was being watched, he made such a hasty exit that he left a letterhead identifying him with the Bureau, which was captured by the Bridges group. What aggravated the incident was that Judge Sears, a special examiner appointed by Jackson to investigate and report whether Bridges came under the deportation act, recently amended so as to apply to him, had filed his report, and there was nothing more to investigate. When all this came out in the newspapers I could not resist suggesting to Hoover that he tell the story of the unfortunate tap directly to the President. We went over to the White House together. F.D.R. was delighted; and, with one of his great grins, intent on every word, slapped Hoover on the back when he had finished. "By God, Edgar, that's the first time you've been caught with your pants down!" The two men liked and understood each other.

I testified before the committee that I knew nothing about the tap, had not authorized it, was not in the habit of approving wiretaps. When I was asked what my attitude to wiretapping was, Senator Tom Connally of Texas, the chairman, objected to the question as being irrelevant, and said to me, "No need of getting into all this. I'll get you through the committee without any trouble." But I told him I would prefer to state my position,

so there could be no question as to where I stood. I testified
that I would permit wiretaps in certain investigations, particularly espionage and subversive activities, but only under my
written approval given on written requests from the head of the
Federal Bureau of Investigation, until the Supreme Court ruled
that the action was illegal. The committee promptly recommended my confirmation. I knew that Jackson had permitted
tapping after the President had written him confidentially on
May 21, 1940:

> I am convinced that the Supreme Court never intended any
> dictum in the particular case which it decided to apply to
> grave matters involving the defense of the Nation.
> It is, of course, well known that certain other nations have
> been engaged in the organization of propaganda of so-called
> "fifth columns" in other countries and in preparation for sab-
> otage, as well as in actual sabotage.
> You are, therefore, authorized and directed in such cases as
> you may approve, after investigation of the need in each case,
> to authorize the necessary investigating agents that they are at
> liberty to secure information by listening devices direct to the
> conversation or other communications of persons suspected of
> subversive activities against the Government of the United
> States, including suspected spies. You are requested further-
> more to limit these investigations so conducted to a minimum
> and to limit them in so far as possible to aliens.
>
> > F.D.R.

The memorandum was evidently prepared in a hurry by the
President personally, without consultation, probably after he had
talked to Bob. It opened the door pretty wide to wiretapping of
anyone *suspected* of *subversive activities*. Bob didn't like it, and,
not liking it, turned it over to Edgar Hoover without himself
passing on each case. When it came to my turn I studied the
applications carefully, sometimes requesting more information,
occasionally turning them down when I thought they were not
warranted. Most of the taps were on Communists, and on suspected spies in the German and Russian embassies and consu-
lates, particularly after war started. We garnered a good deal of
useful information.

The current gossip in Washington was that many of the

government agencies were commonly engaged in this kind of detective surveillance; and that a newspaperman had tapped the President's private wire to Secretary Hull (every member of the Cabinet had a private wire to the White House).

I thought and still think that wiretapping is a "dirty business," but no dirtier than the use of stool pigeons, or undercover men, or informers. Of course it violates privacy; but it is an extraordinarily effective tool in running down crime. However, I do not believe that approval by the Attorney General is sufficient protection against abuse, since he cannot be entirely objective in the matter. Search warrants invade privacy; and under the Fourth Amendment they have to be issued by a court on an affidavit showing probable cause. A similar precaution should be used before a wiretap is allowed. The activity should be centered in the Department of Justice, and all other wiretapping in the District of Columbia be made criminal.

The Senate was debating a tax bill when my name came up from the Judiciary Committee for confirmation. Senator Connally interrupted the debate to ask immediate action as I was preparing to leave the city; and the Senators, who must have been in a good humor, slipped me through unanimously, and went back to their wrangling. I took the oath in the Oval Room of the White House, administered by Bob Jackson, that I would "support and defend the Constitution of the United States against all enemies, foreign and domestic," and would "well and faithfully discharge the duties" of the office on which I was about to enter. Before signing the letter patent the President announced that he was performing an operation on me—he was taking the "acting" out of my system. He added, "Supreme Court Justice Jackson calls my attention to something I have never discovered before in this certificate. In the case of the Attorney General it says: 'Know Ye, that reposing special trust and confidence in the Patriotism, Integrity and Ability of Francis Biddle,' etc. In the case of Justices of the Supreme Court, it doesn't say anything about patriotism. It uses the words 'uprightness, wisdom and learning.' Putting it the other way around, while a Justice of the Supreme Court does not have to have patriotism, the Attorney General of the United States does not have to have either learning or wisdom."

That evening we caught a plane for California to join my brother George, who was teaching art at Pacific Palisades—I remember that we had sleeping berths, with cool linen sheets, like a train, which disappeared with the war and were not again used.

As we flew west I thought over the mistakes I had made as Solicitor General, adding them up, balancing them against what I might have accomplished. I had begun to recognize more clearly my faults—jumping too quickly to conclusions with a lack of the caution that was so essential to a public servant, if it did not interfere with action; the inclination to be too easily convinced by the last comer. I must guard against the desire for popularity, for public approval.

I wondered what I could be proud of? Treatment of aliens? But that was an aspect of the core of our belief—a decent respect for all human beings—that was it. And I thought of our campaign for the Negroes, the long fight which was beginning to tell. . . .

The newspaper comment was friendly. Different reasons were given to explain why I was chosen: that the President wanted a "liberal" at this juncture; that Biddle was sympathetic to business, a point of view so desirable at this time. The Hartford *Courant* approved what it was pleased to think of as the diligence and modesty of the new cabinet member. *Time* spoke of Biddle as the "bright sharp sword in the New Deal." All the newspapers mentioned the fact that his ancestor, Edmund Randolph, had been appointed by President Washington to sit as Attorney General in the first Cabinet one hundred and fifty-two years before.

ATTORNEY GENERAL

❦❧ *Book Three*

*If you think of it, it seems a strange and
ironical arrangement that when the country has
entrusted to a particular group of men the
arduous and delicate task of conducting the
business of the nation, we at the same time
permit them to be harassed by every form of
obstruction and vituperation. It is as if we
had employed a surgeon to perform a delicate
operation and had then arranged that his elbow
should be jogged at the most critical moments.*

LORD MACMILLAN

August 26, 1941

Dear Francis—

Even in these days, when speaking of civilization hanging in the balance is not tall talk but pedantic accuracy, you and Katherine should pause long enough "to hear the kind voice of friends"—as Holmes put it with characteristic modesty. You have been called to a great office—and the greater because you are to represent law in the conduct of war and give signal proof that democracy is not a sham.

In succession you have been called to the two offices of State that excite me most and in which my interest and understanding are longest rooted in experience. Almost the first week of my government service, as an awkward and very shy junior assistant U.S. attorney, in the fall of 1906—just thirty-five years ago—I had the luck to see something of one of your ablest predecessors—William H. Moody. He lacked some of your gifts and "advantages"—but he was worthy of your succession. Dire days are ahead of you, unless I am a very bad prophet—not only those that are ahead for all of us, but those special demands on one's convictions and affections when one has to be indifferent to misunderstanding of friends and to be uncompromising with one's own insights and convictions and to disregard the wishes and views of those with less insight or less disinterestedness. I content myself with saying, as I rejoice in this stupendous opportunity for your versatile talents and character, that I too should like to express the highest praise that Holmes could give to a friend in your situation— "I bet on you."

And of course I cannot separate Katherine in all these feelings, in which Marion warmly joins.

Ever yours,
Felix Frankfurter

THE PRESIDENT AND
HIS CABINET

There hangs in my study a photograph of the Second World War Cabinet, signed by each of the eleven members, plus the President, above his likeness. Next to it is an engraving by Currier & Ives, published in 1876, slightly larger than the photograph, portraying President Washington's Cabinet of four, in which Jefferson and Hamilton had been so hostile, and Edmund Randolph so discouraged because his associates were not able, as Washington had fondly hoped, to form a privy council of advisers, patterned on the British model, who would be *au dessus de la mêlée*. President Washington sits next to his Secretary of War, General Henry Knox, who looks not unlike his namesake at our table. Alexander Hamilton is standing, a hand on Knox's chair, the other tucked in his waistcoat below his ruffled shirt, concentrated and determined, his look suggesting irritation below the slight frown. On his other side sits Thomas Jefferson, holding a piece of paper, his smock very simple and without frills, as became a Republican, his unpowdered hair curly, a line of worry between the eyes. At the other end of the little table is Edmund Randolph, the first Attorney General, my mother's great-grandfather, his right hand separating the pages of a book, his hair brushed away from his forehead and caught in a "horse's tail" back of his neck, a serious young man.

In the photograph of the war Cabinet, Frank Knox, Secretary of the Navy, is at the corner of the long table next to me—short, stocky, straightforward, more prepared to be friendly than hostile. He had been a Rough Rider during the Spanish-American War, and followed his colonel, Theodore Roosevelt, into the Bull Moose Party in 1912. Nineteen years later as owner of the Chicago *Daily News* he became one of the leading critics of the New Deal, and was the Republican vice presidential candidate in 1936, when Alfred Landon was so disastrously beaten for the presidency. Knox and Landon were much alike—amiable, middle class, friendly, with a sort of sturdy averageness about them. When his appointment to the Cabinet was announced, Frank repeated a cliché that every one could understand. "I am an American first, and a Republican afterward!" He was the kind of person on whom you could count for that sort of sound, safe platitude. He died before the war was over, on April 28, 1944. I liked Frank Knox. He was not subtle, but he was healthy and decent to the core.

I sat on Knox's right; and Henry Morgenthau, Jr., the Secretary of the Treasury, was on my other side—we took our places in the order in which our Cabinet positions had been created. Henry had been a gentleman farmer, a neighbor of Roosevelt's in Dutchess County, and had served under him in various state and federal positions. I never could feel close to Morgenthau, although I respected his courage, singleness of purpose, and devotion to the President, a bit doglike at times. The President was fond of Henry, patted him when he looked hurt, teased him in public without striking a spark of humor—humor there was none—and protected him as far as possible against the annoyance which his missionary zeal in fields not the Treasury's occasionally caused the rest of us. He had a tendency to send memoranda to F.D.R. about the work of others—which doubtless touched his own, for almost everything was related by the war effort—instead of first discussing it with them.

I hasten to add that his sights were high, his probity impeccable, and the efficiency of his department well above the average, for on the whole he chose good men to serve under him, and leaned over backward, sometimes unnecessarily far, it seemed to me, to keep away from politicians. We shared the same aims, even if the means chosen to accomplish them, or, more precisely, the method of going about the choice, did not on all occasions lead to a warm sense of team play. One could trust him, except where consideration for the feelings of others entered the picture. How could one be at ease with a man who, suspicious of the present and concerned with the future, recorded your telephone talk with him—"wait a minute, Francis, I would like to put on my secretary to make a record of what you are saying"—to be collected for eternity in those endless volumes of the diary that recorded the minutiae of his daily career?

To Henry Morgenthau's right, at the center of the table sat the President, then came Secretary of State Hull and Secretary of War Henry L. Stimson. Beyond Stimson was Frank Walker, the Postmaster General, and next to him Harold Ickes, Secretary of the Interior, looking belligerently at the photographer. I remember one occasion when Harold was away and his Under Secretary, Abe Fortas, sat in his place. Fortas was a recent appointee and the President, unable to place him immediately, asked Morgenthau about him, who in turn passed the question on to me. "Fortas," I whispered, and his name was relayed to the President, who then wrote on a pad: "not his last name, his *first* name?" And when, going around the table, he came to Abe, the President asked, "Well, Abe, what's been going on in Interior?"

By tradition, the Postmaster General was the political representative of the party in power, and usually chairman of the National Committee at the same time. Although Frank Walker became Postmaster General in 1940, he was not chairman of the National Committee until 1943, and served for a year only. He disliked his political job, but always did what the President wanted him to do, and just then the President wanted the politicians off his back, so that he could get on with the war. Frank was never a professional politician in the sense that Jim Farley was professional or Ed Flynn (who succeeded Jim as chairman) or Bob Hannegan, who followed Walker. Frank was too mild, too decent, too gentle to fill that toughest of all political jobs. But he could and did protect his friend, the President.

Harold Le Claire Ickes was a very different type. If Frank Walker was not a professional politician by temperament there was nothing amateurish about him. People instinctively understood and liked him. Harold Ickes, on the contrary, was the opposite of the politician—a reformer, a liberal (few politicians on either side are liberal by conviction) and an independent—witness his activity as a Progressive from 1912 to 1916. A good cabinet minister should be a competent administrator, and there was none better than Ickes, who sat all through the Roosevelt Cabinet and for a year under President Truman, until he resigned in 1946 with a clarion blast against that President—who was no unworthy opponent himself. He spent the next six years wasting his talents on a syndicated newspaper column that gave him narrow scope for his fierce invective, and occasionally lending his now mild influence to back some liberal measure. Harold Ickes was not a man who, having tasted the satisfactions of public office on a high level, could bear the narrower existence of a critic and gadfly.

I had not fully realized what a suspicious and thwarted human being he was until his secret diaries were published after his death. He had no heroes, and his friends—Tom Corcoran, Ben Cohen, and I were among the closest—remained so only as long as they did not oppose him. Obversely his enemies were those who stood against his strong urges to increased official dominion. Such, for instance, was David Lilienthal. They were both Democrats, both New Dealers, both appointed by President Roosevelt in the same administration. And yet during the Truman administration, when Lilienthal was up for confirmation by the Senate as chairman of the Atomic Energy Commission, and needed all the strength he could muster, Harold Ickes, obviously without realizable ambitions in the public field, attacked Lilienthal in his column, and in private talk, with an unfairness equal to that of Senator Pat McCarran, who suggested that Lilienthal was a Communist, because years earlier Lilienthal would not give him political appointments. Lilienthal had fought for the independence of the Tennessee Valley Authority. Harold wanted it put under the Interior Department—and that opposition was enough to make him the eternal foe of the younger man.

In spite of his faults I liked Ickes, although when he asked me I always refused to be a member of any of the interdepartmental committees on which he sat—committees that the President was delighted to set up in an effort to "solve" the problems that arose when several departments were concerned, and which Harold tried to dominate whenever Interior was involved. I liked to lunch with him in his office in the Interior Department, where, looking like an angry and belligerent Donald Duck, he would let go as much at the Democrats as at the Republicans. I can see him on a particular occasion when he was wartime petroleum and solid fuels administrator. Striding up and down, his hands clasped behind his back, his lower lip protruding, he announced that he had won a terrific victory over some oil barons whom he had persuaded that it was more advisable to play the game, to co-operate with him. Under such circumstances one must either kiss a woman or have a drink: would I join him in a martini? . . .

I had first come into personal contact with him in 1938, when I was counsel for the committee investigating TVA. He called me in Knoxville to ask if I would give him professional advice about whether a political speech he was going to make in Philadelphia was libelous. I flew from Knoxville to Washington— I had some TVA business in the Capital—and read the speech, the secretary's gimlet eyes watching me from behind his desk. The speech was libelous, and so I told him. "Very well then," he quacked, "I'll make it." I remember his last sentence. After denouncing two Republican stalwarts in the city, Moe Annenberg, the owner of the Philadelphia *Inquirer,* and one of the Pews, he ended, "Pew! Annenberg! Annenberg, phew!"

A striking characteristic of Harold's was his ability to fire a subordinate without the slightest qualm or hesitation if he thought him disloyal or incompetent—there was no beating around the bush or trying to place the man elsewhere. Once, after a row in which an Under Secretary of the Interior was involved, the Secretary had decided to get rid of him promptly. Ickes gave instructions that after the incumbent had left for the day the lock on his office door was to be changed—he was not to be admitted to his office or given access to his personal files,

or even allowed to get his hat! The controversy had been going
on for months, and Ickes' ruthless order made it impossible for
his subordinate to get at the material he might need to state his
side of the argument when the press took it up.

Ickes was combative, shrewd, belligerent. He was a very effective radio speaker—he did not *ad lib*—and he had a genius for
what Justice Holmes called "hitting the jugular." He was disliked by many of his subordinates, feared by members of Congress, and highly respected by the public, who regarded him
with a mixture of amusement and admiration. He could not
have been a happy man. He took too much and gave too little
to have understood what love or friendship could mean. Yet the
grains of suspicion and malice in his nature, mixed with fearless-
ness, gave him a sharpness of character, which was a relief after
so much that was soft and sentimental floating on the placid
surface of American life. Harold was never a bore.

Jesse Jones, Secretary of Commerce, sat between Harold Ickes
and Henry A. Wallace, Vice President from 1941 to 1945, three
men as unlike as it is possible to imagine. Frances Perkins, in
her invariable dark dress with two strings of pearls, and three-
cornered felt hat planted firmly and low over her forehead, came
next; and finally Claude Wickard of Indiana, who had succeeded Wallace as Secretary of Agriculture, reflecting in his
amiable person all the sunny, smiling, and friendly, if somewhat
tasteless, qualities of the great corn and wheat states.

The Cabinet was not a group of outstanding men. But they
were competent and offered an experience which reflected the
diversity and range of America. Cordell Hull—he was then
seventy-one, but seemed older—had been in politics for forty
years. He had fought in the Spanish-American War, practiced
law, served in the Tennessee legislature, and had been a judge,
a representative, and a senator before appointment to the Cabinet. As the terrible strain of war built up he tired easily and
had to leave Washington for increasingly longer rests, while Sumner Welles, the Under Secretary, would run things.

Welles was Hull's opposite in every way. A career man, he
had been admirably trained in the old school of diplomacy. He

spoke French and Spanish fluently, had some Italian and German, and knew thoroughly the involved intricacies of Latin American politics and our relation to them. When a foreign diplomat came to Washington, he made a formal call on the Secretary; and then spent two hours with the Under Secretary, who was usually at home in the visitor's tongue. Welles was under fifty, robust, a tireless worker, with correct and formal manners, intelligent rather than imaginative, instinctively "liberal" in a department where that quality was not often apparent. He never walked from the State Department to the Metropolitan Club without his Malacca cane, and in summer wore an impeccable Panama.

Although as a rule a member of the Cabinet consulted only his opposite number in another department when a problem arose, it was accepted that one did not disturb Mr. Hull, but called Welles, who was quick to understand and to act. The Secretary disliked administration and turned over its daily manifestations to others. This choice left him free for the planning of policy. Yet it involved a weakness inherent in our system; no permanent civil servant, reaching to the highest level below the head of the particular government unit, can altogether relieve his principal of the ceaseless grind of administrative decision. Mr. Hull suffered from partial abdication of power.

Secretary Hull stood in high repute throughout the country, for his rugged honesty and independence and was looked upon by members of the Congress with something approaching veneration. He was not very subtle or original. The President counted on him to be his chief liaison with Congress when the time would come to sell the United Nations to the Hill. President Roosevelt was determined not to make the same mistakes that President Wilson's idealistic and obstinate temperament, making co-operation so difficult, had invited after the First World War. From the beginning, Congress was thoroughly and continually informed of the shape that the new union was taking in the minds of the President and his Secretary of State.

I saw very little of Secretary Hull outside of Cabinet meetings. We almost never met socially, and then usually for a meaningless exchange of amenities at one of the formal and solemn dinners that the Secretary gave when the arrival of a visiting potentate made it appropriate, and the President had completed the first gesture, or the visitor did not rank a reception at the top. These dinners took place at the Carlton Hotel—it was before the government had purchased Blair House—and they were not gay. The Secretary was usually tired and worried, but he would not forgo what he considered his duty, impelled, perhaps, by his dislike of his Under Secretary—he did not enjoy Welles stepping into his shoes even on the social side.

I particularly remember a dinner given for General de Gaulle. The President had disliked the general since their first meeting at Casablanca, felt that his bosom harbored the ambition to be a Man on Horseback; and was insistent that we should never "recognize," however indirectly, anyone whom the French people had not themselves freely chosen. We should wait for the time when they could make the choice. Eisenhower was ordered not to sign any agreement with him, nor should there by any with De Gaulle from which a suggestion of "recognition" might be squeezed, nothing formal to which he could later point as conferring authority. . . . De Gaulle, the President said, thought of himself sometimes as General Foch, sometimes as Jeanne d'Arc. He was a bore. . . .

At this dinner for the French general the American Secretary had little opportunity to judge, for he spoke no word of French and his guest was totally deficient in English. No interpreter was present—I suspect that the Chief of Protocol, George Thomas Summerlin, little "Summy" as he was affectionately known, doubtless thought that an interpreter would have introduced an undesirable note of formality. So the Secretary and the general sat stiffly in informal silence, the American drooping a little, the Frenchman solemnly and forbiddingly erect, all the six feet six of him, balancing a chip like an epaulette on each martial shoulder because he had not had his twenty-one guns on arrival.

After dinner Bill Bullitt, the ex-ambassador to France, who spoke the language fluently and had known the general in France, brought up several of us to be introduced to him as he sat in isolated dignity, unsmiling and showing no interest in our tentative remarks. Sol Bloom, chairman of the House Committee on Foreign Affairs, was among the first, and Bill must have murmured in his ear a word or two about the desirability of breaking the ice, an exercise for which Mr. Bloom was eminently qualified, having, in his career as professional entertainer, introduced the lovely Fatima as a belly dancer to the American public. He could be counted on to do his best. Bill stated the congressman's name very clearly to the guest of honor and indicated his importance. Mr. Bloom, bent at all costs on a *rapprochement*, produced a trick cigar from some inner recess, and offered it to the general, who for a moment hesitated. "Take it, take it," the New Yorker insisted. But when General de Gaulle put out his hand the cigar disappeared up Sol's sleeve, withdrawn by some invisible elastic mechanism—"Now you see it, General, now you don't. . . ." Puzzled, suspecting that he was being laughed at, the general turned to his aide. "What does the American statesman wish?" he inquired. The other did not seem to know, and no one dared to laugh. It was not a successful evening. . . .

It was inevitable that the Secretary of State and the Under Secretary should drift apart. When the Secretary was resting at Hot Springs, Virginia, the President would send for the Under Secretary, who admirably supplemented Mr. Roosevelt's imaginative and creative impulses. The President rarely remembered that he was not his own Secretary of State. Together, as a foreign diplomat put it, they would mix an international salad, F.D.R. adding the garlic as he rubbed his hands and tasted the dressing.

Hull came to distrust Welles and finally to hate him. The President knew this long before the Secretary came to him with the final ultimatum—one of them must go. Yet before that the President did little to better their relationship, often by-passing Hull by taking up a matter directly with Welles, and even communicating with him by code outside the regular State Department channels when Welles went to Africa as the President's special representative.

The President cared little for administrative niceties. If someone had remonstrated with him—and I suspect that Mr. Hull frequently did—he would look a little sheepish, apologize, murmur that he had not wanted to "trouble" you with it; and repeat his conduct after a decent interval. Not infrequently he would call Edgar Hoover about something that he wanted done quietly, usually in a hurry; and Hoover would promptly report it to me, knowing the President's habit of sometimes saying afterward,

"By the way, Francis, not wishing to disturb you, I called Edgar Hoover the other day about . . ."

The President had a way of building you up after knocking you down, particularly with Mr. Hull, who under the circumstances that I have related was "touchy," as the President well knew. The building up took the form of an emphatic compliment at Cabinet for the way Mr. Hull had handled something, coming a day or two after the Secretary of State had lost in one of those incessant jurisdictional disputes that infringed so on the President's time.

I think President Roosevelt hated to make the choice between the two men, but it was clear that Welles would have to go. Welles resigned on September 30, 1943, and Mr. Hull, under pressure of ill health, was forced hardly more than a year later to give up the work to which he was completely dedicated. Welles was succeeded by Edward R. Stettinius, Jr., who took Mr. Hull's place in 1944. Stettinius was young—forty-four—for such an important position. Yet he seemed much younger: he seemed like a rosy and friendly sophomore, he wanted to be liked and one could not help liking him. That he had had an enviable career in private business was accounted for by the fact that his father was a partner of J. P. Morgan and Company when Ed was growing up. At twenty-six the son was made assistant to the vice president of General Motors; at thirty-one, vice president in charge of industrial and public relations; and at thirty-five chairman of the board of U. S. Steel. But one can be chairman of a board and remain innocent.

He joined the government in 1939. The job he did best was lend-lease, probably because his contribution to it—an important one—was the establishing of smooth public relations, for Ed Stettinius was essentially a public relations man.

It was a weak appointment. The President wanted to act as his own Secretary of State, and Ed was there to take orders and not to reason why—the war was nearing an end. His first act after his appointment (in December 1944) was to send autographed photographs of himself to the newsmen who went to his press conferences, wishing them a most hearty Merry Christmas. They all liked him and laughed at such displays of well-disposed artlessness. Washington newspapermen are highly intelligent and seldom naïve. I never heard Ed express a judgment; occasionally he would echo one he had heard, handing the words along to us as if he were quoting them, not so much hesitantly as tonelessly, as if he were cautiously reciting from a textbook. We all liked him—and disregarded him.

Although I rarely came in contact with him except at Cabinet meetings, the member of the Cabinet I most admired was Henry Stimson. He was then seventy-four, in his "tough and tranquil old age." He was as loyal to the President as Morgenthau, but stood up to him, which Morgenthau did not. He tired easily, under the new strain of war, and left the office early each day, to keep fit; and he always looked ruddy and clear-eyed. If you had to see him, it was wise to go in the morning—by five o'clock he was weary and peevish. He had no small talk. On those few occasions when we did not talk shop—for instance, when I went to see him and stayed for lunch at the Pentagon when we had not finished our discussion—I found him difficult, rather shy, not forthcoming.

I never thought of calling him by his first name, as did Morgenthau, a familiarity which I felt he resented. I suppose he was old-fashioned. He did not particularly welcome the views of others on matters in his field. He had the Elizabethan sense of humor of a sturdy man, though not often revealed, it came like a gust of wind when stirred. I remember his telling a story about General George Patton, when our troops were moving into Germany. Patton detested rules and regulations, Army forms, and Army reports. After General Eisenhower had warned him that he should pull himself together and follow the fitting formulas, the first of Patton's reports showed that he had taken the suggestion to heart; it was impeccable—succinct, objective, impersonal, strictly according to Army Hoyle—until the last sentence: "P.S. I have just pissed in the Rhine. . . ."

Mr. Stimson used strong language with the men he was fond of, an intimation that to them he could let go. In Washington he was closer to Jack McCloy, who was his Assistant Secretary throughout the war, than to anyone, often dining with him. Once, when Mrs. Stimson had not been feeling well, Jack and his wife went over to spend the night with them. The next morning Mrs. Stimson, entirely recovered, was having breakfast with the Mc-

Cloys. The Secretary's voice, suddenly rising from an adjoining room, broke into the peaceful meal. "I'll be damned if I will," he shouted. "I'll be God damned if I'll do anything of the sort." "It's nothing," said Mrs. Stimson. "Mr. Stimson likes to dictate his journal in the morning, and he often gets rather excited." They could hear him striding up and down the room, as the expletives burst on the air. Then he came in for his soft-boiled egg, relaxed and smiling . . . To me he was a heroic figure of sincerity and strength.

It has been customary for critics and historians to discount the changing role of the Cabinet, as it developed with the times, charging it with ineffectiveness because it had not fulfilled the original function for which it was intended. But what of that? The Cabinet was thought of by the first President as an advisory and authoritative body, an American privy council, to form policy and decide major questions as they arose. Today it is composed of a dozen administrators heading vast departments, who generally meet once a week to discuss their problems and report to the President what they are doing. Though the members are not primarily there to shape policy, their decisions often do. For policy can never be wholly separated from operation and often is developed and defined by the cumulation of action rather than by a reasoned decision taken before the event. And operation down the line, sometimes far down the line among the NCOs of government, can change and modify the original plan or even create a new one, which in the ultimate view is hardly recognizable. The American Cabinet gives some unity to this vast, sprawling, unco-ordinated system and keeps the President informed of what his chief administrators are doing. During my three and a half years there was of course a single overriding consideration which created a sense of unity, the successful prosecution of the war.

President Roosevelt liked to use memoranda—the telephone was more for immediacy. Looking over some of his brief and pungent messages, I am again amazed at the number of matters on which he kept a hand. It has often been repeated that he was not a good administrator; but it may be doubted whether administrative ability is an attribute that is necessary or altogether desirable in a President of the United States. He practiced the far more difficult art of driving a score of subordinate princelings, few of whom could be described as tame, and of keeping their actions in perspective with the needs and the will of the country, settling their disputes, stroking their ruffled feathers, and nicely balancing the need for competent appointments with the political demands of the party system. He had the country to lead at the same time, and finally the war to direct. I do not think that his success would have been as great if he had neglected one function in favor of the others.

As the war went on and absorbed more and more of his time Roosevelt tended to concentrate on his job as Commander in Chief, but never to the exclusion of everything else. Toward the end he became weary of the insatiable details of politics, particularly appointments. I have before me a touching plea: could not I persuade Congress, he wrote me, to get rid of the law requiring him to sign the appointments of notaries public? He was patient until he died; and I sometimes think the little dull burdens were more responsible for his death than the weight of the great decisions.

He grew infinitely tired of the continual bickering between department heads, which went on as if there had been no war; this noisy friction gave the country a sense of disunity and a feeling that the administration did not know where it was going. Differences of opinion were healthy but the jurisdictional fights for power between the departments and the new war agencies, avidly seized on and dramatically exaggerated by a press eager to exploit struggles to achieve power among the temporarily great, created public confusion and blurred the vision of the war effort. The subordinate who disagreed with his superior might give his side of the picture to a newspaper friend, whose code forbade him to reveal the source of his information. One hardly dared to share a confidence lest it turn up in a column. There was no domestic censorship, and the use of information was largely left to the patriotism of the reporters. The military found it easier to clamp down on everything than to exercise the difficult practice of judgment, and the military point of view was continually in conflict with the civilian. I remember soon after war had been declared John Lord O'Brian's saying to me that to a great extent my part in the war effort would be fighting the army. . . .

Every now and then the President would lecture us at Cabinet on the unseemliness of washing our dirty linen in public, or write a letter to the department and agency heads. In the middle of that hot and depressing summer of 1942 he sent out such a communication suggesting that we desist from arguing controversial questions in public. Elmer Davis, director of the Office of War Information, had told him that satisfactory progress had been made toward eliminating much of the conflict and confusion among the departments and agencies so far as their press releases and speeches were concerned. But remarks at press conferences and elsewhere often did not contribute either to the accuracy or the consistency of public information. "If the agencies," the President concluded, "would refrain from resorting to public debate of this kind they would have a good deal more time to attend to their business, and the nation would have a good deal more assurance that the business was being done right."

The language of Roosevelt's memoranda was fresh, informal, and often amusing. "For preparation of a reply"—he wrote once —"with the thought that an offensive's always better than a defensive." He saw that criticisms of my decisions were relayed quickly to me if they touched some essential: "There is a good deal of a howl because the Department of Justice has refused to participate as *amicus* in the Texas Primary case. How about It?" I told him that the "howl" came from Walter White of the National Association for the Advancement of Colored People—the President remembered people, not organizations—that we had established the right to vote in primaries as a federal right enforceable in the federal courts in the *Classic* case, and that, if we intervened here again, the South would not understand why we were continually taking sides. I attached a three-page memorandum from the Solicitor General discussing the legal aspects of the case—the President liked to read that sort of thing. If it bored him or if it was too long, he put it on a pile of papers to be read, and when the pile got too high would tell his personal secretary, "Missy" Le Hand, to take it away.

But usually what the President wanted was to be told what should be done, and how to do it, not a balanced report. As late as January 10, 1944, he wrote me: "Your memo of January sixth is very interesting but it does not tell me what to do. Do please suggest an *out*, a *modus vivendi*, something really brilliant which will go down into history as a judgment of Solomon!" He could be terse, exact, and firm.

One of the most knowledgeable and pungent messages that I received from him concerned the conditions in Hawaii, where martial law had been declared immediately after Pearl Harbor.

Harold Ickes and I had sent out our representatives, with the President's approval, to investigate what was going on. The Army ran everything—food supply and distribution, communications, traffic, hospitals and health, price control, civilian defense, liquor distribution, gasoline rationing, fiscal matters—even to a large extent the courts. General Delos Carleton Emmons, who was in command of the Hawaiian department, styling himself "Military Governor," established and enforced the law by issuing military orders. We examined a hundred and eighty of them. The resulting administration appeared to be autocratic, wasteful, and unjust. A confidential report of the FBI stated that it was common knowledge that blackout regulations were flagrantly violated by officer personnel, and that cocktail parties lasted far beyond blackout hours—Pearl Harbor conditions again after a brief year! Emmons got most of his knowledge of local conditions from a small handful of powerful pineapple planters —"The Big Five," as they were known. Among the population there was deep resentment that did not come to the surface as criticism of the local administration was suppressed by the military.

By the end of 1942 it seemed desirable that the civilian government should be reinstated. After discussing the matter with Ingram Macklin Stainbeck, the governor of the territory, we took it up with the President, who approved our recommendation to end martial law and told us to prepare a proclamation for his signature and clear it with the Army. The "army" in this case meant Assistant Secretary of War John J. McCloy, General Emmons, and General Green, his executive officer, a stuffy, overzealous, unyielding type, who had prepared an elaborate and complicated chart showing the setup. I sent it along with a confidential report to the President, as it told the story with laborious eloquence. I ended by saying that the situation had the makings of a lurid congressional investigation; and enclosed a note to Grace Tully, who had succeeded Missy as the President's secretary, asking her to give it to him at her earliest opportunity.

The President responded promptly and vigorously. I should talk the matter over with Secretary Stimson *in person*, and tell him from the President that the situation was bad, and that from many sources he knew that Emmons got most of his knowledge of conditions from The Big Five. There must be a special Army and Navy investigation into violations of blackout regulations. Hawaii was a thoroughly insidious place for officers stationed there. "That statement needs no argument. There should be a constant rotation of officers and men."

Before Pearl Harbor the President was much concerned with the activities of America First, which he thought of as substantially treasonable. "Will you speak to me about the possibility of a Grand Jury investigation of the America First Committee? It certainly ought to be looked into and I cannot get any action out of Congress." There were too many isolationists in Congress for any such investigation, and there were no grounds to warrant a grand jury investigation, which, the President believed, would show that much of America First's financial support came directly or indirectly from Germany.

There were a great number of memoranda about appointments. "Tom Connally wants Keating for Judge. Has been Attorney General of Texas—just over age. Can we do?" The age limit for federal judges to which the President referred was sixty—an arbitary measure he had fixed on at the time he was trying to enlarge the Supreme Court, and disregarded when it suited him. Or again in longhand: "F. Biddle: Bill Cole of Md. for Customs Ct. in N.Y. Speaker [Sam Rayburn] and John [McCormack, Democratic majority leader of the House] say O.K.???" . . . Sometimes, if the suggestion seemed without enthusiasm and the candidate unpromising, I would table it, and often the President would not mention it again—he had done his bit, and could say to Tom or Sam or John that he had taken it up with the Attorney General.

Now and then I would send him something that I thought might amuse him. When his old friend, Ed Flynn, chairman of the Democratic National Committee, was accused of using WPA work in connection with a private road that he was building, and at about the same time Errol Flynn of movie fame was engaged in more romantic adventures at sea, a little verse by Thomas Hornsby Ferril, the Colorado poet, appeared in the *Rocky Mountain Herald.* I cut it out and sent it to the President:

Flynns Errol, and Ed confuse my head—
I'm daft with yachts and paving blocks;
I'm all mixed up with right behaving,
(Who's without Flynn can throw the first paving)
I'm all mixed up on women and wine
(To Errol's human, but to Flynn divine).

F.D.R. didn't like it—he was a little hurt, or angry, or indignant when his professional friends were under attack; after all he was the most professional of all of them. He rejoined curtly—"You must think you're quite a poet."

But if he did not like this verse about the Flynns, he unreservedly enjoyed a book I sent him, not long before he went to the fateful conferences at Yalta. It was Mark Twain's famous *1601—a Conversation as it was by the Social Fireside in the Time of the Tudors.* It was hard to get, too ribald to send through the mails, and my copy from some anonymous publisher in Canada years before was sent by express. Roosevelt once told me that when he was librarian of the Fly Club at Harvard he had tried unsuccessfully to obtain a copy of this description of Sir Walter Raleigh's unseemly behavior at Queen Elizabeth's Court.

Finally John Biggs secured one for me. I took it over to Cabinet and gave it to him after the meeting—everyone had gone except Jesse Jones, who seemed determined to be the last, as he evidently had something of importance to take up that he did not wish anyone else to hear. The President picked up the book eagerly, began to thumb through it, and called to Secretary Jones, "Come here, Jesse, and listen to this—how little Willie wet the bed." And in his strong resonant voice he began to read to us Eugene Field's poem, which was included in the book, while Jesse, who did not like anything, particularly humor, to come between him and the President, listened with a dark, patient look to a man who at times could be so inappropriately boyish.

After the President died I asked Grace Tully if she had ever heard him speak of the book. She remembered that he had given it to her and told her she must put it away carefully in his library where no one would find it, and she was not to look at it, it was very naughty, and now and then she might remind him where it was—Jesse Jones had given it to him after a cabinet meeting. Thus is history written! I hope the book is preserved in the Hyde Park library. . . .

I tried never to bother the President with anything that was not essential, and to wait until a substantial number of problems —many of them appointments—had accumulated. I would call "Pa" Watson, the President's appointment secretary, and was often summoned for lunch with the President in his study, where we had solid food—an omelette or fish or chops, with plenty of coffee. When he would lean back in his chair and take the first long, deeply inhaled pull at his cigarette, I would get down to business, sometimes submitting a brief memorandum or directive for initialing. In this way I could get in a comfortable hour, except during the last year of his life when he began to resent the accumulation of such burdens, and to postpone them.

His training had made him cautious; he knew that everyone who saw him was in a hurry to get quick approval; he had come to practice the procrastination that brought him a sense of relief. Yet when he wanted to act, particularly where the war called for speed—and war decisions almost invariably did—he would hound the responsible official, often calling him more than once personally. He rarely asked me about department problems, but frequently what I thought of so-and-so. He liked to relax in reminiscence, and I would ply him with questions about his own life, about Cousin Theodore, or about the war. Once I remember suggesting that there were those—I was not one of them—who thought him too pro-British, too much led by Churchill, who had recently been staying at the White House. I hoped he fought back now and then; the British understood that, and always respected a show of opposition. He agreed, nodding his head. He told me of a proposal—half serious, half jocular—that he had made recently to "Winnie," one of several "after the war" arrangements, like the internationalization of Hong Kong, about which his lively imagination used to play, without coming to rest on them. Why not, when the war was over, F.D.R. had said to his guest as they relaxed together over brandy after dinner, why not give the Elgin marbles back to Greece? It would be a wonderful gesture of international friendship, the whole Near East would applaud at the sight of the British lion disgorging. "You know you stole them and you ought to give them back. You could announce that you had been cleaning them and putting them in proper shape." "How did he take it?" I asked. "Take it," he answered. "He almost went through the roof . . ."

F.D.R. took his time about appointing judges, and never considered there was any particular hurry about filling a vacancy. While I was in office there was only one on the Supreme Court, caused by the resignation of Senator James Francis Byrnes on October 3, 1942, to become director of Economic Stabilization. For ten months Byrnes had been on leave of absence from the Court, working with the President in the war effort.

Several times I suggested to F.D.R. that the Court was shorthanded, that Byrnes ought to resign and the President should appoint a successor; but he waved me aside a little impatiently, saying let's keep it open for Jimmy, they can get along. But when the 1943 term opened there were several mildly critical editorials. For nearly two years the Court had felt the burden of the extra work, a load that is always great and at times, when each member is not pulling his full weight, may become intolerable. Chief Justice Stone asked me if I would speak to the President, and I took it up with him again, urging him to make the appointment as soon as he could find the right man. He nodded an unwilling assent, he supposed I was right, he would think it over.

Eventually I convinced him that we could not keep the position open for Jimmy Byrnes any longer. Well then, could we not appoint some old boy for two or three years who would agree to retire when he had reached seventy, so that Jimmy could be brought back? I replied that this would not quite fit in with his often avowed intention to put younger men on the high tribunal. I suppose not, he acquiesced without enthusiasm. I suggested that I might talk to Chief Justice Stone again, and he assented. "See if you can't get me a nice, solid Republican," he said as I left, "to balance things a bit, preferably west of the Mississippi, and not a professor."

When I saw Stone early in November, he said at once that he wanted someone who would "stick"—he had in mind, of course, Byrnes' being taken off for the needs of the war. He wanted a man of broad legal training and experience—a judge from one of the Circuit Courts would fit in admirably. I said I thought the Circuits had little material of first-rate caliber. "Nonsense, Biddle!" he replied, and pulled out a volume of the reports containing a list of the judges. This he read carefully, then looked up. "By gum," he said, "you're about right."

But there were a few: Learned Hand, head and shoulders above all the others; John Parker, Samuel Bratton, who had been on the Tenth Circuit since 1933, a good Democrat, he had been Senator from New Mexico; Orie Phillips, if you want a Republican, also from the Tenth; and there was Wiley Rutledge, who had been on the Court of Appeals for the District of Columbia for four years, after teaching law for fifteen—Rutledge was a good man and young, a little pedestrian but sound. And Charley Fahy? I asked him. He considered, his chin in his hand. They had all liked the way Fahy presented his cases—he was objective, clear, scrupulous. But if we put another Catholic on the Court, he suggested, the Church might feel it was always regularly entitled to two. I mentioned Dean Acheson, but it was clear that Stone preferred one of the federal judges.

Outside of Hand, who was far more distinguished than any of the others, Rutledge seemed to me the most promising, and I had Herbert Wechsler make an analysis of his opinions on the Circuit Court. His views were sound, carefully reasoned, and lawyerlike. He was long-winded, suffering from a sense of obligation to answer everything in the case. He was a liberal who would stand up for human rights, particularly during a war when they were apt to be forgotten. But there was nothing extreme or

Messianic about his approach. He was certainly not a nice solid Republican.

All of which I reported to the President. Where did Rutledge come from, he asked me. He was born in Kentucky, taught high school in Indiana, New Mexico, and Colorado and law in Colorado and St. Louis. "He'll do," said the President, and then, "what do you think about Hand?" I repeated what the Chief Justice had said—head and shoulders above the others. F.D.R. told me that he had had a great many letters from men whose opinion he valued, saying he must appoint Hand. He thought well of Fahy. If Frank Murphy could be offered a job connected with the Army, the President said, that he considered important enough he would resign, and Fahy would be the obvious man. He would like to think it over a little more. I mentioned Benjamin Cohen, whose judgment I admired, but the President said that Ben, who was assistant to Byrnes in the Office of Economic Stabilization, could not be spared.

When I saw him again he was much cooler when I spoke of Hand; and I heard later that he resented what he called the "organized pressure" in Hand's behalf. The President told me that he had determined to appoint Rutledge, and that I should get the papers ready and send them to Grace Tully. But before he made the announcement he wanted to have a talk with Rutledge, after I had seen him.

Rutledge was a modest man and was amazed when I told him—he really believed he was not up to it. Ten years later, when a chance ocean crossing brought Hand and me together in intimacy, I learned to admire his really first-rate qualities of heart and mind, and came to believe that his appointment would have been more suitable, and that I should have urged the President to appoint him in spite of his age. He had the "fire in his belly" that old Holmes used to talk about.

During the discussions and speculation about Byrnes' successor, it was natural that I should have been mentioned. My two predecessors had gone from Attorney General to the Court, and a pattern of precedent seemed to have been established. I was determined, however, not to accept the appointment even if the President wished me to do so. My brief experience on the Circuit bench had not been satisfactory, and I did not wish to

renew the mild level of judicial life on which I had felt cut off
from the world and out of things. The members of the Court in
Washington seemed to me terribly overworked. I loved arguing
cases as Solicitor General; but that was different—I was doing
the arguing, not listening to it.

I dreaded the quiet, plodding, uninterrupted work of a judge.
And I did not want to leave the heart of things while war was
on. I was always more interested in the vivid present than the
future. I said a word to Lewis Wood of the New York *Times*,
whom I knew well as he was assigned to cover the Justice
Department and the Court, and in a story he reflected the
"impression" that I did not want to be appointed.

Once when I was talking to the President about the vacancy
on the Court—did I want it, he asked. No, I said, I did not
wish to leave him during the war, I was happy where I was, I
had not liked being a judge. I reminded him of the time he had
asked me three years before to go on the Circuit Court, and I
had said that being a judge was like being a priest, and he
had unraveled his plan of easing Woodring out and elevating
Murphy. The President was listening, enjoying the recollection.
I added that on that occasion I had asked for an hour or two to
think it over; he had said he was going to a movie and to call
him back; and I had replied that I would call his secretary,
Marvin McIntyre; no, he said, *don't call Mac, call me.* He
laughed again, he was in a good humor that day, and took my
arm. "You are quite right, Francis," he said, now gravely. "You
and I are too young to go on courts; we've got our careers ahead
of us"—he was sixty, I fifty-six. I never liked him more than at
that moment.

One of my early conferences with the President about this
vacancy occurred immediately after the national election in
1942 in which Senator George W. Norris, of Nebraska, after
serving in Congress for nearly forty years, was defeated. His
support of Roosevelt's foreign policy and his vote to declare war
the year before were said to account for his rejection by those
who had so long followed his leadership; but I doubt whether
either factor had much to do with it. Norris, a Republican, was
typical of many Western statesmen, like the older La Follette

and Borah of Idaho, largely independent of party, pacifistic and isolationist—he opposed our entry into the First World War, and ratification of the Treaty of Versailles. He consistently fought the power interests, and turned back directly to the people for his support. He was so firmly entrenched—apparently—that he had come largely to be a representative of national rather than state issues. He was never afraid, however, of standing alone. He supported Alfred E. Smith in 1928, and Franklin Roosevelt in 1932 and 1936, running for re-election successfully in the same year as an independent. But six years later—without any state organization behind him—he was defeated. He had neglected his fences and lost touch with the voters from whom he drew all that was the source of his strength.

I was upset and unhappy about the Senator's defeat, and on the day after the election I wrote him to say that I had come to count on his presence in the Senate with all that it meant to the younger men who were strengthened by the example of his devotion to the common good; without him things would be harder. Norris was in Lincoln's mould. When I thought of him I thought of what Pericles had said: "The secret of happiness is freedom, and the secret of freedom is a brave heart."

The President spoke to me about Senator Norris a few days after his defeat—we must do something for him. Why not put him on the Supreme Court to fill the vacancy caused by Byrnes' resignation the month before? He was eighty-one, and I assumed F.D.R. was expressing a wish that it were possible rather than a serious suggestion. Apparently he mentioned the same idea to others. Irving Brant, the biographer of James Madison, who was then an editorial writer for the Chicago *Sun* in Washington, sent me a letter on behalf of Rutledge, whom he greatly admired. He said that he had read a statement, for which he trusted there was no foundation, that an honorary appointment might be offered to Senator Norris. The thought did credit to the President's heart—but did he realize the unintended cruelty? Senator Norris at his age could not possibly adjust himself to the arduous work of an Appellate judge; and his knowledge that he would not be able to do his share of the work would embitter his remaining years. When the President saw me next week he had it all rearranged. Senator Pope, who was chairman of the Tennessee Valley Authority, would be appointed to fill the vacancy on the District Court in Idaho, and "Uncle George," as he liked to call old Norris, would be put in his place. It would be a wonderful way for the old man to end his career. F.D.R. was a hero-worshiper, and he loved and admired Senator Norris above most men because, perhaps, he had qualities that F.D.R. lacked.

The President asked me to broach the plan to the Senator, and at the same time to ask him about what he thought of the possibility of testing one of the state poll-tax statutes in an action brought by the Attorney General, in case the pending federal bill to abolish the poll tax was defeated. The important thing, he said, was to build up Norris, to seek his advice, since he must be feeling lonely and out of things. It was important to give him a sense of usefulness . . . The President said he had been thinking about the poll-tax problem—he was in one of his fertile moods. Could not I bring some kind of suit to test the Mississippi statute, where the tax accumulated over the years and of course went unpaid, and most of the people did not vote? John Rankin would never last in his congressional district if his constituents voted, but they didn't on account of the tax, and Rankin's total vote was only six or seven thousand out of a population close to a quarter of a million. . . . Well, ask Uncle George what he thinks anyway, it will please him to be consulted, his last fight in the Senate had been in support of anti-poll-tax legislation.

F.D.R. gave me a memorandum explaining his constitutional theory. He had evidently pondered the question, wondering if some new angle could be found, now that a Senate filibuster had prevented the bill abolishing the tax from coming to a vote:

THE WHITE HOUSE
WASHINGTON
November 7, 1942

PERSONAL AND CONFIDENTIAL
MEMORANDUM FOR THE
ATTORNEY GENERAL

It has been suggested to me that the Attorney General study, in confidence the following constitutional problem:

1. It is assumed that the Constitution provides, or at least intends to provide, for universal suffrage.

2. It is recognized that each State is entitled to determine the qualification of voters in carrying out the general requirement of universal suffrage. This brings in the question of reasonability in setting up qualifications—such, for example, as permanence of residence in a given State or Country or Election District; such as simple and fundamental educational requirements of literacy. It has been submitted to me that universal suffrance [sic] being paramount from the Federal Constitution point of view, any unreasonable qualifications by States are subject to determination either by the Congress of the United States or, at the least, by the Supreme Court of the United States in any given case.

3. This being so, and on the assumption that the Congress fails to act, the Attorney General of the United States becomes the guardian of the Constitution.

4. Therefore, the question arises: Does the Attorney General have the fundamental duty of raising the question of unreasonable restrictions by an action at law by the United States against a State either under quo-warranto or an order to show cause, alleging that the election laws of a State impose unreasonable restrictions on universal suffrage. Such an action would, of course, be tried in a lower court and then in the Supreme Court.

Would it be possible, therefore, for the Attorney General to bring an action against, let us say, the State of Mississippi, to remove the present poll tax restrictions? I understand that these restrictions are such that poor persons are, in many cases, prevented from voting through inability either to raise the poll tax or to raise the cumulative tax which has accrued over a period of years.

5. It should be noted that in this procedure the question of race need not be raised in any way, on the ground that in the poll tax States a very large number of whites, as well as Negroes, are, in effect, denied the right to vote.

F.D.R.

The memorandum was patently F.D.R.'s own thinking, not Samuel Rosenman's or that of any other lawyer. It was naïve and breathed a legal innocence that could not be disspelled by his throwing in a "quo-warranto" and "order to show cause." The

"question of reasonability" has an F.D.R. sound. And it all is
so clear and simple—there is not even a reference to the fact
that the states had poll taxes and property requirements for
voting long before the Constitution was adopted; or that one
of the main constitutional compromises was that such qualifications should be left to the states because they could not agree
on them; and the Constitution did not, as he blithely assumed,
provide or intend to provide for universal suffrage.

When I saw George Norris two days later he was moved,
but not tempted. He was old, he said, he felt finished, he was
incapable of doing any more work. The tears came into his eyes.
"My own people have repudiated me," he said. He did not want
any appointment. I spoke about the President's poll-tax theory.
He nodded, but without interest. "Might be," he said. I left,
feeling my own ineffectiveness in the face of his grief. Several
of his friends in the Senate talked to him about the TVA, and
finally the President. But he would not yield—there was not anything more he wanted. . . . He was given a farewell dinner,
and managed a vigorous speech, telling the liberals to keep on
fighting even during a war. In two years he was dead. He had a
strong face, fine and sensitive, clean-shaven, his white hair, not
conspicuously long, brushed back from his forehead, his mouth
firm and large, a face from which had been purged truculence
and pettiness, across which, now and then only, his slow sweet
smile would welcome, or agree.

Norris's fame will rest not on the part he played in changing
the rules of the House, or for sponsoring the Twentieth Amendment to the United States Constitution, the "Lame Duck" amendment, that moved from March to January the date for the
meeting of the new Congress and the inauguration of the President, so as to prevent defeated legislators from making law; but
forever on the Tennessee Valley Authority. Norris, like other
Americans who have achieved leadership in their political
careers based on moral courage and conviction, never dismissed
political considerations. They were adepts in the art of politics
—Jefferson and Lincoln and Franklin Roosevelt; and, on a lesser
scale, Borah and La Follette and Johnson of California. Their
political skill, eternally vigilant, made possible their contributions
to independent leadership.

George Norris—to borrow Stephen Spender's words—was one
of those who are truly great, and who, born of the sun, had
traveled a long way toward the light, and left the vivid air
signed with their honor.

I have often heard innocent theorists, usually businessmen
who had no experience or knowledge of the American living
democracy, argue that it was improper for a President to be
swayed by such considerations as geographical distribution,
religious faith, or party affiliation in making appointments to the
Supreme Court—a man should be appointed solely on his merits.
Such a point of view disregards an essential of a democracy.
Where the Catholic or Jewish or Negro population is not recognized in appointments, and excluded from the courts, resentments
develop. The New England states, the East, the South, the West
furnish different points of view and different problems. Of course
each section of the country cannot be represented on the Supreme Court, but geographical representation should not be forgotten. It would be a sorry thing for our American sense of self-
government if the nine men all came from the East, professed
the Protestant faith, and were graduates of the Harvard Law
School. That F.D.R. knew and remembered.

In New Jersey, George Smathers, the Democratic senator, was
consulted as a matter of courtesy; but Boss Frank Hague of
Jersey City had also to be approached—not directly by the Attorney General but on a lower, more informal level by the
Assistant to the Attorney General. Surprisingly Hague's recommendations for judges—always made with correct protocol through
a Senator—were usually admirable, and did not necessarily have
to be "Hague men" if the boss got the credit for the appointment.
Franklin Roosevelt, like his cousin Theodore, had commerce with
the city and state bosses if they supported him, but did not, like
the earlier President, at the same time attack them as enemies
of decent government when they opposed him. It was part of
Franklin Roosevelt's common sense that he welcomed help from
such divergent sources—from Northern liberals and Southern
conservatives, from artists and eggheads, from Frank Hague and
Ed Flynn, Murphy of Chicago and Ed Crump of Tennessee.

When Judge William Clark decided to join the Army in

1942, for instance, a vacancy was created on my old court, the Third Circuit, which I was eager to fill with a first-rate man. Clark was from New Jersey, and if we could get a good judge there, New Jersey was entitled to the appointment, not otherwise. I asked Gerald McLaughlin if he would let me send his name up. He was from Newark, less than fifty years old, very able, a successful and respected lawyer. He said he would like to think about it, and talk to his sisters—he was a cosseted bachelor—but he had always steered clear of politics, he thought he would have no political backing. The ladies must have approved without hesitation, for the next day he telephoned me that if I could manage it he would accept. Jim Rowe told Hague that I wanted to recommend McLaughlin, and would give Hague the credit of the appointment if he would announce his sponsorship promptly. Otherwise I was doubtful—perhaps Delaware might be considered. Hague responded favorably, and McLaughlin went through quickly, much to the gratification of the bar of the Circuit.

I had to learn by experience when and how far to oppose the President when he wanted to make a bad political appointment. There were times when one could insist on a better man: and he liked to have the satisfaction of supporting one, not so much, I think, because he was concerned with putting men of professional competence on the bench, but rather that, surrounded by the plaudits of the hungry office seekers who favored and flattered, and lay on the threshold of his door, he responded happily to the applause of those of his friends who really counted—Felix Frankfurter and Charles C. Burlingham and George W. Norris—men who were devoted to the necessity of the best, not only from the professional angle, but from the deeper consideration of a humane and broadly liberal approach to life, of which the law was so important an expression.

One night at a dinner at which Charles E. Wyzanski, Jr., was present, soon after I was appointed, Judge Learned Hand and Justice Frankfurter took me aside. Here was my chance, they said, to start my career with a superlative recommendation, Wyzanski was a natural to fill a vacancy on the Massachusetts District Court. Would I back him? I said yes, at once; but irritated Frankfurter by asking if Senator Walsh of Massachusetts had a candidate. Why pay attention to Walsh, he said, he's not a friend of the President's. All the more reason, I answered. Felix, with that charming enthusiasm for men whom he admired, sometimes forgot the difficulties in the way—doubtless a disregard which accounted for so much of his success on their behalf.

When I first knew Charles Wyzanski in 1934 he was solicitor of the Department of Labor; and shortly after that joined the Solicitor General's staff, arguing successfully (with others) in favor of the constitutionality of the Social Security Act and the National Labor Relations Act. His brilliant mind had no touch of pedantry, and his learning—he read Greek easily and with pleasure, and might have a Herodotus in his pocket on a train—was without ostentation. But Senator David Ignatius Walsh—the other Massachusetts senator, Henry Cabot Lodge, Jr., was a Republican and therefore did not have to be consulted—was not sympathetic with the administration, to put it mildly; and was drawn to vote for New Deal legislation only from considerations of political advisability. The first Democrat elected to the Senate from Massachusetts since before the Civil War, Walsh, an elderly politician with a soft tread and low, colorless voice, was an isolationist without enthusiasm, whose concealed and controlled anxieties not altogether centered on retaining his job. He was not personally popular in Washington: but he was useful to his constituents. I found an opening. In Boston almost no Jews had received judicial recognition, and Walsh had publicly commented on the discrimination. He agreed, and the President was pleased—and surprised. He had thought that Wyzanski was too good a man for Walsh to consider. To Jim Rowe, then his administrative assistant, he remarked that he enjoyed the rare luxury of making an appointment on the merits without opposition from a Senator. I sent Wyzanski's name immediately by messenger to the White House so as to close out any chance of a senatorial change of mind, and the appointment was promptly announced.

But let us compare, to show both sides of the picture, another appointment in Missouri a year or two later. I did not know the man. Early recognized by the Pendergast political machine of

Missouri, he spent five terms in Congress, and when he was defeated in 1943, his record as a New Dealer was "darn near perfect" as the St. Louis *Post-Dispatch*, which opposed his elevation to the bench, put it. He was amiable, easy going, and universally popular. He was supported for a district judgeship by Senator Truman, but not by Senator Champ Clark, the other Missouri Senator, who was in chronic disagreement with his associate. It was almost impossible ever to get them together on patronage—a situation not without advantage to an Attorney General looking for an excuse to disregard unworthy recommendations. The FBI report showed that all of the lawyers interviewed in the candidate's small native town considered him an inexperienced and mediocre lawyer, who had never been to a law school, and whose adult life had been spent not in practice but in filling public offices. His local bar association voted twenty-three to one not to endorse him—the one being his former law partner.

I managed to hold up the appointment for a good while, making the best of the split between the two Senators, urging Senator Truman to choose someone else: but he stood firm, as he usually did, then and later. I went down to see him—it was not usual for the Attorney General to call on a Senator, but I was eager to break the deadlock. After I had left he told the press that he had said to me that he would follow the policy that he had always followed, which was to name a single candidate—"I have never believed in compromising in these matters." If the President had not stood behind him Truman would have agreed on another candidate, and would not have held up the appointment indefinitely, as any Senator can if he insists on claiming the personal privilege of objecting to the candidate. But the President had made up his mind to give Truman the man he wanted. As chairman of the Special Committee to Investigate the National Defense Program, he was keeping the Senate off the President's back by his prompt and efficient investigations of war frauds, which might later turn into war scandals. F.D.R., who had a strong sense of history, had not forgotten how the congressional committee on the conduct of the Civil War had harassed Lincoln. And he remembered the fraudulent practices that had come to light after the First World

War, with the investigations begun so late that most of them could not be prosecuted.

He first suggested to me that Senator Truman's candidate could not be as "impossible as you think, for he has the affection and sincere recommendation of practically everybody who has ever known him." I did not think him impossible, but I did not believe he would make a competent judge; and I wrote back to the President summarizing the FBI report. Three days later I got his final word, a lighthearted but peremptory command: "I have your memorandum," he wrote. "This is one—I think the first—occasion where I cannot agree. I have done a good deal of checking and, in spite of what you say about his legal ability, I have a hunch"—F.D.R. often resorted to a *hunch* when his arguments were weak—"that he has as much legal ability as at least half of the people we put on the District bench! What you need on the District bench is old-fashioned, homespun common sense. This is more important than being able to teach at the Harvard Law School." He concluded:

> The above are just a few of the WHEREAS clauses. Now comes the THEREFORE. Please tell Truman that if Clark will go along with it I will send his man's name up, and I think Truman will be perfectly willing to let the other Judgeship go to the southeastern part of the state.

That was the end of it. It was a bad appointment, and the President knew it . . . I never met the candidate. I am told by those in position to know that he has made a pretty good judge.

F.D.R. knew the difference between a good man and a second-rater. He knew, too, that politicians, raised to the bench, would in many cases develop into adequate and sometimes outstanding judges. He shared, to some extent, democracy's innate distrust of the expert. But he always knew when he was making a bad appointment, and usually when he was making a good one. And Roosevelt had the political imagination to realize the importance of appointing Republicans more than occasionally, and to important jobs: Henry Stimson, Frank Knox, William J. Donovan, Gil Winant, Harlan Fiske Stone.

ALIEN ENEMY CONTROL

◆◀┨ ┠▶ Chapter Twelve

Three months after I was sworn in as Attorney General the Japanese attacked Pearl Harbor.

I shall never forget how the terrible news came to me. I was speaking that Sunday at a midday dinner organized by the Slav-American Defense Savings Committee at the Masonic Temple at Detroit to sell defense bonds. As I got up to address a very large audience, my executive assistant, Ugo Carusi, handed me a hastily scribbled note—*Japanese today attacked Pearl Harbor, great U. S. Naval Base in the Hawaiian Islands, and are also bombing Manila from planes probably released from aircraft carriers. The President made the official announcement at 2:20 P.M. The raids are still in progress* . . . I told my listeners that they would always remember the day they held a patriotic rally with the governor of Michigan and the mayor of Detroit, because on that day even as I was speaking the Japs were bombing our country—and I read them the brief, incredible news. There was an instant hush—my listeners profoundly intent on every word I said. I had little to change—for now each word had become felt and real; and the Nazi ruthlessness in Czechoslovakia, in Poland, in Yugoslavia was now matched in the Orient by the Japanese attack on our battleships. From now on we would be at war with the dictatorships. The name Slav, said the Nazis, derived from the noun *slave;* but we knew its true derivation: it came from the word *slava*, meaning glorious. They clapped long, with tense seriousness.

Carusi had arranged for an Army plane to get me back for a Cabinet meeting, which had been called for that night. We gathered at eight o'clock. The President was deeply shaken, graver than I had ever seen him. After he had told us the news, and answered a few of our questions—there was hardly anything to report except that the attacks were continuing and had caused terrible damage—the congressional leaders joined us, and the President told them the story. They were silent for a tense moment; and then Senator Tom Connally of Texas, who had recently been made chairman of the Foreign Relations Committee, sprang to his feet, banged the desk with his fist, his face purple. "How did they catch us with our pants down, Mr. President?" he shouted. And the President, his head bowed, his assurance at low ebb, muttered, "I don't know, Tom, I just don't know . . ." The leaders agreed that we should declare war the next day. The President had made a draft of his message—it would be brief.

I went back to my office, stunned and troubled. In my absence my assistants had prepared the necessary orders for the internment of enemy aliens. The procedure had been carefully worked out. The FBI made the arrests not on its own authority but on warrants issued by the Department, except in emergency cases. But on that Sunday night Hoover was authorized to pick up several hundred without warrants, and this procedure was followed for a short time until the more dangerous had been apprehended.

The special meeting of the Congress came a little after twelve the next morning. The President, still grave but now with a renewed strength of command, enumerated the assaults on the Hawaiian Islands, on Malaya, on Hong Kong, on Guam, on the Philippines, on Wake, and the Midway Islands. He asked Congress to declare that since these were "unprovoked and dastardly attacks," a state of war existed between the United States and the Japanese Empire. It took thirty-three minutes for the House and Senate, sitting separately, to declare war. There was but one dissenting vote. In the House, Jeannette Rankin of Montana, voted nay, as she had voted in 1917. She was the first woman to be elected to the House of Representatives, a pacifist, serving twice and each time while the country was at war. She was sobbing as she answered the roll call. . . .

That afternoon I took the proclamation authorizing the Attorney General to intern Japanese enemy aliens to the President to sign. Most of the first group scheduled for detention had already been arrested. Three days later Germany and Italy declared war against us; and again I brought appropriate proclamations to the White House. The President was with Admiral Ross T. McIntyre, the White House physician. He was swabbing out F.D.R.'s nose—he suffered occasionally from nasty sinus attacks, particularly when under strain. He had left word for me to come in at once. How many Germans are there in the country, he asked. Oh, about 600,000, I told him. And you're going to intern all of them, he said—by that time he was back in the chair. Well, not quite all, I answered. "I don't care so much about the Italians," he continued. "They are a lot of opera singers, but the Germans are different, they may be dangerous." "Please, Mr. President," the admiral pleaded, and his patient sank back, as I hastily withdrew. The color had come back to the President's cheeks. The prospect of action always made him feel better. And from his impulsive and absurdly impractical suggestion I knew that his health had improved. The sinus had plagued him for the last four days.

I was determined to avoid mass internment, and the persecution of aliens that had characterized the First World War. (We had been watching the British experiment. At the outbreak of war there were in Great Britain a good many Germans and Austrians, chiefly Jewish refugees. In the beginning the policy was selective and discriminating and only 568 were interned. But by August of 1940, when it was realized what fifth columnists had done in France and the Low Countries, caution gave way to panic. The government yielded to popular pressure, about 74,000, mostly German and Austrian Jews, and all aliens, were taken into custody and thrown into hastily laid out camps. A reaction soon set in. In a letter to the *Times*, H. G. Wells, with a group of prominent Londoners, told the country that "nothing could be more calculated to dishearten our friends and allies in Germany and Austria than the news that Britain had put under

lock and key her own anti-Nazis of German and Austrian origin."
Sir John Anderson, who as Home Secretary had charge of
internal security, gave his opinion that the wholesale internment
had victimized "some of the bitterest and most active enemies
of the Nazi regime." And by then the British public, who forget
their fears in the face of danger, had undergone a few bombing
raids, and now demanded that the system be changed. Before
long the total had been decreased to 15,000.) With us, except
in the case of the Japanese, which I shall presently discuss,
there was never any demand for mass internment, as the result
of a clear governmental policy, settled well in advance of the
crisis of war, clearly and continuously described to the public,
and firmly adhered to.

I put Edward J. Ennis in charge of the alien enemy control
program. His ability had already been shown as counsel for the
Immigration Service, and he was ideally suited for the position
—imaginative yet practical, able to stand up to the "brass hats,"
and fully sharing my views and James Rowe's views, that everyone in our country, whatever his racial or national origin, should
be treated with fairness. We did not want people pushed around.

Ennis at once set about organizing parole boards; and before
the end of 1941 a number were operating in the cities where
the enemy populations were concentrated. The hearings were
informal, any "fair" evidence could be admitted, and the alien
could be represented by a relative or friend, but not by a
lawyer—an exclusion that greatly expedited action, saved time,
and put the procedure on a prompt and common-sense basis.
The United States Attorney presented the facts to the boards,
who were given authority to obtain further information directly
from the Immigration Service or the FBI. When the program was
completed there were about ninety boards, each composed of
outstanding citizens in the particular community—usually at least
one lawyer on the board. The boards served throughout the war
without compensation, and with marked devotion to their work.
There were a few grumbles about appointments to the boards,
but usually from laymen—politicians don't bother about un-
compensated positions, however honorary.

Under regulations promulgated by me shortly after the first
detentions, enemy aliens were not allowed to travel without

federal authority, were barred from areas surrounding forts, camps, arsenals, airports, power plants and dams, factories, warehouses or storage yards for implements of war; and from canals, wharfs, piers, and docks. They could not change their residence, or travel outside the city in which they lived, except under prescribed rules. They were forbidden to possess firearms, bombs, explosives, short-wave receiving and transmitting sets, signal devices, codes or ciphers, and photographs and maps of any military installation.

In all about 16,000 were arrested, (including Japanese, before their mass internment) of whom 1200 were German and Italian seamen. Only about one third were interned, nearly half of them Germans, and the rest were paroled, released, or (in a few instances) repatriated.

The Department of Justice operated the internment camps. I flew out to visit one in Bismark, North Dakota, chiefly filled with Germans. They were a healthy-looking lot—vigorous, tanned, hard-working. A committee of three of the prisoners had been chosen by the others to talk to the Attorney General in response to my suggestion that I would be glad to hear any complaints as to their treatment. I remember two of them: the thick ruddy captain of a tanker kept saluting and smiling, answering my questions most cheerfully—everything was fine, wonderful, most good food he had had for two years. The other, a Herr Professor-type working in some big chemical laboratory —angular, bespectacled, solemn—had one complaint, but he pressed it obstinately: they did not get enough butter. How much, I asked him. And when he told me I said it was substantially more than I got under rationing. His rejoinder was wonderfully Teutonic. "But that is not the point, Mr. Attorney General. Under the Geneva Convention we are entitled to as much butter as the American troops—and we are not getting it!"

There was little hysteria for the first few months after Pearl Harbor, almost none until the West Coast suddenly discovered that the Japanese were a menace. One excited patriot threw a rock at the window of a store operated by an American-born Japanese; and in Washington an energetic idiot chopped down some Japanese cherry trees. A number of Germans and Japanese were discharged by nervously patriotic employers. I remonstrated in broadcasts against such shortsighted and unfair action. It was stupid, I insisted, to exclude the great mass of skilled labor represented by the enemy alien population. I reminded employers that many of the "foreigners" whom they were discharging had sons who were serving in the American Army and Navy. When I issued an appeal to the governors of the states to take a strong stand against any "molestation of peaceful and law-abiding aliens, whether Japanese, German, or Italian," I was backed almost universally. Fiorello La Guardia, whom while I was in office I came to admire and greatly enjoy, was particularly effective in our campaign for tolerance and common sense.

The wartime measures that I have described were protective and negative. We conceived one program, executed under the authority of the Second War Powers Act, which was positive, and had not, I believe, ever been used during war. We began to naturalize aliens, loyal to the United States, who were citizens of the countries with whom we were at war. There were thousands of applications of Germans and Italians pending when war broke out. These were held up until they could be studied with greater care than was customary under normal peace conditions. Preference was given to applicants who had lived in this country for a long time or who had sons fighting in the Armed Services. We encouraged the naturalization of soldiers on service in foreign countries. Under the War Powers Act we had authority to naturalize them by administrative act rather than by court decree. We sent Thomas B. Shoemaker, deputy commissioner of immigration, to England and France, and to the Pacific—everywhere in fact where there was need. He received petitions, conducted hearings, and administered citizenship oaths. The youngsters applied in mass, very much elated by the service their government was giving them, writing about it to their parents in Brooklyn or Detroit or Boston, and the parents in turn boasted about their soldier sons, and about their country of adoption. . . .

Eight days before Pearl Harbor the President had proclaimed that December 15 should be celebrated as Bill of Rights Day, marking the one hundred and fifty-second anniversary of the adoption of the first ten amendments to the Constitution. The

Library of Congress took the occasion to dedicate the Thomas Jefferson room in the Annex, where four mural panels by Ezra Winter had just been completed. I spoke briefly, trying to choose words that would carry a sense of the reality of the freedoms for which we were at war, and which were so difficult to define— the war would test whether they could endure; and although we had fought wars before, and our personal freedoms had survived, there had been periods of gross abuse, when hysteria and fear and hate ran high, and minorities were unlawfully and cruelly abused. Every man, I said, who cares about freedom must fight for it for the *other* man with whom he disagrees.

I was a little embarrassed but pleased when Roger Baldwin, the director of the American Civil Liberties Union, wrote that I had said the most eloquent and practical words of any public man about civil rights in wartime. How lovely it is to have one's horn loudly blown by another! The sensation was not to last very long.

EVACUATION OF THE JAPANESE

The enemy alien control program involved, as I have said, the internment on a selective basis, and did not invoke any mass incarceration based on nationality. Nor did the department seek to exercise supervision over American citizens of recent German, Italian, or Japanese descent, suspected of sympathy with a country with which the United States was at war, as Great Britain was doing to British citizens under the Defense of the Realm Act. But persons of Japanese origin, citizens and aliens alike, under pressure from the Army and the West Coast politicians, were removed on an immense scale from the West Coast, held in relocation camps, and kept there during the war. Such a program was expensive and troublesome. It diverted large numbers of Army personnel from the more immediate job of getting on with the war, and thousands of civilian workers, particularly Japanese farmers, were rendered idle. It subjected Americans to the shame of being classed as enemies of their native country without any evidence indicating disloyalty. American citizens of Japanese origin were not even handled like aliens of the other enemy nationalities—Germans and Italians—on a selective basis, but as untouchables, a group who could not be trusted and had to be shut up only *because* they were of Japanese descent.

I thought at the time that the program was ill-advised, unnecessary, and unnecessarily cruel, taking Japanese who were not suspect, and Japanese Americans whose rights were disregarded, from their homes and from their businesses to sit idly in the lonely misery of barracks while the war was being fought in the world beyond. The action was unquestionably legal as far as Japanese citizens, *Issei* as they were called, were concerned. But the *Nisei*, American citizens from the day they were born in this country like any other Americans, were also treated like aliens, which they were not. These men and women of a younger generation, whose birthright was American, and who had lived here all their lives, were deprived of their normal way of living, set apart from other Americans, and forced into camps as potential enemies of their country. Their constitutional rights were the same as those of the men who were responsible for the program: President Roosevelt, Secretary of War Stimson, and the Assistant Secretary of War, John J. McCloy, Lieutenant General John L. DeWitt, commanding officer of the Pacific Coast area, and Colonel Karl Robin Bendetsen of the General Staff, who was brought into the Provost Marshal General's office in Washington from a successful law practice on the West Coast, where a strong anti-Japanese prejudice prevailed. In his case this prejudice found expression in his own description of the part he played in the evacuation, in the 1948–49 edition of *Who's Who*—he had "conceived the method, formulated the details, and directed the evacuation of 125,000 persons of Japanese ancestry from military areas." As time went on, and books began to appear highly critical of the evacuation, apparently he became less proud of this patriotic activity, for in the next edition of *Who's Who* all reference to the evacuation is omitted.

The American Civil Liberties Union called the evacuation "the worst single wholesale violation of civil rights of American citizens in our history."

These historic decisions are made by men, and we must look at the men who brought about this determination to understand it, their background and motives, and particularly the pressures which influenced them. One must include in the examination the state and municipal leaders who exerted the pressures, and the congressional delegations working with them—Governor Culbert Olson and Attorney General Earl Warren (now Chief Justice of the United States, who on the Supreme Court is invariably found on the liberal side when civil liberties are concerned) of the state of California and Mayor Fletcher Bowron of Los Angeles. But there were two notable exceptions. Senator Sheridan Downey of California urged the people of his state in a radio address to resist the current hysteria, and to take a humane attitude toward their Japanese-American neighbors; and that suprisingly unpredictable character, Harry P. Cain, then mayor of Tacoma, Washington, so far as I know was the only other elected official on the West Coast to oppose mass evacuation of the Japanese. He expressed his doubt of the wisdom of the government's decision in words that are worth remembering now. "America has always been interested in selection, and I feel it would be preferable to make careful selection, of those who are to be evacuated than just say: 'Let's get rid of our problem by the easiest, most obvious way, by moving everybody out.'" Cain's patriotism could not be questioned—he was shortly to serve with the famous Eighty-second Airborne Division in the Mediterranean and European theaters, and would receive the Legion of Merit and the *Croix de guerre* with palms . . . and his independent and unpopular attitude toward the Japanese did not prevent him from being elected to the United States Senate in 1946.

The curious thing was that there was no serious suggestion to move the Japanese off the West Coast until five or six weeks after Pearl Harbor. There were a few sporadic suggestions by Army and Navy personnel that the government should evacuate the Japanese, but not from the men who eventually persuaded Secretary of War Stimson to take the step.

Take General DeWitt, for instance, who was later to act a leading part in the evacuation. He had seen hard fighting in the Meuse-Argonne and Champagne-Marne operations in the First World War, served in the Philippines, had held important positions before he became the top Army commander on the West Coast in December, 1939. I never met him, and can only reconstruct the picture from his acts and talk during those eventful months after Pearl Harbor. He was a shrewd man inclined to be formal, very keen on reports and memoranda. He was apt to waver under popular pressure, a characteristic arising from his tendency to reflect the views of the last man to whom he talked. He had convictions—but again they did not stick when the final test came. He kept his head at first, and resisted suggestions that the Japanese be herded out of the coastal territory, which was his jurisdiction. The Provost Marshal General, Allen W. Gullion, sitting in Washington, wanted responsibility for the alien program transferred to the War Department. But General DeWitt preferred civilian to military control, and was "very doubtful" about interning 117,000 Japanese in his theater of operations. "An American citizen," he told General Gullion, "after all is an American citizen, and while they may not all be loyal, I think we can weed the disloyal out of the loyal and lock them up, if necessary."

I sent Jim Rowe to California to see DeWitt in the first week of January, 1942; and the general told Jim that any proposal for mass evacuation was "damned nonsense." He wanted the registration of enemy aliens begun as soon as possible on the West Coast—there were a little over a million throughout the country—and this we did. We also agreed with the general to authorize the FBI to make very broad "spot" raids, with powers of search, on the premises of Japanese (these turned up nothing dangerous or even significant); and approved his recommendation for restrictive areas around military installations from which every alien was to be excluded unless he had a pass—a restriction already in use on the docks at all ports.

By the third week in January the members of the congressional delegation from California were pressing me to move out the Japanese from the West Coast. Particularly insistent was Representative Leland Ford, of California, who made it clear that he wished to include American citizens. On January 24 I wrote him that unless the writ of habeas corpus were suspended, I did not know any way in which Japanese born in this country could be interned.

The Report of the Commission on Pearl Harbor, headed by Mr. Justice Owen Roberts of the United States Supreme Court, was released the next day. The report contained no references to sabotage. But it did enumerate in detail the espionage activities of Japanese residents in Hawaii, and helped turn the tide in favor of stricter measures to prevent sabotage and espionage.

General DeWitt came to the extraordinary conclusion, communicated to the Provost Marshal General, that the fact that there had been no sporadic attempts at sabotage showed an "exercised control," and when sabotage came it would be on a mass basis. He was feeling the impact of aroused public opinion, particularly among the "best people of California," as he told Colonel Bendetsen. But he was still opposed to any transfer of authority to the Army.

Two weeks after Rowe's return I assigned Tom Clark, who was at the time in charge of the Antitrust Division office on the West Coast, to co-ordinate the work of enemy alien control with the Army and other agencies on the West Coast. By that time, however, General DeWitt was apparently in agreement with the public officials of California that the American-Japanese population should be removed from the state, and was ready to accept responsibility for such a program. The choice of Clark under the circumstances was not a fortunate one.

It was intended that he should express and explain our views, which were far more moderate than the Army's, and insist that the new program afforded adequate protection. But Clark, a wary but amiable Texan, with a predilection to please those with whom he was immediately associated, construed his assignment as a direction to imply that the Justice Department would patriotically follow the military. If the Army asked for restricted martial law (which it had not) he said he would go to Washington and recommend it. Attorney General Warren, who by that time had come around to endorsing evacuation, on February 7 told the California Joint Immigration Committee, which for years had been hostile to the Japanese, that they should get in touch with Tom Clark—"he is the man who is in direct contact with Biddle all the time and I think the man whose recommendations are taken. You will find him a very approachable fellow, and I think it would be a very good plan for you to talk to him."

On Saturday afternoon, February 1, I asked representatives of the War Department to meet in my office. I was anxious to show the country, if possible, that the two departments were in agreement on the control measures taken to date. I stated at the opening that my Department would have nothing to do with any interference with citizens, or recommend the suspension of the writ of habeas corpus. McCloy, Gullion, and Bendetsen concurred on a rather general statement; but they would not approve a declaration, which I had prepared, that the two departments were in agreement that the military situation did not at this time require the removal of American citizens of Japanese origin.

One cannot altogether blame General DeWitt. Stringent measures were the order of the day. On December 30, 1941, the commander of the Canadian Army's Pacific forces had recommended removal of all persons of Japanese descent, whether or not citizens, from the coastal area; the evacuation began the following February and was completed by October. It was not DeWitt's task to protect the civil liberties of American citizens. He was a soldier, and I suppose in the face of the public clamor he decided that he could not take a chance. But I doubt whether he ever formulated precisely what that chance was. Everyone was after him on the coast to get rid of the Japs—the American Legion, the California Joint Immigration Committee, the Native Sons and Daughters of the Golden West, the Western Growers Protective Association, the California Farm Bureau Federation, the Chamber of Commerce of Los Angeles, and the newspapers, not only the Hearst press but Manchester Boddy's liberal Los Angeles *Daily News*. On February 9 Boddy wrote me that "local white men do not recognize the distinction between Japanese aliens and their sons, there should be a prompt evacuation, and it should include citizens and aliens alike." Even Walter Lippmann, usually cautious and resistant to the hot breath of popular clamor, came out on February 12 for evacuation of the West Coast. It should be treated, he said, as a warship or an airport, and anyone desiring entrance, "no matter what his citizenship or ancestry," should be stopped, identified, and escorted by an armed guard while transacting his business—a system of policing necessarily prevailing in a war zone. He did not mention Japanese Americans as such, and his logic would have had to include German and Italian American citizens as well as Japanese, which would have made a sizable evacuation. In his column four days later Westbrook Pegler seized upon Lippmann's suggestion. "The

Japanese should be under guard to the last man and woman," he shrieked, "and to hell with habeas corpus."

I could not go along with the War Department's views. On February 9 I wrote Secretary Stimson questioning the necessity of excluding Germans and Italians from the areas recommended by General DeWitt, and made it clear that the Department of Justice would not under any circumstances evacuate American citizens. The next day I informed the Navy that I would not approve evacuation of citizens from Bainbridge Island as requested: the Navy could move them if it declared the island a military zone, and then exclude all civilians except those to whom passes had been issued. To put my position unmistakably on record I wrote again to the Secretary of War on February 12 that the Army could legally evacuate all persons in a specified territory if such action was deemed essential from a military point of view; but that American citizens of Japanese origin could not be "singled out of an area and evacuated with other Japanese."

Apparently the War Department's course of action had been tentatively charted by Mr. McCloy and Colonel Bendetsen in the first ten days of February. General DeWitt's final recommendation to evacuate was completed on February 13, and forwarded to Washington with a covering letter the next day. Mr. Stimson and Mr. McCloy did not, however, wait for this report, which contained the "finding" on which their "military necessity" argument to the President was based, but obtained their authority before the recommendation was received. On February 11 the President told the War Department to prepare a plan for wholesale evacuation, specifically including citizens. It was dictated, he concluded, by military necessity; and added, "Be as reasonable as you can." After the conference the Assistant Secretary reported to Bendetsen: "We have *carte blanche* to do what we want to as far as the President is concerned." Apparently General Marshall took no part in the decision.

On the evening of the day they had received the President's approval, McCloy, Gullion, and Bendetsen met at my house. I asked Rowe and Ennis, who were familiar with every step of the controversy, and Tom Clark to be present. General Gullion had an executive order ready for the President to sign. Rowe and Ennis argued strongly against it. But the decision had been made by the President. It was, he said, a matter of military judgment. I did not think I should oppose it any further. The Department of Justice, as I had made it clear to him from the beginning, was opposed to and would have nothing to do with the evacuation. Two days later the President signed the executive order.

I do not think he was much concerned with the gravity or implications of this step. He was never theoretical about things. What must be done to defend the country must be done. The decision was for his Secretary of War, not for the Attorney General, not even for J. Edgar Hoover, whose judgment as to the appropriateness of defense measures he greatly respected. The military might be wrong. But they were fighting the war. Public opinion was on their side, so that there was no question of any substantial opposition, which might tend toward the disunity that at all costs he must avoid. Nor do I think that the constitutional difficulty plagued him—the Constitution has never greatly bothered any wartime President. That was a question of law, which ultimately the Supreme Court must decide. And meanwhile—probably a long meanwhile—we must get on with the war.

I do not mean that he ever spelled that out to me when he spoke of the proposal in terms of national defense. Once he emphasized to me, when I was expressing my belief that the evacuation was unnecessary, that this must be a military decision. When the question arose in Cabinet he said the same thing, although it was never the subject of a Cabinet discussion except in a desultory fashion.

Secretary Stimson, throughout all the negotiations, was expressing to Mr. McCloy his dislike of any exclusion based on racial distinction, though of course he never said that to me—he had to back up his own people unless he chose to overrule them. Just before the evacuation had begun, Mr. Stimson referred to it as a "tragedy," which seemed to be "military necessity," because so many Japanese were located in close proximity to

military installations.[1] And on one occasion he did overrule Mc-
Cloy, who had been pressing me to indict a prominent naturalized American of Italian origin ordered out of an area under a
statute hastily adopted by Congress which made it a crime for
anyone to remain in a prohibited area after the Army told him
to get out. I went over to see Mr. Stimson with McCloy, and
we argued the case for an hour. I said we knew about the
individual—he had been politically prominent—there was nothing against him except that he had been active in the fascist
movement like so many successful Italians, and that the stupidity
of such an indictment might wreck the whole program. If the
Army wanted him to go, they had better put him out themselves
—they had the power. I would not indict him. The program was
pretty edgy anyway, and this was the hell of a test case to pick.
Mr. Stimson sided with me, and the question did not go to the
President.

At first the evacuation was begun on a voluntary basis, the
Japanese finding homes where they could. By February 24 it
was estimated that about 15,000 persons had moved out of the
prohibited zones along the West Coast. But this was not satisfactory. The residents of eastern California did not want them to
settle anywhere in the state; and the officials of the Mountain
States, such as Colorado, made it very clear that there would be
trouble if they sought refuge further east. After the end of March
mass evacuation was placed on a compulsory basis and applied
to all Japanese in California. One hundred and ten thousand
were then moved into camps and kept there during the war,
except that, under the relocation program, several thousand
young people got jobs in the East and moved out of the camps,
and other thousands joined the Armed Forces.

At my suggestion to the President the program was placed
under civilian control after the Japanese had been brought to
the camps by the Army, and Milton Eisenhower, General

---

[1] Of course I did not know all these steps at the time. But they were
subsequently unearthed, and are finding their way into an army
history by Stetson Conn, *The Army and Japanese Evacuation,* a draft
intended to be included as Chapter VI in the volume *Guarding the
United States and Its Outposts* (Western Hemisphere subseries, *The
United States Army in World War II*).

Eisenhower's brother, who was land-use co-ordinator in the Department of Agriculture, was appointed to organize and direct the War Relocation Authority set up in the Department of Interior, which he did with ability, showing a sympathetic understanding of the suffering and needs of the *évacués*.

General DeWitt's Final Report on the evacuation, made over a year after his recommendation that it be undertaken, was compiled by Bendetsen.

The Final Report has been analyzed in various studies that have brought to light the pressures and movements that were behind evacuation. It is an interesting document, and important chiefly because the general's views allegedly constituted the chief basis for the action taken by his civilian superiors, Secretary Stimson and Assistant Secretary McCloy. Yet the facts recited did not indicate any military necessity.

To show the existence of subversive activities the general pointed out that "more than 60,000 rounds of ammunition and many rifles, shotguns and maps of all kinds" had been found in a single FBI raid. He did not add that a truckload of ammunition and guns had come from a sporting-goods store operated by a Japanese alien, and that a large supply of the material was found in the warehouse of the owner of a general store. Most of the "contraband" was harmless, including flashlights, firecrackers, and road maps. In a memorandum to the President in May, 1942, I reported the results of these raids as follows: "We have not uncovered through these searches any dangerous persons that we could not otherwise have known about . . . We have not found among all the sticks of dynamite and gunpowder any evidence that any of it was to be used in a manner helpful to our enemies. We have not found a camera which we have reason to believe was for use in espionage."

The Final Report instanced numerous "unauthenticated" radio communications from coastal areas that had been intercepted; and added that following December 7 "substantially every ship" leaving a West Coast port was attacked by an enemy submarine: this seemed to point "conclusively to the existence of hostile shore-to-ship communication." This was a grave charge, but it was not supported by the facts. J. Edgar Hoover, in a memorandum to me dated February 9, had denied the existence of any information showing that the attacks on ships leaving West Coast ports were associated with espionage activity ashore. Every complaint of signaling, he added, had been investigated; but in no case had "any information been obtained which would substantiate the allegation that there has been signaling from shore-to-ship since the beginning of the war." James L. Fly, chairman of the Federal Communications Commission, on February 26 (two weeks after the decision to evacuate had been made), reported to me the commission's monitoring activities on the West Coast during this period. This service was extensive, and the personnel employed were of outstanding technical competence. He was of the opinion that the Army's equipment was inadequate, and its personnel entirely incapable of determining whether or not the many reports of illicit signaling were well founded.

Fly used pretty strong language about the Army's methods: "I never have seen an organization," he wrote, "that was so hopeless to cope with radio intelligence requirements . . . The personnel is unskilled and untrained. Most are privates who can read only ten words a minute. They know nothing about signal identification, wave propagation and other technical subjects, so essential to radio intelligence procedure . . . It's pathetic, to say the least." Hoover's view that there had been no shore-to-ship signaling was finally confirmed by the historian to whom I have referred. "Actually," Professor Conn writes, "there had been no Japanese submarine or surface vessels anywhere near the West Coast during the preceding month, and careful investigation subsequently indicated that all claims of hostile shore-to-ship and ship-to-shore communications lacked any foundation whatsoever." Toward the end of March, before evacuation had begun, McCloy reported after a visit to the West Coast, that there had been no cases of sabotage traceable to the Japanese population, but that there had been much evidence of espionage. To which Mr. Conn drily comments in a footnote: "No proven instance of espionage after Pearl Harbor among the Japanese population in either Hawaii or the continental United States has ever been disclosed."

Finally, General DeWitt gave three "striking examples" to show the need for military control and evacuation. The first took place on February 22, 1942, eight days *after* the general had recommended evacuation. The last two occurred *after* the Japanese on the West Coast had been removed and incarcerated. Time was not of the essence.

Did the military *really* think that mass evacuation was necessary? Certainly not for six weeks and not in Hawaii, where the foe had struck, where martial law had been declared immediately upon the outbreak of war and the writ of habeas corpus suspended, and where the military had complete responsibility for control of the Japanese. In the Island of Oahu alone there were 118,000—20,000 aliens and 98,000 citizens, more than on the whole West Coast. Evacuation from Hawaii was discussed at Cabinet, and Frank Knox, with his usual boyish but convinced enthusiasm, urged immediate action. But concentration in a big cantonment on the Island of Molokai, guarded by the Army, was thought "impractical" by the Joint Chiefs of Staff; the President was not enthusiastic about moving the Japanese to the United States; the legality of detaining evacuated American citizens against their will was extremely dubious; and, after a few conflicting policy decisions, and the President had declared his unwillingness to suspend the writ of habeas corpus in the United States, the few citizen internees who had been brought over were returned to Hawaii. By the end of March there was little enthusiasm for the original plan. By the middle of January 1943 any idea of mass evacuation had been abandoned.

If the submarine sinkings could be accounted for by shore-to-ship signals from alien enemies among the population, then mass evacuation was far more called for on the East Coast, where the torpedoing was more constant and menacing than on the western shore line, where the sinkings were occasional and sporadic.

Whatever error may have been made by the Army it was not only an error of judgment. It is difficult not to conclude that public opinion played a very large part in the decision, and that the War Department gave way to the clamor of the politicians rather than to a genuine belief in military necessity. Edgar

Hoover sent me a memorandum expressing his view that the demand was "based primarily upon public and political pressure rather than on factual data." With this the Army's historian is in substantial agreement. He writes that in February and March, 1942, "military estimates of the situation continued to indicate that there was no real threat of a Japanese invasion of the West Coast."

It may be even doubted whether, political and special group pressure aside, public opinion even on the West Coast supported evacuation. A confidential report from the Office of Facts and Figures on March 9, 1942, showed that, outside of Southern California, less than one half of those interviewed favored internment of Japanese aliens, and only 14 per cent the internment of citizens of Japanese ancestry. That feeling against the Japanese did not go very deep would appear from the fact that within a year or two after the war Congress was outdoing itself to make reparation for the losses that the *évacués* had suffered —Congress which, three years before, had listened, without protest, to Representative Rankin's plea "to put every single Japanese in a concentration camp for the duration of the emergency." Congressman Jerry Voorhis of California, a sincere and courageous liberal, seemingly influenced by his fear of a vigilante movement breaking out on the West Coast against the Japanese, came to believe that the evacuation order was "a wise and proper move." But fear of violence cannot justify imprisoning those who are threatened. Nor was the fear based on facts. Of course, there were isolated instances of crime and brutality against the Japanese—thirty-six between December 8, 1941, and March 31, 1942, on the whole western seaboard— robberies, extortion, rape, murder, assaults with deadly weapons, the destruction of property owned by Japanese, a sorry story of violence, but not one that told any tale of vigilante action. Seven killings in four months were not an indication that the entire Japanese population was "going to be massacred," as someone wrote to his congressman.

The postwar reaction of Congress and the public generally, suddenly so favorable to the Japanese in the United States, was caused chiefly by the gallant manner in which they fought in our armies, in substantial numbers. But it came also, I suspect, from a feeling of guilt for the way we had treated them, and a desire to make up for it. The Army, who had been keen to evacuate, was particularly laudatory of the behavior of Japanese soldiers. If not much lasting harm was done to the relation of the Japanese to other persons in their communities it was because of the courage and decency of a majority of the Japanese, and in spite of the attitude of those who favored their internment. During the war the Japanese suffered terribly—an immense property loss, chiefly from forced sales resulting from the hegira into the cruel wilderness of the camps; and the far more serious psychological injury, particularly to their youth who had been rejected by their own country. Togo Tonaka, a young Japanese American, wrote me about my life of Justice Holmes— he had read portions of it that had just appeared in *Harper's Magazine*: "I sometimes wonder what advice the late Mr. Justice Holmes would have given me about the situation in which I now find myself: an American living behind barbed wire and military guard in his own native land, deprived of equal opportunity to share the common lot because of his race."

But, after all, the blame for such casual and unsustained judgment cannot be fixed entirely on the military. They had not forgotten that, as Tom Connally said, they had been caught with their pants down at Pearl Harbor. They did not propose to be put in that awkward position again, or to take any chances. Hong Kong had surrendered to the Japanese on December 25, 1941. On January 2, Manila was captured. On January 25, Singapore fell, with 60,000 prisoners of war. At the end of February the naval units of the Allies were largely destroyed at the Battle of the Java Sea, and Burma was occupied early in March. It is against this background of early defeats in the Pacific that the judgment to evacuate must be weighed. I do not mean to suggest that these considerations justified the decision; but they partly explain it.

Although the decision had been handed by the President to the Army, and became primarily its responsibility, it is normal to expect the civilian branch of the government to have a vision less narrowed to see only the conceivable risks, and to balance against them the seriousness of this basic violation of the civil rights. The President, as I have suggested, was not troubled by such a consideration. If anything, he thought that rights should yield to the necessities of war. Rights came after victory, not before. He could probably have withstood the popular pressure without loss to the tenacity of his leadership—pressure of a highly vocative minority in the West. If Stimson had stood firm, had insisted, as apparently he suspected, that this wholesale evacuation was needless, the President would have followed his advice. And if, instead of dealing almost exclusively with McCloy and Bendetsen, I had urged the Secretary to resist the pressure of his subordinates, the result might have been different. But I was new to the Cabinet, and disinclined to insist on my view to an elder statesman whose wisdom and integrity I greatly respected.

Fear is often expressed of the power of the majority in a democracy. This mass evacuation illustrates the influence that a minority, uncurbed and substantially unopposed, can exercise. It shows, too, the power of suggestion which a mystic cliché like "military necessity" can exercise on human beings. Through lack of independent courage and faith in American reality, a superb opportunity was lost by the government in failing to assert the human decencies for which we were fighting. How greatly such an assertion would have contributed to the devotion to the war effort was amply illustrated in our humane and wise treatment of the Italians shortly after the exclusion and quarantine of the Japanese had been finally accomplished.

AND LIBERATION OF
ITALIANS

Chapter Fourteen

Over the years I have come greatly to love the
Italians. Italy was not in the background of my childhood, as
was France. Nor did the romantic Victorian approach to Italy—
the Italy of Shelley and Byron and Browning—much color the
myths of our childhood, although it played a minor part. If
there was an emerging note in addition to England it was
French, with two years in Switzerland as very small boys under
a governess from Alsace, and the other less consequential,
slighter figures who succeeded her on our return to America
before we were sent to boarding school. The recognition that
Italy had produced so many men of genius over the centuries,
so many more than any other country, that she embodied to my
youthful fancy the very essence of genius, was fortified by what
my godmother, Mrs. Owen Wister, Fanny Kemble's daughter,
told me of them one summer (after my freshman year at Harvard), when we shared with her Butler Place, while she would
read the *Purgatorio* in Italian, while I followed in the rather
pedantic Carey translation, and smoked too many cigarettes,
and counted the little orange trees in green pots that lined the
avenue, and wondered what Mother was thinking as she sat

wrapped in her daydreams, not understanding a word of Italian but scorning to follow in a translation. . . .

The masculine quality of the simple Italian—of the peasant— I found later in a client, Doctor Vincenzo Naselli (as he was pleased to rank himself), a masseur with chiropractic trimmings on the side, who now and then would drift into practicing medicine, and would appeal to me to help him escape the disagreeable consequences. He was a skillful masseur and when I was tired after a long day in court, I often visited his "parlor" for a treatment. He would invariably try to waive aside payment, and the gesture became an exchange of good manners between us, his introductory rejection of money—"but you are my friend"—and final acceptance, as he shrugged hopeless resignation under my prolonged insistence. He would always press on me a glass of sour red wine, summoning his wife imperiously to fetch the bottle with a command appropriate to the master in his own domain.

With one friend of Italian descent, of a very different kidney, I have experienced an immediate and continuing recognition of that quality of genius of which I have spoken. It is not that he is an artist, that he writes or paints or composes music in the grand manner—he has no such creative gift. But Ernest Cuneo gives the effect of *éblouissement*. There is no exact equivalent in English, perhaps *dazzlement* would be the closest. His people were Genoese, and Ernest has the thrust, the daring, the edging of pride that we associate with Andrea Doria and his townsmen. He is a superb talker, and talk with him is usually an exchange. What perhaps interests him most is the problem of power—where it is found, how exercised, what are its incidents. A former professional football player, he has put on weight as he reached middle age. His brilliant eyes make you forget this corpulence that so many Italians cannot resist acquiring. He is diffident rather than shy, with a far-reaching memory that supports his splendid exaggerations of emphasis.

During the war Cuneo was active in the Italian underground, leaving this country to operate in Italy as a liaison officer with the O.S.S., and was later decorated by both Italy and Great Britain.

I thought of Ernest Cuneo, complex beyond description, and of Vincenzo Naselli, fundamentally a stupid and simple man, but with his pride to stand on, when we removed Italians from the category of enemy aliens. They responded as he had, telling me I was their friend, proud that they had been trusted, deeply stirred at being treated as American citizens.

It was Ennis, whom I had put in charge of the Alien Enemy Control Section, who made the suggestion. It would put an end to the dishonor—in their minds—that such an enemy status implied. I seized the idea with enthusiasm, and asked him to clear with other interested departments—State, Army, and FBI—before I took the proposal, in August 1942, to F.D.R. He gave his assent immediately—he was, he said, sorry that he had not thought of it himself; it was a masterly stroke of international statesmanship *and* good politics. It was decided that I should make the announcement at Carnegie Hall in New York on October 12, Columbus Day.

I wrote my speech for the occasion with a good deal of care, helped by Ugo Carusi, who had been born in Carrara, and brought to the United States as an infant. He was fluent in Italian and soaked in Italian culture. He understood the outlook of the Italian American, torn between the shoddy glories of the fascist regime and the uncertain assurances of the democratic resistance. They were like children in the misery of the separation of father and mother. I must make them feel that they need not be ashamed—it was the mountebank, Mussolini, who had betrayed them. They were our friends, the Italian people; and they could achieve loyalty by grasping the cause of the Allies, which was also the cause of all good Italians, whether in their new country or in their fathers' land. I would have to stretch things a bit, as many of the leading Italian Americans had been caught in the spurious glory of this shallow dictator. But glory, like everything else to the Italian mind, had its practical limits; and with hardly a qualm or shadow of shame they adopted with enthusiasm the cause of the Allies. Overnight, Generoso Pope, the publisher of *Il Progresso* in New York, high in favor of Tammany Hall, turned over his newspaper, so recently dripping warmly with eulogies of Il Duce, to those who were now engaged in bringing about his defeat.

I talked on an evening program at Carnegie Hall on a nation-wide hookup, after a concert by the Philharmonic Orchestra. Fiorello La Guardia, then serving his last term as mayor of New York, introduced me. My speech was pretty highfalutin', but that is what Italians love and expect, particularly in war.

The Italian people, I said, had time and again resisted the arms of the invader on their soil, the armies of Spain, of France, of Austria. They had often failed, but would not, as Dante put it, put down their weapons "to savor the salt of the bread of others, and knew how hard a road the going up and down another's stairs." Late in the last century Italy had won her independence; but now in the halls of Rome a jackal cowered. . . . They need but recall the great names of the glorious past: Galileo, wanderer among the stars, who heard the command of reaction to keep silent, and would not; Leonardo da Vinci, Michelangelo, Tasso, Ariosto . . . Garibaldi, less than a hundred years ago, on a bank of the Tiber, hopelessly outnumbered by the French, his shirt bespattered with the blood of his legionaries . . .

Such a heritage does not die with the burning of books. The people would not turn forever from their great past, and bow down before the little men of Europe. . . . Here in America 600,000 Italians, technically alien enemies, were joining the revolt, while their sons fought in the United States Army, five hundred on the average in every division. Only 228 Italians had been interned, and, with the approval of the President, they would no longer be classed as enemy aliens, no longer required to comply with the regulations applying to other enemy nationalities. We have trusted you, I ended—you must prove worthy of that trust, so that it might never be said that there were disloyal groups among American Italians.

I suppose all this, so long after the event, sounds unreal, and suggests *opéra bouffe*. But Italians can take a good deal, and it was a moment of history that moved us all. Arturo Toscanini, who did not attend the meeting since he was afraid of reprisal—his niece was in Rome—had heard of the nature of my announcement. He turned on the radio in his sitting room—his secretary told me that he detested the instrument—listened to my words, threw his arms round the machine when I had finished talking,

Fig. 1

Francis Biddle, from a portrait by his brother, George Biddle. *Horydczak-Davis Studio*

Fig. 2

Mrs. Francis Biddle (Katherine Garrison Chapin), 1940.

g. 3

esident Roosevelt signing Francis Biddle's pointment as Attorney General, September 1941.

Fig. 4

Washington and his cabinet. From left to right: George Washington; General Henry Knox, Secretary of War; Alexander Hamilton, Secretary of the Treasury; Thomas Jefferson, Secretary of State; Edmund Randolph, Attorney General.

Copyright 1876 by Currier & Ives, New York

Fig. 5

An autographed picture of the Cabinet in which Francis Biddle sat as Attorney General. From left to right around the table: Claude Wickard, Secretary of Agriculture; Francis Perkins, Secretary of Labor; Henry Wallace, Vice President; Jesse Jones, Secretary of Commerce; Harold L. Ickes, Secretary of the Interior; Frank Walker, Postmaster General; Henry L. Stimson, Secretary of War; Cordell Hull, Secretary of State; President Roosevelt; Henry Morgenthau, Secretary of the Treasury; Francis Biddle, Attorney General; Frank Knox, **Secretary of the Navy.** *Harris & Ewing*

Fig. 7

Attorney General Biddle with his executive assistant (seated), Ugo Carusi.

ig. 6

utographed portrait of Chief Justice
Charles E. Hughes.

Fig. 8

Left to right: James H. Rowe, Jr., Assistant Attorney General; Tom Clark (at desk); the Attorney General; and Edward J. Ennis, in charge of the Enemy Alien Control program. 1942.

Fig. 9

Cartoon presented by C. K. Berryman to the Attorney General with the inscription: "Wishing him all the excitement that is good for him."

Fig. 10

Visit of King Peter of Yugoslavia to National Training School for Boys, June 28, 1942. Left to right: Ambassador Constantin Fotitch of Yugoslavia, Francis Biddle, James V. Bennett then and now director of the Federal Bureau of Prisons, and King Peter.

Fig. 11

Trial of the saboteurs, July 10, 1942. From left to right, front row: the Attorney General, J. Edgar Hoover, and defense counsel Colonel Ristine for defendant George Dasch.

Photo by U. S. Army Signal Corps

held it close while he took in the roar of applause answered, kissed it, turned it off, and burst into tears.

The newspapers were enthusiastic—our action would embarrass the propaganda of the Axis leaders, and would impress not only the people of Italy but the inhabitants of the conquered countries with the sharp contrast between life under the Axis and in the United States. There appeared a charming story in the New York *Post*, headed "There's Joy in Mulberry Street": "The women of Mulberry Street wear black and skin their hair straight back from the forehead as do the women of the Abruzzi. They could not understand why, when they had been giving their sons so generously to the war, they should be called enemies. This morning the street is alive with chattering, and the sound of a new name never heard in these parts before— Biddlé! . . ." My brother George found an echo of my talk in Italy, where he accompanied the American troops on an assignment by the Army to "sketch" the war, in pamphlets that had been scattered across the country urging Italians to separate from the Tedeschi and the Fascisti, and quoting from a speech of Winston Churchill and from my remarks at Carnegie Hall.

The Italians sent me grapes, boxes of candy, bottles of sour, homemade wine; and for a long time I was not permitted to pay for a meal at an Italian restaurant. The telegrams and letters were agreeably unrestrained. Giovanni Parasporo, of Utica, New York, wrote: "I tank you for your speech on the Columbus Day. Reading carefully your speech one may say you was born in Italy. For the fates of the United States, for the liberty and for the freedom of the world, hurrah!" The Russo family thanked me by telegram "from the deepest of our hearts." Father Gattuso, pastor of St. Rocco's Church in Cleveland, told me about the meeting of those who had gathered in the Sons of Italy Hall— "the good, heroic mothers, who were the guests of honor, and the old men who had worked hard for the national progress of this God-blessed country were crying, smiling, gesturing . . . Never one will be found who would ever do anything against this America. Their humble but really sweet home is here— here is their heart . . . It will be my pleasure and duty to explain to my flock your talk this coming Sunday."

And they still remember. I am writing this on the S.S.

Augustus, on the long pleasant lazy southern trip to Gibraltar, Naples, Nice, Genoa. Yesterday Mr. Francesco Fannicelli of Scarsdale, president of the Maid-Easy Cleansing Products Corp., introduced himself to say that at the time of my announcement he was a stateless person. Mussolini had taken away his citizenship, and he was without a country to which to be loyal—one must always be loyal to some country, particularly in time of war. He was living in America, in terror of being interned and sent to a camp. When he had to register he felt he was being branded. He listened over the radio. He had never forgotten.

In 1954 the President of the Italian Republic, acting through the Italian ambassador in Washington, conferred on me at the Embassy the degree of Grand Officer of the Order of Merit— *Al Merito della Republica*—in recognition of my "faith in the destiny of the Italian nation." The award recited that my appreciation of Italy's culture and her contribution to the development of the United States, together with my affection for the Italian people, had helped "in preparing the full recovery of Italy from the dire plight in which the war had plunged her." I was touched, and said so; adding that the two qualities I most loved in Italians were their enthusiasm for life, and the thrust of their humor. "There lurks in the face of every Italian"—so an old saying runs—"a shade of sadness, not because he believes there is anything wrong with the world, but born of the knowledge that some day he will have to leave it . . ." And for their humor, consider this: painted on a little ash tray that my brother George brought me a few years ago, after spending a winter at the American Academy in Rome: La mia moglie l'e come l'America—l'ha sempre ragion lei ("My wife is like America— she's always right").

SEDITIONISTS, FATHER COUGHLIN, AND THE CHICAGO *TRIBUNE*

❧❀❧ *Chapter Fifteen*

Before war between the United States and the Axis Powers was precipitated by Pearl Harbor, the isolationists and pro-Germans, often indistinguishable, attacked the President and his administration scurrilously. In Congress those who wanted to keep the country clear of entangling alliances and at all costs out of war preached an unreal neutrality. Neutrality to Roosevelt and to those of us who were close to him meant to stand by idly while we saw France fall, and England nearly crumble to death under the terrible air assault that followed the phony war. Gradually through the President's leadership and the realization that our turn might come after England fell, the public moved away from a position not so much of isolationism —except in certain sections—as indifference. It was natural that the East, so much closer to Europe in the background of her tradition than the rest of the country, should feel most deeply the desperate threat to her culture. The South shared that concern, not only in the Anglo-Saxon tradition still strong in the Southern states, but because Southerners are always ready for a fight, given a good cause to fight for, and are less easily

upset by having the uneventful flow of their normal lives interrupted by the radical demands of war.

There had been a good deal of German propaganda before
Pearl Harbor; but there was not much pro-German response, not
nearly as much as in the First World War. In the twenty-five
years between the two wars there was little German immigration,
a large number of the older German immigrants had died, and
their sons had been quickly absorbed. But the Irish-American
population, unified by Catholicism, held its immense identity.
Almost all of them were Americans by naturalization or by birth;
and they retained the ancient, well-earned grudge against England. Their isolationism was calculated to prevent linking our fate
with that of Great Britain. There it stopped.

It was part of the ironic turn with which fate plucked at Franklin Roosevelt's career that she should present him, when war
broke out, with a group of men heading several of the most
powerful Senate committees who were isolationists, as during
his two terms as governor of New York he had constantly been
thwarted—and sharpened—by Republican legislatures. Robert
Rice Reynolds, of North Carolina, was chairman of the Military
Affairs Committee; David I. Walsh, of Massachusetts, of Naval
Affairs; and Frederick Van Nuys of Indiana and, after his death,
Pat McCarran of Nevada, of Judiciary. All of them had little
sympathy with Europe's desperate needs, and, for different reasons, were against American aid to meet them. None of them
was an open and outspoken isolationist, like Gerald P. Nye, of
North Dakota, and Robert Taft, of Ohio, in the Senate; or
Hamilton Fish and Clare E. Hoffman in the House. Isolationism,
as a way of American life, had deep if sometimes irrational
roots, going far back into what had been a simpler but not far-
distant past. What gave the word a reproachful connotation,
often unjustifiably, was that many isolationists made common
cause with those who cherished and thrived on hatred: the
Jew-baiters, the anti-English, the pro-Germans and others of their
ilk who at heart despised American democracy.

The extravagant abuse of prosecutions for sedition had been
the most serious example of hysteria in the First World War.
When there were several arrests for "seditious" utterances,
palpably innocuous, I ordered that the men be released and the

prosecutions dropped. Ellis O. Jones told a small group of listeners that the President should be impeached for asking Congress to declare war. Another man, a Danish seaman, had started a barroom brawl by proclaiming that Roosevelt was no good, and that he was for Hitler. Jonathan Worth Daniels noted a few other foolish acts that had followed the declaration of war: a man who booed the President's picture in a Chicago theater got thoroughly pommeled by his neighbors—he explained that he was a Republican who had contracted the habit of booing Roosevelt on all occasions and had not had time to readjust himself to new conditions of national unity. He was fined $200 by a magistrate on Bill of Rights Day.

I directed that thereafter no United States Attorney should institute any prosecution based on sedition without my personal written authority; and that information as to arrests already made should be at once reported to me. I announced that freedom of speech should be curtailed only when public safety was directly imperiled. The majority of the press supported this restraint, some newspapers with a good deal of enthusiasm. The New York *Times* thought it a wise precaution, noted the lack of hysteria in contrast to what had occurred during the last war, when federal judges were "burning with the communicative heat of public opinion," and rendered charges that smacked strongly of the stump.

The fifth columnists and their dupes, the lunatic fringe, unbalanced individuals, some of them shrewd enough to find a not unprofitable way of life in organizing movements based on racial prejudice, took heart at what they considered an official pledge on my part to protect them and allow them to say anything they wanted. A pamphlet, distributed at a West Coast rally, boasted: "Remember: the United States says we have a perfect right to talk—and we will! . . ."

The attacks on our Allies—without foundation of fact and pandering to every possible class and race hatred—increased after war had been declared. These were no longer the voices of isolationists, concerned lest we should be dragged into a war that was not our business, but the cries of defeatists, welcoming a program of domestic fascism calculated to demoralize the war effort. The movement grew. It was not a question of a man's right to his own opinion, but of whether the government should take steps to prevent a campaign seeking defeat, apparently well organized and springing from a central direction. Nor was it a matter of a handful of scattered publications—the *Christian Science Monitor* estimated that there were nearly a hundred of them. The "line" in all was about the same, and was taken directly from or closely related to official German propaganda: America, not Japan, was guilty of starting the war in the Pacific; American aid to Britain was a Jewish plot, and Roosevelt (Rosenfeldt) was a Jew; American boys were being killed to support a tottering British and French imperialism; the secret manipulations of the new money power and the munition makers had brought about the war; fighting was useless against the new order, and we should retire from the war.

William Dudley Pelley was among the most vociferous, and as typical as any of these purveyors of hate. An ardent admirer of Hitler, he launched the Silver Shirts Legion of America on January 31, 1933, the day after Hitler seized power. The Silver Shirts—he told his friends—were modeled on Hitler's Brown Shirts. As soon as they were organized Pelley began a malignant attack on Jews in pamphlets that poured from his press, and in *Pelley's Weekly*. The Silver Shirts platform advocated a plan for registering "all persons of Hebrew blood or extraction under penalty of confiscation of their goods." Resident aliens should be deprived of their civil rights unless they forswore their Jewish allegiance. If the Jews had money, the Gentiles have the numbers: "Within another year the United States will have wakened to the fact that the Jewish problem takes precedence" over all others.

These rabble-rousers had similar characteristics. They were fundamentalists, egotists, and exhibitionists, possessing a flair for recognizing and rousing the obsessions that brought them lucrative returns. They were almost always anti-Semitic and often anti-Catholic. They raised the bedraggled banner of America for white, Protestant Aryans, and talked as their predecessors in this evil tradition had talked—the Nativists, the Know Nothings, the APA, Samuel F. B. Morse, Thomas E. Watson of

Georgia, and William Joseph Simmons and Edward Y. Clarke, who reorganized the second Ku Klux Klan in 1920.

Gerald B. Winrod assaulted Jews and Catholics alike, calling the Jesuits the secret service department of the Pope. Negroes and labor unions were included, Winrod following the noisy trail of Tom Watson. Had not Hitler discovered, he asked, that the centers of vice-nudist colonies, the filthy screen and stage, and poison literature were under the control and direction of "an organization of Jews, who, for money, were willing to tear down the Gentile morals of the nation?" From then on Winrod was openly pro-Nazi.

There was a swarm of such "preachers." Louise Fry, otherwise known as Paquita Louise de Shismaroff, headed the Militant Christian Patriots. George E. Deatherage, of St. Albans, West Virginia, revived the Knights of the White Camellia, which had been allied with the Klan, and became its Honorable Grand Commander, advocating the adoption of a fiery swastika as its emblem. There was the National Gentile League, whose slogan was "vote Gentile, buy Gentile"; the Militant Christian Patriots of Los Angeles; and the American Intelligence Federation, which paid its organizing solicitor forty per cent of all the money it collected; there was Joseph E. McWilliams and his Christian Mobilizers; there was the Mothers and Sisters and Wives of the U.S.A.

And finally there was Father Charles E. Coughlin.

By February of 1942 the mood of the country had become less tolerant of uncurbed free speech in wartime. It was suggested in a column that Edgar Hoover had little sympathy with his chief's view that there should be no prosecution unless the speech or writing directly affected the war effort. The President began to send me brief memoranda to which were attached some of the scurrilous attacks on his leadership, with a notation: "What about this?" or "What are you doing to stop this?" I explained to him my view of the unwisdom of bringing indictment for sedition except where there was evidence that recruitment was substantially being interfered with, or there was some connection between the speech and propaganda centers in Germany. I reported that we were in the midst of a study of the material—

we must have had a ton of it in the Department—and might ask for some indictments, probably one for conspiracy in the District, if we could tie up these strident voices with the enemy. He was not much interested in the theory of sedition, or in the constitutional right to criticize the government in wartime. He wanted this anti-war talk stopped.

We began to feed the grand jury with exhibits. A young trial lawyer in the criminal division, William Power Maloney, was in charge. He made a name for himself before the war by convicting George Sylvester Viereck, whose technical crime was failure to register as an agent for Germany. Maloney was tough and ambitious, his eye never off the headlines. At the moment he was under a favorable public spotlight. The Viereck conviction was on its way to the Supreme Court.

The President was getting a good deal of mail complaining about the "softness" of his Attorney General. After two weeks, during which F.D.R.'s manner when I saw him said as plainly as words that he considered me out of step, he began to go for me in the Cabinet. His technique was always the same. When my turn came, as he went around the table, his habitual affability dropped. He did not ask me as usual, if I had anything to report. He looked at me, his face pulled tightly together. "When are you going to indict the seditionists?" he would ask; and the next week, and every week after that, until the indictment was found, he would repeat the same question. Of course I felt uncomfortable. I told him that there was an immense amount of evidence; that I wanted the indictment to stick when it was challenged; and that we could not indict these men for their naked writings and spoken words without showing what effect they had on the war effort. His way of listening made my explanation sound unreal. At the Cabinet meeting a day or two after the return of an indictment he said, now in his most conciliatory manner, "I was glad to see, Francis, that the grand jury returned a true bill." I cannot remember any other instance of his putting pressure on me. He never tried to interfere with any decision I made, even if he thought it might have serious political repercussions, or might affect the war unfavorably, as when I directed that Harry Bridges be deported.

Twenty-six native Fascists were indicted on July 29, 1942, under the Espionage Act of 1917 and the Criminal Conspiracy Act of 1940—the statute under which, up until then, only one action had been brought, the prosecution of the group of Trotskyites, which I had authorized as Acting Attorney General in 1940.

The defendants were a curious assortment that included Winrod and Elizabeth Dilling—"a true Bible-believing child of God" according to Winrod's estimate—who ran the Patriotic Research Bureau of Chicago. She had given up a career as a concert harpist to enlist in the "cause"; and as early as 1934 had become notorious by the publication of her *Red Network*, which attacked as subversive the Society of Friends and the Federal Council of Churches, and listed many of the country's leading liberals as Reds. Ellis O. Jones and Robert Noble, whom I had set free a few months before in California, were among the company. Jones was head of the National Copperheads and author of the poem *Beware the Wily Jew*, which Mrs. Dilling mailed out from her research bureau. Noble had written a scurrilous article about the President, and was preaching that Germany had won the war and that we might as well accept the New Order. There were George W. Christian, Hudson de Priest, Lois de Lafayette Washburn, alias T.N.T.; and Gerald L. K. Smith, with his sensational *The Cross and the Flag*, whom the America First Party was to run for President in 1944. One of the defendants, Edward J. Smythe, looked, as Paul Ward remarked in the Baltimore *Sun*, like an unfrocked bartender. He charged that the government had exercised entrapment. He threatened a congressional investigation of the Department of Justice.

Senator Wheeler was particularly critical of the manner in which William Power Maloney was handling the grand jury investigations. It was generally assumed that Maloney, who had succeeded in convicting Viereck, and had now obtained an indictment against the seditionists, would try the case against them. But there was merit in the Senator's charge that Maloney was not by temperament and behavior a fit man for this. There was little doubt that he was "leaking" information to the newspapers, and would play up the case for everything that there was in it. It would be difficult enough to get a fair trial during war, and I was afraid that there would be a repetition of the highly prejudicial trials of the First World War unless restraint and decency were exercised. I determined that Maloney should be replaced by someone who could be counted on not to make improper appeals to the jury. I therefore withdrew him from the case, and replaced him with John Rogge.

John Rogge had been in charge of the Criminal Division of the Department of Justice, and had personally tried the series of criminal cases for the government that broke the Huey Long political machine in Louisiana and sent several of its beneficiaries, including a former governor, to jail. He had been a *Harvard Law Review* man, was thirty-eight years old, and had the type of painstaking temperament, springing from his German background, which admirably suited him to cope with the mass of detailed propaganda material that made up the evidence, and to sort and arrange it into a pattern that would support the conspiracy charges. I announced on February 7, 1943, that Maloney had been appointed head of the trial section of the Criminal Division, and that Rogge would try the case.

I was not unprepared for the howl that went up from the press, particularly the liberal press, which was calling for speedy action against the pro-German seditionists who were obstructing the war effort. The New York *Post* saw Maloney's ouster as a major scandal—Biddle's friends had never imagined that he would succumb to political pressure. Why had Biddle done this? Wheeler was chairman of the subcommittee that dealt with the appropriation of the Department of Justice. He had threatened to scuttle it unless Biddle yielded, and Biddle had resisted for a while but now the trial would probably never come off. . . . The Washington *Post* talked of a deal with the Senator in an editorial headed "Appeasement Is Folly." The Charleston *Observer* found something sinister in this yielding to the isolationist leaders in Congress. . . . F.D.R. sent me a brief query: "Why Maloney's removal?"

A month later the Supreme Court handed down its decision in the *Viereck* case reversing the conviction. Chief Justice Stone, who delivered the opinion, stated that the conduct of Maloney was so unfair during the trial that it placed the conviction in jeopardy, regardless of the other issues involved. Maloney's remarks to the jury, the justice continued, were so prejudicial that the trial judge should have stopped counsel's discourse without waiting for an objection. The Chief Justice insisted that prosecutions must be meticulously fair "at a time when passion and prejudice are heightened by emotions stirred by our participation in a great war." None of the newspapers that had lashed me a month before for removing Maloney now admitted that I had been justified. Frank C. Waldrop in his column in the *Times-Herald*, a violent anti-administration paper, was of the opinion that I should have been fired for the bad judgment shown by using Maloney in the first place. Viereck was later retried, again convicted, and sent to jail. He was one of the defendants in the sedition conspiracy case.

The sedition trial was destined to drag through a shockingly dreary and degrading experience. There were three indictments alleging the same conspiracy. Before Maloney had been replaced he made an effort to tighten his original indictment. It had been loosely drawn, and did not sufficiently set forth direct contact between the defendants' publications and the German propaganda machine, which was the essence of the conspiracy. The second indictment traced the conspiracy back to January 1933 when Hitler usurped power, and named Ulrich Fleischauer, publisher of a German propaganda sheet in Ehrfurt, *World Service*, as a co-conspirator. When I appointed Rogge, grand jury proceedings were reopened, and nearly a year later the third and final indictment was filed, adding the National Socialist German Workers' Party—the Nazi party—as a co-conspirator. Some of the defendants previously indicted were dropped, and two prominent conspirators were added, Lawrence Dennis, a Harvard graduate, with half a dozen years in the diplomatic service—one would hardly have thought that such a training would have conditioned him for the intellectual leadership of American Fascists—he was the author of *The Dynamics of War and Revolution;* and Joseph E. McWilliams, organizer of the fascist Christian Mobilizers, who had referred to President Roosevelt as "the Jew King." The theory of the crime differentiated the case from the sedition prosecutions resorted to by the

government in the First World War, which were tied to interference with the operation of the war within the United States
without connecting the defendants in any way with the enemy.
Nothing like the trial had ever happened in an American
court of law. Justice Edward C. Eicher, the trial judge, was
determined to lean over backward to give the defendants a
fair trial. He was an amiable man, once a rather popular member
of Congress, who had later served as chairman of the Securities
and Exchange Commission. He was not well. Nervous, sensitive,
and patient, he was unable, as it soon became apparent, to cope
with the obstinate and unruly defendants—there were twenty-
seven men and two women, and nearly forty lawyers. They
raised every conceivable objection before the trial, and showed
while the preliminary motions to dismiss were being argued a
united front of violent obstruction that was eventually to wreck
the proceeding. On March 3 Lois de Lafayette Washburn appeared in court in a long blue nightgown under her dress,
claiming that the "female attendants" at the District jail would
not let her have any of her clothes.

The bedlam of shouted objections and noise did not begin at
once. Perhaps if the judge had been firmer from the beginning
it might have been checked. But before long the lawyers were
shouting in unison objections to the admission of evidence that
had already been ruled on. In vain Judge Eicher warned the
defendants that he would not entertain repetitious arguments.
"Rising like a nest of disturbed locusts at every attempt of the
prosecution to introduce documentary evidence," as the New
York *Times* put it, "the defense lawyers kept the court ruling
constantly on objections, day after day, week after week. Every
document was attacked—and there were hundreds of them—and
objection was made to every witness, in endless and redundant
speeches by as many lawyers who could get on their feet at the
same time." Turbulent scenes were the order of the day, and the
courtroom was continually in an uproar, the judge fining the
offending lawyers right and left for contempt in a vain attempt
to keep order. Trivial technicalities continually interrupted and
blocked normal procedure. The trial had become a dreary farce.

There was nothing I could do to help the situation. Any interference on my part would have rightly been considered im-

pertinent. But I did send Katherine to the court to sit in as a spectator. She said it was like a great schoolroom with unruly children pounding on their desks, shouting imprecations, jumping up and down, the teacher's efforts to quiet them drowned in the hubbub.

By November 15 the trial had turned into a concentrated effort to wear out Judge Eicher. On November 30, 1944, exhausted and unhappy, he suddenly died. The trial had killed him. It had lasted from April to November, and hardly half of the government's testimony was in. If it had taken a normal course the evidence of both the United States and the defendants should by that time have been completed. But the delays created by the obstructive tactics of the defendants consumed more time than the actual submission of the testimony, which was largely documentary.

Rogge wanted to eliminate more defendants, and bring three or four new indictments, with five or six individuals in each. But there was little enthusiasm to go on with it. Everyone was sick of the farce, the war was drawing to a close, and the propaganda had long since ceased. In that sense, at least the prosecution had accomplished the purpose which the President had in mind. After I had resigned as Attorney General a motion to dismiss for the government's failure to prosecute was finally granted.

Contrast this case with a later trial, not unlike it, except that there were fewer defendants, and a judge who would not be browbeaten. In 1949 eleven Communist leaders were tried and convicted in New York. The Communists attempted the same tactics to irritate and finally wear down Judge Medina that the Fascists had used against Justice Eicher. As Judge Learned Hand said in his opinion sustaining the conviction, the trial judge, "sorely tried for many months of turmoil constantly provoked by useless bickering, exposed to offensive slights and insults, harried with interminable repetition . . . showed considerably greater self-control and forbearance than it is given to most judges to possess."

Father Coughlin was not one of the defendants.

As far back as 1926 in his parish of Royal Oak in Detroit he began his series of radio addresses, which were immediately popular among a certain section of the people. With contributions received from his listeners he built the Shrine of the Little Flower, and organized the Radio League. During President Roosevelt's first term he denounced bankers and lavished praise on the New Deal. But by 1936 he had started his personal attacks on the President, calling him a liar and an upstart dictator.

His savage assault against the Jews and his denunciation of them as Communists came at about the same time. His weekly paper, *Social Justice*, was founded in 1936. The Christian Front was organized "to force capitalism to yield to labor a fair share of its wealth." But—careful to hedge—the Front would never compromise with communism, fascism, nazism, or any movement tending to destroy representative government.

He made a shrewd appeal to the discontented and the frustrated elements of the population, and in a few years it bore fruit. The accusations became sharper and more blatant. The notorious forged *Protocols of the Wise Men of Zion* were published and analyzed—he was not, Father Coughlin kept repeating, concerned with their *authenticity,* he was interested in their *factuality.* He would not vouch for them, but there were the facts; and his newssheet added: "The only unbiased source of truth is Father Coughlin."

Patriotic units (as the priest named them) were organized in Brooklyn and other cities, and violence began in 1939. At a meeting at Columbus Circle in New York a man shouted that he wished "to see Jewish blood flow all over America"; and another that he "would like to see every Jew in the United States hanged." Boys boarded the subways selling copies of *Social Justice,* followed by large crowds who shouted, "Buy Christian only! Save America! Down with the Jews!" While in his newspaper *Der Stürmer,* in Germany, Julius Streicher was calling for the persecution and extermination of the Jews, in New York organized platoons of Christian Fronters and Christian Mobilizers—counterparts of the German Brown Shirts—incited street audiences by anti-Semitic speeches. An investigation of these disorders, ordered by Mayor La Guardia, brought out that 407 members of the New York Police Department were Christian Fronters. A few months later—September 11, 1941—Lindbergh warned a huge America First rally at Des Moines, Iowa, that if the "British, Jews, and the Administration stop agitating for war, there will be little danger from involvement." Fortunately the community as a whole reacted in vigorous protest, and the violence did not spread.

After the declaration of war America First disbanded, and Lindbergh joined the war effort. But Father Coughlin continued his crusade. He was still anti-Semitic; but now more carefully geared in an effort to oppose and block the war and keep out of jail at the same time. On the day after Pearl Harbor he stated categorically: "The United States and Great Britain are planning a post-war program. Vitally related to that program is the confiscation of all raw materials in the world." Great Britain had a "propensity" for deserting her allies "because of her unwillingness or inability to fight her own battles. . . ." Would Americans, he asked, bow down to totalitarian decrees which restricted their sugar, motor cars, and way of life—or would they listen to reason and terminate a war which no one can win now and which "Americans can lose completely."

While he was thus exhorting the nation to failure during those terrible twelve weeks of 1942, the Germans were submarining increasingly large numbers of Allied merchantmen; Manila and Cavite were captured by the Japanese; Rangoon was evacuated and Mandalay fell.

It was time to take action against this troublesome priest.

On April 14, 1942, I wrote a letter to Frank Walker, the Postmaster General, detailing Coughlin's utterances in *Social Justice*, and pointing out that they showed a close resemblance to themes broadcast by our enemies since December 1, 1941, as reported by the Federal Broadcast Monitoring Service. With an estimated distribution of 200,000 copies, *Social Justice* presumably reached persons in the armed services and those subject to induction and enlistment. I cited the Espionage Act of 1917 for the Postmaster General's authority to suspend or revoke the paper's second-class mailing privileges, a power sustained by the Supreme Court in the last war. The grounds for such action were specifically stated by the act—false statements willfully made with the intent to interfere with the operation of the military forces of the United States, or to promote the success of its enemies.

Walker, under the statute, had discretion to act as he saw fit. A Roman Catholic, he was distressed by Coughlin's actions, and worried about the criticism that was being leveled at the Catholic hierarchy and the demands that it put an end to Coughlin's indecent behavior. At the same time he must have hated to move against a priest. Yet, displaying independence and courage, he advised me, the day he got my letter, that he had notified the publisher of *Social Justice* that a hearing would be given him in two weeks to show cause why the second-class privilege should not be revoked. The postmaster at Royal Oak was told to withhold dispatch of any further issues.

Father Coughlin was no longer—according to his own statement—editor, owner, or publisher of *Social Justice*, and was not therefore included in the order to show cause. The grand jury, which was gathering material on sedition, was directed to investigate the ownership of the newspaper. On April 20 the father wrote me that he was ready to appear at any time before the grand jury, to waive immunity and testify to the facts with respect to the publication of *Social Justice*, adding that if the criminal laws of the United States had been violated, he alone was guilty. His letter was released the same day. He was a skillful operator; and was looking forward to the far more exciting role of martyr.

This role I was determined to prevent. The priest had a large audience, a substantial following, and was made for the part. Once indicted, a majority of Catholics who had up till then been critical of him, or who had held off, would close ranks and rally to his defense. The isolationist newspapers, savagely anti-administration—the Chicago *Daily Tribune*, the New York *News*, and the Hearst papers—ever since the war had been sympathetic to his line, and would espouse his cause as representing freedom of the press. The day before Frank Walker's letter the *News* stated that "millions who love the truth and the facts concerning this country and its preservation love and listen to Father Coughlin"; and five days later, with an obvious eye on a possible clash, declared that the mail ban on his paper should be a bond to unite Catholics and Protestants against suppression of freedom of press and speech. The case—whatever turn it took—would be appealed. One could count on its being dragged out for at least two or three years—the very years when national unity was essential to our success.

I asked Leo T. Crowley, a Roman Catholic and a close friend of the President, whom I knew well and trusted, to lunch with me. He was then chairman of the board of the Federal Deposit Insurance Corporation. He was very skillful at settling rows and cleaning up messes. I went over the father's past activities—and his future—in some detail. If the grand jury indicted Coughlin, I told Crowley, the country would be thrown into a rift that would do infinite harm to the war effort. Why could we not appeal to the Church hierarchy to silence Coughlin? Surely the Church did not want that kind of a fight—and we must go through with it if we started. The point was to win the war—not to indict a priest for sedition. Who was the man, I asked him, to whom we could appeal, a man of real power, who could and would act? The grand jury might indict Father Coughlin any moment.

Archbishop Edward Mooney, he answered at once, the Archbishop of Detroit, the only prelate who had authority and would exercise it. Father Coughlin was directly under him. "Do you know him?" "Well," he said. "Will you see him *at once?*" He agreed, he was certain he could persuade the Archbishop. He would fly out to Detroit the next day. Should we talk to the President first? On the contrary, Leo said, that would embarrass both of them. "I'll bring it back tied up—then we can tell the President."

In three days he was again in my office, smiling and rubbing his hands at the success of his mission. The Archbishop had agreed at once, without any stipulation or condition. He had sent for Father Coughlin and told him that he must stop all his propaganda, on the air or by pen, for the duration. *Social Justice* should not be published again. The Archbishop wanted his word now. The alternative was being unfrocked. The priest agreed; and the Archbishop confirmed his understanding of the arrangement in a brief letter to the President. F.D.R. was delighted with the outcome. That was the end of Father Coughlin.

I have said that there was no condition attached to the exercise of the Archbishop's authority. Crowley, who did these things with finesse, never asked me for an assurance that no action would be taken against Father Coughlin if he were silenced, and I doubt whether the suggestion arose in his talk with Archbishop Mooney. But it was a matter of course between the two of us. The whole point of the arrangement was to avoid a trial. Archbishop Mooney's action was reported; and Marquis Childs in the St. Louis *Post-Dispatch* spoke of the Archbishop's letter to the President. But no word got about as to how this result had been achieved, and I doubt whether many people know about it today. *P.M.* and the "liberal" newspapers such as the New York *Post* and the Philadelphia *Record* were crying for Father Coughlin's scalp. Bob Allen of the *Record*—it was not long before he was to enlist, and lose an arm at the front—prodding me at one of my rare press conferences, demanded to know categorically whether I was protecting Father Coughlin because he was a priest—was he or was he not to be indicted? Why was he being treated differently from anyone else? I answered that it was a matter for the grand jury to decide, they were considering the case. "You mean they wouldn't indict, Mr. Attorney General, if you told them to? You don't really mean that, do you? . . ."

The administration was continually having trouble with the isolationist press, particularly the Chicago *Tribune*. These newspapers published material that was probably as seditious as anything put forth by *Social Justice*, although they were not anti-Semitic or rabble-rousing. In several instances we were tempted to take action. But I did so only once in a criminal presentment charging illegal use of secret information, and involving the Chicago *Tribune*, owned by Robert R. McCormick, the New York *News*, a tabloid owned by his cousin Joseph Medill Patterson, and the Washington *Times-Herald*, "Cissy" Patterson's paper.

Secretary of the Navy Frank Knox had granted the *Tribune* the privilege of having a special correspondent with the fleet in the Pacific—an unusual arrangement. This correspondent, Stanley Johnston, assigned to the *Barnett* during the battle of Midway, had come across a copy of a secret dispatch giving information obtained by breaking the Japanese naval code, and listing the Japanese vessels as they approached Midway. Pocketing the cable, he got it to the *Tribune's* office in Chicago, and on June 7, 1942, the newspaper published a list of the warships, and said that the strength of the Japanese forces "was well known in American naval circles several days before the battle began." The list of ships was so accurate that Japan must have known that her naval code had been deciphered, and at once changed it. We had lost an important advantage in the campaign for control of the Pacific Ocean.

A law adopted in 1940 made it a crime willfully to publish secret naval or military information, and provided that an offending newspaper should be prosecuted in the jurisdiction where it was published. The Navy was upset, and demanded that I prosecute immediately. I told Frank Knox that the essence of the case was the harm done to the national safety. Except for that, the violation of law was purely technical. It would be necessary therefore for me to put on witnesses to testify that the newspaper stories showed that we had broken the Japanese code. At first the Secretary and his associates demurred—it would be a mistake to make all this public. Very well, I said, I won't prosecute. Finally, however, after consultations with Admiral Stark, chief of naval operations, and other officers, Knox, with some reluctance, agreed this proof would be forthcoming; and I accordingly made arrangements to go before the grand jury in Chicago. I persuaded William D. Mitchell, who had served as Attorney General under President Hoover, and was one of the leading lawyers in the United States, to present and try the case. After studying the evidence for two weeks, he was convinced that we had a case *if* we could persuade the jury that the United States had been injured by the disclosure, but not otherwise. I again called Knox, who confirmed our understanding that we should present testimony to this effect. On August 7, I announced that the investigation had begun.

In the House of Representatives, Holland of Pennsylvania, a Democrat, assailed the three newspapers owned by the McCormick-Patterson families, as members of the "vermin press" which were preaching "defeatism" among our civilians and "mutiny" among our soldiers—they belonged to the same category as the Pelleys and Coughlins. In the Senate, Brooks of Illinois, a Republican who owed his election largely to the *Tribune,* denounced the investigation as a "smear" to defeat his re-election, instigated by Secretary Knox, whose paper, the Chicago *Daily*

News, competed with the *Tribune.* Representative Clare Hoffman introduced a resolution calling for an investigation of
Secretary Knox's motives, a suggestion which Secretary Harold
Ickes met by answering an obviously planted request for a comment at a press conference by saying that the Chicago *Tribune*
"not only had given aid and comfort to the enemy but is continuing to do so." Senator Taft assailed the investigation as
menacing the freedom of the press.

As Mitchell was developing the case in Chicago before the
grand jury Frank Knox telephoned me to say he had recon-
sidered the matter on further extended consultations, and that
as a result he had concluded that it would be a grave risk to the
protection of our naval code if the Japanese got word that we
had broken theirs. The United States must not put on any
evidence of this nature. He was terribly sorry . . . I was annoyed
and angry, and told him so; but there was nothing for me to do
but call up Mitchell in Chicago and explain the situation to him.
He was a good sport about it, and went through the form of
presenting the other evidence to the jury. The members of the
jury wanted to know whether they should be asked to indict the
correspondent and those responsible for publishing the story for
what apparently was a technical offense, without apparent damage to the national safety, particularly when the officers on the
ship were guilty of gross carelessness in letting a copy of the
cable lie around, and nothing was being done to them. They
resented the fact that Mitchell would not take them into his
confidence, and refused to indict.

The *Tribune* and Patterson papers were unusually restrained,
praising the fair way in which the case had been handled, and
there was no great stir anywhere largely owing to the fact that
Bill Mitchell had refused to say anything before the grand jury
had acted—and then only briefly. He stated that he had been
asked by the Attorney General to conduct an inquiry, and in so
doing to see that the grand jury had all the facts; this he had
done "as fully and fairly" as he knew how; "the jury had considered the case fully, and its conclusion that no violation of law
was disclosed settled the matter." He had conducted the whole
sorry business with dignity and fairness. I felt like a fool. It was
an instance of what so frequently occurs to public officers, where

a word that could at once clear up an ambiguous situation cannot, for the sake of the public good, be spoken. The irony of all this was that more than one newspaper, after the grand jury had acted, publicly mentioned the code in editorials, while the Department of Justice had to be silent in the secret proceedings before the jury. Jim Rowe sent me a memorandum, ending: "I do think the idiocy of the Navy should be pointed out to the President. It seems that everyone in the United States except the grand jury knows the facts."

THE DEPARTMENT
OF JUSTICE

❦❧ Chapter Sixteen

The Department of Justice had grown considerably since the days when the first Attorney General, my mother's great-grandfather, pointed out to Congress that he had need of at least one clerk, and President Washington had made his recommendations the basis of a special message—but Congress took no action. In 1934 the Department moved into its present quarters on Constitution Avenue, covering the block between Ninth and Tenth streets. When I took office it had about 35,000 employees.

The flow of letters to the Attorney General was substantial, always some from cranks, mothers of inmates, and criminals in asylums. Now and then came an appeal for legal advice. An individual from Pekin, Illinois, was worried about what would happen:

1. If a man sends money to a girl for her to use as traveling expenses to visit him, and also to visit other friends or relatives at the same time, could that be construed as a violation of any law?

Having introduced his theme, the gentleman became more specific:

2. If the girl uses the money to travel interstate, does visit

the man, spends a night out with him and "stays for breakfast," would this be construed as a violation of the Mann Act?

3. If this would be construed as a violation of the Mann Act, and were brought to the attention of the proper authorities, would prosecution be automatic or would it be necessary for some interested person to sign a complaint?

4. For what length of time afterwards would prosecution be possible?

Will you please answer each question separately?

They were interesting queries . . .

To run a big department effectively in the government two things are essential: the head of the department (and his first assistant) must keep his hand on the personnel, and know the details of his budget. Keeping a hand on personnel also meant knowing what was going on—who was being hired or fired, what was our relation on this count to the Hill, how were we working as an organization. It was seldom wise, for instance, wasting patronage on a Republican even if he had helped you get a controversial bill through the Judiciary Committee, as such a gesture made the other Republicans expectant and the Democrats mad since there were never enough plums to go around. The price you paid for being left free from the Hill and the chairman of the Democratic National Committee to appoint really competent men—and you had to distribute your favors between these two centers of power—was not very high if your assistant knew how to use the comparatively modest fraction of jobs that were at his disposal for this purpose.

To the outsider such considerations usually appear improper or irrelevant, although he seldom hesitates to use political influence to obtain a government contract. Part of the folklore of American society is that the politician—particularly when he is contrasted with that blameless figure, the businessman—seeks public service because he is incompetent to make a living in the hard field of business enterprise, and must be supported from the public purse since he cannot support himself. Nothing could be further from the truth. The world of politics produces unusual men, far more able to govern the country than the businessmen who almost always underrate them, naïvely identifying the ability to "meet a payroll" with the difficult and intricate art of governing the American people.

For smoothly-working administration the assistant to the A.G. should be his alter ego, his vicar for almost every conceivable matter, acting for him not only in matters political but sharing questions of policy, and sitting in from the beginning on decisions that are not routine. There was no position exactly corresponding to this in any other department, or even on the President's staff. An under secretary was of course comparable. But other departments did not have, either in kind or in amount, the same pressures brought to shape their work. There was the mass of litigation in which the government was involved; and almost every man who was indicted for tax violation, or ran into antitrust difficulties, or was discovered in a fraudulent bankruptcy, seemed to be able to get political as well as legal representation. The pressure was unending and never to be avoided. The load had to be taken off the Attorney General's back if he was to function at all.

From Jackson I inherited as Assistant Attorney General, Matthew F. McGuire, who was appointed to the District bench soon after I took office. He helped break me in, and when he was appointed was succeeded by James H. Rowe, Jr., who had begun his interesting and varied career as Justice Holmes' secretary the year the justice died. He finally became an administrative assistant to the President for three years before coming to me late in 1941. He knew the setup, knew everyone in the government on the Hill. He was aggressive, and could stand up and fight. He was a Catholic—and recognized and respected power. He had imagination, and employed it. He had a sense of humor that was wry and idiomatic. Cynical on the surface, he was romantic beneath it. He was interested in government on two levels: that of efficient administration, which he believed possible within unavoidable human limits; and in the play of politics, which he took to like a gull to water. He was obstinate within reasonable bounds, disliked not having his own way, believed that his chief should be permitted to deal with policy and that he, the Assistant Attorney General should run the Department; knew the necessity

Fig. 12

Sewell Avery, chairman of Montgomery Ward, being carried out of his office, 1944.

Wide World Photo

Fig. 13

The Attorney General and Philip Murray, president of the CIO; delegates at large from Pennsylvania at the Democratic Convention in Chicago in 1944.

Fig. 14
Francis and George Biddle at George's house at Croton-on-Hudson shortly after Francis' resignation as Attorney General in June, 1945. *Colten Photos, New York*

Fig. 15
Francis Biddle, American member of the International Military Tribunal, Nürnberg, 1946.

Fig. 16

Members of the International Military Tribunal hear indictment read as Nürnberg trials open. Left to right are: A. F. Volchkov, alternate for the USSR; Major General I. T. Nikitchenko, member USSR; Justice Birkett, alternate for Great Britain; Presiding Member, Lord Justice Lawrence, Great Britain; former Attorney General Francis Biddle, member for the U. S.; Judge John J. Parker, alternate, U. S.; Henri Dounedieu de Vabres, member for France; and Robert Falco, alternate for France.   *U. S. Army Photograph*

Fig. 17

Nazi defendants stare intently at a chart of the party organization introduced in the third day of the trial.   *U. S. Army Photograph*

Fig. 18

Hermann Goering entering the courtroom in the Palace of Justice for a morning session. Prisoners came up from the jail in this elevator, but Goering, because of his size, had to make a slight turn to negotiate the narrow doorway.

U. S. Army Photograph

Fig. 19

Rudolf Hess put in much of his time read Here his current interest is *Jugend* by Er Claes. *U. S. Army Photog*

Fig. 20

Francis Biddle reading a portion of the judgment at the Nürnberg trials.

U. S. Army Photograph

of publicity, had friends everywhere; was partisan; had strong
likes and dislikes. Ever since he came to work with me he has
proved a devoted and delightful friend.

I don't remember any segregation in the Department, although
in one instance a mild attempt at segregation was made. I had
finally wangled enough aluminum out of Donald Nelson, chairman of the War Production Board, to install virtually a new
cafeteria. I took a look at the plans before the work began. They
provided for a sort of segregation—some bright designer thought
it would be nice if the Negro help, who had been taking their
meals separately, had their own place to eat, in a corner of the
main room. I had the plans changed so that there should be no
distinction. And a few colored employees, when the changes
had been put into effect, rather shyly took their places at tables
where white employees were sitting. I asked my colored Department chauffeur how it worked. "Well," he said, "at first they
stared at us as if we were something that jumped out of a cage.
Now they don't pay any attention to it."

Dr. Alain Locke, a sensitive and cultivated Negro professor
of philosophy at Howard University, who had graduated from
Harvard two years before me, once told me that when he came
to Washington during the First World War the only restaurant
where a colored man could sit down for a meal with a white
man was at the Pennsylvania Railroad Station. Today every
hotel in the Capital and all theaters are open to both races. But
the change had hardly begun at the time I am describing, some
twenty years ago. Washington was a Southern city, and the
habit of Negro discrimination was strong. I was made an honorary
member of the Federal Bar Association, and I threatened to
resign when I heard that Negroes were being excluded. Before
long they were admitted, and no one any longer seemed to care.
We employed a few Negro lawyers, but not enough. The division heads, honestly showing a desire to increase the proportion, found it extremely hard to get well-trained Negro
lawyers.

In 1943 Jim felt he should join up, and served as intelligence
officer in the Navy, chiefly in the Pacific. He was cited for
gallantry in action while under fire on the carrier *Suwanee*
during an operation off the Japanese-held island of Leyte: *When*

an enemy fighter-bomber damaged his ship, causing extremely heavy casualties, he manned a fire hose, most of the trained firefighting crew having been decimated by the attack. With complete disregard for his own safety he advanced to the forward part of the flight deck and island, thus contributing materially to the saving of his ship.

James Patrick McGranery, who succeeded Rowe, was also an Irishman and a Catholic. He was one of the leaders of the New Deal group in the House, a Philadelphia lawyer whom I had known well for years. He was an excellent mixer, with a warm heart and fierce hatred for those whom he considered his enemies. He had a good deal of influence on the Hill, and could be trusted to handle a difficult personnel matter with a shrewd ability. He was made a district judge in 1946; and resigned from the bench to serve as Attorney General under President Truman during the last year of his administration. It was a wise move, for Jim is fundamentally an advocate, not a judge. He asked Herbert Wechsler and myself to join him when he returned to private practice in the District of Columbia in 1953. We were both tempted, but each for a different reason refused.

I found it hard to consider how any particular action of mine might affect my career—I never really thought of myself as having a career in public service—and both Jim Rowe and Jim McGranery were continually on the lookout to protect me from some inadvertent mistake. Washington was then, as it always is, full of intrigue, and I suppose I was rather innocent. I found it difficult to be suspicious, and did not recognize disloyalty until it slapped me in the face. There were of course the usual jealousies and jockeying for place. But there was also, I think, pride and *esprit de corps*. Most of my associates trusted me, as I did them, and were loyal to me, and believed in disinterested and competent work.

A group of human beings, organized or acting for a single purpose, takes on a life of its own, with the characteristics of a living organism. It may be religious, athletic, or political. To nourish and sustain this sense of life, touching it here and there in the individual member of the group, is at the heart of good administration.

One's responses to such a sense are soon tested. Three days after I had been sworn in as Attorney General I received a long anonymous letter, verging on the incoherent, which recited with indignant reiteration the wrong which the writer, who described herself as a young lady clerk in one of the divisions, wished me to believe she had suffered at the hands of another employee. She was careful to give no hint of how or where she could be discovered for future reference. Her accusations were definite and factual—he had borrowed money from her frequently, and not repaid it. He was a liar, and undependable—everyone in the Department knew that, said she. He had treated other girls that way; and from the final accusation—now less specific and more agitated—I gathered "that way" was intended to indicate that he had loved and left her, apparently still on the premises.

I sent for the young man who had been thus accused, asked him to sit down, and handed him the letter. He read it slowly, the blood mounting to his head and suffusing his face. He looked up at me, crestfallen and unhappy. "I know who wrote this," he said. I put out my hand for the letter, and tore it up. "I'm not interested in anonymous letters," I said. I stood up and held out my hand again. "But I thought you had better know about it." From that moment I could count on his devotion.

It was largely in order to bring Edgar Hoover more into the center of things that I arranged weekly policy conferences. His bureau was in essence a service organization for the other divisions, investigating facts and preparing cases for trial. He was not concerned with policy decisions, and eschewed them, taking the position that the investigator should not draw conclusions from the evidence. This constituted a broad and safe defense against criticism, and tended, I think, to add to the efficiency of his work, and to take it out of the temptations of politics. But he was too valuable a man not to use in discussing and determining departmental policy. It was a small group—Charles Fahy, the Solicitor General; Jim McGranery; Hugh Cox, who, as Assistant Solicitor General, drafted my opinions to the President; Herbert Wechsler, who ran the War Division; and Edgar. The Council, as we called it, met regularly once a week for an hour. There were often sharp differences of opinion which, thus openly voiced, tended toward greater understanding and a better solution of the problems involved.

For nearly twenty years Hoover had been director of the Bureau, and his admirable record, at all times clear of any breath of corruption, had made him a career man in the truest sense, unaffected by changes in administration. His appointment was by the Attorney General, not for a term of years but during good behavior; and no Attorney General would have thought of discharging him.

Edgar Hoover's character interested me. He had already achieved an extraordinary reputation as an expert in his field, which since then has not failed to grow. In Washington public figures come and go—Presidents and congressmen, Cabinet members and diplomats: Hoover remains. The myth that has gathered around him crowned him as indispensable. Chief Justice Stone had appointed him when Stone was Attorney General; and Stone gave me a key to Hoover's complex character: if Hoover trusted you he would be absolutely loyal; if he did not, you had better look out; and he had to get used to his new chief each time.

I had come into office with the stamp of a "liberal," and Hoover must have suspected that I would be too soft, particularly now that a war was on; too soft with Communists—so many liberals had not yet realized what the Communists were after. I think the word "liberal" included in his mind a large number of individuals whose views were considered radical by the conservatives of church and state. and carried a sense of irresponsibility. Temperamentally Hoover was a conservative, although such an easy classification hardly describes a temperament which was clearly not reflective or philosophic. Edgar Hoover was primarily a man of immediate action.

I sought to invite his confidence; and before long, lunching alone with me in a room adjoining my office, he began to reciprocate by sharing some of his extraordinarily broad knowledge of the intimate details of what my associates in the Cabinet did and said, of their likes and dislikes, their weaknesses and their associations. It was as if he were saying to me that he trusted me enough to know that I would not repeat information which, except to his Chief, it would have been highly indiscreet of him to communicate, and would have been embarrassing had his revelation been communicated to the V.I.P. whom it concerned. Edgar was not above relishing a story derogatory to an occupant of one of the seats of the mighty, particularly if the little great man was pompous or stuffy. And I confess that, within limits, I enjoyed hearing it. His reading of human nature was shrewd, if perhaps colored with the eye of an observer to whom the less admirable aspects of behavior were being constantly revealed.

He knew how to flatter his superior, and had the means of making him comfortable. The Attorney General, when he was traveling, could count on an agent to meet him at the station, to settle him on his plane with an armful of newspapers, to take him in an FBI car wherever he wished to go. But he also showed a friendly thoughtfulness on more than one occasion when it was not called for, and made me feel that our relationship was not without cordiality on both sides.

When I was in Nürnberg in 1945 serving on the International Military Tribunal, Hoover did something for my wife, which I cannot forget. My son Randolph, who was in the Army, was down with a bad attack of malaria in a Chinese hospital. Through the intercession of Bob Lovett, then Assistant Secretary of War for Air, he had been brought home, and Katherine had taken him to Tucson in Arizona. She returned to Washington after a few weeks, leaving him in the West, and ran into a severe snowstorm as the train, almost twelve hours late, drew into Washington in the early hours of a wet and howling morning. There were no porters, no taxis: but an FBI agent was there to meet her on the train and take her home. Hoover apparently had kept himself in touch with her movements.

I suppose these things are trivial, and I cite them to show a human side of Edgar Hoover with which he is not always credited. To be efficient to a degree not achieved by other men has built up a figure in the public imagination that excludes the warmth as well as the weaknesses of other men. And his absolute self-control strengthens the image. Behind the control is, I suspect, a temper that might show great violence if he did not hold it in on leash, subject to the domination of a will that is the master of his temperament. Of course, like all men of action, he cares for power and more power; but unlike many men it is power bent to the purpose of his life's work—the success of the Federal Bureau of Investigation.

External standards make the safest judge of character, and Hoover must be described in the light of his work. Can the reader recall any other American police force about which there has never been a breath of corruption? He has been head of the FBI now for almost forty years, and its slate is clean. There have been suggestions of the use of third degree—that terrible cancer which seems at one time or another to attack those whose duty it is to keep order. But Roger Baldwin, for many years director of the American Civil Liberties Union, after investigation, reported that the suggestions were without basis of fact.

Talk to a police captain who has been trained in an FBI school, and he will tell you that those six weeks gave him a professional outlook and experience that he could have found nowhere else. The Bureau's efficiency has been built up without the use of civil service, like the TVA, and both government agencies have furnished outstanding benefits to the country, chiefly on account of the ability and singleness of purpose of the men at the top.

Hoover prided himself on working co-operatively with the local police, and it must have been peculiarly distasteful to him to develop, in the deep South, evidence of the maltreatment of Negroes on which to bring prosecutions, in many cases against local police who had joined in violating some constitutional rights. Yet when I discussed these cases with him, suggesting that he might add to his reputation by thus espousing the liberal cause, he raised no objection to making test cases, although we both knew that his success might be at the price of intense resentment of such "Yankee interference." Without his co-operation the test cases would have never been put together.

Hoover has had immense appropriations for his work and has achieved a position of power which no other man in public service has wielded so long or with such universal approval. Yet I do not believe his power has corrupted his work; and I venture to think that withholding power—a practice so deeply inherent in democracies—may often prove more corrupting than its grant. That, however, is a generality that I begin to doubt as soon as

I see it on paper. In this particular claim I do believe that the immense authority which Edgar Hoover has been given is justified by the record. I know his weaknesses—his passion for the limelight, his obsession with the Communists that tends to include in his net fish that are hardly worth catching, his hypersensitiveness to any criticism of his beloved Bureau. But the limelight, so skillfully used, is an asset of his success, and his preachings about the Communists are not without value in our so easygoing American ideology. Weighed against his concrete achievements they do not tip the scales.

A more disturbing question is the future use of this great machine of detection with its ten million personal files, its reputation grown sacrosanct—human agencies should court criticism rather than wear halos—its obvious possibilities of misusing the trust it has won. When Hoover resigns or retires or dies, what will happen—can the same freedom be given to another man, the virtual freedom from control? I do not believe it can. But the tradition of good work over these long years will carry it along and perhaps hold it above the corruption and misdirection which has infested so many police forces. A successor to Hoover must be found who is outstandingly competent, but who is also humane.

Some divisions ran themselves; or to put it more fairly were so well run that they needed little supervision. I think particularly of two; the Tax Division under Sam Clark (a brother of Charles Edward Clark, now senior judge of the Second Circuit), who had graduated with a *magna cum* from the Yale Law School in 1928; and the Claims Division (now the Civil Division) headed by Frank Shea. Sam Clark was friendly, polite, and thoroughly informed about every case of importance. His politeness did not prevent him from saying no to a congressman. I soon established a general rule not to discuss a pending case with anyone outside the Department without the head of the appropriate division sitting in. The facts were seldom accurately reported by the congressman who came to see me; and when Clark would straighten him out he usually agreed that nothing could be done. Before very long the reputation of a particular division would be established—a tradition for incorruptibility

(not the phrase used by the congressman) that made a visit to
the Attorney General a waste of time, except for the record.

With Clark and Shea I could rely not only on their scrupu-
lousness and competence, but on their choice of personnel.
Frank Shea would visit the Harvard or Yale or Columbia Law
School each year to pick out top honor men for his needs.

Charles Fahy was Solicitor General with me through the war
years (he is now a member of the Court of Appeals of the
District), and was respected and liked by the members of the
Supreme Court. His arguments were like tentative judicial
opinions advanced for the consideration of the Court. He was
not, like me, a convinced advocate, but balanced and objective,
developing the government's point of view with such quiet skill
and fairness that it was sometimes hard to realize that he was
representing the United States.

During my first year in office the eager flame of reform burned
more brightly in my bosom than later, when greater experience
with the ways of Congress had somewhat dimmed its luster.
One could do something, but not all at once, not very quickly,
probably not very fundamentally, and only with infinite patience
and constant rebuffs. It was not hard to get good men, for everyone who could not join the Armed Forces was eager to work
in some way for the government. The difficulty was to get rid
of the dead wood. If an individual had been serving his country
for even a few years ("eating out of the public trough" was
the other way of putting it) he achieved a certain vested right
that was difficult to dislodge, and was recognized and supported by the congressmen, even if he had no particular political claim to protection. There he was and there he would
stay.

I well remember an instance of this after I had been in office
about a year. Eager to save money and particularly manpower,
I decided, after a study by the Bureau of the Budget and much
consultation, to eliminate the Bonds and Spirits Division, which
had been set up to enforce the Prohibition law, and had lingered
on as a sort of vermiform appendix in the body politic long after
its usefulness had disappeared. I transferred what mild activities
it had been engaged in, connected with certain revenue laws,

to the Claims Division, and places were found for some of its personnel, although in most cases at lower salaries. The Division had employed thirty lawyers and as many clerks, and the savings were substantial—about $150,000 a year. A good deal of pressure was brought to find a position for the director, who had been in charge since Bonds and Spirits was founded; but I was not willing to appoint him to any position carrying a similar salary, and he left.

One lawyer, drawing excessive pay—$8000 a year if I remember rightly—to perform some trifling clerical job, was dropped, turned out to have been under the protection of the redoubtable Senator Kenneth Douglas McKellar of Tennessee. In twenty-four hours that worthy burst into my office, sweeping by my frightened appointment clerk, his gray hair flying in the wind, the black bow string cravat that he invariably wore askew, breathing fire and brimstone. Why had not he been consulted? The man was his friend, his schoolmate, and I was throwing him out on a cruel world, not even trying to find another place for him. Senator McKellar had been in the Senate since 1926, and was chairman of the subcommittee that had charge of the appropriation of the Department of Justice. He was not therefore a man lightly to offend. I waited until the storm had blown over—he was glowering at me and breathing heavily—and then said, "Why did you not tell me, Senator, he was a friend of yours?"

"I thought you'd have known!" he snorted.

"With thirty-five thousand employees?"

"Well, somebody ought to have known."

"But Senator, mistakes will happen."

It took a little time to cool him off, to quiet him down, to flatter him into friendliness. When he was amiable again, I suggested that we could find a job for his friend somewhere, but at that salary level it would be difficult. When I told him what we paid his friend he was genuinely shocked, not by the waste to the government, but to think of such a snug berth going to someone who, after all, was nothing but a friend. He declared that the gentleman in question was not worth half of that; and when I suggested that we might pay him such a sum he nodded his head in satisfaction—that would do very nicely, there was no good exaggerating things. After that we got on admirably. When I wanted help, if there was no conflict of interest, he gave it to me, and now and then he would get an appointment. He was one of the most powerful men in the Senate—obstinate, vindictive, shrewd—and he never forgot. But these qualities are not uncommon. Like a dozen other Senators his influence came from one source, his seniority.

There were a few untouchables, like Senator McKellar's classmate. They are found not only in every branch of government, but in every large business, where nepotism corresponds to political protection, with approximately the same results. The world would be very different without its quota of such favorites, a world in which every executive would act on a cool moral level from which the temptations of friendship were excluded and the claims of blood ignored.

One of the most picturesque of the untouchables was Mary Ward. With limitless ambition and a matching vitality she never stopped talking until she got what she wanted. She had been kept comparatively peaceable by a position in the Immigration Service. When Earl Harrison, the commissioner, discovered that she did nothing justifying her retention, he wanted to fire her and appealed to me, since her job was by no means clerical. I had never heard of Mary, but soon did from Jim Rowe, to whom I referred Earl's suggestion.

Mary Ward—Jim reported in one of his inimitable memoranda—was once a Democratic politician with some weight in Massachusetts. Being one of the faithful she was properly rewarded as Commissioner of Immigration, in the days when they had District Commissioners. She got along all right because she had nothing to do and people liked her. When the reorganization plans came along, the President quite logically abolished these useless jobs. He soon heard from Mary on the subject, and since he takes his orders from her just like the rest of us, she was quickly back on the payroll where she has resided ever since, with the exception of sporadic efforts by the Department of Justice to get rid of her. We almost got her once. Schofield fired her, Matt McGuire backed him up, and when she got to the White House, I backed Matt up. It was a terrifying experience, and I still wonder how I had the courage

to go through with it. You would not understand unless you had
been face to face with Mary. Bob Jackson left town when he
heard she was coming . . . Mary had six Democratic Congressmen from Massachusetts working at top speed for her
. . . It was much easier to push Presidents around than explain
to Mary that really she shouldn't be on the payroll if she
wouldn't do any work. I recall having an impression that Mary
drove the Congressmen down Pennsylvania Avenue in tandem,
much like a dog team with Mary cracking the whip.

To be brief and succinct the President signed a truce of
unconditional surrender. Mary went back on the payroll, and
there she stays . . . Before you fire her I suggest you have the
signature of the President, of the esteemed Democratic Chairman, and of your honorable self on one piece of paper, in the
form of a ukase . . . If you decide to fire her, please give me
advance warning—so I can get out of town . . .

When Ugo Carusi succeeded Harrison as commissioner he
sent for Mary Ward, talked over the situation with her, and she
promptly and pleasantly, to everyone's surprise, tendered her
resignation.

Our difficulties with members of the Congress were not, however, confined to patronage. They got into trouble now and then
and expected to be treated considerately by members of their
party in the executive departments of the government. I remember particularly two cases of powerful members of the
House who had overstepped the limits of innocent behavior.
Against the first, Edward Eugene Cox of Georgia, ranking member of the powerful Rules Committee, and, except for Speaker
Sam Rayburn, as influential as any member of the House, no
action was taken. He was a bitter foe of the New Deal and opposed most of the measures backed by the administration. The
other, James Michael Curley of Boston, one of President Roosevelt's ardent and effective supporters, was indicted, convicted,
and sent to jail.

Cox, a shareholder in the corporation which owned station
WALB, tried to persuade the Federal Communications Commission to renew its license, and his letters to the commission
were a matter of record. At the time the FCC was under in-

vestigation by a committee of the House of which Cox was chairman, and of which the obvious purpose was to "get" James Lawrence Fly, the chairman of FCC. The FBI investigation showed that Cox received a check for $2500 after the license was granted. The president of the corporation told the agent who investigated that the fee was a retainer for future services, and that Mr. Cox had received nothing for the work he had done in getting the license renewed. If the fee had been for services rendered, Cox would have been guilty of a crime, punishable by a $10,000 fine and two years in jail, under a statute which forbade congressmen to accept compensation for practicing before federal agencies. Since payment of the fee had been in Georgia the United States District Court in that state had jurisdiction. It was suggested that he might also be indicted in the District of Columbia; but it was improbable that the District had jurisdiction. He would not have been convicted by any Georgia jury. In fact a judge in that state might have directed a verdict for Cox on the ground that the only evidence as to guilt was in favor of Cox—the statement of his client that payment had been for future services. If we had brought criminal proceedings and lost—as appeared almost certain—there was no telling to what extent his retaliation might have injured the Department and the administration.

I decided, after long and anxious consideration and discussion with my associates, not to bring the case before a grand jury. It was a hard decision to make. The papers would have applauded my fortitude in going after a congressman, or called my action vindictive (the FCC had supplied a good deal of the evidence against Cox), depending on their political slant. As it was, most of those that commented used pretty strong language. The Washington *Post* spoke of my "pusillanimity," and talked about "weak-kneed officials who lack the stamina to stand out against corruption and smearing" when politics were involved.

The case weighed on my conscience, particularly on those rare occasions when I ran into the Honorable Cox at a Democratic convention or dinner—and he would greet me with a grateful cordiality, and ask where I had been keeping myself—words that touched my face like a kiss of degradation. Many of my friends were unhappy about the decision. Bob Allen told Charlie

Malcomson, my press relations officer, that I was too God-
damned decent—"for a real fighting man when the going gets
rough give me a slugger like Corcoran, Ickes or Hugo Black.
They know how to dish it out."

Curley, besides being prominent in local and state politics,
had been half a dozen times elected a member of the House. He
had been mayor of Boston and governor of Massachusetts. His
chief business activities appeared to be as a director of the
Hibernia Savings Bank and in connection with the Curley Luck
Gold Company. He was convicted with half a dozen others in
the District of Columbia for using the United States mail to
defraud the public. His profit had been trifling, his activities
hardly more than lending his name to promote a fraud. When
I told the President that we would put the evidence before
the grand jury he was a little startled. Curley had always been
loyal to him, he said, he was an important figure in Massachusetts politics. "I'd like to give him a break, if it were
possible." "What sort of a break?" I asked him. He thought for a
moment. "Would he be permitted to appear before the grand
jury on his own behalf? He's very persuasive." I could see no
objection if he wanted to submit himself to examination; it was
a little unusual. Curley appeared before the grand jury shortly
afterward. He did not testify, but made a speech about himself
for an hour. The jury promptly indicted him.

The pressure from the Democratic politicians to have the case
dropped was strong—it was as if I had betrayed my friends. The
President stood firm, refused to interfere, or to discuss the matter. He sent me a letter Curley had written him, with the
notation: "for your eyes only, and for personal preparation of a
reply." Yet the letter would not have injured the President if it
had been made public. "I have hesitated," Curley wrote, "to
write to you about my problem, which is meaningless as contrasted with your major ones, but to me personally it is monu-
mental . . . Four of my sons are in the armed service and one
a novice in the Jesuit Order, and you, a father like myself, can
well appreciate the seriousness of the infamous charges levied
against me . . . A dear friend, outraged by the false and cruel
charge, recalled to me the words of Shakespeare in the address
of Cardinal Wolsey to Cromwell—'Had I served my God with

one-half the fervor that I served my King, he would not leave
me in my old age naked before mine enemies.'" It was a shrewd
insinuation. Curley was confident, he added, that the lines of
Shakespeare would never be applicable to a friendship extending back nearly a third of a century. I advised the President
that the letter should remain unanswered; and enclosed him a
colorless answer if he decided to answer it, to the effect that
he felt certain that the issues would be fairly and promptly
determined.

But Curley's account of the episode in his autobiography,
I'd Do It Again, is very different. Apparently he believed that
the President was "behind" the persecution: no mere Attorney
General would have dared to strike so high. When charges were
made against a congressman, he says, the procedure was for
the Attorney General to bring them to the attention of the
President who would "table" them. In this case, he continues,
Attorney General Anthony Drexel Biddle (sic), "getting a green
light from F.D.R.," gave instructions to bring in the evidence before the grand jury. Roosevelt was out to get the big city bosses,
Tom Pendergast, Ed Kelly of Chicago, and Frank Hague—and
"Curley apparently was next on the list . . . I had never truckled
to the man," he writes proudly, "and I told the press after my
indictment that I had refused to be a rubber stamp while serving
as a member of Congress." Indictments and threats could not
deter him from doing what was best for the American people.
. . . Curley adds that he went to a congressional reception at
the White House and told the President he ought to have the
case thrown out of court; and that the President said he was
not a dictator—if he were he would have it thrown out. Curley
was satisfied that the President alone was "responsible for fram-
ing" him—he still bore Curley a grudge because Curley had
once "declined the Ministry to Poland," and had criticized the
President sharply on many occasions.

How can one ever trust the history books if the principal
characters involved vary so widely in their accounts?

But the mayor's triumphal return to Boston after his conviction
on January 18, 1946, cannot be questioned. As he puts it: "Brass
bands and thousands of cheering supporters met me at South
Station; tied up traffic for nearly an hour, and followed me

home in a noisy motorcade, while a band played *Hail the Conquering Hero Comes.*" While serving his sentence of six to eighteen months at the federal prison at Danbury, he was re-elected mayor of Boston. "Bostonians," Howard Brubaker dryly remarked in *The New Yorker*, "have again disproved the charge that they are narrow-minded people. They can see merits in James M. Curley not visible to anyone else." An extraordinary man, Curley—eloquent, persuasive, popular, Irish to the bone, and a true son of the Church, which he must have regarded as a kind of benign political organization. "Thanks, dear God . . ." he remembers saying when informed of his pardon by President Truman.

ANTITRUST
ENFORCEMENT

❦⟨⟩❧ Chapter Seventeen

The vital need of production for war soon ran into the enforcement of the antitrust laws under the agile and ubiquitous hands of Thurman Arnold. Graduating from the Harvard Law School in 1914, he practiced in Chicago and in Laramie, Wyoming; taught at the College of Law of West Virginia University and at Yale; and for five years had been Assistant Attorney General in charge of antitrust violations. His energy was prodigious. He knew how to get at the evidence which showed price-fixing (in itself an infringement of the statute), the illegal use of patents to control production, combinations seeking to dominate the market, or cartels providing for territorial agreements excluding outside competition. It was really very simple, and Thurman perfected the method if he did not invent it. When a company would not let the government inspect its books and correspondence, Thurman asked a grand jury to begin a criminal investigation, and that body would issue subpoenas for so many files that were in confidential or constant use that it soon became advisable to let Thurman's investigators in without resistance.

Thurman had a remarkable staff of men to help him. There were as many economists as there were lawyers. They were not particularly intellectual—I doubt if many of them had read

Kafka; they were not addicted to any particular ideology, and in their hours of leisure did not pursue the higher pleasures of the mind. But they were young, they were vigorous, and they liked to prepare cases and to win them.

Thurman's small-business advisory section helped the little fellows on antitrust problems, and—a service particularly popular during the defense effort and the war—how to deal with the government under the tangle of new orders and procedures, so perplexing and confusing. He took up their problems and usually straightened them out with war agencies like the Priority Section of the Office of Production Management. He got the government to redraft specifications for bidding that excluded small concerns and could only be met by the great ones.

When the war came and his staff had less to do, he began to supply the Board of Economic Warfare with information about Axis production, the availability of raw materials, and bombing objectives, which he had gathered in his investigations of foreign cartels. The British Ministry of Economic Warfare soon began to send him specific requests for information. His reports would indentify geographical landmarks in the Stuttgart area with photographs and maps attached, in Berlin, in Danzig, and on the Hamburg docks and the Ploesti oil fields. Or he would furnish information on the Japanese machine-tools and light-metals industries volunteered by the engineer who had built Japanese aluminum plants. Details on the capacities of high-frequency electric crucible furnaces used in the production of ferro-alloy steels in the Axis countries were supplied by a Philadelphia company producing this type of furnace under a license agreement from a Swedish firm . . . and so it would go. The description for bombings was surprisingly exact: the Bleischarley mine was the focal point for blasting the zinc operations in Upper Silesia, and the crucial spot was "the elevated head frame with hoisting machines situated at the top"—if this were destroyed it would take four or five months of day and night construction work to replace the equipment and resume operations. The mine was destroyed. It was a small world.

Thurman was a born politician. He had been elected mayor of Laramie, and had served two terms in the Wyoming legislature so that the professionals—which in Washington means the members of Congress—respected him. He had entrenched himself on the Hill firmly as soon as he arrived. If the Attorney General tried to limit his field or control his pronouncements, the Attorney General would shortly hear from some powerful Senator—they were behind Thurman on both sides of the political line. It was essential to back him unless you were ready for a first-rate row.

I believed in the theory of the act (always with a small hesitant doubt in the back of my head), and its enforcement. Bob Jackson was more doubtful, and went along halfheartedly, and during his year as Attorney General was continually nervous about what Thurman would do next. I think this apprehension was unfounded; but the two men did not get along too smoothly, and Jackson before he left warned me to watch Thurman. As a matter of fact Thurman was the one who was watching me; and when he saw that I was behind him, there was no one more co-operative. I do not mean that life with Thurman, as I styled it at a dinner in his honor when he resigned to go on the Court, was peaceable or without surprises and occasional irritations. But on the whole we saw eye to eye, and both felt that enforcement should be on as tenacious a scale as our budget and personnel would permit.

Nor should it altogether be turned off during the war; for in war things must be done quickly and the orders go to the big boys who come out far stronger at the end than they were before. Technological improvements are forced by manpower shortage, and only the most powerful corporations can take advantage of the new kinds of mass production. But while small businesses still exist it is worth the effort to sustain them in order to delay —if for no other reason—a too complete and sudden uprooting of our long ingrained way of living by the comparatively new mass culture.

After a year of war, steel, chemicals, and textiles began to grumble. How could they get their work done and the material off the assembly lines if they had a score of New Deal reformers in the office, asking for this letter, messing round in the files, probing and nosing around, while Army and Navy people were on the company's back to speed production? Even before the war, immunity from action by the government under the Sherman Law was occasionally granted, and this arrangement was formalized by statute not long after war had been declared. Where a manufacturer complained that a suit would interfere with the war effort and requested postponement, the antitrust division took up the request with John Lord O'Brian, general counsel for the War Production Board. At that point the matter was usually settled. If there was no agreement, and this happened less than a dozen times—it was referred to the Secretary of War (or the Secretary of the Navy) and the Attorney General for decision. The whole procedure was prompt, informal, and highly successful. It eased tensions, and responded to the reasonable demands of manufacturers. The satisfactory result was chiefly owing to John O'Brian's wise and informed judgment. He was soft-spoken, open-minded, and prompt: and his experience in antitrust enforcement under prior administrations had given him a sympathetic view toward these attempts to break up restraints of trade and monopolies.

I have cited these procedures in somewhat tedious detail because they seem to me to illustrate rather aptly the Anglo-Saxon genius for using compromise as the chief tool of government.

But gradually the progress of the war crippled Thurman's efforts. It was not only that the trials of more and more cases were being postponed, but that he lost a large part of his staff. Because they were young the war took many of them. Restless and immensely energetic, used to living under the stimulus of high pressure, he did not have enough to do, and when, at my suggestion, the President offered him a place on the Circuit Court for the District of Columbia, he accepted, although with some hesitation. He was on the bench for two years before plunging into an active and varied private practice. The dinner in his honor was attended by a large number of the business tycoons he had been prosecuting, many of whom were destined to become his clients when he went back to practice. The whole affair was incredible—an epitome of the folklore of the American business world that Thurman so wittily satirized in *The Folklore of Capitalism.* Almost every speaker recited worn-out platitudes. Henry Kaiser stumbled through a tedious piece obviously constructed for him by an overworked public relations man; and Joe Martin's effort, in the congressional style, was so dull that

Henry Mencken, when it was over, sadly shook his head as he mourned the decline of American demagoguery. . . .

Six years ago some of my former associates in the Department of Justice, with a few other friends, gave me a surprise dinner on the occasion of my seventieth birthday. Thurman presented me for the occasion with a silver mug on which was inscribed: "From one of the world's two greatest living ex-judges to the other."

Americans like to have their cake—and eat it. An example of that preference is found in the way business, big and little, subscribes without hesitation to the principle of free competition. But when, acting under a law that had been on the statute books for many years, we tried to make effective that ideal condition by bringing bills in equity to cut Gordian knots that prevented the free play of the absolute law (as they believed it to be) of supply and demand, or sought to punish the offenders by criminal action (I do not remember any case during my administration in which prison terms were imposed or asked by the government), the business world cried out in the name of free enterprise that we were stifling industry! What they wanted was freedom from interference with their right to suppress competition. If they had said competition is outmoded, the small unit out of date, the giants should run the show—that would have been arguable. But in a democracy they could not very well proclaim that small business was no good. So they announced from the house tops their belief in the little fellows, or more accurately at the meetings of the Chambers of Commerce, even if in private they did not believe in them, putting their obeisance to the little man, as it were, in the plate which was passed around for the Sunday collection, to pay the toll required to give them an open road for the other six days of the week.

F.D.R. distrusted businessmen and the philosophy of businessmen. It was not merely because they feared and fought him at every step, but because he knew their insensitiveness to human and individual values. Of course he made exceptions, and would have liked their support, and occasionally courted it. But he believed that there could never be any peace with them except on terms that he could not accept. They had become used to running the government and they ran it with their power concentrated, pervasive, and alert, slipping into the vacuum that is always created when those in whose hands political power is vested fail to use it. It had happened under Harding, when the political powers not only stepped aside but welcomed the business marauders to join them in collecting the loot. Under his successor, Calvin Coolidge, whose philosophy of withdrawal was matched by his passive temperament and personal distaste for hard work or careful thinking, the process continued, shorn of its spectacular dishonesty. And Hoover, slipping into the depression, covering the weakness of his leadership by resort to the old shibboleths of *laissez faire*, was temperamentally unable to act with the imaginative vigor that would have made him disregard the maxims on which he had been brought up. When it came to President Eisenhower's turn twenty-five years later, he saw—but not until after his first term was over and he had begun his second—that it was necessary to fight in order to bring about the moderate measures that he advocated and which he had once naïvely assumed his party also wished to see enacted. A trained commander in the military field, he had no conception of how to do battle in this confusing jungle of business and politics. And meanwhile the business interests flowed back into the vacuum which his initial stepping aside had created—a sort of constitutional bow to the principle of the separation of political power, while he waited, hat in hand, as they swept through the gates.

I have never been able to make up my mind as to just what attempts to enforce the antitrust laws have accomplished. The freer and more dynamic any economy is, the more quickly combinations that restrain trade will develop, born of cut-throat competition. Justice Holmes used to say that the theory of the act was that you must compete, but no one would be allowed to win the competition. For to win a competitor will of course try to destroy or swallow its rivals. That is the law of nature. But laws of nature are not sacred, and human society will inevitably try to tame the jungle in which it seems destined to live. However, the Sherman Act would preserve a partial jungle lest civilization make us stagnant, and our incentives to destroy and to swallow be atrophied. The antitrust laws have come more and more to be used not merely to outlaw combinations in restraint of trade and monopolies, but to watch and regulate them to the extent of keeping them from reverting to their former dominant positions. The Court often keeps jurisdiction over a suit, perhaps for several years, and sees that the provisions of its decrees are carried out.

We know almost nothing about the effect of antitrust enforcement on the American economy. To most Americans antitrust enforcement has meant protection from the inroads of monopolies on their business opportunities. Recently (1958) The Twentieth Century Fund published a study of this effect in twenty industries. Except for the statement that there is nearly unanimous agreement that American antitrust policy is sound, but that such a policy applied to Europeans would not meet their needs, the committee, appointed to review the study and consider the problems that it disclosed, permitted themselves no other generalities, but underscored the need of finding answers to a good many practical questions: Why have cartelized Germany and Switzerland been so prosperous? Is it possible to disentangle the effects of antitrust policies from other causes? What types of enforcement are the most successful? On what grounds should enforcement be based?

I don't know . . . I am inclined to think that this miraculous American economy has flourished more potently than others partly because the feeling against big business, against consolidations, trusts, and monopolies expressed in the Sherman and Clayton laws, has tended to keep the economy a little more open, a little more alive. But when I am tempted into such a generality I am apt to pull back and limit it in certain fields and for certain periods of time. I do not know what the suits against Standard Oil and the tobacco companies, and the dissolution of producers of movies from the ownership and operation of theaters, have accomplished.

But one such proceeding, decided finally in favor of the government by the Supreme Court, was salutory—the civil suit against the Associated Press asking the court to declare it a monopoly, and to set aside those provisions of its bylaws that effectively prevented competition.

Of the three newspaper services in the United States the AP was by far the largest, with its 1400 newspaper members, hundred "bureaus" in the United States, and large staff of correspondents abroad. It was a highly successful and efficient cooperative, incorporated in 1900 to furnish its members with news. But it was not open to all alike. No newspaper could be elected over the objection of a competitor; and from 1929 to 1941 four efforts to obtain AP franchises by election failed. Nor could the AP or any of its members furnish news to anyone not a member. Moreover the costs might be prohibitive. An amendment to the bylaws required that an applicant publishing in the same field (morning or evening) as an existing member should pay to the association for distribution to the member affected a sum of money (based on a complicated formula) which, in Chicago, would amount to from $400,000 to $600,000, and in New York to a million or a million and a half. The Chicago *Sun* had been unable to purchase a morning membership, to be used only for Sunday circulation, for $250,000. The result was to prevent the competition of new papers starting. If a paper folded, none took its place. The public was served in most cities by one morning and one evening paper only, and often limited to a single point of view.

All this we set forth in a bill of complaint, finally filed in New York in the late summer of 1942, charging a conspiracy in restraint of trade and a monopoly by the Associated Press, its board of directors, and the newspapers with which the directors were affiliated, which included such powerful publications as the Chicago *Daily Tribune*, the Baltimore *Sun*, the Philadelphia *Evening Bulletin*, the Cleveland *Plain Dealer*, the Atlanta *Constitution*, the Washington *Evening Star*, and the Kansas City *Star*. Three very able judges sat in New York in the trial of the case—Learned Hand, Augustus Hand and Thomas Walter Swann, all from the Court of Appeals of the Second Circuit.

As was to be expected, editorial comment was critical and partisan: the President wanted to control the press; the case smelled of bias; the country was being regimented; Mr. Roosevelt's obsequious Justice Department was seeking revenge; the

suit was an attempt to punish this great news-gathering agency
for refusing a franchise to Marshall Field's pro-administration
Chicago *Sun,* which was not a legitimate newspaper, but "part of
an alien and radical conspiracy against our Republican form of
government." Mr. David Lawrence in his gloomy column put
forward the suggestion that perhaps a communal press, regu-
lated as to every detail of its operation by the government, was
in prospect. There was talk in Congress about an investigation.

Our action was not a last-minute move on the part of the
government. The AP had been given every opportunity to mend
its ways. There had always been doubt as to the legality of
its setup, and John G. Johnson had refused at the time it was
organized to give an opinion that it was free from the taint of
illegality under the Sherman Law. Almost two years before suit
was instituted two applications for membership were made, and
both refused by the board—the Chicago *Sun,* and Eleanor Medill
Patterson's Washington *Times-Herald.* Thereupon the Department formally notified the AP that the refusal conflicted with
the law. In April, 1943, Thurman Arnold presented to the AP
board at its annual meeting a written statement, outlining the
Department's views in detail. As a result, the bylaws were
amended to eliminate the rights of protest, and substitute a
majority for a four-fifths vote for election of members. On paper
this seemed a large concession. But it was not—as immediately
appeared when the *Sun* and *Times-Herald* again applied and
were again rejected. We believed that any newspaper should
be admitted that could and did pay its proportional cost for
AP services. Accordingly, Arnold, with my approval, which was
required before an antitrust suit could be filed, notified the AP
that he was authorized to proceed. Again he presented his views
to the board.

Several months before the suit was filed Robert McLean, who
was president of the AP, dropped in to see me, and to persuade
me that it would be a grave mistake to bring such an action in
time of war when we should all unite and forget our differences.
We were old friends, but every angle had been discussed *ad
nauseum,* and there was nothing new to say. I had come to the
conclusion, after studying the case carefully, that we should win,
and that there was no reason for further postponement. I had

received the President's blessing before giving my approval to Thurman. Later that afternoon Bob came back, beaming with premature pleasure. He had just lunched with the President, and was certain the suit would not be brought. Just *what* F.D.R. had said he could not remember, but Bob had left him with the conviction that he need not worry. But so had others; and I warned Bob that we were going to file the bill at once. He left unshaken, and imbued with the comforting certainty that the President would not "buck" the press, and went to Bar Harbor for his summer vacation.

I thought it wiser to see the President again. The last time that I had bucked the press, in 1935 as chairman of the Labor Board, he had slapped me down pretty hard, and there was no good taking chances. I pointed out that he would have almost all the newspapers of the country up in arms; to which he replied that was nothing new, 80 per cent of the newspapers were always against him. I said that the suit would be criticized for bias, for favoring a newspaper that had consistently supported him: and he asked me whether I thought he should confine his help to those who were against him. He was at his best, cool and relaxed, having considered the pros and cons carefully. When I suggested that he initial a brief memorandum for the record, approving the action, he smiled, and appended his loose, sprawling initials. "The suit won't do you any good, Francis." And I answered that that was all right as long as we were both pulling in the same boat. . . .

Judge Learned Hand, writing for the court, found for the government; and on June 19, 1945, the United States Supreme Court sustained the judgment. Justice Black said that the First Amendment (protecting freedom of the press), which the defendants were invoking, rested on the assumption that "the widest possible dissemination of information from diverse antagonistic sources" was essential for the welfare of the public, and that the AP had impeded that dissemination by imposing restraints on newspaper competition. He pointed out that the competitive advantage enjoyed by AP members did not spring from any superior enterprise but from their collective power. Justice Roberts dissented on the unrealistic ground that if a newspaper could not get into the AP all it had to do was set up a news service of its own.

I resigned as Attorney General ten days later, well satisfied that I had had a hand in removing from the otherwise free American press—the greatest press in the world—this impediment to its most complete, democratic effectiveness.

It is true that since the Court's decision the International News Service was unable to continue in business and was acquired by the United Press. At first glance this net result would not seem to have stimulated competition among the news services—there are now two whereas before the suit there were three. It has been suggested that as long as newspapers could not readily become members of the AP, or acquire access to its services, there were always newspapers in the market for a competing service; that such a market, as a result of the decision, has now virtually disappeared, and as a result the INS did not get enough patronage to keep going. Whether this is the true explanation of what happened is, however, beyond the point. The purpose of our action was not to increase competition among news services but to open them on an equal and equitable basis to all comers. That has been accomplished; and if the services, which are owned by the newspapers, now operate in effect as a public service, it would hardly seem to be a serious objection that there are now two instead of three. A freer competition among the newspapers themselves was the end in view.

MEN WITHOUT WOMEN, PARDONS, TRAITORS

◆{}◆ *Chapter Eighteen*

The work of one division—the Bureau of Prisons—interested me as much as anything in the Department. It was different from any other division, and like the FBI and the Immigration Service was run largely independently of central administrative control. Because it presented such intensely human problems, and the convicts with their strange lingo, their touching struggle, their hopelessness, and their special wry humor made a unique world of their own, I have been tempted into treating it at some length.

James V. Bennett, the director of the Bureau, had scheduled a trip for me to Atlanta in the December following my appointment, but this had to be delayed on account of Pearl Harbor. The prison paper, the *Atlantian*, sent me "A Memorandum of Faith," signed on behalf of the inmates by the editor, Morris (Red) Rudensky and couched in a perfervid yet moving style: "We who have forfeited our liberties . . . recognize the peril confronting this Nation even more vividly than do our free brothers outside . . . We are prisoners, true—but we are AMERICAN prisoners. Beneath the thin veneer that is our felony [Red's veneer was mail robbery, and he had spent nearly twenty-five years on what he called 'service with the government'] we are

Americans as good as those who will fight in the front lines."
Those "who are on the wrong side of the Justice Department's
walls" were happy to have at the "helm of their destinies" a
man "whose humanitarianism was a conviction rather than a
convenience . . . who had placed red tape on the list of wartime
non-essentials, and had removed the blindfold from the eyes of
the lady he serves. Mr. Attorney General," he ended, "give us
our use, give us our function."

I was able to get away at the end of the following January,
accompanied by Bennett, and was joined by the excellent
warden, Joseph W. Sanford, and half a dozen notables. The
occasion involved the presentation by me of an Award of Merit
to the prison, and individual certificates to twenty-five of its
2500 inmates. The place was seething with excitement as we
trooped through the prison gate followed by a swarm of
photographers and reporters. The prisoners were in a good
mood, they liked the fuss and feathers—"all these important
people here at the institution for the whole day to pay tribute
to a bunch of mugs like us," as one of them wrote a friend. They
knew they were being publicly applauded, and for good reason:
in the past year they had spectacularly stepped up their production of war materials—tents and mattress ticking—by voluntarily increasing their work from thirty-six to fifty-six hours a
week.

We all made short speeches and they stamped and whistled
when Representative Louis Rabout mentioned his nine children,
and roared gleefully after Judge Marvin Underwood of the
Northern District of Georgia said that he had had "dealings"
with many of them. Red, a past master of the art of publicity,
accepted the award as he took my hand—"Hold it, Red!"—the
camera snapped and the convicts cheered.

The reaction in Berlin to the little ceremony at the Atlanta
penitentiary was typically German. The newspapers solemnly
declared that in America the war was so unpopular that it was
necessary for the President to force prisoners into war work! The
Nazis could not conceive that 200,000 men in federal and state
prisons (18,000 in United States institutions) could co-operate
with the government.

Red's term had been stretched by an unsuccessful attempt to escape. He managed to get himself nailed up in a coffin; but when it was being taken out of the prison, no longer handled by any of his friends, it was stood on the wrong end, and Red's wails of discomfort gave him away. But the interesting thing about Red's long and dramatic criminal career—vagrancy, burglary, assault, concealed weapons, manslaughter (in the Army during the First World War), and successful escapes from at least three penal institutions—the extraordinary thing about Red was his complete change, while still in prison, from a continually rebellious to an enthusiastically co-operative inmate.

He was released during my term of office, and I ran into him again when I was addressing a joint meeting of the Bar Association and Chamber of Commerce at St. Paul. Red, who was working for Brown & Bigelow, was in the audience. I had told them the story of my first jury trial, when I successfully defended a safe-cracker; and described the chips of yellow soap that were found near the safe, used, as I had been informed, to quiet the sound of the drilling. Red came up afterward to the platform to shake my hand—and to put me straight on what he called a "technical" error. Soap was not used to quiet any sound, but to prevent the "soup" (nitroglycerin) from running out of the seams. He was ashamed of my pulling a boner like that in public. He had a feeling of personal loyalty to me which previously had found expression in a personal attack in the prison paper, the *Atlantian*, on Walter Winchell when Winchell had been critical of my reluctance to bring sedition indictments. Red referred to Winchell as the "high priest of hysteria . . . back to your boudoir keyhole, Sir! and your Sunday night bragging sessions."

Red was one of some two hundred federal ex-convicts employed by Brown & Bigelow, whose president, Charles Allen Ward, had once been a convict himself. Charley Ward's story is one of the most unusual I have ever come across in this most romantic of countries. Like all sagas it had developed into a gilded legend before I ran into him. What I say here I submitted to him before he died not long ago, and he told me that the account is substantially correct.

Ward was self-made—miraculously made. He was born in Seattle and managed to get a high school education before starting his life of adventure. In accordance with the American recipe for self-made men, he peddled newspapers at the age of seven, and shined shoes. A sailor at seventeen he shipped to China and Japan on a freighter. He tried his luck in Alaska for several years—as a fisherman, prospector, dog-sled driver, and hotelkeeper. His pockets almost empty, he headed south. He organized a stage line and sold out at a profit. He went further south to Tiajuana, where he owned a gambling place; and got out one jump ahead of the Rurales.

Moving east in Mexico he met with Pancho Villa, the Mexican bandit and revolutionary leader, who made him a captain in Villa's commissary. Ward "liberated" the beef animals belonging to the rich Mexican *rancheros* and sold the hides across the Rio Grande in Texas, on his own account.

Heading north for Denver, Charley was arrested for the possession of narcotics. He vigorously denied the charge, and claimed that it was a "bum rap"—to put it technically—and that the package had been planted in his room by men who wanted to get him. But the jury did not believe him, and he was given a term in the federal pen at Leavenworth.

In the cell next to him was Herbert Huse Bigelow, at the time president of Brown & Bigelow, serving a brief stretch for income-tax evasion. The two men became friends, and Bigelow, no longer young and impressed with the other's quickness of wit and eagerness to settle down and succeed, offered to give him a job, when they got out, in his small calendar factory at St. Paul. But when they began to work together the two did not get on. Ward considered his boss mean and timorous; and doubtless the old man thought young Ward reckless. In a few years the great depression descended, and Brown & Bigelow teetered toward bankruptcy. By 1933 Ward had worked his way up from bench hand to vice president. In September of that year Bigelow decided to take a canoe trip with a friend on one of the lakes in northern Minnesota. Before they started, the Indian guide was worried as he sniffed at the wind—a storm was brewing, he said, they needed two guides and a bigger canoe. Bigelow hesitated—no, he could not afford it, he had worked out his budget, he would take a chance. The three of them took the chance, and were all drowned that evening. Bigelow left Ward a quarter of the stock in the company, worthless at the time. In ten years Brown & Bigelow was employing 5000 men, and Charles Ward was a millionaire with half a dozen companies under his wing, a beautiful, rolling farm where he bred Belgian horses across the border in Wisconsin, the Rancho Roca, Roja Rimrock, and the Lazy T. Ranch at Campe Verde in Arizona, and a pretty wife, whom he married at fifty-three. His wild oats were sown, and he had settled down to fantastic—and comfortable success.

Perhaps it was because he thought he had received a square deal from the Department of Justice, or that his luck turned when he was a prisoner and he got his chance, or that what he experienced of the life of prisoners moved him to a compassion for them, that accounted for his employing ex-convicts in his business on so large a scale. The percentage of recidivists— of those who did not make good—was very small indeed, and Charley Ward was proud of his convicts, and of his trust in them. He would take you down the main corridor of his office building, introducing you to one former inmate of a state or federal institution after another. Jim Bennett told me that Ward presented him to a former jailbird, with the statement: "Here, Mr. Bennett, is John Blank, who spent five years with you for defrauding his company and transmitting fake securities through the mails. He has been our assistant treasurer for several years."

When as Attorney General I would go to Chicago or Detroit, to St. Paul or to Denver to make a speech, there would be a basket of fruit, a bunch of roses, and a bottle of admirable whiskey in my room from Charley Ward. He was showing his gratitude to me as the head of the Department of Justice that he considered had taught him something about the way to live. Until he died he sent Katherine and me presents each Christmas.

I visited, always with Jim Bennett, half a dozen other federal penal institutions—the women's reformatory at Alderson, West Virginia, the Lewisburg prison in Pennsylvania, Alcatraz in San Francisco Bay, and McNeil Island off the state of Washington. At Alderson, where Katherine and I motored with the Bennetts after I had spoken at a bar association meeting at Hot Springs in Virginia, Miss Helen Hieronimus, the competent and devoted warden, asked Katherine to read some of her poetry to the inmates. She chose *Plain Chant for America* (later used as the title of her third book), a poem that extols freedom—"salt in our blood and our bone shape"—contrasted to the "blackshirt cruelty," the "goose-step mind." The girls liked it; and "Marie K" and "Mildred L" in the summer edition of *Eagle*, published by the reformatory, expressed their appreciation in a poem that described their emotion at feeling the "Spirit of America swell and pound about their ears." They had seen the "clear, white light of Freedom."

I also was honored. A Negro baby was born the day we arrived. His mother hesitated between calling him after Joe Louis, who since 1937 had been United States heavyweight boxing champion, and Francis Biddle; but, unable to cope with such an alternative, finally compromised on Napoleon Bonaparte.

There was usually no announcement of my proposed visit, yet it was curious how quickly word got around through the prison grapevine. My trip to Alcatraz was in the summer of 1944, and I had gone to the West Coast with Jim McGranery to visit the offices of the United States attorneys in Washington, Oregon, and California, and (incidentally) to talk at Democratic political rallies. The visit had not been suggested until I reached California; yet James A. Johnston, the warden, told me that the news got out immediately. When I reached the island almost every prisoner was busy writing a petition for habeas corpus— the United States Supreme Court was extending the scope of the constitutional right to use of counsel. I lunched in the long prison cafeteria with several hundred prisoners; and when we were back on the launch after the "inspection" was over Jim Bennett told me that two years before one of them had suddenly seized an aluminum tray and hit the warden with the edge on the back of his neck during an otherwise peaceable lunch, almost killing him. Two FBI plain-clothes agents, who had been detailed to guard me, walked around the gallery above us watching the crowd below in the cafeteria. The warden would not allow anyone to carry firearms, and the agents told Jim it was the most disagreeable hour they could remember.

I talked to a dozen prisoners, and among those in D block, the special treatment unit, was Robert Stroud, the birdman, who was a dangerous killer. He had prepared a rather persuasive petition, and talked to me quietly, logically, earnestly, his great hands gesticulating through the bars. . . . Stroud had first come to the attention of the authorities in 1908, in Juneau, Alaska, where, at the age of eighteen, he worked as a pimp for an elderly streetwalker and dope addict. One morning she returned to him with the story that she had spent the night with one of the local bartenders who had paid her only two dollars instead of the customary ten. Stroud bought some shells from a neighboring hardware store, went to the bartender's house, killed him by shooting him three times in the body, robbed him of the money on his person, and took it to the woman. He was permitted to plead manslaughter, was sentenced to twelve years, and committed to the United States penitentiary at McNeil Island. There he stabbed an inmate for "snitching," and was given another six months. He was moved to Leavenworth, where, a few months before the end of his term, he killed one of the guards in the dining room in the presence of 1200 convicts, walking quietly up to him when the guard had granted him the right to leave his seat temporarily, and jamming a self-made double-edged dagger into the guard's heart—it must have taken Stroud several weeks to sharpen this piece of steel to perfection. He was tried three times on account of technical errors that crept into the government's case. After the third and final conviction President Wilson commuted the sentence to life imprisonment. It was significant that the commutation was accompanied by an order of the Attorney General that Stroud should thenceforth be kept in solitary. Stroud once said that he could not endure being with other people. He hated society, hated authority, and above all hated the Bureau of Prisons with a burning savagery. In the last few years he tried suicide twice, by swallowing drugs and by slashing his groin in order that he might bleed to death. He was a killer, and killed each time for a reason. Yet he was not insane under the present definition followed by most American courts. He was a compulsive psychotic—he could not, under given circumstances, resist the urge to kill.

Stroud hated men but loved birds. At Leavenworth he managed to tame two sparrows and make pets of them, and when they died he was allowed canaries, who sang happily from cages hung in his cell. He set up a little research laboratory to study the diseases of birds. In a few years he became an authority on bird diseases, and wrote a book, published by his brother, on this new, strange hobby.

Bennett, who soon became and has remained my close friend, is a devoted public servant who had spent most of his life in the field of criminology, a profession that absorbed him (he was awarded the Civilian Order of Merit by President Eisenhower in 1959). Gradually but steadily he introduced sound and humane techniques into prison management. A trained lawyer, he followed criminal legislation, and through excellent judgment has been able in most cases to persuade both Republican and Democratic Attorneys General under whom he has served to back more humane and intelligent federal legislation. He is considered "advanced," which means that he favors psychiatric treatment of prisoners, believes in treating them like human beings, that criminals must be restored as well as punished, and that prisons should be instruments of salvage rather than detention areas. He has a sense of timing, and knows when not to push reform too hard. His play of humor never deserts him, even when the joke is on himself. He likes to quote a grateful letter from a former convict. "I write to tell"— it ran—"how much your training has meant to me. When my revenoo case came up in the Tennessee court they showed my still. The judge and jury all looked it over most kerful and admitted to a man that it war the finest piece of coppersmittin they had ever seen in these here parts, barring none . . . I just wanted you all to know I owe it to yor sheet metal course."

Bennett's human understanding of his charges—like a wise schoolmaster—does not blind him to the fact that some of them are incurable and therefore dangerous, and cannot be trusted to act normally, and therefore can never be safely released. He is aware of the terrible plight of homosexuality that infects all prisons, all armies, all men without women, and that adds to the malice and treachery among prison inmates. I believe that this is a root evil; and that the separation of men from their women is the chief dehumanizing factor in their lives, for which work, and exercise, and recreation can be a relief but never a substitute. In England, in Germany during the Weimar Republic, in Spain and Mexico and other countries with a Spanish culture, the prison authorities permit many of the prisoners to go home at regular intervals for a few days, where their behavior warrants the treatment, a sort of experimental probation. The results have been on the whole successful. A similar treatment has come about in several states, particularly in the South, in Alabama, Mississippi, Texas, and Florida, without formal or statutory authority, but through the exercise of a broad discretion of the individual warden. Public opinion, however, has not yet come to consider such a step possible as a recognized practice, even though the risk to the community would be negligible, and most prisoners would soon be released in any event, smarting from the bitterness that such an enlightened treatment would tend to soften. Such a furlough should be granted not only for the purpose of easing the tensions of prison life, but also to enable the prisoner to hunt for a job, and to rebuild his relationship with the community from which he had been cut away, or with a new environment that he might choose.

Our treatment of conscientious objectors during the war, though more humane and intelligent than in the past, lacked the recognition that human beings object to war on grounds other than religious conviction. The courts had interpreted the statute to apply only to persons who professed a religion that held that war was evil, and those who rejected war on moral grounds irrespective of religion were not exempted. Roger Baldwin served a prison sentence in the First World War because he believed it was evil to kill, but did not belong to any church.

The most difficult cases to handle were the young men who refused even to register on the ground that such an act would admit the validity of a law which they considered immoral. They were indicted, convicted, and sent to jail—a clumsy and stupid way of handling persons whose obstinate and belligerent attitudes almost always could be traced to early parental cruelty, broken homes, and hidden psychological pressures of which they

themselves were usually unaware. The cumbersome legal paraphernalia that attaches to formal trials should be avoided so far
as possible. Jehovah's Witnesses were not allowed, as they insisted they should have been, to claim exemption because each,
since he testified for the Lord, should be granted the status of
a minister. Several thousand of them, therefore, were sent to
prison, where from an administrative point of view they were
exemplary inmates, working hard, keeping clean, obeying the
rules once they had been committed. They had little chance to
proselyte, kept largely to themselves, and did not get on too
well with the other prisoners. One of them, a sturdy and incommunicative farmer who was certain that there was but one
way to salvation, goaded to fury by the gibes and laughter of
his companions, suddenly burst out, "That's all right. You wait
till He comes back to Earth again, He'll clean up all you dirty
bastards in no time!"

President Roosevelt's exercise of the powers of pardon and
commutation of federal convicts reflected his sense of pity for
the trespasses of human frailty. I would send him my recommendations, based in turn on those of Daniel Lyons, the pardon
attorney. The President studied the accompanying files with a
good deal of care, not from any overscrupulous feeling that it
was his duty to do so—he could have delegated most of this
work to someone else—but because it involved the personal
considerations that always tempted his attention. He enjoyed
dealing with human beings, their weaknesses, their virtues, the
possibility of a decent future. Here he was at his best, moved
by the Christian virtue of compassion, remembering more the
teachings of the New Testament than the lessons of the Old,
which he knew still lay at the base of so much of our conception of justice, that suffering be paid for by the compensation
of suffering.

I remember a particular memorandum which he sent me in
connection with granting an application for commutation of a
moonshiner's severe sentence: "Send word to Claude W. Blackman that the President of the United States expects him to go
straight, to keep sober, to make no more whiskey, and to take
care of his family." He rarely failed to follow my recommen-

dation, although now and then he would send a file back for
further information. I do not recall any determination on political grounds.

The first treason case in the war presented a difficult question
of judgment. Early in 1942, Lieutenant Hans Peter Krug, a young
German bomber pilot, escaped from a Canadian prisoner-of-war
camp, rowed across the Detroit River, and landed in Detroit.
There Max Stephan, whose restaurant had been a popular meeting place for members of the Bund, sheltered him and helped
him in an effort to escape to Mexico, which did not prove successful. Stephan was convicted—the first conviction under the treason statute since 1794 when a Pennsylvania leader of the Whiskey
Rebellion had been found guilty. Krug was sentenced to death.

Should his sentence be commuted? I discussed the question
with the President, who was torn between making a stern example of the case by letting the conviction stand, or—because
of the man's aid and comfort to the enemy had not been very
serious—commuting his sentence to life, and waiting for a more
apt case about which to be stern. He was wavering until Judge
Augustus Hand wrote him, suggesting clemency, pointing out that
there were different degrees of treason, as there should be; and a
due sense of proportion would be lacking if the penalty was
allowed to stand—he would have given Stephan twenty or thirty
years. Other treason cases would be coming up, "and you will
have to boil them in oil or crucify them if you give this man a
death sentence." All doubt was removed, and Stephan's sentence
was commuted to life imprisonment.

There were other traitors, too, of a different caliber, during the
war. By 1943 the Army became concerned about the Nazi short-
wave propaganda, broadcast by Americans, reaching the
United States. Robert Patterson, the Under Secretary of War,
called me up one day to ask if I knew anything about it—had
I ever listened to any of the programs and commentators? He
thought that for the morale of the country the propaganda ought
to be shown up for what it was—blatantly pro-Axis. I told him
that I had never listened to any—I thought that most radio news
comments were a bore, except Elmer Davis's who began broadcasting at the end of 1945, and who was wonderful—just, lucid,
funny, dry, American to the bone. I said to Patterson that I knew

the Axis line, it was very much like the cranks and isolationists here: scurrilously anti-Jewish and anti-Roosevelt, pro-Hitler, defeatist. Only a few nuts paid any attention to it. But Bob thought we ought to take action—if we branded this talk as criminal it would stop people listening to it. But why stop them, I said. It just made them mad, and probably was helping the war effort . . . but I promised to take a look at it.

The broadcasts were unquestionably treasonable. Traitors, under the Constitution and statute, were Americans who adhered to the enemies of the United States, giving them aid and comfort within the United States or elsewhere. So we indicted eleven of the worst of them, seven men and four women. A majority were employed by the German Reich, and broadcast from Berlin and other points in Germany.

Of the eleven accused of treason, five—Axis Sally, Tokyo Rose, Mr. Guess Who, Paul Revere, and Joe Scanlon—were convicted and sent to prison. Lord Haw Haw and Mr. Anders died before they could be brought to the United States, Anders in a Russian prison camp. The charges were dismissed against three others.

Ezra Pound's was the last case to be disposed of. He was brought to the District of Columbia soon after we had won the war, and entered a plea of insanity. He was adjudged insane and sent to St. Elizabeth's Hospital in Washington.

In 1948 the Fellows in American Letters of the Library of Congress, established by Archibald MacLeish when he was Librarian, were asked by the Bollingen Foundation—Paul Mellon's generous and imaginative creation—to make an annual award of $1000 to an outstanding American poet. My wife was a Fellow at the time, with Allen Tate, T. S. Eliot, Robert Lowell, Louise Bogan, Robert Penn Warren, Willard Thorp, Katherine Anne Porter, and Karl Shapiro. Leonie Adams was resident consultant in poetry. The Fellows decided to honor Ezra Pound with the award for the *Pisan Cantos*, which had recently been published. But since several could not attend the meeting—Katherine and I were in Rome—it was decided to take a vote by mail. Katherine voted with one other of her associates against the award. She felt that it was unwise for the Library of Congress of the United States to single out a traitor for recognition; and that the traitor could not be separated from the poet—his anti-democratic, anti-Semitic fulminations ran through his whole work. She believed, too, that such a choice would do incalculable harm to the work of the Fellows. The others insisted that nothing should be considered but Pound's standing as a writer: his influence on a whole generation of younger men was germinal, he had never been given appropriate recognition, it was pusillanimous to back down before the politicians, before public opinion. . . . The award to Pound was announced in 1949.

There was not much excitement until the *Saturday Review of Literature* published a series of "patriotic" articles attacking the Fellows, and darkly hinting that their action was the result of a Nazi plot, although the object of the plot was never made clear. The public remained rather indifferent, but certain members of Congress, seizing the rare chance to be ahead of their constituents, demanded what the Library of Congress was trying to do—decorate a traitor?—and introduced a resolution for an investigation. . . . At the suggestion of the Librarian the Bollingen Foundation withdrew the annual award for poetry from the hands of the Fellows and turned it over to Yale. Katherine was a good deal upset by the incident, and I remember that summer her reading a headline in the New York *Times:* Parliament to Investigate Pound, and saying rather forlornly, "Parliament, too?"

For a dozen years Pound lived at St. Elizabeth's while a constant stream of friends and admirers went to see him, a famous anchorite, withdrawn from the outer life, mystic and remote. These pilgrims reported that he appeared to be sane enough unless something tempted him into his old demonophobias that were the source and inspiration of his treason: his abomination of democracy—"jewocracy" as he called it—of bankers, who were all "usurers," of President Roosevelt ("Roosenfelt" he would say venomously), and of the Attorney General, who had sent him where he was. From St. Elizabeth the *Cantos* continued to pour forth; and the recognition of his distinction as a poet flourished. Caught in the ugly turmoil and slobbering madness of the other inmates, he was not a forgotten man in the great world of letters outside the little world of an asylum. From time to time suggestions were made that he should be given his freedom. Such distinguished poets as T. S. Eliot (an intimate friend of Pound's

in the old days) and Archibald MacLeish (who never knew
Pound, he told me, but thought that he should be freed) vaguely
interested themselves in his case. The war had been over for
more than a decade and it was a good tradition that political
prisoners be given amnesty after a war.

Then, rather casually, on a warm day in April 1958, Thurman
Arnold, representing Mrs. Pound, argued briefly in the United
States District Court in Washington that the indictment be dismissed. Pound was hopelessly insane—so ran the argument, supported by appropriate medical affidavits—and could never be
tried; but was not too dangerous to be returned to the community. The United States agreed that in the interests of justice
the motion should be granted, and Judge Laws announced from
the bench that he would dismiss the indictment. Shortly afterward Pound was released from the hospital. Behind these formal
actions was the intercession of Robert Frost, then eighty-four,
the well-loved dean of American poetry. He was New England
to the core, and never overstated a position. He told the Attorney
General that he did not like what Pound had said, but he did
not think he should be kept in an asylum at the age of seventy-
two. Frost was paying off a debt to Pound, for it was Pound who,
more than forty years before, living in England, where Frost
had been published and was known, used his influence with
American men of letters to obtain recognition for Frost in the
United States. But Pound was not grateful—he was annoyed
that Mr. Frost had been unable to turn up at the hearing, and
said so emphatically.

When Pound moved to Rapallo many years before the war,
my brother George went to see him and made an excellent
lithograph of the poet; and later called on him at St. Elizabeth,
hoping to be allowed to draw him again. But Pound would not
agree. When George asked him to autograph a book in August
1957 he wrote George one of his funny half-mad letters:

"Dear Jarge"—it ran—
"I will do anything in reason, but NOTHING that wd. force
my infinitely patient wife to wrap up parcels and tote 'em
to the post office. She got 'nuff to do luggin in stuff people
send to her instead of direkt to me at the orsptl . . . Ain't
it time fer yr. bro. I mean ain't he young enuf to turn over a

new leaf and admit the country warn't invaded when they stopped habeas corpus or other irrigularities I mean the dems might even git some kudos for going anti-Javitts kulchurl uplift an all that. If history don't brand F.D.R. as one of the worst stinkers, it cant avoid seein that he was a cad and a liar who perjured himself every time he tukk oath of office. And the causes of war have been defined in Fuller's Military History etCettyroar, merely certain lies and evasions putt out 12 years ago are being revived, etc. He knows damn well I didn't betray anybody.

He knows

Yorz
Ezra

HARRY BRIDGES
—COMMUNIST?

Chapter Nineteen

One of the first, and certainly one of the most difficult decisions I had to make after I had been sworn in as Attorney General, was whether I should deport Harry Bridges as a Communist. That clever and tender cartoonist of the Washington *Evening Star,* the late C. K. Berryman, must have sensed my dilemma, for he depicted me in a drawing plucking the petals of a flower as I murmured, "He is, He isn't, He is."

The issue was one of those nightmare contests between the government and an individual that never seem to end. In 1939, Secretary of Labor Perkins, as I have already related, appointed James M. Landis, dean of the Harvard Law School, as a special trial examiner to report as to whether Bridges should be deported. Two questions of fact were involved: was he a member of the Communist Party of America; and did that party advocate the violent overthrow of the government of the United States— grounds for deportation under the statute? The Supreme Court had construed the act to apply only to the time when the action for deportation was taken, and not to membership before that. Landis on December 28, 1939, held that the evidence did not show that Bridges was a member when the warrant was issued, and that evidence as to his previous membership was irrelevant. He did not decide whether the Communist Party of America was the kind of revolutionary organization contemplated by the law. The Secretary accepted Mr. Landis' recommendation, and canceled the deportation warrant. Several members of Congress promptly demanded that she resign. Miss Perkins appeared before the House Judiciary Committee and explained her conduct of the case with her usual courage and coolness. She told the President, according to report, that she would resign whenever he would let her—she would never embarrass him—but he smiled, and told her not to talk foolish.

After the Landis decision Congress amended the act so as to broaden membership to apply to the time after the arrival of the alien in the United States. Bob Jackson as Attorney General, thoroughly disliking to have his hand forced, ordered the FBI to investigate once more to determine whether under the amended law grounds for deportation existed. His dislike of continuing a course of action which many of his liberal friends had come to regard as political persecution was not lessened by Edgar Hoover's injudiciously expressing the opinion that Bridges was a "Red"—a statement which the public might easily have concluded could not have been made without the acquiescence of the Attorney General.

A good deal of new evidence was turned up, and Jackson appointed Judge Charles B. Sears, a retired judge of the New York Court of Appeals, as a special examiner to take evidence and recommend appropriate action. On September 26, 1941, soon after I had been appointed, he filed his decision. Bridges, Sears found, was a member of the Communist Party of America; and the party was, in the words of the statute, "an organization that believes in, advises, advocates, and teaches the overthrow by force and violence of the government of the United States."

Bob Jackson asked me to come to see him in chambers. He was concerned, he said, about the Bridges case. He suggested that I bypass the Board of Immigration Appeals, and order that Sears' findings and the evidence supporting them be sent up directly to me for decision. He had the impression that the board might be "pro-Bridges," and would overrule Judge Sears' conclusions, so that, when the case came to me, I should find another obstacle to my sustaining Sears—that is, of course, if I agreed with him. The case was so important that it would not be out of line if I had it sent up to me directly. If I bypassed the board and simply sustained my own inspector, a former member of the highest court in New York, the case would eventually go to the Supreme Court in the best possible shape.

The Board of Immigration Appeals was one of those convenient intermediary fact-finding departmental bodies, created not under any statute but by administrative order of the Secretary of Labor, for the purpose of taking the vast load of immigration decisions off the Secretary's back. It had no power to put into effect warrants of deportation, and its findings were purely advisory. It was composed of five men whom I considered conscientious and fair. Ninety per cent of its decisions were affirmed without question by the Attorney General. Only occasionally I would send back a case involving a question of policy or statutory interpretation for reconsideration; but rarely overruled the board.

Thinking the suggestion over, I could not agree. I had no foregone conclusion. But if I bypassed my own board and then decided against Bridges, it would surely be said by those who supported him that I had already made up my mind. I could see no reason for not treating the case like any other, and deciding it in due course.

Jackson's prophecy was right. The following January the board held that the record did not sustain Judge Sears' findings, reversed him, and entered a tentative order that the warrant of arrest be canceled, and execution of the order of deportation be stayed pending the decision by the Attorney General. The case was now before me for action.

Harry Bridges, a gaunt, mordant, shrewd man, was born in Melbourne in 1901 and came to the United States in 1920. He joined the longshoremen almost immediately, and led their strike in San Francisco in 1934, which soon spread over the whole waterfront, tied up shipping, and created such violent disorders and dislocation of business that the governor declared martial law. Bridges became popular among the turbulent elements of the labor movement on the West Coast, and was elected president of the International Longshoremen's and Warehousemen's

Union, a CIO affiliate. His union, in sharp contrast to the shipping conditions on the East Coast, was free from corruption.
Under his mettlesome leadership the men's working conditions
improved enormously, and much higher wages—long overdue—
were secured. After the strike charges were made that Bridges
was a Communist. But that accusation was often made against
tough and tenacious labor leaders, and Bridges was both. By then
he was the most hated man on the West Coast, except among the
members of his local, who adored him. When the war broke
out in Europe he consistently followed the Communist line, a
position which had nothing to do with advancing the interest of
his followers.

Seventeen days after the strike Germany invaded Russia, and
the Party's policies changed overnight. Bridges immediately
shifted his effective leadership to all-out production. The vessels
carrying ammunition were loaded with a new burst of enthusiasm, strikes were of the past, Bridges declared he was fighting
for the democracy of his adopted country, the United States—
three times he had begun naturalization proceedings, and each
time had let them lapse—and he was now an overnight patriot.
The Navy paid him a tribute for his effort against the Axis
powers. He was asked to address the Commonwealth Club in
San Francisco—the ultimate accolade in California. So that when
Judge Sears' ruling was handed down three months after Russia had joined the Allies, Bridges had largely reinstated himself
by his "patriotic" action in the war effort.

After studying the evidence I was convinced that Harry
Bridges was a Communist, and that the Communist Party of
America was an organization which advocated the overthrow of
our government. Although occasionally deviating from the original Marxist line for temporary tactical purposes, the Party had
never abandoned the belief in the compelling necessity—should
it arise—of using force.

But the more difficult question was Bridges' connection with
the Party. To show "affiliation" would have been enough to
bring Bridges under the statute—his party "line," his activity
in distributing Communist literature, his intimacy with acknowledged Communists. But association was a loose word, and

I believed the courts would look on it with distaste. I need not consider association if actual membership were established.

The evidence dealing with membership was not overwhelming. Much of it had been excluded by Judge Sears on the ground that it was inconclusive, unreliable, or contradictory, including the testimony of seven ex-Communists that at one time or another they had seen Bridges at Communist meetings. Sears based his finding on the testimony of two other witnesses. Harry Lundeberg, a prominent AF of L West Coast labor leader, testified that he dined one night at Bridges' house with Bridges and Sam Darcy, a well-known Communist. Darcy asked Lundeberg to join the Party, saying that Bridges was a member, and Bridges said, "Nobody has to know you are a member of the Communist Party. You don't have to be afraid, because I am one, too." Another witness, James D. O'Neil, publicity director of the CIO, who shared offices with Bridges, made a statement to two FBI agents in 1941—it was taken down stenographically—that he walked into Bridges' office one day in 1937 and saw Bridges pasting assessment stamps in a Communist Party book; and that Bridges told him that he had been attending Party meetings. On the evidence I had little doubt that Bridges was a Communist and was therefore deportable.

Before Germany invaded Russia one of the most serious threats to the Allied war effort had come from the shipping unions, known over the world to be impregnated with Communists opposed to the Allied cause. Now they were with us; and it was proper to consider the effect on the war effort that the removal of Bridges might have.

Would the decision to deport Harry Bridges affect our international unity—meaning our relation to Russia? I thought not. I remembered that many years before, Kemal Ataturk, the President and dictator of Turkey, had gathered several thousand Communists living in his country on a freighter, and caused the vessel to be towed into the middle of the Black Sea and there sunk. Shortly afterward Ataturk and Stalin entered into an alliance establishing close political and economic collaboration. Alexis Leger told me of an episode a few years later, further illustrating Stalin's point of view. In 1935, as permanent Under Secretary at the Quai d'Orsay, he had accompanied Pierre

Laval, French Minister of Foreign Affairs, to Moscow, where a Franco-Russian treaty was negotiated with Stalin. One evening after they had come to an understanding, Stalin, relaxed and talkative, puffing at his comfortable pipe, asked the French Foreign Minister why his government was not rearming—Germany was arming, and even England; what was the matter with France, why was not France building up her military strength? It was a blunt question, much to the point. Laval answered that Stalin should know the reason, since it was the French Communists in the *Chambre des Députés* who were blocking the necessary appropriations. Stalin looked at him, grunted, and asked, "Why don't you liquidate them?" He would not care a straw what we did with our American Communists so long as we supplied him with arms to fight the Nazi invaders.

Moreover the Bridges case would move into the District Court (by habeas corpus), and thence eventually to the Supreme Court. That would take at least two years, probably three for a final decision, and meanwhile Mr. Bridges would be out on bail, performing his patriotic duties along the waterfront. The war would be over before the final decision was reached.

Turning the matter over in my mind, I tried to take a long view of history, beyond the war. I did not go along with the current disinclination to think about the kind of world that might emerge from the war. It was considered improper to indulge in such irrelevant speculation. I had regular reports from the FBI on the activities of our allies, the Russians, who were trying to obtain all possible information about our factories and shipping. We were allies to win the war, and that was all. Such an alliance did not involve permitting the Soviet to build her disruptive tactics in our labor organizations—the Communist leadership at that time was particulary strong in certain CIO unions. As the New York *Times* said in an editorial, immediately after my decision to deport Bridges had been announced, it was useful to have the finding of what the Communist Party advocated "placed officially on the record" in order to clear away the misleading notion, so sedulously fostered by the Communists themselves— and, the *Times* might have added, and by not a few American "liberals"—that communism and democracy had much in common. That this was untrue, the *Times* concluded, did not contribute an argument against all-out American aid to Russia. There was a perfectly clear distinction between activities of Communists on the Russian front and their activities in the United States.

Immediately before making public my decision I went over to the White House to tell the President what I proposed to do. I did not ask his advice but spoke in some detail of the reasons for my action. He whistled, drew deeply on his cigarette, and for a moment was concentrated in thought. "I'm sorry to hear that," he said. Then his face cleared; he screwed the butt of his cigarette in the ash tray. "I'll bet," he said, "that the Supreme Court will never let him be deported." Then he said with a smile, "And the decision is a long way off." "Precisely," I said—and that was the end of it. He thought I was making a mistake—his mind was altogether centered on the immediate job of the war; and at that time he did not take the Russian "threat" very seriously. He always lived intensely in the present, and the war filled every chink of it. He did not try to dissuade me. He never attempted to influence my decision or to suggest how he would like me to decide any particular case or resolve a problem, except on the one occasion that I have mentioned when he pressed me to hurry the sedition indictment. I wanted to take all the pressure possible off his back—after all, it was not *his* decision; and at my next press conference I stated flatly that under the law the President had no power to revoke the deportation order.

The reaction of the press was divided. Liberals and conservatives, radicals and reactionaries were in wordy disagreement. The newspapers were puzzled. I had long been pigeonholed as a liberal; liberals were supporting the war effort, and many of them were urging a greater unity with the Communists. It didn't sound "consistent" for me to deport Bridges. *The New Republic* for instance suggested that I had missed the opportunity to make at least an approach to dissolving the distrust and contempt with which so many American liberals viewed the Communist Party, a point of view that colored our attitude toward the Russian government itself, and so became an obstacle to co-operation with our greatest ally in war and *our potentially most powerful ally and promising collaborator in peace.* The words I have emphasized seem to me typical of the ambiguous and naïve attitude of so many liberals of the period.

Finally a dozen clergymen, innocent and earnest, voicing their unhappy reactions through a "front" group, the National Federation for Constitutional Liberties, deplored my regressive and dangerous precedent—the most shocking news since the attack on Pearl Harbor, as the chairman of the Committee on Industrial Relations of the Hartford Federation of Churches put it. Looking back, it is hard to understand why so many good people believed that Russia, victorious after the war, would suddenly become democratic and collaborate with us in the new peace; and why they should think the German invasion of Russia somehow changed things. It was an example of the lack of realism behind so much American thinking in the war years, stemming from a flaccid optimism and innocent of the cumulative facts of Russian history.

To some extent, I think President Roosevelt shared that cheerful outlook. It was not so much that he was counting on the impact of his charm to persuade Joseph Stalin to co-operate on the morrow, as that the habit of success, and F.D.R.'s Christian certainty that right would triumph over evil, was still enduring in his heart. It was that self-reliant conviction that led him to announce, foolishly, I thought, that the pardon of Earl Browder, the general secretary of the Communist Party, was "in the interests of international unity." He had commuted Browder's four-year sentence on a conviction of fraudulent misuse of a passport, two weeks before I held that Bridges should be deported. The newspapers pounced on what they believed to be the inconsistency of the two actions. I had recommended that Browder's term be shortened—he had served six or eight months—because I thought that the sentence was far too severe, not as a friendly gesture to the Soviets. I thought the President's phrase unfortunate, and told him so when he sent for me to discuss the matter. If any further unity with Russia was achieved it would not result from the commutation of Browder's sentence.

Time, without expressing dissent at my deportation of Bridges, accused me of developing a "sudden passion for the letter of the law." Ralph Ingersoll had a two-page signed editorial in *P.M.* —as might have been expected—castigating me in disdainfully ironic terms. "What Is A Biddle?" it was headed: I had not moved against Father Coughlin's *Social Justice* until I was pushed into it; when was I going to march against the Hague machine in New Jersey, or the Kelly-Nash machine in Chicago, or the Pendergast machine in Kansas City? and *when* was I going to clean up the New York waterfront? The *innuendo* that the Russians were in any way interested in the overthrow of our government was absurd. For several issues *P.M.* published a boxed coupon to be cut out and sent to me, with the appropriate space for the reader to mark: "I agree, Mr. Biddle, you and the Nazis are right . . . I disagree, Mr. Biddle, you and the Nazis are wrong . . ." Four or five hundred coupons were torn out and sent to me—one greeting me with a "Heil, Biddle!" signed "Adolf Hitler."

The labor unions were divided. Philip Murray, protesting vigorously, asked the President to reverse me. At that time I think he had little conception of the extent to which the Communists had come to control a substantial number of CIO unions. He did recognize this after the war, and fought with courage and success to oust them from the CIO and to break them. When I was Solicitor General nearly a year before we entered the war I had expressed my concern to Jackson of this situation, and suggested to him that we approach some of the union leaders—particularly in the CIO—to see if they would not quietly police the unions where there had been infiltration, avoiding publicity, and keeping known Communist leaders out of the key war industries. Jackson telephoned the President, who suggested that I see Murray.

Murray greatly relied on his chief counsel, Lee Pressman, a Harvard Law School graduate, who had held several important government jobs, and now headed the legal staff of the CIO. We suspected Pressman of being a Communist, an association which, a few years after the war, he confessed. He was sitting in Murray's office when I came in. I said to Murray that my business with him was private—could I speak with him alone. He looked at Pressman, and then back at me. "There is nothing," he said, "that I do not share with Mr. Pressman." There was a pause. Pressman turned red, got up, and left the room without a word. Murray must have heard what we believed about him;

but it was like him to be loyal to his assistants until the proof was convincing. He was one of the most courageous and upright labor leaders I have ever known, with an abiding sense of the virtue of compromise in spite of his Scotch moral obstinacy— he was born in Lanarkshire and came to the United States as a lad of sixteen, succeeding John L. Lewis as president of the CIO in 1940.

Lewis had been elected president and Murray vice president of the United Mine Workers twenty years before, and the two men had worked together closely and with substantial results. But Lewis could not forgive a man who became his successor, so it was natural that when Murray attacked the Bridges deportation order Lewis should come to my defense. He was unpredictable to anyone unfamiliar with his labyrinthian temperament: his shrewdness, his single devotion to the cause of his men; his arrogant egotism and vanity; his jealousy; his rumbling humor and instinctive common sense; and his elaborate, resounding, old-fashioned phrases that nevertheless told and stuck, smacking of the Bible, fitting like a rough coat his own extravagant and rhetorical character. John Llewellyn Lewis disliked any man who wielded more power than himself. He was very nearly a great man.

My supporters made up a motley group. There was Representative John Elliott Rankin, the venemous and rabid Negro-hater, born in Itawamba County, Mississippi, who was soon to attack me as vigorously as he now praised me, for enforcing civil liberties in the South. There was the American Legion National Commander Lynn V. Stambaugh—the Legion was not usually lyrical in my praise; and there was the Hearst press, particularly on the West Coast. Sumner Welles, Under Secretary of State, called me up to express his enthusiastic approval of my decision.

Harry Bridges, smiling and cool, sent a telegram to Donald Nelson, head of the War Production Board, saying that in spite of Biddle's outrageous decision, he would do everything possible to offset any effect it might have on production and labor-management unity; and would urge all workers and unions to redouble efforts to "win the main fight, the fight against the Axis . . ."

On November 11 of the same year, while the case was pending in the courts, Bridges attacked me in a speech at Harvard, saying that my order to deport him was blocking the war effort. My son Randolph, then a junior at Harvard, who had come to hear what he would say, rose to his feet and asked, "Mr. Bridges, why were you an isolationist until Russia entered the war?" Mr. Bridges answered, "The lad means why did my attitude change after Hitler invaded Russia. The answer is simple. I believe in industrial unionism." It was a meaningless and evasive retort. The American Legion wired Randy its congratulations. I was proud of him—it is comforting to be backed by one's son.

The argument for the government was made before the Supreme Court in April 1945 and the Court handed down its judgment on June 18, thirteen days after Field Marshal Montgomery, Marshal Zhukov, and General Eisenhower assumed full control throughout the German Reich, and my belief that the war would be over before the Bridges case was decided was substantially accurate. The Court ruled that there was not sufficient proof that Bridges was a Communist or even affiliated with the Communist Party, and canceled the order to deport him. Justice Douglas spoke for the majority. The opinion did not suggest that the deportation clause in the statute was unconstitutional; or deny that a purpose of that Party was ultimate, violent revolution. It observed that the link by which it was sought to tie Bridges to subversive activities was exceedingly tenuous. But there had been no attempt to link Bridges with any subversive activity except membership and association with the Party—and if that was not sufficient, the case fell.

I was in Court to hear the opinions read. Frank Murphy thought he should "concur" with the majority in a separate opinion. I sat directly in front of him at the Attorney General's table and he read his opinion at me, glaring and glowing with emphatic righteousness: Bridges, he said, had been denied the protection of the Bill of Rights; there was not the slightest evidence to show that either Bridges or the Communist Party seriously and imminently threatened to uproot the government by force and violence. "The record in the case," he pronounced, "will stand forever as a monument to man's intolerance to man . . . When the immutable freedoms guaranteed by the Bill of

Rights have been so openly and concededly ignored, the full wrath of Constitutional condemnation descends upon the actions taken by the Government . . ." What a windbag he was, I thought, as I watched him warm up to his scolding. The three most judicially-minded judges—Stone, Roberts, and Frankfurter (Jackson did not sit) dissented. Chief Justice Stone expressed their views, pointing out that the testimony of numerous witnesses, much of it uncontradicted, showed that Bridges had long and continuously associated with Communists and Communist organizations, and that all the Court had to consider was whether Bridges' membership was supported by the evidence. He believed that it was.

In a handful of years the Court was to sustain convictions for conspiring to organize the Communist Party as a group to teach and advocate the overthrow and destruction of the government.

SEIZURE OF
MONTGOMERY WARD

❧ *Chapter Twenty*

No act of mine as Attorney General caused more sharp resentment and blame than the part I played in connection with the seizure by the government of the Chicago plant of Montgomery Ward & Co. The criticism came chiefly from those who were opposed to President Roosevelt and the New Deal, supported by the press, of which more or less 80 per cent were habitually against his administration. But the seizure was, I regret to say, unnecessarily melodramatic, and had the quality of *opera bouffe*, for which I must share the blame. Yet it was essential for the war effort that the step be taken. And the legality of the action, tested in a second seizure of the property of the same defiant corporation, was sustained by the courts.

Sewell Avery, the sixty-nine year old chairman of the board and president of Montgomery Ward, was a shrewd and thoroughly reactionary individualist who fought organized labor all his life, and believed that, even in wartime, he was entitled to run his business as he damn well pleased without interference from any government bureaucrat, including the President of the United States. Mr. Avery was one of the dominant figures in American business. A director of Armour, of Northern Trust Company, of U. S. Steel, of the Pullman Company, and of

Peoples Gas and Light, he ran Montgomery Ward with the enthusiastic support of a board of directors who, like him, represented the ultimate in industrial power. U. S. Steel adopted a resolution, shortly after the seizure, that it was "proud" to have Avery on its board. He could count on his own shareholders, to whom regular and satisfactory dividends were paid on a sound business basis. It should be added that the turnover among his employees—little skill was needed in the distribution of goods by a mail-order house—was strikingly high.

It was inevitable that he should tangle with the Labor Board. The American economy was open and substantially free from government interference until Pearl Harbor changed it overnight into a highly restricted and government-controlled operation. The two most difficult domestic jobs during the war were to keep production moving at the spectacular new pace that the war required, without lockouts and without serious strikes, and to hold prices at a reasonable level without undue inflation. Both these tasks were accomplished.

It was necessary to obtain from labor an agreement not to strike during the war, based on the corresponding assurance that such a pledge would not be taken advantage of by industry, which, freed of the threat of a strike, could easily avail itself of the opportunity to break unions. This had occurred twenty-five years before during the First World War, and organized labor had lost much of its strength as a result. The President, then Assistant Secretary of the Navy, had been active in helping to smooth out some of the threatened strikes at that time. He knew the necessity of keeping the workmen in line. Organized labor was infinitely more powerful than it had been then, and the problem was correspondingly more difficult.

Immediately after war broke out the President called together representatives of industry and labor. After a meeting held on December 17, 1941, he made public a letter, written to both sides, in which he accepted their agreement that there would be no strikes or lockouts; that all disputes would be settled by peaceful means, and that the President would appoint a board to handle them. The War Labor Board was promptly created by executive order.

The men who would handle these disputes must seek not

consistency to a formula but the application of a balanced and thoughtful judgment—*when* to overlook, *when* to insist, *what* was essential. They must not be labor leaders, or necessarily pro-labor; but they must have some knowledge of labor, and be trusted by the labor leaders—labor had been let down too often in the past. Above all they must be men of sensitive imag-ination. They could never keep all the problems off the Presi-dent's shoulders, but they must not overburden him until the issue got to the ultimate point of decision, and for that reason they had to know thoroughly the President's policies and point of view. They had to create and maintain a general stability of pattern essential to hold the confidence of the people.

To carry out this difficult assignment the President chose two men ideally suited for the work. James Francis Byrnes had resigned from the Supreme Court in October 1942 to become director of the Office of Economic Stabilization. In May 1943 the President made him director of War Mobilization, with powers second only to his own, which Byrnes exercised with tact and common sense. His place as economic director was taken by Frederick M. Vinson, who was at the time a judge of the Circuit Court of Appeals for the District, and would later be Secretary of the Treasury, and finally Chief Justice. Vinson's experience as chief judge of the Emergency Court of Appeals, created to hear appeals from price-fixing decisions, made him particularly suited to head an office organized to stabilize the economy, and to prevent the inflation that usually accompanies war. If wages had to be held down, so did the prices of food and rent and clothes. The War Labor Board was responsible for wage stabilization policies, and for keeping workers on their jobs. The Office of Price Administration, the OPA, tried to hold prices on an even keel. There was a certain amount of healthy internal pull in difference of opinion between the two organ-izations; but on the whole they operated as a single unit, under Vinson's skillful direction.

Byrnes and Vinson, working closely together in a wing of the White House, were old friends. Each had served in Congress. During the President's first term Byrnes in the Senate and Vinson in the House had led his legislative program. Byrnes was shrewd, agile, imaginative; Vinson supplemented his associate's qualities by seeing issues in simple, direct lines. A better team would have been hard to find. The success of the stabilization program was shown by the results. On October 2, 1942, the Office of Economic Stabilization was established by statute. From October 15, 1942, until April 1943 the cost of living index increased 4.3 per cent. The President then issued the Hold-the-Line Order, giving the Office greater powers to hold prices and wages, and saying, in effect, that there should be no more increases. From April 1943 until Vinson's resignation in April 1945 the cost of living rose only 3.2 per cent: and this was during the huge inflationary pressure of war. In the twenty-two months that followed the abandonment of the order, the increase in the cost of living was 20.2 per cent. Those two men did an amazingly good job, and, largely because of their fairness and firmness, they had pretty solid popular support.

Labor disputes under the new controls went automatically to the War Labor Board, made up equally of representatives of the public, of industry, and of labor. Its chairman, William H. Davis, a successful New York patent lawyer—he was then sixty-five—had had extended experience in labor adjustments. He was highly respected by both sides. He was able, patient, and human. The public representatives on the board included Frank P. Graham, president of the University of North Carolina, who later would be United States Senator from that state, and Lloyd K. Garrison, then dean of the Wisconsin Law School, who succeeded Davis as chairman in 1945.

At the time of the seizure of Montgomery Ward on April 29, 1944, the board had established an excellent record, and had kept strikes to a minimum—strikes never disappear from a free economy, even in a war. The board had broad powers to settle disputes, but its powers were purely advisory. If no agreement could be reached, it made findings of fact and recommendations, which were sent to the President for enforcement. The Labor Disputes Settlement Act, the so-called Smith-Connally Act, was adopted over the President's veto—he thought the bill too drastic and largely unnecessary—as a result of John L. Lewis's defiance of the President's efforts to get the coal miners back to work in 1943. Before the statute was passed the President took over and operated the coal mines through Secretary Harold Ickes and the Interior Department. He seized the property of Montgomery Ward, however, under the provisions of the statute. The chief difference between the two cases was that after seizure Lewis told the miners to go back to work, whereas Avery defied the government.

A dispute between Montgomery Ward and its employees had been going on for two years when the government's seizure took place. The company had been doing everything in its power to destroy the United Mail Order, Warehouse and Retail Employees Union, a CIO local. Never at any time very strong, its recognition as the workers' sole bargaining agency was essential if it was to make any headway. On February 12, 1942, it won a plant election, and was declared by the National Labor Relations Board to be the bargaining agent for the company's Chicago employees. Negotiations for a contract broke down, and, in accordance with the standard procedure, the War Labor Board took jurisdiction. After four months of investigation and hearings it directed that a contract be signed that would include a maintenance of membership clause, under which union members had to remain in the union or be discharged—a not uncommon provision.

For nearly a year Montgomery Ward delayed signing the contract. Twice the President, under his war powers, directed it to sign. Finally it complied. On December 18, 1942, after the agreement expired, the company again refused to recognize the union, claiming that it no longer represented a majority of the employees. The union objected to another election—it was not usual to hold one after so short a period—but the National Labor Relations Board ordered one, on the understanding that the union should continue as the recognized bargaining agency until the men themselves repudiated it. The company refused to comply with the Labor Board's unanimous order to maintain the contract and the *status quo* for thirty days until the election. Such unanimity was unusual in a closely contested issue, the industry members often refusing to go along with the labor and public members. After another four months in which the union made prolonged and fruitless efforts to have the contract extended, it called a strike on April 12, 1943. The President promptly ordered the men to return, and the company to recognize the order. A few days later the strikers were back at work; but the company refused to comply.

The seizure order directed the Secretary of Commerce, assisted by the Army, to take possession of the Chicago plant and operate it. I never understood why he picked Jesse Jones to undertake the job. In the other seizures, with the exception of the coal mines where the Interior was used, the Army was chosen, and had built up an effective unit for this purpose. I suspect that the Secretary of War, Henry L. Stimson, resisted—and the President then turned to Commerce, deeming it not inappropriate to delegate Jesse Jones, himself a sizable tycoon, to put another tycoon in order, and was probably amused at Jesse's disrelish at the prospect. Jones managed to slip out of any personal involvement in the distasteful episode by directing his Under Secretary, Wayne Chatfield Taylor, to do the job for him. Jesse was not one who stuck his neck out in a crisis, and his capacity for pulling it in was one of the qualities that accounted for his enviable success. Taylor was a rich and respected Chicago businessman, with a conservative turn; and I suppose the Secretary thought that his popularity in his own city would tend to offset the indignation over this silly business—as he must have thought of it—in a territory which by no stretch of the imagination could be considered sympathetic to the President. I had discussed the matter with Byrnes and Fred Vinson, and then given my formal written opinion to the President that he was specifically authorized to seize the plant under language of the Labor Disputes Settlement Act. I added that under his aggregate powers as President and Commander in Chief, granted him by the Constitution, he had general authority to act. I had not talked to the President—he was away, trying to get over a cold that was hanging on—but he knew about the case, and I rather think Byrnes discussed it with him by telephone.

On the night of April 26, Jimmy Byrnes called me at my house. He said that he was concerned about the situation; nothing seemed to be happening. Taylor had gone to Chicago and displayed his order, the Army was in possession, but Sewell Avery had told him, without marked politeness, that he did not recognize the right of the government to seize his business. Byrnes was afraid that there would be a stalemate, with the government sitting about and Avery operating the plant as usual. Before long we would be the laughingstock of the country. Could I fly out and put a little life into the seizure? He would put a government plane at my disposal immediately.

I agreed—far too hastily—telephoned to Hugh Cox and Benedict Deinard, two of my assistants, and reached Chicago at four o'clock the next morning. My executive assistant, Ugo Carusi, was already there, having at Wayne Taylor's request gone out with him the night before. We got in touch with Albert Woll, the United States Attorney in Chicago; and, after a brief consultation, Taylor, Carusi, and I went to Sewell Avery's office at about eight-thirty in the morning, accompanied by a small detail of soldiers.

When we left for Chicago we had decided to petition the United States District Court for an injunction against Sewell Avery and Montgomery Ward from interfering with the government's possession. After an early breakfast consultation in Chicago I asked Cox and Deinard to prepare the necessary papers with Albert Woll. Meanwhile, in order to exhaust every effort to gain peaceable possession before going into court, Taylor, Carusi, and I repaired to Mr. Avery's office soon after eight o'clock.

Mr. Avery walked into his office at five minutes before ten. He had evidently got wind of our arrival—there was a reporter at the airport when we got there. I told him that we were extremely sorry to interfere with his business, that we were obeying orders, acting under the President's direction issued under the statute. I asked him to co-operate. He bluntly refused to do so. I suggested he direct that the company's books be turned over to the government bookkeepers, so that a new set of books could be opened. This, too, he declined. He said that he was the boss, and would do things his own way. Taylor suggested that he call a meeting of his staff and ask them to work with us. Avery said he would do just the opposite. After further discussion, we asked him to leave the office—we could not let his presence interfere with the government's possession. He said he would do no such thing—"to hell with the government." There was a pause . . .

I was deeply shocked. This reckless old man was paralyzing the national war effort that had been built up with such infinite pains. Turning to Taylor, I said, "Take him out!" Avery looked at me venomously, summoning the most contemptuous words he could think of; and finally—"You New Dealer!" he managed to say. Taylor suggested to the officer in command of the half-dozen soldiers who were waiting that, "on advice of counsel," he should remove Mr. Avery. Under the directions of the officer, who kept apologizing to Avery, two soldiers gingerly picked him up and put him on a "hand seat," crossing their hands and gripping each other's wrists under him, while he sat, comfortably relaxed, and as dignified as the circumstances of his ride permitted, his hands crossed benignly over his stomach. They put him on an elevator, which bore him to the ground floor, and finally deposited him near a "no parking" sign where his car and chauffeur were waiting. He bowed to the crowd, smiled frostily, and stepped into his car. One photographer who somehow had been locked out of the building when the government took over was there when this solemn and absurd little group arrived, and managed to get an excellent photograph of Avery, still carried by the soldiers, before he got into his car—an exhibition that was destined to flame with accompanying headlines in every paper across the country: U. S. Troops Eject Avery . . . Avery Evicted by Army. The picture did more to rouse the country to Avery's defense than any argument on the merits of the controversy.

Jesse Jones called me from Washington. "I hear you've been wrapping packages all day," he said. "Only one," I told him.

All that afternoon and most of the night, Hugh Cox, with Deinard's help, prepared a bill of complaint, setting forth the history of Ward's recalcitrance. It referred to the company's gross annual sales of six hundred million dollars, and profits of thirty million; its 75,000 employees and thirty million customers, its six hundred branches—this defiant action was bound to interfere with the war effort. Seventy-five per cent of Ward's customers were farmers engaged in the government's war-food program. Substantially the entire economy of the nation was a war

economy, delicately balanced and synthesized. The resistance
to the War Labor Board's decision by such a powerful corporation would necessarily affect the stability of all labor relations,
and therefore jeopardize the continuity of war production.

To bring the company under the provisions of the act we
stated that Ward had extensive contracts with the government
for lend-lease farm machinery and parts; that $185,000 worth
of machinery had been shipped to New Zealand; that over a
million dollars worth of shoes had been sold to the United States
to be used for citizens of liberated countries; that 36,000 priority
ratings for material based on war necessity had been issued to
Ward; and that the Hummer Manufacturing Company, a wholly-
owned subsidiary of Ward, was making gun mounts and airplane
parts.

Late on our second day in Chicago our papers were ready;
and at ten o'clock that night United States District Judge William
H. Holly granted a temporary restraining order, and fixed a
hearing for the next day at two o'clock. The arguments began
that afternoon and lasted through the next day.

In arguing the case I stressed the danger of any defiance
of the Labor Board, by a company or by a union, spreading into
other fields—a sympathetic strike had already pulled in truck
drivers, and might soon reach the railroads. If labor felt that
its rights would not be protected it could not be expected to
forgo its fundamental prerogative to strike. If one company
could defy the Board others would follow.

Ward was represented by Silas Strawn as its chief counsel.
Strawn was then nearly eighty, a leader of the American Bar and
a thorough-going conservative. He had been president of the
American Bar Association, and was a director of railroads, of
banks, and of Montgomery Ward. As president of the United
States Chamber of Commerce he remarked in 1932 that "the
best public servant is the worst one . . . A thoroughly first-rate
man in public service is corrosive. He eats holes in our liberties."
He did not argue the case. That duty was left to his junior, Mr.
Harold Smith, who spent most of his time talking about Magna
Charta, an association of ideas which fitted admirably into the
Montgomery Ward publicity approach. Mr. Strawn advised Mr.
Avery on every step, and conducted the publicity with great

shrewdness, keeping in the background, now and then ejaculating a pious and earnest generality or note of shocked gravity to serve as a text for the reporters.

There were two issues of law, the first comparatively simple, the other covering an uncertain constitutional ground: Did the Smith-Connally Act apply to Montgomery Ward? The seizure, I argued, was authorized by the Act, since, in reading not merely one phrase but the entire statute, it was apparent that the law was intended to include businesses engaged in distribution as well as manufacturing. It was hard to conceive that Congress intended to leave a dangerous gap in the law by excluding distribution. To narrow the act to a segment of the economy would have been too limited a grant of power to meet the occasion.

I added that, irrespective of this particular law, the President had general powers to make the seizure. President Roosevelt's use of his war powers had not been very different from those of other wartime Presidents. Before the passage of the statute he had taken over industrial facilities in nine instances where operation had been interrupted, and this was the first time possession had been resisted. President Wilson, without statutory authority in the First World War, seized the Commercial Cable Company and placed it under operation of his Postmaster General, and the United States District Court upheld the seizure. Lincoln, during the Civil War, had taken possession of a railroad, confiscated property, called for 80,000 volunteers although Congress alone had specific authority to raise an army, and finally had freed the slaves on the ground of military necessity. I could not point to any specific clause in the Constitution saying that the President could seize this property or that, but three great war Presidents had acted on the assumption of that power. If the President had waited until strikes began to spread, he would have been guilty of irresponsible hesitation.

Strawn gave the publicity "lead" in a statement immediately after Avery's ejection that "the government had no more right to seize property than it has to come into your home and seize your goods." The analogy was false and misleading, as was the comparison of Montgomery Ward to the little corner store—if you could seize Montgomery Ward you could seize any little store—

a phrase which the press seized on. A little corner store did not and could not obstruct the war effort. Montgomery Ward could and did.

But the cry was taken up, and across the land it was reiterated that no farm, no home was safe, no one was immune from the assertion of arbitrary power by the New Deal, and "that Man in the White House." The administration, the press cried, was "following the footsteps of Hitler"—it was a dictatorship partaking of fascism and communism. The Fort Wayne *News Sentinel* rose to extraordinary eloquence. "It could be," it suggested editorially, "that Mr. Biddle has had, all along, the conviction that he was writhing in the womb of destiny, and that one day his time would come . . . It is government not by law but by bayonet." The Denver *Post* added that "a more infamous outrage had never been perpetrated under the cloak of government: Hitler's thugs, in the palmiest days, never did a more efficient job." In the Chicago *Tribune* I was cartooned as the "Axe Man," with the black cap of an executioner, holding his enormous bloodstained axe against the block, over a sign that read: "No Business Is Immune from Our Power."

When an exciting public issue seizes the press, it is not long before it gets into the Congress. In the Senate Harry Byrd of Virginia asked if Mr. Biddle had "an ambition to become an American Himmler"—we had apparently reached the state where directions of federal bureaus were enforced at the point of the bayonet. Senator Pat McCarran sent out to Chicago an "investigator" who sat busily taking notes during the long argument before Judge Holly. I wrote the Senator asking that I might appear before the Judiciary Committee, of which he was chairman, to state my case. He refused—there was nothing new that the Attorney General could tell the committee—"he would try to apply the law unswayed by emotional argument." Representative Leo Elwood Allen, of Galena, Illinois, a Presbyterian, Mason, Elk, Odd Fellow, and Republican, went further, demanding my impeachment. The government's power to seize the plant under the act was not discussed.

A small section of the press and several influential columnists took the view that the seizure was justified on account of Sewell

Avery's recalcitrance, and the serious consequences that would flow from a failure to enforce the orders of the War Labor Board. Dorothy Thompson in her column and news broadcasts made an admirable analysis of the issues at stake, particularly of the War Labor Board's record. Since its organization, she pointed out, the Board had recommended seizure in seventeen cases out of the 6000 referred to it for action, ten involving unions and seven with respect to corporations, Montgomery Ward being the seventh. This record hardly supported the charge that it had been biased in favor of labor and against management. The only way to enforce an order was to seize the plant. The Weimar Republic had fallen because the government was too weak to enforce law and order in a crisis. It was utterly absurd to compare F.D.R. to Hitler. Mr. Roosevelt had not made it a crime punishable by imprisonment or death to criticize his person—if he had, there would not have been enough concentration camps for his critics. Nor had he declared that he would reverse any court decision he chose.

Life, publishing the telling photograph of Avery being carried out feet first, was fair. Congress, it thought, had been conspicuously unwilling to fight a total war. "To count [Mr. Avery] a true martry, you would have to believe that the administration is really plotting, or at least willing, to overthrow the Constitution. It isn't."

The President got back to Washington from his cruise on May 7, thoroughly refreshed and rested. An election had been fixed at the plant, and it was believed that it would be held without interference by the company, and that the government should then withdraw. The President said at a press conference two days after his return that, if the election showed that the union did not have a majority of the employees, that would end the case; if the union did have a majority, Ward had declared that it was willing to continue its contract, and the dispute would be over. The issue had been grossly exaggerated and distorted. The facts were simple, the government's tactics necessary and right.

The union won the election and the government withdrew. As it abandoned possession the newspapers ran a picture of a

mail-order clerk, Dorothy Stokna, kissing a private good-by—the
final curtain to the comedy. Neither side was satisfied—the union
declared that the seizure had been a farce, and Avery said the
election showed the dominance of racketeers. The struggle
would soon be renewed.

Meanwhile the country was seething with my denunciation,
and my mail was choked with letters, almost all of them hostile,
many scurrilous and anonymous. "Maybe the gangsters from
Washington," wrote a woman, "who have been feeding at the
public trough so long may think such tactics will keep them in
office—through the vote of hoodlums—but We the People know
different."

The Republican press predicted the effect that the seizure
would have on the election—there had been nothing like it since
King John was forced to sign Magna Charta, one historically
minded columnist exclaimed. The Chicago *Tribune* carried a
cartoon—"One Picture Suggests Another"—of F.D.R. being
carried out by the voters the following November. But the President knew that the Montgomery Ward episode had solidified
him with workingmen all over the country. He liked the dramatic, and he enjoyed an impulsive action. Even the Gallup
poll indicating that 61 per cent of those polled thought the
government had not done the right thing in seizing Montgomery
Ward, and the "Congressional mail sacks bulging with letters
from furious constitutents denouncing the seizure"—as *Time* put
it—did not shake his opinion that the Republicans would not
make this an issue in November. They would be afraid to touch
it. And he was right. At the end of a long month the episode
was forgotten. The press had overreached itself, the country was
becoming bored, opinion began to veer around. In the campaign of 1944 the famous seizure was never mentioned, in spite
of David Lawrence's prediction that Attorney General Biddle
would become the principal issue.

The President's mood found expression in a brief and thoroughly typical note that he sent me just before I testified before
a special House investigating committee. "Dear Francis," he
wrote, "rumor hath it that you will probably be getting up on
the Hill this week. Don't let the boys get you down. Good luck

to you." After signing it, he wrote in his own hand: "bite 'em!"
The hearings before the House committee were held in May.
Robert Ramspeck, the chairman, had been in Congress since
1929. He was the Democratic whip, a member of the Democratic
campaign committee and one of the most highly regarded members of the House, in striking contrast to Senator McCarran, who
was conducting the Senate investigation. Ramspeck had a re-
assuring habit of keeping his head while those about him were
losing theirs and blaming it on the Executive in hallowed congressional tradition. William Davis, chairman of the War Labor
Board, testified that if the President had failed to back up the
Board by seizing Montgomery Ward's Chicago properties the
nation's wartime policy would have blown up. The Board had
gone out of its way to be fair to the company, and "his face was
red" because the Board did not move faster against it. "If you
want to fool with this dynamite," he said to the committee,
"come down and help me some time. No one can sit where I sit
and have any doubt that the Ward strike adversely affected the
war effort."

When my turn came—I testified for five hours, for the greater
part of the time under cross-examination by the Republican
members of the committee—I argued again the government's
legal position, which was completely misunderstood.

The House committee approved the seizure. I did not get
a chance to appear before the Senate subcommittee, which
thought it unnecessary to call any witnesses, and permitted its
chairman, like some malevolent spider, to spin the web of his
own facts and law out of the depths of his belly. Supported by
Chapman Revercomb from West Virginia, the Republican member of a subcommittee of three, Pat McCarran "reported" that the
Attorney General had "misadvised" the President when he said
that he had authority to issue his executive order under the War
Labor Disputes Act. In a press release the day his report was
made public I cited the only court decision on the point, handed
down two weeks before, and which the subcommittee had failed
to quote, which held that, irrespective of the War Labor Disputes
Act, the President had power under the Constitution to take
possession of the property and operate it.

After the election had been won by the CIO local, Ward refused to sign a contract containing the maintenance clause, and would not bargain with the union in an effort to reach an agreement. Sporadic strikes broke out. The company disregarded an order of the War Labor Board granting the union certain pay increases. The Board again sent the record to the White House with a recommendation for a second seizure. It was decided that certain of the company's properties in Chicago and six other cities should be seized—this time the Army would take possession. But the Secretary of War would not agree, and we met again in the President's office to hear his objections. He made them with his usual graphic language that carried a sense of profound personal conviction. We had all spoken—Jimmy Byrnes, Fred Vinson and I—reiterating what we had said to the President the day before: the Army had the experience and the organization, no other department could do the job as well. Mr. Stimson—he was seventy-seven, almost at the end of his extraordinary career—speaking against the background of the present war (General Karl von Runstedt had begun his sudden drive in the Battle of the Bulge against the thin American lines in Belgium and Luxembourg, and the Allies were suffering heavy losses) pleaded for his army: every man was needed in the *war* effort; it is a great army, Mr. President, it must not be sent to act as clerks to sell women's panties over the counter of a store; the men will feel it as a disgrace to the army, Mr. President . . . The President felt sorry for him, but not convinced. "Harry," he said, "the majority seem to be against you." He signed the order.

The War Department, knowing what the outcome would be, had everything ready. It took over the properties on December 28, 1944, and the government brought suit in Chicago asking the district judge for a declaratory judgment in its favor. A month later Judge Philip L. Sullivan entered a judgment against the government, but, pending its appeal, held the case in *status quo* —the Army remaining in possession—until the Circuit Court had spoken. The Army managed to get along better with Sewell Avery—perhaps he thought that one gesture of defiance was enough—and meanwhile the War Labor Board's order was enforced and the union's position sustained.

The President asked me to try to get some lawyer of national reputation, preferably a Republican, to argue the case in the Court of Appeals. I told him that Hugh Cox, who had written the brief and argued it before Judge Sullivan, was soaked in the legal and constitutional questions, and would argue them better than any lawyer I could think of. But if we lose, he said, we had better lose through someone on the outside. I tried at least a dozen men, but none of them would touch the case. One or two hesitated for a few days. Others thought our position weak, or were unsympathetic to it, or were frankly—or guardedly —afraid to take hold. I remember two in particular—George Wharton Pepper of Philadelphia, most eminently top-shelf, and Charles Evans Hughes, Jr., of New York, who had been President Hoover's Solicitor General, and had resigned on the appointment of his father as Chief Justice. Both were men of great ability, and impeccable in their political orthodoxy. Each professed to be tempted, but both were able to resist.

Cox argued it with conspicuous and successful ability. He is today one of the leaders of the American Bar. The Circuit Court of Appeals in a two to one decision reversed Judge Sullivan and upheld the government's action, ruling that Congress had intended in the War Labor Disputes Act to give the President power to seize a mail-order business. Congress meant the word *production,* the court said, as I had maintained a year before, to include *distribution.* Having held that the President was entitled to seize the property under a specific statute, it was unnecessary to go into the constitutional powers of the President. The decision constituted a clear victory for the administration—if we had a right to seize Montgomery Ward it followed that we had the right to eject Sewell Avery. The Supreme Court refused to review the judgment.

There was hardly mention of the decision in the papers; and an issue which had rocked the country a year before quietly sank into oblivion.

I am not certain that the Court would have refused to recognize the President's "aggregate powers" to seize without an authorizing statute had the question been argued under the persuasive heat of war, or on a stronger set of facts. But it was not; and when President Truman took over the steel mills, the existing emergency was born of the cooler issues of peace, and the Court turned him down, and settled an issue which had often arisen but fortunately had never before been adjudicated. There were two dissents, by Justice Stanley Reed, a cautious and balanced jurist, and the Chief Justice, Fred Vinson, who from his experiences as a war administrator knew the necessity of concentrating in the hands of the Commander in Chief all power reasonably calculated to carry on war. The two dissenters spoke out strongly of the danger, particularly in wartime, of such a narrow construction. To what extent the case will control or curb the actions of Presidents in future wars remains to be seen— if there is a survivor to review his action.

In introducing this discussion of the Montgomery Ward episode I said that no act of mine as Attorney General had caused more resentment than my part in the Montgomery Ward seizure. I must add that I look back on the whole business with distaste. To paraphrase the old song, it was not so much what I did, as the "narsty" way I did it. As Walter Lippmann aptly put it: "It was the manner in which the troops were used far more than the legal issues involved which has made the affair so notorious." I acted impetuously—an old fault. An Attorney General with greater caution—Homer Cummings or Bob Jackson—would not have stuck out his neck quite so far. It would have been more appropriate if I had not gone to Chicago myself—an impulsive act, which dramatized a situation that should have been played down. It is no particular consolation to reflect that, in the long run, I hurt no one but myself.

THE TEN SABOTEURS

❧ *Chapter Twenty-one*

On June 13, 1942, four German saboteurs—Peter Burger, Heinrich Harm Heinck, Richard Quirin, and George John Dasch—clad in marine fatigue uniforms, landed on Amagansett beach, Long Island, in a rubber boat dropped under cover of night by U-boat No. 202, the *Innsbruck,* which managed to elude our destroyers and escape the vigilance of the United States Coast Guard patrols. Dasch was in command. Four days later Herbert Hans Haupt, Edward Kerling (the leader), Hermann Otto Neubauer, and Werner Thiel, wearing swimming trunks and caps of the same service, similarly transported, clambered off their rubber boat on Ponte Vedra Beach, Florida, twenty-five miles south of Jacksonville. Each group possessed a substantial supply of TNT and other high explosives and fuses, timing devices and detonators, which, in the hold of a boat or in a locker of the waiting room of a railroad station, set off at a crowded moment would have caused unimaginable damage and loss of life. These adventurers had plans of key railroad centers and bridges and of the locks on the Ohio River from Pittsburgh to Louisville. They carried the layouts of three plants of the Aluminum Company of America, of the Niagara Falls hydroelectric plant, of the New York water supply system, and of a number of key industries. Kerling's men were to concentrate on railroads. They all possessed forged birth certificates, automobile drivers' licenses, and selective service and social security cards. They had plenty of cash, each team captain $70,000, and each of the others $4000 in money belts and $400 in small bills in their wallets. For months after the declaration of war by Germany against the United States they had been trained at a sabotage school at Quentz, west of Berlin, in the use of explosives and in methods of secret writing, and learned carefully the new parts they were to play. From Quentz Lake the saboteurs were sent to a submarine base at Lorient, in France, where they boarded the U-boats. Nothing must be left to chance.

Nothing that is excepting the character of two of the men involved. Peter Burger had been a supporter of Roehm, whom Hitler, Göring, and Himmler had caused to be murdered in the infamous *putsch* of June 30, 1934, and had spent seventeen months in a concentration camp. George John Dasch seemed to me, as I listened to him testify in court, glib, vain, and essentially unsteady—hardly a man who could be counted on to take heroic risks. When he began to serve his sentence the prison psychiatrists considered that he was suffering from an "obsessive, compulsive, neurotic, hysterical personality disorder." For methodical people the Nazi administrators were curiously careless at times, missing the central issue in their plodding collection of the irrelevant.

On the dim Long Island beach a coast guardsman surprised Dasch and his three companions, who were burying their explosives and uniforms in the sand. One of them had told the others not to shoot him—they were threatening him with revolvers—and another had forced $350 into his hand to keep his mouth shut. The young American acted with courage and intelligence, and took the money and his story immediately to his superior. The FBI was on the job in a few minutes. The four Germans who landed at Ponte Vedra were able to get into civilian clothes and disappear into the night without being seen.

Dasch, who had formerly been a New York waiter, took a train to Washington, went to the office of the Federal Bureau of Investigation and told his story. It sounded utterly incredible: but not so incredible, perhaps, when one remembered the fearful "Black Tom" explosions at Kingsland, New Jersey, in 1915, resulting from sabotage accomplished, as it was later proved, under the direction of the German High Command. Dasch was not certain where his comrades of the first boat had gone. But he knew their general plans, and gave fairly accurate descriptions of their looks. Even before he left Germany, he insisted, he was determined to turn state's evidence—he spoke English well, having, like the others, lived for a good many years in the United States before returning to Germany between 1933 and 1941.

All of Edgar Hoover's imaginative and restless energy was stirred into prompt and effective action. His eyes were bright, his jaw set, excitement flickering around the edge of his nostrils when he reported the incident to me. He was determined to catch them all before any sabotage took place. He had steadily insisted that this war could be fought without sabotage. But he was, of course, worried. The immediate problem was whether the Coast Guard and patrols along the Atlantic beaches should be alerted, indeed whether the public should not be told—other submarines might be landing as we talked; or whether FBI agents alone should work on the capture of the eight, and every effort made to prevent the news of the landings getting into the papers and being read by the quarry. We both thought the latter course was preferable; but I wanted the President's approval, and telephoned him. He agreed.

On June 27, ten days after the second landing, Hoover called me to say he had apprehended seven of them, and would soon have the last. The same night Katherine and I were dining with our friends, Constantin Fotitch, the Yugoslav ambassador, and his wife, and I can still feel the flood of relief that poured over me when Edgar called again. Yes, he had the last of them. I had had a bad week trying to sleep as I thought of the possibilities. The saboteurs might have other caches hidden, and at any moment an explosion was possible. Would it not have been better to alert the country, even if we lost our quarry?

I called the President, who was at Hyde Park, and told him the news. I added that we had collected $175,000 from them, and had dug up the explosives and other wrecking paraphernalia. As so often happened, his relief from anxiety found expression in humor. "Not enough, Francis," he answered. "Let's make real money out of them. Sell the rights to Barnum and Bailey for a million and a half—the rights to take them around the country in lion cages at so much a head." And I think he would have enjoyed doing it. He had a smack of the Old Testament retributive justice about him—a tooth for a tooth . . . he kept chuckling, and I knew that he too was immensely relieved.

We released the story of the landings, describing the caches in the most general terms and the swift apprehension. It was a short release—nothing was said about Dasch's long, minute rambling signed confession. The country went wild. The coast guardsman became a national hero, and was elevated to the rank of coxswain. Speculation as to how the second landing had been discovered was in every newspaper; and it was generally concluded that a particularly brilliant FBI agent, probably attending the school in sabotage where the eight had been trained, had been able to get on the inside, and make regular reports to America. Mr. Hoover, as the United Press put it, declined to comment on whether or not FBI agents had infiltrated into not only the Gestapo but also the High Command, or whether he had watched the saboteurs land . . .

What to do with them? The problem was not without difficulty; and I was anxious that there be no false move, and no delay. There was little suggestion of espionage that we could squeeze from their detailed and meticulous instructions; they had not committed any act of sabotage. Probably an indictment for attempted sabotage would not have been sustained in a civil court on the ground that the preparations and landings were not close enough to the planned act of sabotage to constitute attempt. If a man buys a pistol, intending murder, that is not an attempt at murder. The broad federal law covering conspiracies to commit crimes applied; but carried a penalty grossly disproportionate to their acts—three years, as I remember. However, they could be charged before a military court with penetrating in disguise our line of defense for the purpose of waging war by destruction of life and property, for which under the law of war the death penalty could be inflicted.

But there was a troublesome Civil War case that seemed to stand in our way. *Ex parte Milligan* was decided by the Supreme Court in 1876, a decade after the Civil War, at a time when the tide of opinion was running strongly against the excesses indulged in by the Executive while war was being waged—Lincoln, in suppressing rebellion, had not been overtender with civil liberties. With his approval thousands of civilians were arrested without warrant, held on suspicion of disloyalty, without charges being preferred against them, at the will of the administration, often without bail, and released at its discretion. As early as 1863, in an act suspending the writ of habeas corpus, Congress, already in reaction against such high-handed proceedings, provided that the names of detained citizens (other than prisoners of war) should be filed with the courts at the places of their residences; and if thereafter a grand jury should sit and fail to indict, they should be discharged on order of the court.

Milligan was arrested by the military in Indiana, found guilty of conspiring against the United States to aid the rebels—he had obtained military supplies from northern arsenals and sent them to the Confederates—of inciting insurrection and violating the laws of war. He was sentenced to death, and his sentence approved by President Lincoln. The grand jury sitting in Indianapolis had not indicted Milligan, and he accordingly petitioned the court for his discharge under the statute. When the case reached the United State Supreme Court it decided unanimously that Milligan should have been released in accordance with the act of 1863. But five of the justices went further in a long and vehement dictum to the effect that if a statute had permitted trial of a civilian by a military commission, the statute would have been unconstitutional. No civilian could be held for military trial, the opinion stated, as long as the civil courts were open and properly functioning, and courts could not be closed except where martial law had been declared, based on actual invasion rendering the courts incapable of performing their functions. Indiana had not been invaded. This pronouncement was quite unnecessary to the decision of the case. It was *obiter dicta;* but there it was, rolling down the years and occasionally given fresh life by a judicial pat on the back.

We thought we could overrule or get around *Ex parte Milligan,* and would argue that it had no application to modern war in a case in which saboteurs, members in fact of the enemy's armed forces, penetrated our line of defense. When that happened, captives had always been subject to the swift penalty of military trial. These men had penetrated battle lines strung on land along our two coasts, and guarded on the sea by our destroyers, and were waging battle within our country.

I dispatched a memorandum to the President briefly summarizing our conclusion, and recommending that as Commander in Chief he appoint a special military commission to try the prisoners. He had been thinking along the same lines, and a note from him, dated June 30, crossed mine:

> I have not had an opportunity to talk with you about the prosecution of the eight saboteurs landed from two German submarines nor have I recently read all the statutes which apply: [Note the Rooseveltian touch, as if to say: I know all about law, and anyway I don't have to read all the statutes: this is War.]
>
> It is my thought, however:
>
> 1. That the two American citizens are guilty of high treason. This being war-time, it is my inclination to try them by court martial. I do not see how they can offer any adequate defense. Surely they are as guilty as it is possible to be and it seems to me that the death penalty is almost obligatory.
>
> 2. In the case of the other six who, I take it, are German citizens, I understand that they came over in submarines wearing seamen's clothes—in all probability German Naval clothes—and that some of them at least landed on our shores wearing these German Naval clothes. I think it can be proved that they formed a part of the German Military or Naval Service. They were apprehended in civilian clothes. This is an absolute parallel of the case of Major Andre in the Revolution and of Nathan Hale. Both of them were hanged. Here again it is my inclination that they be tried by court martial as were Andre and Hale. Without splitting hairs I can see no difference [i.e. don't split hairs, Mr. Attorney General].
>
> F.D.R.

The comparison was not inexact. Nathan Hale, volunteering for espionage work, was captured on Long Island behind the British lines and hanged the next morning. Major John André, adjutant general in the British Army, returning from his negotiations with Benedict Arnold for the surrender of West Point, was caught in American territory in civilian clothes, his boots stuffed with incriminating papers, on September 29, 1780. He was tried by a board of officers appointed by General Washington, which concluded that he was a "spy from the enemy, and that agreeable to the law and usage of nations . . . he ought to suffer death." He was hanged on October 2.

From the beginning it was clear that the right of the government to hold the court-martial would be argued and decided by the Supreme Court. Our problem was narrowed if not simplified by the President's saying to me when we again discussed the case: "I want one thing clearly understood, Francis: I won't give them up . . . I won't hand them over to any United States marshal armed with a writ of habeas corpus. Understand?" I understood clearly, but his words did not make things any easier for his Attorney General, who was under a very special obligation to obey the law, even if the words had the historical echo of some of his obstinate predecessors, who, in times of crisis, had resisted what they considered judicial interference with the President's duty to act.

I urged the President to appoint me prosecuting official before the military commission. The Judge Advocate General of the Army, Major General Myron Cramer, had practiced briefly before entering the regular Army in 1920, but had not argued before the United States Supreme Court. "We have to win in the Supreme Court, or there will be a hell of a mess," I said. "You're damned right there will be, Mr. Attorney General," replied F.D.R. grinning back at me, and told me to see Stimson. The Secretary of War did not like it, it was most irregular, it had never been done before—a civilian prosecuting for the Army. But he knew how eager I was to try the case myself, and smiled, and said, "Talk to Cramer." As it turned out the Judge Advocate —the "Jag" as he was called—was relieved not to have to take charge, and we sat most amicably together in trial and argument. He was unwilling to take any active part in either. The Secretary chose Colonel Kenneth C. Royall—in association with Colonel Cassius M. McDowell—to defend the prisoners, which he did with perseverance and skill.

Royall was a special assistant to the Secretary, and would later serve from 1947 to 1949 as Secretary of the Army under

President Truman. He was immensely tall—six feet five or six—on occasions as hard and sharp as steel, yet with admirable court manners and presence, warmed by a pleasant, deep-chested North Carolina drawl. It was typical of Royall that he defended his clients up to the hilt, and at the same time wisely notified his chief, the Secretary, before taking any important step on their behalf, particularly when he filed the petitions for habeas corpus, so that the Secretary should have an opportunity of registering an objection should he wish to do so.

The Department of Justice drafted an executive order, which, signed by the President on July 2, set up a special military commission—as distinguished from a court-martial—consisting of seven general officers. The order provided that the prosecution should be by the Attorney General and the Judge Advocate General; designated the two-defense counsel; directed that the commission should try the eight Germans on July 8 or as soon thereafter as possible for "offenses against the law of war and the Articles of War"; and added a requirement that the concurrence of only two thirds of the members of the commission should be necessary for conviction or sentence—the Articles of War governing courts-martial required a unanimous vote for the death penalty.

It was a distinguished commission, made up of some of the best-known officers of the Army, four major generals and three brigadiers. The president was Major General Frank McCoy. He had been particularly cordial to me when, as a youngster, thirty years before I had spent a year in Washington as Justice Holmes' secretary, and I had grown greatly to admire him. He had been aide-de-camp to General Leonard Wood when that officer served as military governor of Cuba, and when I first knew him was associated with General Wood when Wood was Chief of Staff. He commanded the Sixty-Third Infantry Brigade in France during the First World War, and during its march into Germany after the Armistice. He was a first-rate administrator and skillful negotiator. After his retirement in 1938 he was called on constantly to serve on important boards and commissions.

The prisoners, at the President's direction, were handed over to Major General Albert L. Cox, who was in command of the military district of Washington. I rather think he expected an attempt at rescue, though from what source or by whom it would have been hard to say. One day, when for a few minutes the court had recessed, one of the prisoners—they all spoke English fluently—asked General Cox for a cigarette. The general was upset—he was a nice man, and I grew to like him—he was sorry, there was no Army appropriation for such a purpose, he said a little wistfully. Edgar Hoover, standing next to me—he was easily and often irritated by the unaccountable ways of the Army—whipped out a package and offered it to the young man.

The District jail was turned into a military prison. Sentries with bayoneted rifles and steel helmets patrolled the doors, the courts, and the corridors. They were posted outside the walls, and each acquired a little following of neighborhood small fry, who kept their distance behind him, but walked post with their hero. Every morning during the trial the prisoners were placed in two armored vans and brought to the Department of Justice, guarded by two cars of soldiers manned with machine guns, accompanied by nine motorcycle police. Traffic was halted as the heavy iron gates of the Department swung open on the courtyard, and closed on the crowd of spectators. The photographers, who were not allowed in the building, their movie cameras anchored on top of automobiles, waited in vain through the long mornings. Outside the entrance fifty soldiers stood guard. A hundred curious spectators lingered near the building, and hot-dog and ice-cream vendors for a while did a thriving business, as the crowd waited to see the procession of vans and motorcycles thunder in each morning.

From the beginning General McCoy laid down a strict rule that no reporters should be permitted at the trial, and no news should be given out by the commission. He had the kind of authority that carried conviction, and there were no leaks. Now and then—very rarely—the reporters put two and two together, and did some clever guessing: Haupt, when arraigned, had a bandage on his left wrist and was handcuffed by the right wrist to a deputy marshal. He was reported to have torn his wrist artery with his teeth in a vain attempt at suicide. The fact that pretty Mrs. Gerda Melind, a Chicago divorcée, formerly engaged to Haupt, had taken the stand on the first day was treated as immense news, but the nature of her testimony

was not known . . . the country, on edge for news, got nothing.
The press was highly indignant.

Elmer Davis was then in charge of censorship. He had left
the Columbia Broadcasting System to direct the Office of War
Information, which exercised a voluntary censorship that was,
with few exceptions, respected during the war. Anyone who has
been connected with the government in Washington realizes
how difficult it is to prevent leaks. The reporters, who knew the
ropes and had friends everywhere, were familiar, as they always
are, with most of what was going on. But except in a few rare
instances they did not use their information improperly, and
the secrets did not get out if Elmer said "no." And how terribly
they must have been tempted at times—when the African landing was being readied, for instance. This admirable restraint
was largely because they had confidence in Davis, and knew
that he would not be bullied by the brass hats, and, if he could,
would release news that was not harmful to the war effort. On
paper his power was absolute. The President's order appointing
him used clear and precise language, and it may be doubted
whether he would have otherwise taken the job of controlling
information. He had authority "to issue such directives of war
information as he might deem necessary or appropriate," and
these were "binding upon the several Federal departments and
agencies."

He did his best to pry something loose, to give the country
some idea of what was going on in that mysterious room in the
Justice building, a classroom for the training of special FBI
agents. He talked to the Secretary of War, he talked to the
President, he begged me to intervene with the Secretary when
the President had refused to interfere. A suggestion for a limited
press coverage was vetoed by the Commission. Davis proposed
censored accounts. The proposal was rejected. How could it be
expected, he said, that newspaper editors and reporters would
respect the voluntary censorship, the gentlemen's agreement not
to divulge military secrets, if they were not allowed to get some
information on this most spectacular trial, with the country
stirred to the marrow, and the newspapers filled with speculation? What was the need of all the secrecy? I thought at that
time that the censorship was overdone. The Germans must have

known the substance of the evidence, and indeed there was little if anything that had to be concealed, except the confessions of Dasch and of Peter Burger.

But Elmer Davis' pleas were of no effect, and only little laconic and uninformative driblets issued from the commission, regularly twice a day: three FBI agents testified; the trial was proceeding satisfactorily according to schedule; the prosecution had closed its case—that sort of thing; but not a word about how the prisoners had been caught, or what their instructions were, or anything that was not already old news. In spite of the President's directive to Davis, the Army continued largely to control military information. Mike Monroney of Oklahoma, then in the House—he was elected to the Senate in 1951—lashed out not inaccurately at the "stiff and inadequate Army communiqués that suppress all news under the guise of withholding military information."

Finally eleven carefully selected newspapermen were admitted by General McCoy for a quarter of an hour to make observations; but, to their scornful disappointment, the proceedings were suspended while they looked around in almost total silence. General Cox told them that the commission would permit no questions to anyone but him; proper decorum must be followed; notes could be taken. He mysteriously added, "Anything you record with your eyes you may write about." He identified all the prisoners—that is all except one who kept his silence, and Werner Thiel startled everyone by calling out his associate's name, which the general had momentarily forgotten. The reporters expressed themselves as surprised to find the saboteurs ordinary-looking individuals, not "burly, booted storm-troopers," as Lewis Wood, of the New York *Times*, romantically put it. They were not handcuffed, and looked pale under the glaring artificial light—they had not seen daylight since their capture . . . Heinck crouched behind a pillar, till General Cox ordered him to lean forward. The generals did not wear full-dress uniforms, or place swords on the table before them. . . . On a table at the opposite end of the room from the bench rested some of the prosecution's exhibits—dungarees worn in the submarines, spades, a metal can, which had contained explosives, two brown valises, a fatigue cap with a swastika emblem, Burger's draft

card and social security card . . . that kind of trivia was all
the reporters could report.

After they had been there for fifteen minutes, General McCoy
said, "We are under pressure, gentlemen. We will allow you
three more minutes."

Burger stood out sharply from the other prisoners, who were
a sorry-looking lot, their eyes dim with the certainty of death—
I don't think any of them except Dasch and Burger even considered the possibility of anything else—the dark circles beneath
their lids a little heavier each morning as they took their places.
None was outstanding; none except Dasch and Burger could
be differentiated from the average young German soldier, his
hair cropped, his cheekbones prominent, personality gone from
his face, trained to obedience the way a child might be trained
to obey by the slap of ruler over the knuckles, or a clout on the
head. While Burger was at the concentration camp his wife had
a miscarriage. This was not surprising, as the Gestapo were trying to get "information" out of her about her husband, and had
told her that he was guilty of an infamous crime.

Burger's eyes were hard with the memory of past tortures,
but he would not talk about them. He said in a statement to the
FBI that he had vowed from the beginning to betray Adolf
Hitler at the earliest opportunity. But at first he refused to testify.
He was afraid reprisals would be taken against his wife and
parents if the news got back to Germany that he had turned
against the Führer. He would rather die than take that chance
—and we believed him. He would not talk to escape death;
while Dasch, to save his skin, pleaded and begged and whined.
We finally persuaded Burger to give evidence on the promise
that what he said would be kept secret.

We proceeded promptly with the trial. It was obvious that
the reliance of the public on their government would be im-
measurably strengthened if these would-be saboteurs were disposed of promptly. As I have said, the last German was captured
on June 27. On July 8 the trial began, in accordance with
schedule. Edgar Hoover sat next to me, handing me typed summaries of the evidence of each witness just before he went on.

By July 27 all the evidence for both sides was in. On July

28 the prisoners, through their appointed American lawyers, applied to the District Court for leave to file petitions for habeas corpus, and their application was immediately refused. Kenneth Royall and I flew up to Philadelphia to request Justice Black, who was staying with Justice Roberts on his farm at Chester Springs, Pennsylvania, to urge the Chief Justice to call a special term of the Court. This Stone did "in view of the public importance of the questions raised, and of the duty which rests on the courts, in time of war as well as in time of peace, to preserve unimpaired the constitutional safeguards of civil liberty." He fixed the next day for the argument. Application for leave to file the petitions, answers to the petitions and a stipulation of facts were filed the same day in open court. While the argument was proceeding, Royall, on behalf of his clients, filed appeals from the orders of the District Court to the Circuit Court of Appeals, and petitions to the Supreme Court for certiorari to the Court of Appeals before judgment, pursuant to the provisions of an act allowing the Supreme Court, in its discretion, to take this short cut. The Court granted certiorari, and in accordance with a stipulation of counsel, treated the record, briefs, and arguments in the habeas corpus proceedings as the record, briefs, and arguments upon the writs of certiorari. All of these steps—which will not interest any lay reader, but may stir the technical imagination of the lawyer—were necessary because the jurisdiction of the Supreme Court, except in a few matters expressly stated by the Constitution, is appellate and not original. The Court, generally speaking, cannot take a case until a lower tribunal has passed on it.

When the Court opened on July 29 every seat was filled, with a scattering of officers in uniform who had received special permission to attend. Two justices were missing. Justice Murphy dutifully answered the summons and returned to Washington in uniform, where he permitted himself to be photographed on the steps of the Supreme Court building, but disqualified himself on the ground that he was an officer on "active duty" with the Army (for the summer), and therefore not qualified to pass judgment in a case involving military authority. Justice Douglas, flying from Oregon, got to Washington the next day. Chief Justice Stone announced that the rule giving each side one

hour for argument would not be enforced, and we could have
as much time as we needed. Royall took all the first day, although
the Court did not adjourn until six o'clock, and finished the following morning. He was on his feet about four hours, facing a
ceaseless barrage of questions. My argument lasted about three
hours. When Royall got up to make the first argument a page
handed him a telegram—I suppose from a lawyer—which he
looked at, and passed to me with a smile. It read: "Have you
considered *Milligan* case. Am interested only in constitutional
aspects." So were we; and Milligan had never been out of our
minds.

Did the famous dictum of *Ex parte Milligan* apply, that, as
long as the civil courts were open and functioning, civilians
must be tried by them? If not, what law did apply? I argued
that *Ex parte Milligan*, having but enunciated a dictum, quite
unnecessary to the decision of the case, was no binding precedent, and that the Court should now take the opportunity to
sweep away any lingering authority that the case still carried.
Nor was the case intended to apply to the situation here presented. Our coasts were lined with defenses against the constantly attacking submarines, which had landed these soldiers
behind our lines.

I talked of the law of war, a well-recognized body of law,
which occasionally the Supreme Court had referred to in
opinions in the past. Their questions showed that several of the
justices had but a dim idea of what the phrase meant—I was in
the same uncertainty until I began to prepare for argument two
days before. The conception held in the phrase, although definite
enough for recognition and application, derived its scattered
roots from divergent sources: from treaties, from the construction of treaties by sovereign powers, from the actual practices
of nations at war—the André trial, for example—from the principles embodied in the Hague Convention, and those which found
place in military codes. A very ancient and universally accepted
doctrine of the law of war was that enemy spies, penetrating the
battle line, could be shot. Under the Military Manual, however,
spies were entitled to court-martial if not caught hot in the act
but later arrested.

The Supreme Court filed a *per curiam* decision on July 31, the day after argument was completed, affirming the order of the District Court. Arguments before the commission were closed on August 1, and all eight defendants were sentenced on August 3, to the death penalty. Following my recommendation, the President, in consideration of their having turned state's evidence, commuted the sentence of Burger to life, and of Dasch to thirty years. On August 8 the six saboteurs condemned to death were electrocuted in the District jail. Exactly six weeks elapsed between the last arrest and the ultimate carrying out of the sentences. The defendants had been given every right afforded by our law, and were represented with unusual ability and perseverance by lawyers assigned to them by the country to which they had come in order to wreck war plants. It was an extraordinary example of justice at its best—prompt, yet fair— in striking contrast to what was going on in Germany.

About five years later there was an attempted jail break in the federal penitentiary at Atlanta, in which a group of criminals, most of them "lifers," got hold of three guards and held them as hostages while they bargained with the prison authorities over the "conditions" of their surrender. One of their chief complaints was that they had been forced to share the same prison with George John Dasch, a dirty German Saboteur (Burger had been transferred elsewhere), an indignity which they considered calculated to make the blood boil of any decent American forger, con man, or kidnaper. In 1948 President Truman commuted what was left of the prison terms, and both men were deported to Germany. I have no doubt that Dasch, one of the most unhaltingly voluble men I have ever encountered, has by now generously embellished the strange story of his capture and release as he keeps recounting it to a younger generation.

All through these weeks I received a stream of letters and telegrams insisting that these men should have been shot at once—they were murderers, swine—why should not they be treated as an American would under similar circumstances in Germany? . . . In his patriotic enthusiasm for reprisal Senator Dennis Chavez of New Mexico suggested that "some of the strong-arm boys in the FBI should be allowed to sock the Germans around a little" to produce more information—an utterance

that must have riled the members of that organization who were
particularly proud of a record which excluded the third degree
. . . General McCoy's wife told me many years later that, when
she was lunching at a restaurant in New York, her waiter—an
elderly man with the usual look of patient submission that belonged to his trade—asked her with a quiet shyness whether
she would plead with her husband that he be given a job as
one of the hangmen when the time came.

There are usually two sides to the coin. The saboteurs were
waging a desperate war for their country, not without pluck. It
must have required skill and courage to undertake their desperate and dangerous adventure.

The Court handed down its full opinion, written by the Chief
Justice, on October 29. "From the very beginning of its history"—
the opinion declared—"this Court has recognized and applied
the law of war as including the status, rights and duties of
enemy nations as well as individuals." Four years later the International Military Tribunal, of which I was the American member, quoted this passage as authority for the proposition that
international law was concerned with the actions of individuals
as well as of sovereign states, and that, under it, individual offenders could be punished for offenses against the law of war.
Stone went on to say that it was unnecessary to consider whether
the President as Commander in Chief had constitutional power
to create military commissions without the support of legislation,
since Congress had authorized such trials, and that the only
question was whether it was within the constitutional power of
the government to try the prisoners before a military commission
for the offenses with which they were charged. Spies and enemy
combatants without uniform, coming secretly through the lines
to wage war by destruction of life and property, were, by
universal agreement, not entitled to the status of prisoners of
war, but were offenders against the law of war, and subject to
trial and punishment by military tribunals.

The Court dealt briefly with the *Milligan* case. The sweeping
language of the majority opinion in that decision that the law
of war "can never be applied to citizens where the courts are
open and their process unobstructed" was construed as having
particular reference to the facts before the Court. Chief Justice

Stone wisely added, to keep the door open, "We have no occasion now to define with meticulous care the ultimate boundaries of the jurisdiction of military tribunals to try persons according to the law of war." From this it was clear that the Court reserved the question of the power of Congress to restrict the President's authority to conduct military trials.

The Chief Justice had great difficulty with the final opinion, doubtless increased by a sharp attack of lumbago at Peckett's in New Hampshire, which descended on him a few days after he had returned to his summer home on Sugar Hill from Washington, and was partly due, as he wrote Charles Evans Hughes, to two strenuous days climbing over mountain trails—he found it difficult to be more discreet at seventy than at twenty-one. He was irritated with the secrecy surrounding the military trial, of which the habeas corpus proceedings contained no record. There was nothing to show, when the argument was made, whether or not the prisoners had already been sentenced—and perhaps executed.

It was not clear, Stone felt, whether the Articles of War governed the procedure of special commissions, such as this, and required unanimous judgment of the military tribunal instead of two thirds, as the order provided, and review by the Judge Advocate General, in spite of F.D.R.'s direction that the record be sent "directly to me for action thereon." There was no way of determining whether the judgment of the commission had been unanimous, or if the JAG had—personally or through a deputy—reviewed the evidence. The only question that had been raised was whether the prisoners could be tried by a military body rather than a judicial one. But what plagued Stone was whether they could be tried under the rules set down for this particular commission. Suppose the two surviving saboteurs raised this question now, with a record that properly presented them, and the Court agreed with their view of the law: it would place the Court—as he put it in a memorandum to certain of his associates—"in the unenviable position of having stood by and allowed six men to go to their death without making it plain to all concerned—including the President—that it had left undecided a question on which counsel strongly re-

lied to secure petitioners' liberty." Yet he was reluctant to pass
on a question that was not raised by the record before the
Court, and to decide "a proposition of law which is not free
from doubt upon a record which does not raise it."

I still occasionally carry on my watch chain a small piece of
aluminum, about as big as a fifty-cent piece, cut into the likeness
of a porcupine by one of the saboteurs who was in the submarine that landed off Long Island. He told Hoover, who gave
it to me, that it was their "mascot." He did not say whether
they carried a real porcupine, or why they had chosen that
unapproachable animal to bring them luck. It has not, so far as
I can discover, had any particular influence for good or ill in my
own case. But then I am an American on whose skeptical and
casual nature such occult mysteries do not appear to operate.

Two years after these first landings a German U-boat brought
two espionage agents, Erich Gimpel, a German radio expert,
and William Curtis Colepaugh, to Crab Tree Point, not far from
Mount Desert Island in Maine. Willy Colepaugh . . . the name
stirred faintly in my mind, until Katherine, whose memory is
much clearer, reminded me. Twenty years before we had spent
a summer, one of four, at Black Point, Connecticut. Attached to
the cottage which we rented was a windmill that pumped our
water supply, and not infrequently needed attention. Mr. Colepaugh, who looked after everyone's windmill, had a son Willy,
I suppose about sixteen at the time, who must have been something of a problem even then, for I can remember our neighbors
saying, when the boy got into some mild scrape, "I wonder what
will happen to Willy Colepaugh." He became a renegade American in the war, but without enough courage of conviction to see
through an adventure in sabotage. He sought out the FBI and
confessed, perhaps getting momentary excitement from his new
role. Colepaugh remembered that Gimpel was accustomed to
buy Peruvian newspapers—he had lived in Peru for several
years—at a newsstand in Times Square in New York. Four days
later two FBI agents picked him up at the stand as he was
purchasing a magazine. Both men were tried by a military commission, found guilty, and sentenced to death by hanging. The

President commuted their sentences to life imprisonment. Gimpel was released for deportation on August 11, 1955, but Colepaugh for some unexplained reason not until May 10, 1960. He is doing very well on parole.

VISIT TO MEXICO

In the spring of 1943 Morris Cooke telephoned that he would like us to see his friend Dr. Salomon de la Selva—did we know him?—he had a plan for us to visit Mexico, and we should at least listen to it, and besides we would enjoy Salomon—he was unique. Dr. de la Selva had tea with us one Sunday afternoon, and we found him unlike anyone we had known. He was a little man, with penetrating bright blue eyes, and delicate hands that flew in and out of his talk. He had lived everywhere and known apparently as many North Americans as Latin Americans. Born in Nicaragua, he had spent a good many years in New York, and then settled in Mexico. In New York he had been an admirer (to put it mildly) of Edna St. Vincent Millay, and had been her companion—so he assured us—on that ferry boat which she immortalized so characteristically. "Don't you remember," he said, "it had a Spanish title, *Recuerdo*," and began to recite:

We were very tired, we were very merry—
We had gone back and forth all night on the ferry.
It was bare and bright, and smelled like a stable—

. . . .

His proposal had all the generous sweep of hospitality that makes a Latin American occasionally hard to resist: my wife and I were to go to Mexico, accompanied by my brother George and his wife, not at the formal invitation of the Mexican Government—that would be standard, and we would have to go through stuffy ambassadorial channels—but from Carlos Pellicer, the renowned poet and distinguished director of the Institute of Fine Arts, and from the rector of the National University. One of Katherine's three ballads that had been set to music would be performed by the Mexican orchestra—preferably *And They Lynched Him on a Tree;* my brother George, "the celebrated painter," whom he had not yet had the honor of meeting, would decorate one of the most beautiful public buildings in the city with appropriate murals, and his wife would add noble bas reliefs; and I was to speak, preferably in Spanish, to the Mexican Bar Association. In the middle of the war it was "necessary" that I should thus unite our nations; and who better than an Attorney General with a poet for a wife and an artist for a brother, and a sculptor for a sister-in-law? If only we would not say "no," he, Salomon de la Selva, would arrange it all. . . .

Katherine and I looked at each other—how could we say no? After Salomon left we smiled and shrugged and forgot this pleasant prophecy—things like that never happened—but it was certainly a charming Latin gesture on Dr. de la Selva's part. . . . Wait and see, said Morris Cooke, who knew him better; and wrote me a little later that de la Selva had confirmed the arrangements to him in a letter: "The invitations mentioned," wrote Morris, "seem adequately to cover the fields of music, art, literature, and public life. Quoting Wendell Willkie, 'I would wish' that the Biddle family had produced, let us say, a horseshoe thrower and a tap dancer. Certainly if these could have been added to the galaxy of talent already listed, Mexico, from the Rio Grande to the Isthmus, would fall like a ripe apple in the family lap."

To our amazement—and delight—the invitations arrived after a couple of months, each separately issued by the appropriate dignitary: to George and to my wife by Dr. Pellicer, and to me by the acting rector of the National University of Mexico, Licenciado Alfonso Noriega, Jr., who was also dean of the law school. "The Faculty of Law and Social Sciences is honored to invite you to visit its centennial halls and to place them at your disposal so that, before a gathering of professors and students, you may expound the development of the science of law in your country—a subject on which this school recognizes you as a great and noble master. In recent years, especially during your tenure of office at the head of the Department of Justice in the Cabinet of President Roosevelt, the concept of *right*, and the vision of the ends of the Law have undergone a development in your country which tends to recognize human values ever more firmly." This development Mr. Noriega begged me to explain "in terms that would gain our comprehension." Cordial hospitality and the opportunity to know Mexico was offered "in exchange for the contribution of the wisdom" I would give them.

Katherine and I accepted after I had told the President our plans but without talking to the State Department—I was not long on protocol—and everything was made ready for a ten-day trip in September 1943. I should of course have cleared with the ambassador, George Messersmith, and when our visit was announced in the Mexican newspapers the ambassador was hurt, and said so in a long, friendly letter of remonstrance. It was not often that a member of the Cabinet came to the country to which he was accredited, and he and Mrs. Messersmith would have liked to have had the pleasure of having us stay with them during our visit to the city. But that was precisely what we wanted to avoid—the fatigue and boredom of polite exchanges, the dinners and luncheons, necessarily dull—I did not know the Messersmiths but I knew embassies. We wanted to see Mexico and the Mexicans, particularly some of their artists and poets and men of letters, and knew we would see them more convivially through the understanding eyes of de la Selva, entering by the back door, as it were.

Actually we entered by Monterrey—Mary Winslow had told us that we must not waste precious time in flying, but approach the wonderful city lying on a great high plateau through the mountains. As we climbed off the train at seven-thirty we were met in the freshness of a clear morning by a young lady in white satin with an enormous bunch of roses, followed by a reception committee: Pardo Aspe, a justice of the Supreme Court, Jose Vasconcelos, an internationally known philosopher who had been minister of education under President Obregon, Dr. Noriega, representing the University, and our friend Salomon,

who, as appeared in the next few days, had no official standing
on the committee, but was clearly entitled to an unofficial place
in its activities. He was at the time associated with a lively
weekly called *Hoy*, and the current number contained his translation of Katherine's poem *Plain Chant for America*. Vasconcelos
spoke fluent English—he had written a book on Ralph Waldo
Emerson—and Aspe and I could communicate in a combination
of French and English; but Noriega—"Chatto" or "Pug Nose" as
he was nicknamed—was limited to Spanish. But he was so gay,
so quick, so friendly and funny that the language barrier was
almost surmounted. We had two cars, and there was a third
automobile with guards, which followed our leisurely procession
through the mountains. The weather was perfect. We spent the
first night at Valles, and stopped for lunch the second day at
Tamazunchole (Thomas and Charley, as the gringos call it),
and I have never known a less formal or more cordial journey.

The escort increased in size as we entered Mexico City,
chaperoned by four screaming motorcycles. We were lodged in
the De Sota, a well-appointed little modern duplex apartment
house, the living room bursting with flowers, the Frigidaire—displayed by Salomon with an amused, casual pride—full of whiskey
and Coca-Cola. We had been assigned a cook, Herminio Lucia,
who had been valet to the most loved of all American ambassa-
dors to Mexico, Josephus Daniels; and Lucia's wife who did
everything else. For a week I did not discover that I also had
a private secretary. He would turn up every morning as we
were sitting down to a late breakfast, and ask me what my do
sires were for the day. I was laboring under the illusion that
he was the manager of the apartment house; and when I suggested that something might be done to make the hot water
run, he would bow and smile, as if mention of such details between us could only be taken as some international joke, at which
it was the part of good manners to be amused. Two young
officers were detailed to guard us. They were evidently instructed never to lose sight of us; and at first we thought it
would be a bore. But they were so smiling and easy, so useful
and discreet and attractive, and finally so boyishly affectionate
that we enjoyed their chaperonage, as they slipped out of a
shadow to stand at attention while we climbed into their car,

always ready to pick us up at any hour of the day or night. One of them, P. DeKoster Fuentes, spoke a little English, acquired at the University of "Techas," as he pronounced it, and still sends us a Christmas card addressed to Mrs. Biddle and family.

Our arrival had been somewhat casual, and the members of the American Embassy were, not unnaturally, put out that everything had not been according to Hoyle—my speech had not been submitted to the ambassador until the last moment, and only in response to his politely phrased request that he might be permitted to take a look at it. Mr. Messersmith had not been given an opportunity to meet us on arrival, and in the upper hierarchy the spectacular entrance of our noisy cavalcade was frowned on as not being *comme il faut*.

When we had been in the apartment a few minutes, looking at everything with enthusiastic exclamations, laughing and generally making merry, a gentleman was announced, who informed us that he represented the ambassador. He was upright, stiff, formal, correct—clad in the most rigid of cutaways, speaking the most impeccable American English. He seemed troubled, reticent about something, and not without embarrassment. When we had surmounted the usual preliminaries he cleared his throat. He thought it was his duty to inform me that—he hesitated—a "person" had been trying to get in touch with me at the Embassy, had in fact been telephoning me every two hours. "She" had left her name and address and telephone number on a bit of paper. He extracted this from an inner recess and held it out to me at arms' length, as if it polluted the very air that separated us. On it was written "Paulette Goddard." What did she want, I asked? How should he know, answered the young man; but she was very anxious to talk to the Attorney General. I said I did not know her and could not see her—after all I was on a holiday. The young diplomat looked almost gay, he was so relieved. He mopped his brow; the thought that I should see Paulette, presumably on ambassadorial *terrain*, had been almost too much for him. At the time she was engaged to Burgess Meredith, of whom we were very fond. She had tangled with the Customs, and presumably needed help.

George Messersmith was hard-working and intelligent. F.D.R.

had moved him from consul general in Berlin, where he had been for a long time, to be minister to Austria, and then to Mexico. He liked the Mexicans, and those who came in contact with him returned his friendliness. But the larger public noticed only his superficial gaucheries. One of these—slight perhaps, but the sort of thing that is easily misinterpreted—we witnessed. During our visit, when General Marshall had reviewed the troops, he decorated a Mexican general at the Embassy. Messersmith took Marshall aside, and began to whisper to him. The Mexican looked upset. But in spite of his slightly uncouth manner, Messersmith was an excellent ambassador, an American and a man, in refreshing contrast to the little oh's and ah's who once tiptoed in and out of our embassies, with their cherished French accents, and allusions to Paris restaurants that only the select were supposed to know about, happily a diminishing group, a hangover from the days when "gentlemen" who could pay their way lounged about the foreign service.

Katherine had been led to expect that her ballad would be under way when we got to Mexico in September. Dr. Pellicer would take the part of the narrator, and Julian Carrillo, a composer and musician, would have charge of the orchestration and musical rendering. They wanted to confer with her in order to discuss how the lines should be read. We hurried back from Taxco, with its beautiful church like a ripe fruit, to meet them. Neither was available; and we were told by Vasconcelos that a most disconcerting thing had happened: the performance was to be under the auspices of the Red Cross, and no such function could succeed without the help of the American Embassy. The wife of the president of the Red Cross had been refused an "engagement" with Mrs. Messersmith—was it perhaps because the Embassy did not approve, or, more accurately put, would not "lend its approval" to such a subject? Could I see the ambassador? I could and did, at once. Mr. Messersmith said it was all a mistake, his wife had been tired and resting when the Red Cross lady called, he would attend to it personally at once, would subscribe for two hundred seats, and would see that the whole American Embassy (there were about six hundred of them, counting the Office of Economic Warfare, Lend-Lease, and similar organizations) would attend. Back we went triumphantly

to Vasconcelos. But he then informed us that the musicians were
all out of town, there was hardly time—could we not wait over
until they could be gathered? He was afraid there would be a
slight delay . . .

The slight delay lasted for a year, but at last *And They
Lynched Him on a Tree* was performed with éclat and enthusiasm, if not with a sense of tragedy. Dr. Richard Lert, a well-
known European conductor (and Vicki Baum's husband) heard
the performance and reported to Grant Still (who had written
the music) with enthusiasm. The chorus was very fine, they were
not afraid to sing, these music students from the Academy
Nationale—the Conservatoria. Carlos Chavez placed it with the
first beat—and there it was. The contralto, who went by the
wonderful name of Conception de los Santos, performed with
great style . . . Peggy Rosenbaum, who had married and was
then living in Mexico, thought, however, that the ladies of the
chorus, with elaborately swirled coiffures interwoven with flowers,
sang in rather thin, reedy tones, and that one missed the warmth
of a broad-bosomed Negro contralto. Pellicer was the narrator,
and recited—*Era un hombre* (He Was a Man)—with clarity and
dignity. The performance was completely sold out.

My brother George could not at the time "decorate beautiful
buildings" as he was busy with his job as chairman of the War
Department's Art Advisory Committee, which he had organized
to obtain a pictorial record of the war—when Congress neglected
to continue the modest appropriation to pay the expenses of a
dozen artists to do this work at the front, *Life* magazine took
over, and the record was made. He went through the African,
Sicilian, and Italian campaigns, living with the GIs, carrying
his own pack, following them on the night marches, sleeping
with them in the rain, the only correspondent living with the
troops. He was fifty-eight, and stuck it out for seven months,
losing twenty pounds, but otherwise unharmed. He felt the experience deeply, and wrote about war in moving words[1]: "the
discomfort of lying night after night in wet clothes; the smell of
cold sweat and vomit; the misery of old men and little children;

[1] *Artist at War* (New York: Viking Press Inc., 1944).

feeble, starved, hunted, afraid; staggering, half-clothed under weights that are too heavy for them to bear—going nowhere, driven relentlessly on, seeking a cave into which they can crawl, straw on which they can lie; destruction of peasant homes, of the warm shells of the poor of this earth, more terrible than the destruction of palaces, churches, monuments . . ."

The following year, after the plan for the murals had been put to sleep in the official files of the Mexican Government and finally prodded out and approved by two ministers—the jurisdiction of each seemed uncertain—George and Hélène went to Mexico City for a year, during which George painted frescoes and Hélène executed bas reliefs in the Supreme Court building.

My talk to the Mexican lawyers was delayed only a week, until the day before I left. I had taken a good deal of pains in its preparation. Katherine and I had been taking Spanish lessons —we never got very far—with an attractive and cultivated young Chilean connected with the Pan American Union, Francisco Aguilera. I wrote my remarks out, Aguilera translated them, I practiced reading them aloud, and read them, duly broadcast, at the meeting. Noriega gave me a friendly introduction, quoting at length from what I was about to say.

I spoke of the different aspects of democracy. There was political democracy—and I talked of its development in the United States—in which legal rights were fundamental: universal suffrage, impartial justice, trial by jury. But there came a time when a true democracy must concern itself with economic as well as political ills; and I instanced some of the federal legislation adopted under President Roosevelt. In speaking of political and economic functions, I had not meant to exclude the inner virtue below and behind all government—*la democracia del corazon*—"the democracy of the heart." It was instinctive, it was charming, it knew no caste, was not blinded by the color of the skin, or race, or by poverty or ignorance.

The United States had interfered at times, I continued, with the internal affairs of Mexicans, had not always been a good neighbor . . . Mexico should be developed for Mexicans; utilities must be operated by Mexican skill and for Mexican interests. But the past was past, and our eyes were on the future. I reminded my audience what Walt Whitman had once written:

> We have frequently printed the word Democracy. Yet I cannot too often repeat that it is a word the real gist of which still sleeps, quite unawaken'd, notwithstanding the resonance and the many angry tempests out of which its syllables have come, from pen or tongue. It is a great word, whose history, I suppose, remains unwritten, because that history has yet to be enacted.

Just before we left Washington, Jesse Jones had recommended a loan to a public utility owned and operated by an American company in Mexico City. When the President asked me about it I had objected on the ground that such support would be flying in the face of our good neighbor policy, which for the first time in our relations with Latin American countries, particularly following the satisfactory adjudication of the Mexican oil dispute, largely as a result of the efforts of the United States representative, Morris Cooke, the year before, was taking the shape of reality. The President turned down the loan; and when I told him I was soon to speak in Mexico City he had suggested that I say something about "Mexico for the Mexicans." Franklin Roosevelt was a heroic figure in Mexico, and something of this worship was vicariously reflected in the vociferous applause that greeted my talk. The audience crowded around me, leading members of the government and bar were introduced. I was asked what was evidently a leading question—there was a hush, while those in the circle crowded forward to hear my reply. There was no use avoiding the truth any longer. "I do not understand a word of Spanish," I said. Some of them smiled and shrugged, evidently thinking it was a discreet way of avoiding an answer.

I left Mexico with mixed impressions—we had seen so much in those ten flying days. The tendency to a rapid war inflation was already causing anxiety and some suffering. The Indians tried to live almost exclusively on corn, hanging on to the stony edges of life. . . . Mexicans are extraordinarily polite to foreigners, and sharply spiteful about each other. They would respect us more if we traded—a hard but honest bargain—rather than gave them things; for they are a proud and sensitive people, preferring neither to be exploited nor to be nursed. . . . President Manuel Avila Camacho and former President Lazaro Cardenas were everywhere admired, while Maximino, President Camacho's brother, who seemed to have a hand in most of the night clubs, was generally distrusted. . . . The hardly-suppressed anti-United States feeling was rising again, perhaps had never much retreated. Our propaganda—and there seemed to be a good deal—should exchange cultural accomplishments rather than emphasize battle strength, an emphasis which largely accounts for the distrust.

The Mexican Government's idea of friendly propaganda was to translate Emerson into Spanish, and follow with Jefferson, Whitman, and Mark Twain. In Mexico it is more important to be a poet than a politician, but one can be both, and every member of the government whom we met seemed to have written a book. Jaime Torres Bodet, who was the assistant minister of Foreign Affairs, and would later head UNESCO, and Carlos Pellicer, both distinguished poets, presented Katherine with volumes of their poetry *en recuerdo* of her visit to Mexico; and Padilla, the Foreign Secretary, after inviting us to a pleasant informal luncheon, gave me a copy of his book, *Considerations on the Mexican Interpretation of The Good Neighbor Policy*—bound in leather with my name tooled in gold letters on the outside, and my title in Spanish—Procurador General de Justicia de Los E.U. de N.A.—to all Latin Americans we are North Americans.

The wonderful markets . . . the warm, sweet smells in the shrine at Guadalupe . . . the disease and filth and sadness of the Indians . . . the gaunt fortress-churches mounted in high places, the snow peak of "Popo" among the clouds, and the Pyramids of the Sun and Moon . . . we longed to see the baby volcano, but there was not time . . . we looked down from the windows of the old Palacio on the surging crowd in the great square, under fading eighteenth-century portraits of Spanish grandees and their ladies and of the doomed Maximilian, whom Lincoln would not recognize, and his Belgian empress Carlotta, and the glittering chandeliers and polished floors . . . Conscription had just been introduced tentatively. The youngsters were clean-cut-looking and marched with rhythm and pride, before the inspection of General Marshall, who sat as guest of honor on President Camacho's right.

THE FOURTH TERM
CONVENTION

◆{}◆ Chapter Twenty-three

In April of 1944 I was elected a delegate at large from Pennsylvania to the Democratic convention that was held in Chicago in July. A large majority of the delegates had come pledged to vote for Roosevelt for a fourth term, and there was no contest over the nomination. From the beginning the interest centered on the nomination of the vice president. President Roosevelt would not declare himself for anyone, although he could have had, in accordance with traditional practice, any running mate he wanted. It was evident that he did not want Henry Wallace. He remembered the famous letters that had turned up during the campaign four years before, and his trust in Wallace's judgment had been shaken. As in 1940 he preferred to give the delegates the feeling that they were making a free choice, and at the same time quietly steer the decision to the candidate he preferred. Very few delegates knew who that candidate was. Frank Walker, also a Pennsylvania delegate, received word indirectly that it was Truman, and told the other members of the delegation that they should vote for him. But how could they be sure? Similar assurances as to other candidates were flying around, and something more direct and positive was needed. The Pennsylvania delegation was a large one, with a substantial Wallace vote, but not pledged to any candidate.

I had gone to the convention believing that Justice William O. Douglas would be the best candidate we could choose. He was still under fifty, a man of great ability and vitality, deeply liberal in outlook. Although there was no organized Douglas movement before the convention several of the most powerful Democratic leaders thought he was a "natural," as Ed Kelly, the boss of the Democratic machine in Chicago, told me. There was something earthy and "folksy" about Bill, he looked like a handsome plow-boy come out of a field, with his clear humorous eyes, wrinkled forehead, and easy, serious smile. And those who knew him knew that he had the political shrewdness and savvy essential for the job. He had strong though spotty support in the convention. If one of the professionals had managed his campaign I think he might have been nominated. I do not believe that F.D.R. would have rejected such a selection, and I think that he meant what he said in the famous letter to Robert Hannegan, the national chairman, that either Douglas or Truman would be a suitable candidate.

In that particular convention power was distributed in three groups: among the city "bosses"—Ed Flynn, Ed Kelly, "I Am the Law" Frank Hague; the congressional leaders—Sam Rayburn, Senators Scott Lucas of Illinois, Millard Tydings of Maryland, Harry Byrd of Virginia, Carl Hayden of Arizona, and others, many of whom headed their delegations; and finally the labor delegates, who were far less united and influential than most of the press credited them with being. The mouthpiece for organized labor was Sidney Hillman, vice president of the CIO, who was not a delegate but was influential and active behind the scenes. Philip Murray, president of the CIO, a delegate from Pennsylvania, sat next to me on the floor of the convention. The American Federation of Labor, less politically minded than the CIO, was not active in the convention.

Henry Wallace was still a knight in shining armor to the "liberal" and—a much smaller but more vociferous group—the radical labor delegates, chiefly in the CIO, some of whose affiliated unions had not yet been cleared of their Communist control. Wallace had received the endorsement of a sizable number of delegates in the primaries, and came to the convention with substantial backing. But his strength was illusory.

I did not believe that at any time he had a chance of being nominated. The political leaders of the convention, however divided among themselves on a candidate, were solidly opposed to Wallace, whom they could not understand and distrusted. It was hardly conceivable that he could have swept the convention against the professionals, as Wendell Willkie had swept the Republican convention in 1936, and William Jennings Bryan the Democratic in 1896. Politically speaking, Willkie and Bryan were unknown figures; Henry Wallace was too well known.

His vote was so strong on the first ballot that Hannegan and Rayburn, afraid that he might carry the convention if the balloting immediately continued, caused an adjournment at the end of the vote. Everyone went into a huddle. Wallace's strength was Sidney Hillman, who stuck hard, uncertain about Truman and not yet prepared for a compromise. The leaders were afraid of a drawn-out battle, which they believed should always be avoided if possible, as it has the appearance of disunity. The delegates—by that time bored, sleepy, and beginning to be worried about their hotel bills—started to slip home, not caring much who was nominated for vice president.

The strategy of the scattering of delegates who hoped to see Douglas nominated was to deadlock the convention between Wallace and Truman so that Douglas could be pulled out as a compromise, a candidate with the look of something fresh and vital. The Wallace group were playing up the old comparison—Wallace was the hero of the unbossed delegates, of the country at large; Truman the choice of the bosses emerging from a smoke-filled room. There was a good deal of Douglas talk on the floor; he received a small scattering of votes on the first ballot; and when we sounded out some of the large delegations, particularly in the Northwest, his name was well received.

As a symbol there must have been something peculiarly compelling about Henry Wallace for such a shrewd and tough-minded man as Hillman to have preferred him when Douglas could have been put in the field. I could understand Hillman's doubt about Truman—Truman had not yet proved his independence, liberalism, and courage, and the albatross of Pendergast lay heavy about his neck. I believed that if Hillman had said to Hannegan that he would accept Douglas as a compromise,

Douglas might have been chosen. Harold Ickes, another Pennsylvania delegate, and I went over to see Hillman and urge him to shift to Douglas. He had managed to get himself cooped up in a strangely inaccessible penthouse at the top of some hotel, in order to avoid the politicians, and we found ourselves in the uncomfortable position of crawling up a fire escape, while a joyful news photographer, perched in a commanding spot, took photographs of our undignified approach. These were plastered the next morning over a press that tried to make it appear highly improper for two delegates to call on an influential labor leader to enlist his support for their candidate.

But we were unable to get anywhere with Hillman. The leaders of the convention had broken the Wallace strength. They saw to it that word got around that President Roosevelt wanted Harry Truman—not Douglas or Truman as he had written; and the tired delegates fell into line.

DEATH OF THE
PRESIDENT

❧❦ *Chapter Twenty-four*

It was April 12, 1945. It had been an extraordinary spring—copious, pervasive, beautiful. Katherine was to give a poetry reading that night at the National Arts Club. She wanted a spring poem poignant enough for the season, and as she was walking in Montrose Park that afternoon, a couplet from the Rubaiyat kept returning:

I sometimes think that never blows so red
The Rose as where some buried Caesar bled;

. . . .

I was with Edward Stettinius and Jim Forrestal, discussing at the President's request the formation of a permanent counter-intelligence service. Several tentative plans had been proposed, including a suggestion to place it under Edgar Hoover's competent direction—his background and experience suggested such an arrangement. Major General William J. Donovan, who had been director of the Office of Strategic Services since June 13, 1942, was mentioned for the job—OSS already operated in the foreign field, and could continue to function permanently after the war. But it was generally felt that since the new organization would work on a highly secret plane it should start from scratch and be on its own from the beginning. Its functions would not be the detection of crime like those of the Federal Bureau of Investigation, but the gathering and weighing of information in the foreign field. These should be sharply separated from any association with criminal investigation.

As we discussed the various suggestions we were interrupted by a message from Stephen Early, the President's secretary, that Stettinius should come immediately to the White House. There was no inkling of the terrible news which he brought back with him in a few minutes: the President was dead. I remember that we sat there, stunned and uncertain for a few minutes. Stettinius had never met Harry Truman. He asked us what it meant; what would happen—would there be another Harding regime?

We went to the White House. There were about two dozen persons gathered in the President's study, still too dumb with misery to realize what had occurred. I think all of the Cabinet were there. I remember Frances Perkins, crying quietly. There were a few representatives from the House—Sam Rayburn, John McCormack, Robert Ramspeck, Joe Martin, the minority leader. I do not remember any senator. I telephoned for Chief Justice Stone—the new President was to be sworn in at once—and when he arrived we could not find a Bible, and there was a fumbling delay, no one seemed to know where to get one. It was as if there were a gap in time, time was empty, nothing was planned, the instinct to postpone the flood of realization for as long as possible was for a brief moment satisfied by an immediate act, the next thing to be done, and it had to be done at once, the staggered mind thought, *at once*, or the world would fall apart . . . Margaret Truman came in with her father and mother, and I wondered what was in her mind, unable to bear what was in mine . . . Frances Perkins was sobbing now, and little Isador Lubin, who had served under her as commissioner of Labor Statistics and was a close adviser to the President on economic matters, had an arm around her . . . there was no sense of direction or guidance—what next? Felix Frankfurter and Bob Jackson were there from the Court, General Philip Fleming, Leo Crowley, Fred Vinson, John Blandford, and the White House reception secretary, William Simmons . . . The Vice President, his wife standing by his side, held the Bible in his left hand, his right hand a little below the hand of Chief Justice Stone, as he administered the oath . . . Nothing was said afterward—for the moment there was nothing to say.

When I got home it was nearly eight o'clock. Katherine held me in her arms for a moment; and something was loosed in me, and the pain began. She said that when a friend told her the news over the telephone she could not take it in, the words had to be repeated twice. She called Mary Winslow, and the colored maid answered, and when Katherine told her of what happened there was a pause, and then, "Not *our* President, Mrs. Biddle?" . . . We sat down to supper but I could not eat. Radio station WOL called me—would I say a few words on the air? I scribbled something on a piece of paper, and we went out. When I got there, there were two or three others connected with the government, I can only remember Senator Connally. I spoke hardly three or four sentences. I remember saying that when I heard the tragic news I thought of all the people of the world who loved the President—the oppressed, the minorities, the plain people whom Lincoln loved. "They will miss him," I said. "May God help America, and the world, suddenly made lonely, in our hour of need." It was hard, but I got through. . . .

The next afternoon I held a memorial service for the employees of the Department and the Great Hall, which seated over a thousand, was packed and overflowing and very quiet. Felix Frankfurter had come, and Bill Douglas, and Senator Carl Hatch, and Senator Joseph O'Mahoney. I asked Katherine to stand near me. I repeated what I had said the night before, adding a little more, but not talking over five minutes: it was fitting that we should meet together to share our sense of loneliness over the death of the President. He had come to serenity within his spirit before he became President in the dark days of the depression—and now in this hour of our sorrow we drew strength from what he said then, that there was nothing to fear. His courage was unconquerable, and his strength was measured by a faith in the people which could not be shaken . . . Bob Jackson, who spoke after me, was at his best, his words a little faltering. Power to the President, he said, was never an end, but a means to a better world where men might live their chosen lives, rear their families in decency and security, safely think and speak their thoughts. The President's "patience with blundering" was sometimes past understanding; but it was "mighty comforting" when the blunder was your own. The President would have been pleased that we were meeting in his memory, not because he would have wanted a personal tribute, but as a sign of our dedication to things he stood for . . . A resolution was offered. We sang *Abide with Me.*

Ruth Cunningham, who worked in the personnel office of the Department, told me that her boy, aged four, when he was saying his prayers the night the President died, after invoking the usual blessings on father and mother, added, "And especially Mother, God: she's just lost her President."

There were of course many tributes and messages of sympathy —I received a letter from Jesus T. Pinero, the resident commissioner from Puerto Rico, transmitting a resolution of the island House of Representatives, that ended, movingly, I thought. "The House, standing . . . fervently prays Almighty God to receive in his bosom the soul of the greatest contemporary citizen and the most fervent champion of the liberty and democracy of the world."

Writing to Mrs. Roosevelt I spoke of her husband's patience— even with lawyers: and Katherine quoted a phrase of Rebecca West's, that my wife thought described the President's leadership—he had kept the face of his people turned toward the sun.

After the service at the Department we drove to the White House to see Anna Boettiger. Mrs. Roosevelt had flown down to bring her husband's body home from Warm Springs. Anna's little boy was suffering acutely from a mastoid infection, and all the arrangements for the funeral services had been left to her. They were to be in the East Room; and she said the floor was so weak that the invitations had to be cut to the bone—would it be all right to ask the diplomatic corps without their wives?— and that was agreed on. "Ma says she won't have any lying in state; he didn't want it . . ." Anna was collected, strong and simple, more like her father, who had leaned on her heavily these past few years, more like him than any of the boys. We had supper with Jim Forrestal and his wife at their house on Prospect Street, sitting on the terrace and watching the movement and gleam of the Potomac, very broad at that point, at our feet.

The funeral service was early the next afternoon, a Saturday. The crowds still filled Lafayette Square. In the East Room of the White House the flag-draped casket lay between tall portraits of George and Martha Washington. Six servicemen, combat veterans, stood at attention. It was very warm. At the left sat the Supreme Court, with former Chief Justice Hughes, erect and fragile, and Mrs. Hughes, and the Cabinet and government officials. Almost no one noticed the new President and Mrs. Truman, with Margaret, slip quietly into the seats on the front row that had been saved for them. Mrs. Roosevelt, looking even taller in black, walked in on Elliott's arm, and we rose. Jimmy, flying back from Manila, was too late. The other boys could not be reached at the front in time.

"O God," prayed Bishop Dunn, "we thank Thee for the qualities of heart and mind which Thy servant brought to the service of our nation and our world—for steadfast courage in adversity, for clear vision of danger, to which many shut their eyes; for sympathy with the hungers and fears of common men." We sang two hymns, Senator Barkley's deep contralto voice immediately behind Katherine, and she cried a little, and he put an arm about her . . .

As we drove down Constitution Avenue that evening soldiers lined the streets, and people waited to see the casket drawn slowly to the station to be put on the special train; and all night they stood along the tracks to get a glimpse of it. . . . On the train we breakfasted opposite West Point with the Chief Justice, and watched the Hudson, beautiful in the clear, cold day. At Hyde Park lilacs were in bloom and apple blossoms. After three volleys were fired over the grave, Fala, the dead President's Scotty, barked three times—then taps, as Katherine said, the saddest sound in the world . . .

We climbed on board the train to go back to Washington. Harold and Jane Ickes came to our compartment. Harold asked if anyone had a drink; and Frank Walker produced a bottle of whiskey . . . We talked about F.D.R. Frances Perkins spoke of his good looks as a young man, of his arrogance, of his solemnity as a youthful reformer, and how all that changed after his paraly-

sis. Jonathan Daniels brought in his father, who said he did not
mind our drinking if we liked to poison ourselves—and we
laughed and joked and felt more normal. I went up to say a
few words to President Truman. He was with Bob Hannegan
and Jimmy Byrnes, who clung to him as if they were afraid
that he might be captured by someone else.

Looking over what I have recorded from the tugging memories
of Franklin Roosevelt gives me a sense that I have not offered
a balanced picture, that I have talked a good deal about the
small characteristics that stood out when one saw him in the
close and constant relationship that does not make a man heroic
to his valet. But on the contrary he was—at least to this particular
observer—a great man, even if in certain aspects he was not
heroic. Against the stature of that greatness must be measured
the faults: his passion for manipulation, his lack of frankness, his
streak of vindictiveness, his often amateur approach to the problems of government. Yet weighed in the balance, these failings
do not affect the ultimate achievement of his long career. His
gift of leadership would not have made him great were it not
for the quality and direction that it took. As John Gunther has
said of him, he lifted people above themselves. He gave them a
vision of what their country could be, convinced them that life
might be both secure and adventurous.

But it was more than that. He brought into the service of the
country the ablest group of men the government had ever known.
In the first two terms he did more for the American people
than any President had ever done. He was not, like Woodrow
Wilson, obsessed with any vision, except to do now and continuously what was needed for their welfare. Then came the
war; and, having achieved the unified support of the country,
he led the people to the victory that made the United States for
a brief space of time the democratic leader of the world.

Six weeks after President Roosevelt died I got a telephone
call from Stephen Early, who had been the late President's
secretary, and was still with the White House, to say that
President Truman wished my immediate written resignation, to
take effect at the end of June.

The new President was reorganizing the Cabinet, and I had assumed that he would not wish me to continue as his Attorney General. I knew him slightly. We had been in conflict on several matters that included the few appointments that came from Missouri, and he was a little cool to me. Maurice Milligan, the United States Attorney for the Western District of Missouri, had prosecuted the Pendergast organization of Kansas City, and sent several of its members to jail; and Senator Truman, loyal to the man to whom he owed his successful start in politics, opposed Milligan's renomination for office when his term expired in 1944. I had worked against Senator Truman's nomination for vice president at the Democratic convention in the summer of 1944, ten months earlier. I had no political influence in the Democratic Party, although a good many friends in the administration. I had been waiting for some time for the new President to let me know when he wished me to go.

However I thought, and so told Steve Early, that the manner of my dismissal was abrupt and undignified. I telephoned to the White House for an appointment. In an hour I was alone with the President. He was at first stiff, formal, and a little self-conscious. I said that of course I would send in my resignation at once, but that I was surprised at his way of asking for it—did he not think it would have been more in keeping with our official relationship if he had sent for me? He assented at once. He had not felt like facing me, he said, I told him that I understood perfectly that he should want me to go—the relationship was a highly personal one, lawyer to client—he should have his own man. He looked relieved; and I got up, walked over to him, and touched his shoulder. "You see," I said, "it's not so hard." He smiled.

I asked him if he would mind answering two questions: Was there anything particular in my record with which he was not satisfied; and, would he mind telling me who my successor was to be? No, he thought I had done a good job (what else could he say?); and he did not mind at all telling me who was to take my place. "You'll be pleased," he said. "He is someone in your department—Tom Clark." Tom Clark was then head of the Criminal Division, and I asked the President if he knew him. As a matter of fact, he replied, he had never met Clark. I told him that I was not pleased and would not have recommended him. I suggested that he talk to Jim McGranery, whom the President knew well, before making the announcement. He said he would; but he never did, and a few days later my resignation, and those of Frances Perkins and Claude Wickard were announced, with the names of our successors.

Since Clark had been appointed head of the Criminal Division he had become close to Robert Hannegan, the chairman of the Democratic National Committee, who had been in charge of Harry Truman's successful bid for nomination as vice president the year before. Clark also had the backing of two very influential Democrats from his state, Sam Rayburn, the Speaker of the House, and Senator Tom Connally. In 1949 Clark was appointed to the Supreme Court.

In his *Memoirs* President Truman remembered the incident somewhat differently. "Francis Biddle"—he wrote—"had been a good Attorney General and there was no ill feeling between us. I did not ask him to quit. He quit voluntarily. I do not believe he was as well satisfied with me as a liberal President as he had been with my predecessor. This was his right . . . I asked Biddle whom he would recommend to take his place, and he suggested Tom Clark, who of course, was strongly endorsed by the whole Texas delegation."

In this particular instance President Truman's memory was at fault.

THE NÜRNBERG TRIAL

❧ *Book Four*

Civilization does not expect that you can make war impossible. It does expect that your judicial action will put the forces of international law, its precepts, its prohibitions and, most of all, its sanctions on the side of peace, so that men and women of good will in all countries may have "leave to live by no man's leave, underneath the law."

> Robert H. Jackson, opening for the Prosecution, November 20, 1945

The nightmare of many a man that one day nations would be dominated by technical means was all but realized in Hitler's totalitarian system . . . In five or ten years the technique of warfare will be able to destroy one million people in the center of New York in a matter of seconds with a rocket . . . invisible, without previous warning, faster than sound, by day and by night . . . May God protect Germany and the culture of the West.

> Defendant Speer in his closing statement, August 31, 1946

THE INTERNATIONAL
MILITARY TRIBUNAL
IS ORGANIZED

≪{}≫ *Chapter Twenty-five*

We were spending a few weeks with Mary Winslow at North Hatley in Quebec Province, when Jimmy Byrnes, in September 1945, called me on the telephone to ask me if I would be willing to accept the President's appointment to act as the American member of the International Military Tribunal to try the major German war criminals. The trial was scheduled to begin as soon as possible, the indictment was ready, the defendants in custody. It should take, he said, in answer to my question, not more than three or four months. Could he have my answer immediately? I told him I would call him back that morning.

As Attorney General I had discussed the advisability of a trial with President Roosevelt and Secretary of War Stimson, and, in greater detail, with the Assistant Secretary, John M. McCloy. We cleared each step with the State Department, which was usually represented at the conferences, although I do not remember that it took any positive position in the matter. The heads of several of the Allied nations, including the United States, had from time to time announced that the "war criminals" would be punished, and we felt committed to take action. I was of the view that this should not be merely political—the execution of the leaders out of hand, or after a drumhead court-martial—but that there should be a serious and fair trial. The three departments came to the agreement outlining a general procedure, which was approved by the President. This preliminary plan he took with him to the Yalta Conference; but through an oversight, or on account of the pressure of more immediate plans, it was not discussed with Winston Churchill and Marshal Stalin. When he got back President Roosevelt turned over the project to his assistant, Judge Samuel I. Rosenman. After the President's death, President Truman asked Rosenman to take it up with representatives of the other members of the Big Four at the San Francisco Conference in April 1945. I delegated Herbert Wechsler, who was familiar with the negotiations, to act with Rosenman. Several conferences were held at San Francisco, which included Sir Anthony Eden, Vyacheslav Molotov, then Russian Commissar of Foreign Affairs, Secretary of State Stettinius, Jack McCloy, and a representative of the French. At one of them Eden said that his government had not wanted "a full-dress parade," which would afford the Germans an unparalleled opportunity for propaganda; but—and he bowed to Molotov and particularly to Stettinius—he would defer to the wishes of the Allies of his Britannic Majesty, and agree to a trial.

Justice Robert Jackson had written an article in the *Atlantic Monthly*, setting forth, with his usual clarity and eloquence, the scope and importance of such a trial, and President Truman appointed him after an Allied agreement had been reached at San Francisco, to act as chief prosecutor for the United States. On August 8, 1945, the London Agreement and Charter were executed by the United States, the Provisional Government of the French Republic, Great Britain, and the U.S.S.R., providing for international trials.

I had no plans for the immediate future. I had been offered partnerships in one or two New York firms, but had declined. I was not particularly eager to go back to private practice after nearly ten years of almost continuous public service. I felt a certain obligation to accept if the President wanted me—there was no adequate excuse to decline. And the prospect of being back in public work, and of having the decision of what I should do thus temporarily solved for me, was not to be resisted.

When I saw President Truman a few days later in Washington we were both standoffish. He looked well—as indeed he always did—but was still consciously living under the heavy shadow of his great predecessor. He was not a naïve man, except in certain fields; but he was neither fluent nor subtle, and often expressed himself in a naïve way. He was then still conscious of this, and perhaps thought of me as moving against a background of Groton and Harvard that was Roosevelt's, but not his. This did not irritate him, but it hardly made our relationship easier.

I remember some days after my resignation as Attorney General going to one of those stiff protocol stag dinners at the White House, which during the war President Roosevelt had instituted and his successor carried on. Half the Cabinet was asked at a time (Secretary Stimson never dined out), the remainder on the next occasion, flanked by alternating members of the House Foreign Affairs Committee and the Senate Foreign Relations Committee, the generals and the admirals relieving our black civilian monotony, finally the lesser lights, usually a White House assistant or two. On this particular occasion the visiting fireman was His Royal Highness Abdul Ilah, Regent and Crown Prince of Iraq, a young and handsome bachelor. The Crown Prince sat on the President's right, and on his left the prince's aide de camp, Lieutenant Colonel Ubayd Abdullah, next to whom I had been placed. Chief Justice Stone was on the prince's other side. I found the colonel delightful, cultivated, speaking a fluent and graceful English. He had known Lawrence of Arabia well and spoke of him with unaffected admiration. Did I know that Lawrence had mastered a dozen Arab tongues? I did not. At that moment the prince had turned to the Chief Justice, leaving the President disengaged, crumbling bread. I leaned forward and repeated to him what the colonel had said about Lawrence. The President looked at me and smiled. "Gosh," he said, "I can hardly speak English." The colonel did not understand. What, he asked me, did the President mean? Was it perhaps a joke?

Before I went to see the President, Katherine had said to me when I expressed the hope that Judge John J. Parker would be my alternate—Jimmy Byrnes had mentioned the possibility—"Remember that Mr. Truman is President. Don't tell him what he ought to do, whom he ought to appoint. Ask his opinion." Excellent advice . . .

The President told me that he had first offered the position he wanted me to fill to Justice Owen J. Roberts, who had recently resigned from the Supreme Court. He was very anxious that the four powers should co-operate in this new and complex undertaking, and that the world should be impressed by the fairness of the trial. These German murderers must be punished, but only upon proof of individual guilt at a trial. He would do anything to make my task easier; he admired Bob Jackson's careful, patient, and successful preparation. The agreement among the four nations had been signed three months after Jackson had been appointed.

"I'll do it, Mr. President, if you want me to," I said, and got up.

He put out his hand. "I'm glad, General, that I can count on you." He did not call me by my first name for the next year or two, not until our relation had become more intimate.

"I have only one condition," I continued; and, to his glance, surprised and faintly annoyed, I answered, "I want to take Mrs. Biddle with me." He acceded at once, and sent me a letter to be used if she ran into difficulties, which she soon did.

"Whom are you planning to appoint as the American alternate?"

"Judge Parker of the Fourth Circuit," he said. "Do you know him?"

I was delighted. I knew Parker slightly. He was a Republican, which afforded a desirable political balance. He was presiding judge of the United States Circuit Court of Appeals for the Fourth Circuit, able, liberal enough to know that he lived in a changing world, a leader in progressive law reform, admired by the American Bar Association, in which he had been active for many years. President Hoover had nominated him to the United States Supreme Court in 1930, but the Senate refused to confirm him by a tie vote. Vice President Dawes had been absent, and his vote would have put Parker on the bench. Dawes rushed over to the Capitol but arrived a few minutes after the Senate had adjourned. Parker never got over it. The opposition, chiefly from labor, had been based on his following the Supreme Court's decision that statutes outlawing "yellow-dog" contracts, under which the employee agreed never to join a union as long as he was employed, were unconstitutional. He did not share that view but felt constrained to bow to the judgment of the brethren on high when the question came up to his court for a new test. A reconstituted Supreme Court less than a generation later sustained a similar law.

I hesitated before leaving, and finally said, "Mr. President, am I right in thinking that your appointment says to the country that you have confidence in me? I left last June under a cloud. Didn't you have that in mind?"

This pleased him, and drew us together as he acknowledged his motive without stressing it, and I expressed gratitude. That moment was, to me at least, the beginning of a friendship which, as I write, is pleasant to remember and to record. Mr. Truman's nature included a keen sense of fairness, and he wanted to make up for the abruptness of my dismissal.

I called up Parker in Charlotte, North Carolina. He was skeptical, not very much interested, troubled about leaving home and his comfortable, well-defined life, somewhat concerned with the effect his absence would have on the court over which he presided with dispatch and tact. But what troubled him chiefly was that as an alternate he would be a voteless cipher, except when he replaced me if I were sick—like a vice president with nothing to do. I said that, except for the single point of voting, his status would be identical with mine, he would join in all discussions with complete freedom to express his opinion, whether or not it differed from mine.

Judge Parker agreed to go, and I do not think his doubts survived very long after we got to Germany, or that he regretted his decision, or felt any sense of trespass on his dignity, except perhaps on one unfortunate occasion when, entering the courtroom at Nürnberg, which had been at last made ready, to take our seats for the first time to hear some preliminary application of German counsel, we discovered that, although in splendor of upholstery the eight judges' chairs along their raised platform were identical, the alternates' seats were smaller and lower, not

mean or hard, but less exalted . . . Parker was visibly angry.
At the noon conference of the members he at once raised the
question of the status of the alternate members of the Tribunal.
Why should they have lower status—a deliberate belittling of
the position of alternates. The issue was far more important,
however, than this petty, gratuitous insult. What part does the
alternate play as a matter of right, he continued, shaking a long,
solemn forefinger at us, a gesture which we came to know well.
"The people of England will blame Sir Norman Birkett [the
British alternate] just as much as if he were an actual member!"
An alternate should have the right to be called for the expression
of his opinion, to set forth his views, to ask questions from the
bench, even to disagree with his member should the occasion
arise. At this point the British representatives, without raising
it as an issue, indicated their disapproval of such national disunity; while the French member, Professor Donnedieu de Vabres,
enthusiastically emphasized the sacred right—nay, the duty,
should the occasion arise—to differ, even eloquently, with one's
associate. . . . We all supported Parker. The next morning the
Army removed the lesser thrones, doubtless highly disapproving
of our timid sense of protocol, and replaced them with greater
seats, so that, examining only their chairs, a spectator could not
distinguish between member and alternate.

Actually Parker was the most considerate and unselfish of
associates, resourceful, just, hard-working. His training as a judge
tempted him occasionally to refer to how such and such a problem of practice had been solved in the Fourth Circuit; and once
the Russian member, I. T. Nikitchenko, who liked to tease us
now and then as we all grew to be friends, when he saw Judge
Parker straighten in his chair and clear his throat, murmured to
me in English, a language which he was not supposed to speak,
"Here comes the Fourth Circuit!"

Just before we left Washington I asked Chief Justice Stone
to swear me in, but he refused, a little testily. He was annoyed
at Jackson's taking so much time off, which would greatly interfere with the business of the Supreme Court—there were
several cases in which a divided vote postponed decision until
Jackson's return. To what extent this and the added burden on

the other judges may have influenced the Chief Justice's view of the trial is hard to say; but he expressed his disapproval in a letter to a friend in unmeasured terms—he could let go on occasion—writing about Jackson's "lynching expedition."

I knew that an immense amount of work would have to be done to bring orderly procedure and rational justice out of the trial. It was hard enough to reconcile European and Anglo-Saxon law—which the Charter set out to do—let alone Russian conceptions of jurisprudence, with which we were totally unfamiliar. I chose my associates carefully. I must have an international law expert to keep us out of the pitfalls of that boggy and uncertain territory. I persuaded Quincy Wright, a professor of international law at the University of Chicago, to join us. I needed a first-rate criminal-law man. Herbert Wechsler was scheduled to resign from the Department of Justice to go back to Columbia, where he had taught for many years, and he managed to postpone his return for six months to help me. Jim Rowe, whom I had not seen since 1943 when he had resigned as Assistant Attorney General to join the Navy, also agreed to go. He was skilled in public relations, and would be able to handle the military, whose language he spoke with appetizing fluency. Adrian Fisher, one of my assistants in the TVA investigation, had been a bombardier in the Pacific and was still in the service, accepted without a chance to see his young wife before joining me. Later he was to serve as solicitor to the Department of Commerce, under Averell Harriman, general counsel for the Atomic Energy Commission, and legal adviser to the State Department.

We sailed on the *Queen Elizabeth*, still pretty shabby from the troops, whose initials were carved all over the railings. William L. Shirer, Ed Murrow, Mackenzie King, Lord and Lady Portal, Dennis Brogan, were among those on board.

I spent a good deal of time with King, and found him charming—modest, tired, not impressive and perhaps for that reason more effective, a man whom you instinctively trusted. He had been Prime Minister of Canada for eighteen years, losing only once out of seven general elections. He told me about his meeting in the spring of 1937 with Hitler and Constantin von Neurath, Hitler's Foreign Minister, and one of the defendants

in the Nürnberg trial. It had been arranged by Joachim von
Ribbentrop, at the time German ambassador to Great Britain,
after an Imperial Conference in London, and had the approval
of Chamberlain and Eden. The discussion was frank. Hitler said
he had to arm—European governments respected only armed
force—an argument that was to be repeated during the trial with
telling effectiveness by Horace Greeley Hjalmar Schacht, accused of conspiring to wage aggressive war when as Reich
minister of Economics and president of the Reichsbank he found
ways of financing the rearmament of Germany. Hitler disliked
Eden and his Eton manner, but disliked Chamberlain and his
umbrella even more, and said so. But he had no quarrel with
England, who was entitled to control her empire, that is if she
let Germany be the master of Europe. Nor had he any disagreement with France—the inference being that Russia should be the
first to be immunized. The Führer expressed a desire for further
intimate discussions; and in the summer of 1939 sent word to
King that he would be delighted to pay for a Canadian depu-
tation to Germany—twenty if King wanted—if they were not
prejudiced persons. King got the impression that Hitler wanted
peace with England, "at least at that time."

We talked long and intimately about Franklin Roosevelt, whom
King admired and loved. He spent three days at the White
House two weeks before the President went to Warm Springs
for the last time. "When I saw him," said King, "my old friend
looked so badly, so haggard and worn, that I almost sobbed. I
went up to him and kissed him on both cheeks . . . No, I
cannot remember whether anyone else was there." King gave
me a copy of his book about the Ludlow massacres, which John
D. Rockefeller, Jr., had asked him to investigate.

Judge Parker had selected as his aide Major Robert Stewart,
the son of an old friend from Charlotte, fresh from active service in the Battle of the Bulge. He had that essential quality
of a capable officer, the ability to handle men without friction,
not uncommon among Southerners. He was young, attractive,
unattached; and it was pleasantly appropriate that he should
have, in a very short time, found it unreasonable to resist the

charms of Tania, one of the best of the Russian interpreters, the very young, very pretty wife of an absent Russian brigadier. She spoke slangy American, read *Life* and *Newsweek*, adored American movies—*Gone with the Wind, The Great Waltz, For Whom the Bell Tolls;* and dressed and danced to perfection. After a few months she departed suddenly to rejoin her brigadier in Moscow. Doubtless she was having too good a time, and had been so reported by the representative of the N.K.V.D. at Nürnberg (People's Commissariat of Internal Affairs—the secret police), who stalked joylessly about the corridors in ill-fitting incognito, his dour eye on citizens of the Union of Soviet Socialist Republics, or in and out of the Grand Hotel, the former Reichsparteitag Goesthaus (Guest House for the Nazi Party Conventions), where members of all nations went to relax and eat passable food, and drink, and flirt, and witness vaudeville performances of tumblers and jugglers and thin, overpainted, half-starved German girls, not very young any longer, who danced . . . The Soviet secret agent touched everything, enjoying with a fixed and frowning solemnity the pleasures of the flesh, a little violent when he touched drunkenness, relaxing now and then at one of the Russian parties, which were always informal, after the first hour of slow unbending; or singing a gypsy song to his own piano accompaniment, the others joining in the choruses under his beacon eye, then all of them letting go in the final burst.

The best translator for the Russians was young O. A. Troyanovski, son of a former ambassador to the United States, who had been at school and college in America and spoke fluent English. He had picked up American idioms, turns of humor, and ways of thinking, and seemed like an American boy, friendly and easy. We all liked him. I suppose it was conceived that he might be contaminated, for I can remember one evening, when three or four of us were lounging in a corner, laughing and gossiping, seeing him leap to his feet and leave the room as if he had suddenly remembered an engagement, when the N.K.V.D. man stalked by, pausing to frown for a split second. Troyanovski left for a conference of ministers in Paris shortly afterward.

During the crossing I met constantly with my associates to discuss the Charter, possible procedures, and problems of international law that might arise. At my request Wright drafted a memorandum of the principles of international law which he believed were involved. He took the position that the definition of crimes in the Charter was declaratory of pre-existing international law; that an individual cannot avoid responsibility for his acts on the ground that they were authorized by a government if it lacked power under international law to give such authorization; and finally, that states had no authority under international law to resort to war except in necessary self-defense, or as permitted by appropriate international procedure.

Ultimately these three principles, elaborated but not substantially modified, found their place in the judgment of the Tribunal.

The Charter provided that the permanent seat of the Tribunal and its first meeting should be in Berlin, and the first trial in Nürnberg (there never were any subsequent trials under the Charter).

When we reached Berlin the black market was at its height, watches selling for $400, cigarettes for $100 a carton. The loot was smuggled back into the United States, and a clever operator could make enough in six months to buy a farm in Michigan—so my guard told me—and since everyone was doing it no one could get caught. The first thing you did, he continued, when a Kraut surrendered was to strip off his wrist watch, but toward the end you shot him first and then stripped him, just the way the Germans would kill you when you put your hands up. So there were a good many watches. It was not pleasant to see how casually he spoke about it . . . Parker and I wandered down through a black market in the Tiergarten, which was swarming with Germans and Allied soldiers, bartering anything they had left or could lay hands on, clothes, shoes, often not matching, a woman's opera cloak, an outdated gramophone with a big horn, a hammer, a pair of striped trousers. The prison guards collected autographs from Göring and sold them. Medals commemorating distinguished service to the Fatherland fetched three or four cigarettes apiece. It was illegal for soldiers to use the market, and a Russian general had been nabbed the night before in the

British zone. When we heard this, Parker and I hastily retreated to our car, trying to look unself-conscious and dignified.

The British representatives arrived just before us, and we had tea with them October 8. They both wore wing collars, striped trousers, black coats. Mr. Justice Geoffrey Lawrence, now Baron Oaksey, my opposite number and a few years my senior, said when we met—apparently not remembering his "briefing," and confusing me with A. J. Drexel Biddle, Jr., who in London during the war had been ambassador to the governments in exile of eight of the countries conquered by the Germans—that he "realized the advantage" of my "diplomatic training"—he was "nothing but a simple barrister and judge." He looked like John Bull—rubicund, healthy, a twinkling eye and pleasant English humor, friendly and attractive. As time wore on we became close friends. At that time he was a member of the Court of Appeals and soon after the trial was made a Law Lord. He reminded me of Galsworthy's Soames Forsyte, I think on account of his instinctive feeling for art values, a fresh and discriminating enjoyment with no particular intellectual background or subtlety of informed taste. He was typical of an English tradition which has by no means disappeared—conservative, land-loving, sturdy. He raised Guernseys at his place, Hill Farm, Oaksey, near Malmsbury in Wiltshire. He had strength, an understanding of men that came from a human friendliness rather than any turn of shrewdness, and a very real personal dignity.

There was a ruddy, outdoor quality about Lawrence, which he must have inherited from his father, Alfred Tristam Lawrence, First Baron Trevethin, who had died when, trout fishing at the age of ninety-three, he had leaned forward from a stone in the bed of the stream, lost his balance, and been swept down by the current and drowned before his gillie could reach him. He was appointed Lord Chief Justice by Lloyd-George in 1921 to fill the vacancy caused by the resignation of Lord Reading to become viceroy of India, but served for only one year, it was said by an agreement he had first made with the prime minister.

Lawrence's alternate, Sir Norman Birkett, was very different. Lawrence was short and roundish, Birkett towered above him, six feet three, beak-nosed, reddish hair, lean, angular, hawklike.

He had wit, was broadly read, particularly in poetry; was impulsive and generous.

I liked Birkett at once. He had left a large and lucrative practice as one of the leading barristers of England two or three years before to accept an appointment on the Court of King's Bench. He had often spoken in the United States at meetings of the American Bar Association and was very popular with our bar. Proof of his popularity at such occasions was afforded by a story which he liked to recount of a highly inebriated member, after one of the dinners, with an arm round Birkett's shoulders, assuring him that "What I like about you, Sir Norman, is that you're not one of those condescending sons of bitches that they so often send over." Birkett talked pithily, with an apt sense for a fitting quotation, and a well-stored and accurately catalogued memory. He had been the British Government's first choice as member, but when the matter had been referred to the Foreign Office, it had insisted that a Lord of Appeal should be appointed rather than a nisi-prius judge, and the choice had fallen to Lawrence, Birkett gracefully agreeing to go as his alternate. I don't think the two men were close friends—temperamentally they were very different—but they appeared to get along well, their relationship marked by more than usually good manners. I was saddened when Birkett died in 1962.

The two Frenchmen also exhibited contrast. M. Donnedieu de Vabres was a short, stout professor from the Ecole de Droits in Paris, with a quick, overbalanced, slightly uncertain gait. He was a recognized authority on international law, a little pedantic, with formal, old-fashioned manners, very courteous. He had great sweeping moustaches, which he liked to twirl upward with a flourish after speaking or eating. When his earphones were attached something warlike was added, and he looked like the drawings of Vercingetorix in school editions of *Caesar's Commentaries*. He was familiar with German, but knew only three or four words of English, usually out of context, but which on occasion he liked to exercise. When his wife joined him some weeks later I ran into them at the Grand Hotel; and with an old-world flourish he introduced me to her. "Mon cher collègue permit me to introduce you to—my woman!" Madame Donnedieu de Vabres, who understood and spoke English, turned crimson.

The French alternate, Robert Falco, was a member of the Cour de Cassation, the highest court in France. He had been a captain in the First World War, and had been decorated for gallantry in action. Skeptical, ironic, hard-working, sharing my preference for understatement, he made a very pleasant companion as well as a resourceful associate.

Major General Nikitchenko, vice chairman of the Supreme Court of the U.S.S.R., was in his forties, the youngest member of the Tribunal. He was grave, dignified, thin-lipped, capable, I thought, of using cruelty when it seemed appropriate; restrained, subtle. He knew what the rest of us were like, knew the score, kept in mind a few essentials. After he got to trust us, or at least to understand us a little better, he did not bother quite so much with the meticulous passion for detail which the Russians felt called upon to exhibit during those first few slow weeks. Out of a limited and childlike sense of humor something apt now and then would emerge. Nürnberg had been selected largely because its immense Palace of Justice had hardly been touched in the concentrated bombing that almost destroyed the old city. As we walked by it together for the first time, Nikitchenko turned to me, saying, through his interpreter, "I suppose your pilot must have had the trial in mind when he skipped the courts. You Americans think of everything!"

His alternate, Lieutenant Colonel A. F. Volchkov, a member of the Soviet District Court, could carry on a limited conversation in English—he had lived in London for several years—and was a pleasant, easy-going Slav who became quite affectionate when he had dined pretty well. He had an unclear mind, and never seemed to grasp the point of what was going on. He bored Nikitchenko, and was a little afraid of him.

The Russians had brought with them Professor A. N. Trainin, whose little book, *Hitlerite Responsibility*, edited by A. Y. Vishinski, and translated into English, sought to define the basis of international crime, which according to the learned author consisted of "an infringement of the foundations of international communion."

Nikitchenko had negotiated and signed the London Agreement on behalf of the U.S.S.R.; Robert Falco for France; Jackson for the United States; and Lord Jowitt, who was then Lord Chancellor, for Great Britain.

In Berlin, Lawrence took the chair at the first meeting at once as a matter of course, and continued to act in that capacity for the first three or four meetings. Nikitchenko led me aside and suggested that perhaps we could take turns in presiding— was not that according to international precedent? Lawrence, when I passed on the suggestion, immediately accepted it with a disarming smile. "Of course, my dear fellow, you are quite right. It never occurred to me." We decided to rotate at the organization and private sessions of the Tribunal, a different member acting as chairman at each session, morning and afternoon.

At the third organization meeting, Lawrence, still in the chair, handed us what he called an "agenda," written in a clear public-school hand. The first item was "dress." What should we wear? The reactions of the members were typical of their national characteristics. At that time, and for the first few weeks, a stenographic record was made of all our discussions, but discontinued as we got to know each other better. It consumed endless time as it had to be translated into Russian and French, and we were apt to talk less freely under the knowledge that every casual word was being framed for reference. I have before me the minutes of that particular meeting.

> Lord Lawrence: Now, do you think we can pass to some of those procedural matters which are of less importance than what we have been discussing? Does any member wish to express any view about the dress of members?
>
> General Nikitchenko [cautiously]: On that particular point, I have nothing to suggest at the present time.
>
> Lawrence: Does that mean that the question remains open?
>
> Biddle [with a trace of irritation]: Can't we settle some of these minor problems now? The dress is not important. I will agree to any arrangement that is made about dress in advance.
>
> Nikitchenko [solemnly, feeling his way]: The gown reminds me of the medieval ages . . . What about black suits, business suits?
>
> de Vabres: We insist on black robes and absolute quiet for

those on the bench, and we insist on something to conform to our intelligence and dignity. That is one precedent there is and there never has been any protest against it—the gown. Thus, because of the things we have been used to, I insist on a black gown.

Biddle: I move that the members of the Tribunal dress as they choose.

de Vabres: I do not see that personal preference should play such a large part in a military trial. It calls not for uniform but for uniformity. A military tribunal should at least have some discipline. I would strongly object to judges being mistaken—they must have distinctive clothes. Magistrates and judges should have robes.

Nikitchenko: I do not think that the form of the robe, the kind of robe, or the cost, would really mean the dignity or authority of that person who is wearing it.

The sequel was that the Russians wore military uniforms, the rest of us gowns. I suggested to Parker that to liven things he and I occasionally wear the hoods of our honorary degrees, but he shook his head—this would hardly do. The French wore jabots and elegant little ruffles at their wrists; and on Falco's gown was a touch of ermine. They looked like Daumier's lithographs of a hundred years ago, still as living and trenchant as ever. One hangs in my study, as I write, the drawing of the judge representing immobile, inscrutable authority, waiting for an answer to his question, the prisoner standing, lean, shabby, a hand moving from explanation to protest:

Vous avez eu des moyens d'existence; qu'en avez-vous fait? J'ai existé avec. (You've had means of existence; what did you do with them? I existed.)

The delicate international balance of power having been adjusted by rotating the chairman of our administrative sessions, the question as to whether rotation should be introduced into the trial itself—this first great international trial—had to be decided. The British and Americans were convinced that there should be a single presiding judge all through the trial. We believed that rotation would be confusing if every day or every week a different judge presided, trained in a different jurisprudence and practice from his predecessor. On this, as indeed on almost all questions, the British and Americans saw eye to eye. The

Charter, although permitting rotation, seemed to favor one presiding judge for each trial. "The members of the Tribunal shall," it provided, "agree among themselves upon the selection from their number of a President, and the President shall hold office during the trial, or as may otherwise be agreed by a vote of not less than three members. The principle of rotation of presidency for successive trials is agreed." General Nikitchenko would certainly have preferred rotation at the first trial. There might, he pointed out with exact foresight, be no second trial, and rotation would follow the practice of the Allied Control Council, the presiding member changing at regular intervals. But he conceded that apparently the Charter favored a single president.

Donnedieu de Vabres thought we might have rotation by topics—when crimes committed in the East were being presented a Russian would preside; crimes in Europe, a Frenchman; crimes on the high seas, a Britisher; the conspiracy, an American. "This splitting up," he pointed out, "would be quite rational; and the president in each instance would have the greatest knowledge of the subject matter before the Tribunal." If that arrangement were followed the prosecution would present all the evidence on one topic at a time. It might involve a witness testifying two or three times, but that could not be helped—it would draw into the trial the greatest degree possible of "clarity and unity." He kept coming back to this, what his interpreter called the "division of the objects of the trial." Nobody paid much attention to him, particularly Nikitchenko, who was seldom more than stonily polite when forced to listen to what he regarded as the impractical unrealities of a medieval scholastic.

The principle of a single president having been finally conceded, who should be elected? This was important, particularly since in any case, where the votes of the members were evenly divided, the vote of the president was decisive, except that convictions and sentences could be imposed by a vote of not less than three to one. Nikitchenko nominated me—it was at the time when the Russians still assumed that our two countries would divide the world between them. Donnedieu de Vabres suggested Judge Lawrence. Neither of the other two were considered.

I had discussed this with my associates coming over on the

boat, and we had agreed that I should decline if my name was put up.

Robert Jackson's tireless energy and skill had finally brought the four nations together—a really extraordinary feat, I came to reflect, as the trial proceeded. It was to be held on American-occupied territory—Nürnberg had already been agreed on as affording the greatest conveniences of courthouse and prison. All but two of the proposed defendants had been apprehended by our Army. The Americans, under Jackson, had collected and would present most of the evidence. If any international flavor was to be preserved it was essential that an American must not preside, and it would seem that the best choice would be Lord Lawrence.

Jackson felt strongly about this, and was relieved when I told him my decision as soon as we arrived in Berlin.

I withdrew in favor of Lawrence, who was thereupon elected, and made a modest and appropriate little speech about his selection not being "a personal matter but a tribute to the confidence and trust which exists between all our four nations." He would "guide our deliberations to a just and righteous conclusion." It sounded bully at the time, although why the selection of an Englishman more than of a Russian evidenced the existing confidence among the four powers may have puzzled the Russians.

I said I thought that, when we had elected a presiding officer for the Nürnberg trial, we should choose another member to officiate at the opening meeting in Berlin, where the indictment was to be filed. Donnedieu de Vabres proposed Nikitchenko for Berlin, whom I warmly seconded, murmuring something about his "outstandingly co-operative attitude," and he quickly agreed, pleased I think by our action. We were all drawn together, and a sense of unity had been established. Lawrence wrote me a grateful and friendly line: "I should not like you to think that I am unaware or ungrateful that your influence was principally responsible for my selection as President today, and I hope you will believe me when I say how sincerely I should have enjoyed working under your Presidency. I shall trust you to let me know whenever you think there is anything in the conduct of the trial which can be improved."

Jackson was in the United States in the late summer of 1946, between the closing of the evidence and the delivery of the judgment, and while in Washington made arrangements with the Government Printing Office to publish selected speeches and documents, which subsequently appeared in nine volumes, under the title of *Nazi Conspiracy and Aggression*. On September 9 he cabled me that he would like to say in the preface: "I should note in this connection that upon assembling it was generally known that representatives of all nations were ready to agree upon the American Member, Francis Biddle, as Presiding Officer. However, the United States was to be host to all the nations at Nürnberg, had as its prisoners most of the defendants, had captured the bulk of the evidence, and had been delegated a leading part in the prosecution. Under these conditions, for the United States also to take the Presidency of this Tribunal would tend to make the trial too predominantly an American enterprise in the eyes of Europe, and to relieve our associated powers too much of responsibility. Mr. Biddle in the interests of the United States declined the honor when it was clearly within his reach. Such accounts of self-denial are sufficiently rare to deserve recording."

I cabled him back my thanks, but that I did not think it was appropriate to publish the story in view of my very cordial relations with my associates, particularly the British. He replied that he would, of course, withhold publication, adding that he rather wished he had not asked me, as the incident should be made known, and some day it would have to be.

Our new unity was at once to be tested. Nikitchenko announced some "very disquieting news." The indictment would not be ready for filing as planned. It appeared that the Russian prosecutor had been misinformed as to his facts and was not prepared to go ahead. But, we argued, we were advised that the texts of the indictment in each language had been approved and were ready for filing. All arrangements had been made for simultaneous releases in Washington, London, Paris, and Moscow. The press would say there had been a disagreement, that there would be no trial. The only inaccuracy in the indictment related to the number of persons alleged to have been murdered in Russia by the Germans in half a dozen instances. These had been understated. In all but two instances modifying words were used before the number, such as "over" and "more than." Why not amend the indictment? The Charter did not expressly permit amendment, but a majority of us had little doubt as to the Tribunal's power to grant an amendment if requested by the prosecution.

General Nikitchenko was obviously very much upset. He considered that "a sad occurrence of the highest order," but the press should not be considered, the press should never be given more than they deserve.

We took a recess, had a brief tea—at first we laughed at the insistence on tea by our British brothers, but soon came to count on it—and sent for the prosecutors.

Sir David Maxwell Fyfe—dark, thickset, powerful, a man from the North, with a streak of Scottish in him—who had been Attorney General in Winston Churchill's caretaker government, and was to become Home Secretary when the Conservatives went back to power in 1951, and Lord Chancellor in 1954, was deputy chief prosecutor for the United Kingdom. Substantially the whole burden of presenting the British case fell on his shoulders. He was worried. The impression had got about most unfortunately that there had been a real divergence over major matters between the prosecutors. He thought it highly inadvisable to postpone, as did his French and American colleagues. An amendment would solve the difficulty.

But General R. A. Rudenko, chief prosecutor for the U.S.S.R., was adamant. Rudenko was an impressive figure, with his broad shoulders and the youthful insensitive vigor so characteristic of the modern Russian, in the brown uniform and white epaulets with gold stars of a public prosecutor. How could the Russian text be presented tomorrow, since none existed? The text in all three languages, he insisted, must be in agreement. It was pointed out to him that if the other powers voted to file the indictments as they were, the U.S.S.R. under the Charter would be bound. Rudenko to this said he recognized the responsibility of being bound by the majority, "but I have no way at all of presenting a Russian text tomorrow for signature."

The prosecutors withdrew and the members of the Tribunal went into a huddle. I was concerned. Berlin was crowded with newspapermen from all over the world. To postpone the filing of the indictment the day before it was expected would loose an avalanche of conjectures about the ultimate disposition of the case—was the vaunted unity of the Big Four going to pieces? —that sort of thing. The atmosphere of Berlin was tense and skeptical. It was evident that the prosecutors who opposed any postponement were moved by this consideration. Yet were we not, particularly the Americans, too much troubled by press reactions? If the Russians as well as the rest of us wanted to go ahead with the trial, which I believed to be the case, the postponement would be forgotten in a day or two. But what if we refused to postpone?

The Russians were obviously nervous, but as obviously insistent on the delay. It was evident that they were taking their instructions directly from Moscow. The reason for their obstinate and inflexible attitude lay in fear of being laughed at if the Russian portion of the indictment showed glaring mistakes—an attitude which I found, as I saw more of them, was characteristic of an oversensitive approach mixed with adolescent toughness.

I watched Nikitchenko's firm chin and glazed eye. I think he would have bolted if the other three powers had gone ahead without him. He was much more on the spot than the rest of us.

Lawrence moved that the public meeting be held the next day, the Russian prosecutor preserving his right to file the Russian text later, and to amend. The French member seconded the motion. Nikitchenko, tense and a little angry, said that the meeting could not take place; the Tribunal could not compel the prosecutor to sign a faulty indictment; the meeting must be postponed. Filing the text as it was would harm his country, the country which had suffered most in the war with Germany. There was as yet no question of disagreement, no suggestion that action be postponed for more than a few days. But if we really wished to avoid a disagreement, we had better accept the lesser of two evils.

I suggested that the Russians retire for a few moments while the rest of us conferred. When they had gone out I said I disliked any further delay but thought the Russians would resign and go home if we filed the indictment without them, and we had better postpone it for a few days, on the understanding with Nikitchenko that it would not again be put off. We agreed, the general was summoned, he was pleased and grateful, and expressed his "extreme indebtedness" to his colleagues. We gave a brief notice to the press that at the request of the Russians there would be a three-day postponement. We adjourned for supper at about half past eleven, tired but much relieved.

ROMAN INTERLUDE

We sat in Berlin on October 18 to receive the indictment, then adjourned, the French to go home to vote, the British to fly back to England, and I to Rome for a few days with Katherine's older half sister, Marguerite, who had married Roffredo Caetani, then Prince Bassiano, the second son of the Duke of Sermoneta. With General Eisenhower's plane went a crew of youngsters who looked as if they had just broken the shell. Before we started, the chief pilot asked Jim Rowe if he would speak to me about bringing his girl friend along. He had better, I said to Jim, talk to me directly. There was a "person," the pilot told me, who had to go to Rome on important business, and he thought perhaps it would be only decent to find room . . .

"Man, I suppose?"

"Well, no sir, not exactly."

"Old lady, perhaps?"

"Well, I wouldn't say that, sir."

"Have you known her long?"

"Not very long . . . two or three days, sir."

"Favorably?"

"Very favorably, sir."

He relaxed, and when the time came a charming little red-headed Red Cross nurse slipped quietly on board and found her place next to the pilot . . . I got along admirably with my crew.

We left at eight o'clock in the morning, flew over Lyons, grounded and lunched at Marseilles, then over the Ligurian Sea, Monte Cristo, Corsica, clear and blue and romantic; circled Rome a few times to get a good look at it—none of us had been in Rome before—and made a perfect landing, three minutes before we were due, for five precious days in Rome.

The Palazzo Caetani, where my sister-in-law lives when she is not at Ninfa, is on the little Via Botteghe Oscure—the street of dark shops—and from my sunny balcony at breakfast, eating fresh eggs for the first time since we had left the United States, and sweet butter from Ninfa, and drinking bitter Italian coffee, I had the sense of buoyant life rising from the courtyard, of balconies and roofs, the geraniums and chickens. I spent enchanting hours rambling through the streets with Roffredo. The oleanders were in bloom. It was too warm for even a light coat. In contrast to Berlin's twisted and tortured buildings and streets, the trees in Unter den Linden gutted and dying, and the creeping, frightened, half-starved ghost people, Rome touched my senses with its serenity and endurance. Before lunch we sat on a balcony high over the city with little orange trees and petunias in boxes, sipping Cinzano with a dash of gin, watching the light drift upward to touch the domes of the neighboring churches.

I got a car from the OSS and turned one of my pilots into a chauffeur. My crew continued to be a progressive lot. The two pilots took the little nurse to the opera, with another "friend." One of them called up "Mom," for twenty dollars, somewhere in Arkansas, his girl sitting with Mom. But he didn't waste any talk on his girl. He had his portrait painted for Mom for another twenty dollars by a Roman artist. I took them to meet Marguerite at the palazzo, and with her pleasant way of making people feel at home—her exclusions are equally effective—she released their talk, and they forgot to stare at the great, vague, dusty, faded pictures and tapestries, and to drawl, "Yes, Ma'am," and then talked with a rush of vivid recollection about flying wounded soldiers over the English Channel, ten to twenty feet above the waves, dodging boats as they went . . .

Marguerite was closed into herself, after her son, Camillo, had

been killed two years before in the Albanian invasion, and she
filled my time with people at tea, at lunch, at dinner. They were
all immensely interested in the coming trial. They wanted to explain to me the complications of Italian politics in a sentence
or two . . . Countess Karolina Lauckaronsky, Roffredo's rather
handsome mannish cousin (one of his grandmothers had been a
Polish woman, Countess Calixta Rzewuska, whose grandmother
had fallen a victim of the French Revolution on the same day as
Queen Marie Antoinette) poured out her adventures in German
concentration camps over two years, as a result of her activities
in the underground, disguised through a local Red Cross organization, of which the books of accounts carried a code system
containing the names and addresses and telephone numbers of
her co-workers. Roffredo had saved her from death through the
intervention with Hitler of the Prince of Savoy. She spoke with
horror of the German police guards at the camps, huge women
with enormous hands, cruel, handsome, given to rather casual
copulation under the trees with SS troopers. "One is always
dirty and starving," she remarked, "but disgust sets in when
one's nails begin to rot away."

Ignacio Silone came to lunch with his pretty Irish wife, a vivid
putting-forth about her, a little overcertain of her own values.
Silone by then had left the Communists. Italians had learned,
he said, that Russians will never co-operate. They always destroyed, as the French had learned before the war, and we
would all learn in time. America, he kept reiterating, was the
hope of all Italy, of all the world indeed, but you must understand, take time to understand, it is not too simple. . . .

Count Carlo Sforza and his wife dined with us. He was an
old-fashioned diplomat—correct, innocently vain, and if not
"liberal" in our sense, anti-fascist to the bone, refusing to conform or to toady to Mussolini as so many had crawled and
fawned. He was soon to be foreign minister, after Churchill,
who distrusted his independence, had withdrawn his opposition to the appointment . . .

Roffredo motored me to Ninfa, built in the twelfth and thir-
teenth centuries and named in honor of the nymphs of the "Inner
Sea," as the Mediterranean was called, the daughters of Zeus,

"those female divinities of a lower rank." It was thirty-five miles south of Rome, on the edge of the Pontine Marshes, a lovely ruin, partly restored, with one square medieval tower mirrored in the lake, an arch of bridge and broken nave of a church clustered about a clear trout stream rushing out below the mountains. Although the wide area of the Pontine Marshes is now drained and become fertile pasture, the green expanse of Ninfa, with its orange and lemon groves, its cypress, its luxurious mimosa and triangular garden patches of box, lavender, and roses, rises out of the earth at a sudden turn in the road, and vanishes as quickly, folded in among the hills. When Katherine first came to it, the following May, flying down from Nürnberg, all she could think of was Keats' *La Belle Dame sans Merci*. She tried to capture its quality in a poem that she called *Legend:*

Traveler, traveler coming from the marshland
What of plague and famine, the enemy on the hill?
Is there death in the pale lake below the single tower?
Who rolls the thunder stones if the gods are still?

Thirteen hundred feet above perched Norma, where a branch of those one-eyed lawless giants, the Cyclops, was reported to have dwelt, forging thunderbolts and lightning for Zeus, trained in the business by Vulcan, the old god of furnaces. Six miles to the northeast stands Sermoneta, from which the Caetanis derive the ducal title, an immense, grim fortress, carved out of the gray-green rocks. As we left our car to make the last steep stretch on foot to the castle the peasants flocked out to see us, pulling their caps, asking after the *bambina*, Roffredo's daughter Lelia, who was then thirty-two. Roffredo told me that during the Ethiopian war it housed five thousand troops for a night or two. A little girl carrying an immense tin of water on her head to feed the pigs who were thirsty, she said, stopped to look us over . . . The peasants, Roffredo told me, do not domesticate the small wild horses who run in the mountains, but occasionally round them up to shoot for food. Muting the grimness of Sermoneta three miles away, the little monastery of Val Vasciola, with its tiny thirteenth-century Romanesque church, still held five monks.

The Germans had moved into Ninfa, seizing and carrying

away the long-horned cattle from Roffredo's farms; and the Caetanis took refuge in Sermoneta, where a few rooms had been made livable by Roffredo's younger brother, Gelasio. They were followed by the peasants with their children and beasts and chickens, streaming in from the country on all sides—a crowded Breughel canvas—filling the courtyard. Gelasio Caetani, an engineer who had been trained at the Columbia University School of Mines, and was appointed the Italian ambassador to the United States in 1922, had successfully drained the Pontine Marshes, which ran from the mountains to the sea, and freed them of malaria, after unsuccessful attempts by many an emperor and Pope, starting with Appius Claudius three hundred years before Christ. We could make out Anzio from Sermoneta twenty miles away on the coast, where the Allies two years before had made their famous landing. From the sea, below Anzio, rises Montecirco, where once the sorceress Circe, the daughter of the Sun, charmed Ulysses to forget.

Harold H. Tittmann, assistant to Myron Taylor, the President's personal representative to the Pope, went with me to the Vatican for an audience. I was alone with His Holiness for fifteen minutes. He was interested in the trial. Frau von Papen had requested that he intercede for her husband, and the Pope asked me to do what I could to see that he had a fair trial, and I assured him I would. He looked lean and dry, spoke English perfectly, asked about California, which he had visited in 1936. The future, he said, was in the hands of the United States. A great responsibility, I replied; and told him that I had been sworn in as a member of the Tribunal on a Bible given me by Cardinal Denis J. Dougherty of Philadelphia—your only Cardinal in America, I added; at which he smiled, and I saw in the evening paper that Spellman had just been appointed Papal Secretary. I am told that the Vatican considers the preponderance of Irish in high places in the Church in the United States unfortunate.

Mrs. Tittmann drove me out through the Campagna. We stopped at the Ardeatine caves, where, in reprisal for the throwing of a hand grenade, the Germans had shot 325 Italians, seized from all walks of life, and thrown their bodies into the caves, the city refuse dump. Mourners were silently moving about, placing flowers and candles and little images of the Virgin on the wooden coffins, crying to themselves. . . .

My pilot, the weather being bright, cold and still, persuaded me to fly back through the Brenner Pass. We missed it the first try in a violent wind, but a second time sailed through, winging over Innsbruck and Munich, arriving at Nürnberg for lunch.

ROSENBERG, FRANK, LEY, AND HESS

✦❘❭✦ *Chapter Twenty-seven*

In Nürnberg I found that the business of the court was virtually at a standstill. The four secretaries of the Tribunal—one from each nation—without experience of the difficulties of functioning in occupied territory, were unable to handle the flood of applications and motions that were pouring in. It soon became apparent that order could be established only by an army officer with full backing from the top.

With this in mind Parker and I motored over to see General Eisenhower at Bad Hamburg, near Frankfort. He gave us a pleasant lunch with several members of his staff—*truite meunière* and our first fresh vegetables in Germany. He had swapped six hundred goldfish from a little pond for a hundred trout, which he fished until they grew wary of flies, then drained the pond in our honor. He showed us a chamois pelt, skull, and brush which he had shot in the Austrian Tyrol—no easy feat. He was amusing about some of the problems with the Russians that grew out of basically divergent conceptions. General Zhukov, his opposite number, recently had come in to see him, very angry, holding a copy of some American periodical, *Time* I think, with a drawing of a young lady stooping over and looking through her legs while she made a face at Stalin. It must be suppressed at once, said the general, and the people who were responsible for this vicious and vulgar attack on our great leader punished, severely punished. The American general tried his best to explain not only the limits of his own power, but the American theory of freedom of the press. The Russian listened stonily. He put his finger on the girl's bottom. "Do you call that freedom of the press? You keep saying, every day you say it, that you are friends of the Russians, friends of your Russian ally: and yet when, in the name of my government, I ask you to suppress this filthy libel—a small thing to ask—you say you will not do it. I cannot understand." He stalked out . . .

I found General Eisenhower very good company. "Gentlemen," he asked us after lunch, "what can I do for you? I received a cable from the President soon after you were appointed telling me to do everything I could. I hope you are comfortable, and that you are being well looked after."

I assured him that we were, and thanked him for assigning me one of his personal planes, which was making all the difference to my comfort. There were two matters however with which he could help. I explained to him the lack of any organization in the secretary's office, the enormously increasing flow of work, the confusion. We must have a general officer to take charge.

"When do you want him?"

"At once."

He sent for his Chief of Staff, Lieutenant General Walter Bedell Smith, who the next year was appointed ambassador to the U.S.S.R., and, after serving two years as director of the Central Intelligence Agency, was named Under Secretary of State by his old chief in 1953. General Eisenhower told him to arrange for a brigadier general to report to me the next day at nine o'clock.

"And the second point?"

The Tribunal had appointed a number of lawyers to represent defendants who had no lawyers of their own, I explained. We had no funds to pay them. If they were not paid they would go home—even Germans must live—and the trial might be again postponed, perhaps indefinitely. We had applied to the Control Authority, who "had it under consideration . . . but you know what that means, general; we must have the money now, at once."

"How much?"

We planned, I told him, to recompense them at the rate of $300 or $400 a month, out of which they would have to pay their assistants, stenographers, and traveling expenses. He seemed to think this a modest request, and again rang a bell. To the officer who answered, General Eisenhower said, "Print enough money to keep Judge Biddle going." And that was that. Brigadier General William D. Mitchell reported promptly, and in his efficient and tactful hands order gradually shaped itself out of chaos, and a vast load of detail was removed from the Tribunal's back.

Back in Nürnberg one of the first things we had to do was to test the system of simultaneous translation. It had been used only once before, at an International Labor Organization meeting on a smaller and more limited scale. At the meetings of the United Nations and elsewhere the system is now a commonplace; but at that time its use seemed a very daring experiment. It proved highly successful, largely owing to the skill and tact of Colonel Leon Dostert, the chief of interpreters. The interpreters greatly varied in their rendering of the evidence. Some were casual, unemphatic, relaxed; others spoke with a rush, often dramatically. One particularly young lady, who had recently graduated from a high school in Minneapolis, threw her whole being into the work, acting each part, hands and face and voice, smile or frown. And since she wore a towering and complicated hairdo, magnificent to watch as she worked, she became known as the "Passionate Haystack." At a dance where we met she seemed a little stiff and could say only "Yes, Judge," "Oh no, Judge," "You don't say, Judge," handling her glass with a stiff and polished little finger, almost at right angles, emphatically elegant. Thinking that it would be easier than conversation I asked her to dance. If her cheek to cheek was still formal we were at least on a level. Judges were like other men . . .

The earphones were of incalculable advantage in saving time. We had all expected that the defects would be from human factors—the strain of fast, concentrated translation. This is an expert field, in which intimate knowledge of two languages is by no means enough to insure proficiency; it is essential to seize and render the substance of what is said—translation must not be too literal or the core of the meaning will be lost. To everyone's surprise, although the mechanism occasionally broke down, the interpreters were extraordinarily proficient, and only now and then one had to be taken out. Ina Talbert, who rendered Russian into English, spoke nine languages. Several translators had not long before left concentration camps. Genia Rosoff, who had been at Ravensbruck, was later to interpret at the United Nations meetings. George Wassiltchikoff, a Lithuanian, stuttered in conversation, but never in his interpreting.

Lieutenant Colonel A. M. S. Neave was in charge of applications and motions. He was one of those extraordinary Englishmen who were always getting into breathless adventures during the war and wriggling out of them. Dropped here and there in Germany for espionage work, he was constantly being arrested and escaping from prison. Once, he told me one night at dinner, he was incarcerated with a dozen other fliers in an ancient *schloss* not far from Nürnberg. They tried tunneling out. After two weeks they broke into an excellently-stocked wine cellar. That delayed progress. For two weeks they drank their host's admirable Rhine wines—there was a particularly good Liebfraumilch. The excellent morale of the English prisoners became the subject of comment. He paused.

"And what," I said in answer to the pause, "did you do with the empty bottles?"

He grinned. "We filled them with an unmentionable liquid . . . the Camp Commander was a rather fastidious chap—old school, monocle—you know—pretended to be a connoisseur of wine. We used to picture him holding a bottle up to the light, saying it looked a bit cloudy . . ."

Rosenberg was recognized as the Party's "ideologist." His book *Myth of the Twentieth Century* had a circulation of over a million copies. He proposed to establish this ideology as a defense to the acts of cruelty with which he had been connected. He petitioned the Tribunal for leave to introduce into the record twenty-two books on philosophy, chiefly by German professors,

including the *Myth*, to prove that, in his own words, his "intuitive method of perception and irrational philosophy had a predecessor in the French romantic movement, and that the German neo-romantic movement took the German spiritual life with
elemental force, and was also represented by recognized
scientists in the universities; and that it has been proved by
historic-philosophic realizations that every historical appearance
becomes degenerate against its will."

In January 1940 Hitler appointed Rosenberg to supervise the
entire "spiritual and ideological" training of the Party. For this
purpose he saw to it that copies of *Mein Kampf* were officially
presented to all newly-married couples. One of them was offered by the prosecution as an exhibit. It bore the inscription:
"To the newly married couple, Friedrich and Else, née Zum
Beek, with best wishes for a happy and blessed marriage, 14th
of November 1940."

As Governor General of Poland, Frank stated that his mission
was "to make Poles understand that a master race is reigning
over them," and later referred to in his diary to his "task of
pacifying Warsaw—that is, razing Warsaw to the ground." In
Poland, Frank carried on a lawless and ruthless exploitation of
the economic and human resources of the country, introducing
widespread shooting of hostages, establishing the notorious Treblinka and Maidanick concentration camps, liquidating, as he
told a police conference, "the leading representatives of the Polish intelligentsia," reporting as early as August 1940 that he
could supply 800,000 slave laborers for the Reich, killing and
burning the Jews, estimating that by January of 1944 there were
only 100,000 still alive, out of an original population of two or
three million . . . Frank tried suicide three times. Finally he
was condemned to be hanged.

It was extraordinary with what minute exactitude Frank recorded his daily doings, his reactions, his cruelties and crimes,
for the posterity of a court, as if, masochist that he was, he had
tasted night after night, as he posted up the forty-two volumes,
which were later to convict him, the poignant thrills of self-
martyrdom. Generals such as Jodl and Halder kept voluminous
and loquacious journals. And if the other defendants did not
contribute such comprehensive personal records, the stories of

their official misdeeds were carefully preserved in innumerable orders and memoranda. The neatly crated collection of all of Alfred Rosenberg's official and personal correspondence was discovered behind a false wall in a Bavarian castle. The records of the German Foreign Office from 1837 to 1944, 485 tons of them, were taken from a castle near Marburg. Eighty-five notebooks with the minutes of Hitler's secret conferences had been carefully preserved. For the trial 100,000 documents were examined by the prosecution, and about two thousand put in evidence. What a record of the "inner workings and the outward deeds of the German Government and of the Nazi Party!"

A month before the trial began one of the defendants, Dr. Robert Ley, leader of the German Labor Front, committed suicide in his prison cell by strangling himself with a noose made from an army towel and tied to the toilet pipe. Another, Gustav Krupp von Bohlen und Halbach, who had married Bertha Krupp after whom the giant guns were christened in the First World War, was dying of senile softening of the brain at his shooting lodge at Blübach, near Werfen in Austria. A committee of physicians representing the Tribunal—the French member had the engaging name of Professor Piedelievre—reported that he could not be moved without endangering his life and would never be fit to appear before the Tribunal. Robert Jackson, followed by the French and Russian prosecutors, took the extraordinary position that Alfried Krupp, who since 1940 had been president of the company and owner of the vast iron and steel works, should be substituted in place of his father, since it was essential that a "representative" of the family should appear before the Tribunal! The resulting delay need not "exceed a few days," Jackson told us, because the work which had been done on behalf of his father would be available to Alfried, who might even be willing to "step into his father's place." I was amazed that Jackson, in order to save the symmetry of his design, should suggest to us such a shuffling.

The only member of the prosecution who kept his sense of the reality of justice at this moment was Sir Hartley Shawcross, the chief British prosecutor, who, except for making the opening and closing speeches, rarely appeared at the trial. He was Attorney General in the recently elected Labour Government. Comparatively young, extraordinarily handsome, with a high color and clear eye, he gave one a sense of courage and directness mixed with a quick temper that might flare up from a passionate yet controlled nature. Little known before his appointment, he became after he left the government one of the most successful barristers in England. When arguing to the various motions, he reminded us that this was "a court of justice, not a game in which you can plug a substitute, if one member of the team falls sick." The application on behalf of Krupp must be treated on its merits. The part played by the industrialists could be fully established without the joinder of any particular industrialist. And there must be no postponement.

At our conference Volchkov, in Nikitchenko's absence, was the only member favoring the proposed amendment, but did not insist that his dissent should be announced in court. This established an understanding that we should so far as possible speak publicly as a unit without indicating differences of opinion. The dissents went into a "secret record," established at the suggestion of the Russians, obviously for use if any questions were raised on their return to Moscow after the trial.

The Tribunal entered an order granting Krupp's motion for a postponement of the proceedings against him, but directing that the charges be retained on the docket for trial thereafter in case he were ever well enough to stand trial. The motion for substitution of his son was summarily declined.

Ideas spread and took on new possibilities quickly among the master race. Evidence was given that a certain Dr. A. Pokorny, "specialist on skin and venereal diseases," addressed a letter to Himmler as Reich Plenipotentiary for the Consolidation of German Folkdom, in which he wrote that, "prompted by the thought that the enemy must not only be conquered but exterminated," he felt obliged to submit the results of Dr. Madaus' research into sterilization by medicaments. "Maudaus discovered that the juice of the plant *Coladium Segiunam*, swallowed or injected, produces, after a certain time . . . a lasting sterility." Dr. Pokorny was struck by the "enormous importance of this medicament in the present struggle of our people . . . a new and very effective weapon." He was thrilled by the thought that "three million Bolsheviks now in German capivity could be sterilized, so that they would be available for work but precluded from propagation." Thorough people, German scientists, particularly when they are working for the Fatherland . . .

Hess's trial presented a problem. There was little doubt that his mental condition had been deteriorating, indicated even to the casual observer by his indifference, his appearance of glazed abstraction, and his jerky, goose-step manner of walking. The report of a commission of neurological experts, appointed by the Tribunal to examine him, was not free from doubt—Hess was a "psychopathic personality." His abnormal obsessions were a reaction to the failure of his mission on his famous flight to England. He suffered from a persecution complex, fearing that he would be poisoned by the English under the hypnotic influence of the Jews, and his death would be represented as a suicide. He had attempted suicide twice. Amnesia developed late in 1943, and he resisted attempts to be cured. Hess was unwilling to submit to a narco-analysis, which had been recommended to "clarify" the situation. The amnesia, the report continued, was hysterical, and might terminate when he was brought to trial. This loss of memory would not "entirely" interfere with his comprehension of the proceedings, but would affect his ability to make a defense. He was not insane "in the strict sense of the word."

We heard oral argument on the motion. Maxwell Fyfe presented the problem. In English jurisprudence it had never been held to be a bar either to trial or punishment that a person who comprehends the charge has no memory of what happened at the time. To put a simple case: after a motor accident a man charged with manslaughter cannot be heard to say that because of the accident his memory had failed, so he should not be tried.

After some discussion we permitted Hess to take the stand in person, his lawyer having indicated that he desired to do so. I urged Lawrence to allow this, and Donnedieu de Vabres backed me; but Lawrence, supported by Nikitchenko, hesitated —it might create a disturbance. Hess announced that he wanted to take part in the proceedings alongside of his comrades. He had been simulating loss of memory. Although his ability to con-

centrate had been somewhat reduced, his capacity to follow the
trial and to defend himself had not been affected. He said that
he was taking full responsibility for everything he had signed
or countersigned. He sounded clear and normal; and we announced the next morning that he should stand trial. Several
months later Dr. G. M. Gilbert, the prison psychologist, reported to us that Hess did in fact recover his memory on that
day in court. The doctor had told him (as a challenge) just
before the hearing that he might be considered incompetent
and excluded from the proceedings. He seemed startled, said
he was competent, and gave his declaration about malingering,
apparently as a face-saving device, for later he told Dr. Gilbert
that he had not been malingering. During December and January his memory was in order, and his lawyer had ample opportunity to prepare his case, which came up in March, although,
by February, Hess had relapsed into a state of almost complete
amnesia, and his memory span was only about a one-half day.
At the early sessions he read to himself a German translation of
Jerome's *Three Men in a Boat*. A guard thought this disrespect-
ful of the court, and took the book away from him, but we
deemed it a harmless pastime and ordered it returned.

THE TRIAL BEGINS—
GÖRING, SCHACHT, AND
THE KATYN WOODS

❧ *Chapter Twenty-eight*

On the twentieth of November, 1945, the actual trial began, "in a high solemn moment of extreme importance," as the Soviet member, General I. T. Nikitchenko, put it. Lawrence made a brief statement before the indictment was read as required by the Charter (it took nearly two days to read it in four languages, a tiresome drain on everyone's patience). Every defendant, he said, has been in possession of the indictment for more than thirty days, and all were represented by counsel, chosen by the defendants themselves in most cases, in a few appointed by the Tribunal. Reporters were impressed with Lawrence's dignity and sincerity; and the sense of authority so thoroughly British in quality that he brought to the courtroom largely accounted for the orderly days in court that followed. "Incidents" had been feared, but there were none. Germans were used to bowing their heads to those in command.

Robert Jackson's opening statement was eloquent and moving. The wrongs here condemned, he began, were so devastating that "civilization cannot tolerate their being ignored, because it cannot survive their being repeated. That four great nations, flushed with victory and stung with injury, stay the hand of vengeance and voluntarily submit their captive enemies to the judgment of the law is one of the most significant tributes that Power has ever paid to Reason." We must never forget, he continued, that the record on which we judged these defendants today will be the record on which history will judge us tomorrow. If these "men of troubled conscience" were the first war leaders of a defeated nation to be tried they were also the first to be given a chance to plead for their lives in the name of the law.

He outlined the organization in 1921 of the Nazi Party: the formation the next year of the SA, the Storm Troops, committed to violence under semimilitary discipline; of the SS, distinguished by the cruelty of its members and its fanatical devotion to the Führer; of the infamous Gestapo, the secret police. He summarized the swift consolidation of Nazi power, culminating the morning after the Reichstag building fire on February 27, 1933, in the decree obtained by Hitler from the aged and ailing President von Hindenburg suspending the constitutional guarantees of civil liberties, so that secret arrest and indefinite detention without charges, without evidence, without hearing, without counsel became the order of the day. "The German people were in the hands of the police, the police were in the hands of the Nazi Party, and the Party was in the hands of a ring of evil men." He touched in some detail on the abolition of the labor unions, the battle against the churches, the crimes against the Jews—a continuous and deliberate policy; segregation into ghettos, forced labor, expulsion from professions, expropriation of property, prohibition of any cultural life; and finally the tortures, the burnings in concentration camps, the ultimate liquidation. Civilization, he said, "does not expect that you can make war impossible. It does expect that your juridical action will put the forces of international law, its precepts, its prohibitions and, most of all, its sanctions, on the side of peace, so that men and women of good will in all countries may have 'leave to live by no man's leave, underneath the law.'"

Sir Hartley Shawcross, when he opened the British case on December 4, emphasized individual responsibility. "The State is not an abstract entity. Its rights and duties are the rights and duties of men. Its actions are the actions of men." Politicians who embark upon an aggressive war should not be able to "seek immunity behind the intangible personality of the State."

To me, François de Menthon's summary of the French case—he was their chief prosecutor—was more interesting than any, and in many ways more moving; more interesting because he sought to distinguish and to understand the German soul within the dark cloud of German action; more moving because he thought and spoke of Germans as members of a group to which all human beings belonged. The philosophy of the National Socialist Party, he argued, logically resulted in a war of conquest fought without respect for any human values. The vast organized criminality sprang from "a crime against the spirit," which aimed to plunge humanity back into barbarism, not the spontaneous savagery of a primitive race, but a reaction conscious of itself, utilizing for its ends the material means put at the disposal of mankind by contemporary science.

This doctrine, de Menthon pointed out, was based on the monstrous theory of racism, "the commandments of the blood," modern Germany turning back to find primordial refreshment in the dreams, the rites, the myths of primitive life. The nation is equivalent to the race. The end is the absorption of the personality of the citizen into that of the State, and the intrinsic value of the human being is finally denied. Anyone whose opinions differed from the official doctrine was asocial and unhealthy. Humanism is condemned as decadent. Reason is replaced by the romance and the virility of war; violence becomes the test of manhood. Nietzsche's will to power is the guide. The sanity of war is reaffirmed in Fichte's dictum: "The moral health of nations is maintained thanks to war, just as the passing breeze saves the sea from stagnation." National socialism in modern Germany, he concluded, is the "ultimate result of a long evolution of doctrines," raising "inhumanity to the level of a principle." The regime creates a logic of crime which obeys its own laws.

General Rudenko, presenting the Russian case three weeks later, talked of crimes in the Slavic countries in a speech calculated to cover about as much time as his predecessors. He referred to the defendants, doubtless for some semantic reason of his own, as "Hitlerites" and "Fascists"—never as "Nazis"—"with the morals of cannibals and the greed of burglars." The prosecutors, he ended, were presenting the defendants with "a just and complete account which must be settled."

Of the defendants Hermann Wilhelm Göring was the most kaleidoscopic. He would occasionally forget himself in a blaze of anger. For so gross and heavy a human being he could move with extraordinary quickness.

Lahousen was the first witness called. He took the German oath that we had prescribed: "I swear by God the Almighty and Omniscient that I will speak the pure truth—and add nothing." After the *Anschluss*, Lahousen had been transferred from the Austrian Intelligence Division to a corresponding position in the German Army under Admiral Canaris, who was chief of the Abwehr, the German Intelligence. Canaris, his subordinate testified, was "pure intellect" who hated violence as such, and war, and abominated Hitler. Canaris kept a diary, a habit during that period of both American and German public officials—to which the witness "contributed much." On September 12, 1939, shortly before the fall of Warsaw, there was a special conference in the Führer's private train, with Von Ribbentrop, Jodl, Keitel—all three defendants—Canaris and others, men moving in and out, the group forming and re-forming. Keitel told Canaris that the bombardment of Warsaw had been agreed upon directly between the Führer and Göring. Canaris then protested against the proposed shooting and extermination measures that had come to his attention, directed particularly against the Polish intelligentsia, the nobility, and the clergy, "and of course the Jews," saying that some day the world would hold the Wehrmacht responsible for these measures. Keitel answered that all this had been decided by the Führer, and if the Army was unwilling to carry through, the SS would be sent in, and a civilian officer appointed to function with each military commander in this "political house-cleaning," as the Führer put it. All the farms and dwellings of the Poles, said Ribbentrop, should go up in flames, and all the Jews be killed. On other occasions Keitel put pressure on Canaris to kill General Weygand, who was then in North Africa; and ordered

Canaris to "eliminate"—one got quite used to the word—General Giraud after he had escaped from Königstein in 1942. This was worth remembering when later, in the United States, one heard protests against the trial of a soldier simply because he had, like a loyal man, carried out his military duties.

Göring, in his double-breasted light gray uniform of a Reich Marshal, which he had designed for himself, now faded and baggy, without decorations, sat in the corner of the defendants' box, a rug across his knees, so that all the witnesses had to pass near him as they left the courtroom. When Lahousen left the stand, Göring, leaning across Hess, remarked to Ribbentrop in a clearly heard voice, "That's one we missed on July 20" (July 20, 1944, when an attempt to assassinate Hitler failed). And, when Bach-Zelewski, a high ranking SS general who was in command of the anti-partisan warfare on the Eastern Front, had finished his testimony about the terrible atrocities committed there, Göring was suddenly on his feet. He spat in the face of the witness as he left the room, and shouted *schweinhund!* —then seated himself, straightened his tunic, and beamed jovially at the MPs who had rushed up. There was nothing to do.

On occasion Göring could be coolly and politely insolent, deferentially impudent. It was no wonder that this attitude—sly and quick and skillful—should irritate the cross-examining prosecutors. When Justice Jackson was cross-examining him about the minutes of the working committee of the Reich Defense Council in 1935, which contained a phrase translated "preparation for the liberation of the Rhine," Göring suggested that Mr. Jackson had made a "great mistake." The phrase had nothing to do with any contemplated occupation of the Rhineland, it meant simply that the river should be kept clear in case of mobilization for defense against attack from the west, or from the east for that matter.

Jackson: You mean the preparations were not military preparations?

Göring: Those were general preparations for mobilization, such as every country makes.

Jackson: But were of a character which had to be kept entirely secret from foreign powers?

Göring: I do not think I can recall reading beforehand the publication of the mobilization preparations of the United States.

The answer was really innocuous, and Jackson should have let it pass. But he lost his temper. For some time Göring had been trying to put him off balance, and had finally succeeded. It was a long cross-examination, lasting a couple of days, and Jackson, already overburdened and tired, felt the strain. He made the initial mistake of not holding his witness psychologically, letting him go. He should never have dropped his eyes from Göring's face. Instead, he kept occasionally looking at his notes while the witness was answering, as if he was not thoroughly prepared, and the impact was lost.

Maxwell Fyfe, on the other hand, held on like a bulldog; held on without ever noticing the witness's impertinence, his sallies, his wit and sneers, which gradually died down; held on the way Edward Carson held to Oscar Wilde during that famous trial, while Wilde laughed at him and the spectators egged him to further witticisms; held on until Wilde made his first break, and Carson had him against the wall, stammering and frightened.

"I respectfully submit to the Tribunal that the witness is not being responsive," Jackson appealed to the bench: It was "futile to spend our time if we cannot have responsive questions . . . this witness has adopted an arrogant and contemptuous attitude toward the Tribunal which is giving him the trial which he never gave a living soul." He asked that the witness be instructed to answer the questions "yes" or "no," and leave explanations to the end of his testimony. I suggested to Lawrence that now was a good time to recess, not to give an immediate ruling, to let things cool off overnight. We adjourned—it was almost the usual time—and met in chambers. We were all of the opinion that witnesses after answering should be allowed to explain their answers at once, as was the usual practice, and not be forced to wait until the examination was over.

After the recess Jackson, profoundly upset, came to see me and Parker. He said we were always ruling against him, and intimated that I went out of my way to oppose him. He thought he had better resign from the trial and go home . . . We did our best to soothe and mollify him, to stroke his ruffled feathers by telling him how much we all admired him, how well he was conducting the trial. At the time I thought it was merely his irritated reaction to Göring's calculated and telling impudence. Later I became convinced that some more enduring sense of failure or of disappointment haunted him. It is not improbable that appointment as Chief Justice of the United States would have eased that brooding misery. But I do not think any achievement would have altogether banished it. Missing some subtler value, he may have tried in vain to persuade his ambitious heart that the externals were all that counted. That wonderful year he had all the glittering acclamation that anyone could long for —degrees, decorations, a press almost universally won over to the adventurous value of his achievement. Why should he not have everything he wanted?

In the eight years that followed Nürnberg he came nearer than he ever had to finding a serenity of mind that filled most of his conscious being—he loved his work on the Court, and his work was of a very high order—thoughtful, lawyerlike, and wise. He was deeply admired by the bar. His pungent style, personal and fresh, framed his opinions for later generations. Only when his face was in repose did the inner light disappear and the commonplace set in, as if the emptiness had been waiting at the edges of his vitality. We would see each other occasionally in Washington after the trial, and it was friendly, there was no tension. But we were not again intimate. He may have associated me with some disappointment he had suffered abroad. A friend said he had changed since Nürnberg. It would have been more revealing to suggest that he had there abandoned something which his friends had loved in him. Until he died in 1954 I did not realize how much I cared for him.

The next morning Jackson renewed his motion. He was confronted, he said, with the choice of allowing Göring's improper answer to stand or, at considerable expense of time, to rebut it. The difficulty, he continued, was that if the witness was permitted to make "statements in cross-examination" there was no opportunity to object until his statements—nothing but German propaganda—were placed on the record. That was of course true,

but it is true about all cross-examination, a fact which makes a
practiced lawyer wary of a hostile and clever witness. We ruled
against Jackson, and the trial continued.

Schacht was a witness of a different kidney. Wrapped in a
Teutonic self-esteem, which fitted him like a pair of suede
gloves, he remained cool, never surprised, disdainfully self-reliant. He listened to each question, very straight and stiff in his
five-inch collar, looking over and beyond the others, occasionally
breaking into English. He sounded more like a professor re-
proving an overeager pupil than a prisoner fighting for his life.
Had Mr. Justice Jackson taken a course in economics in school?
Perhaps if he, Schacht, explained in simple language . . .

He hated Göring with a scornful, jealous bitterness, for it was
Göring who had forced him out of power. Göring, Schacht said
in an interrogatory, "endowed by nature with a certain geniality . . . was the most egocentric being imaginable. The assumption of political power was for him only a means to personal
enrichment and good living. The success of others filled him with
envy. His greed knew no bounds. His predilection for jewels,
gold and finery, *et cetera,* was unimaginable. He knew no comradeship. In his personal appearance . . . one could only compare him to Nero, appearing at tea once in a sort of Roman toga
and sandals studded with jewels, his fingers bedecked with innumerable jewelled rings . . . his face painted and his lips
rouged." And, Schacht added, his competence in the economic
field was nil.

Frau Manci Schacht, writing to her husband from Winsen
Lube, Hanover Province, like any wife to any husband, told him
she was very well, only the toilet was out of order. "The prosecution speeches are terribly boring. All the Congo bestiality is
being rehashed. Instead of the Gestapo and the SS being convicted here, the Government, General Staff, and even our brave
GIs [sic, in the translation] are being thrown into the same pot.
Only Hitler and his cronies are deserving of death. A German
court would have been better . . . Take care of yourself, darling."

Before the trial Dr. Gilbert gave the defendants a series of
psychological tests. Schacht was at the top of the class, with
an IQ of 143; Göring was third, his IQ 138, and Julius Streicher

at the end, with 106. Dr. Gilbert also reported in his interesting book *Nuremberg Diary* that, when he asked each of the defendants to autograph his copy of the indictment, Göring, typically enough, wrote: "The victor will always be the judge, and the vanquished the accused!" Whereas Schacht complained: "I do not understand at all why I have been accused."

Cross-examination of course varied from nation to nation, and it was natural that the French should be less good at it than the British and American, for it was not a French technique. The Russian idea of cross-examination was to read a long incriminating question, and, looking up at the witness, expect him to admit to everything. Thus their chief prosecutor, General Rudenko, cross-examined Rosenberg:

> Rudenko: Do you admit that Nazi Germany, having prepared and pursued war against the Soviet Union, aimed at plundering the economic riches of the Soviet Union, the extermination and enslavement of her people, and the dismemberment of the country. Answer yes or no.
> Rosenberg: No.
> Rudenko (with the height of sarcasm): You deny it? All right. Let us turn to a new document.

The Russians were used to co-operation from a defendant, and were rather put out by what among themselves they probably referred to as the careless preparation on the part of the Americans. It was not to be expected that they would understand our practice when the purposes of their trials were so different. The Russian trial must conform to the policy of the State, not oppose it. When, for instance, Rosenberg's lawyer applied for leave to call a witness to prove that the Soviets had employed slave-labor practices in Latvia, Volchkov was genuinely shocked that we should even listen to such a suggestion. To him it was libelous, and he said so, obviously libelous because it was an attack on his nation's sovereignty.

The Katyn Woods incident was typical of the Russian attitude.

The inclusion in the indictment of the allegation that the Germans had massacred 11,000 Polish officers and civilians in the Katyn Forest, on the banks of the Dnieper near Smolensk, was dictated by political considerations. Since there was no evidence that any defendant was remotely connected with the killings, the charge was irrelevant. Although he had not seen the reports indicating that the Russians might be guilty, Jackson sensed trouble, and did his best to persuade them to omit the charge. But Rudenko insisted on including it. The matter was at that time highly controversial, and the evidence inconclusive. In addition to spreading in detail on the record the report made in 1944 by the Special Soviet Commission, he produced three witnesses to establish German guilt. This took a week. When he had concluded Dr. Otto Stahmer, counsel for Göring, against whom the charges had been leveled in the indictment, since he was considered the highest-ranking officer among the defendants, petitioned the Tribunal for leave to produce three witnesses to show that the Russians had killed the Polish prisoners. Rudenko indignantly opposed the motion.

When we came to consider it in chambers, General Nikit-chenko threw all his weight behind the Soviet prosecutor. It was obvious that he attached great importance to our decision. I do not think that many things were expected of him by his superiors in Moscow, but there can be little doubt that they were eager to have the Tribunal brand the Germans as the perpetrators of these systematic and sordid killings.

To the rest of us it seemed trifling to argue that, having per-mitted the Russians to introduce the hearsay evidence of their own self-serving report, and to support it with eye-witnesses, we should not allow the Germans direct evidence in their de-fense. The general's argument—and he spoke with conviction for a solid hour—was based on a phrase in the Charter which pro-vided that the Tribunal need not require "proof of facts of com-mon knowledge, and might take judicial notice of official govern-mental documents . . . including the acts and documents of the committees set up . . . for the investigation of war crimes." Under this language the Russian report was obviously admissible. But the phrasing was unfortunate. "Facts of common knowledge" were coupled with "Government documents"; and in the Russian translation the two phrases might have interlocked. "Judicial notice" must have been hard to translate.

Not however for the Russian member. Since, he insisted, governmental documents had been given special treatment, and recognized for what they were—statements of the true facts— how could their contents and conclusions be denied? We had no right to disregard the Charter, to flaunt its provisions.

He was as emphatic as he had been on the former occasion when I had pleaded with my brethren to go along with him lest he withdraw from the Tribunal. And this issue must have been more important to him than a postponement to correct an error in the indictment. And yet I thought he would not; he was too far committed, and such an action would appear like an admission of guilt. But whether he bolted or not we *must* let the Germans call their witnesses, who had examined the corpses on behalf of an International Medical Commission formed by the Germans on April 30, 1943, two weeks after they had discovered the bodies of four thousand Polish officers, in uniform, in some cases shackled, with pistol bullets in the back of the neck.

We announced our decision the next morning. The Russian prosecutor immediately filed a petition for a rehearing of the question. It was the only petition for reargument we received. Its language was intemperate: the court, Rudenko claimed, had misconstrued the Charter, violated its duty, and was grossly in error. The petition followed Nikitchenko's argument and indicated his co-operation.

The occasion warranted action. At our conference the next afternoon I asked my *confrères* to permit me to speak on a matter of personal privilege not on the agenda, but of the most vital importance to all of us. For it concerned the integrity of the members of the Tribunal, their honor, and their competence.

The brethren were by now giving me their attention.

One of the prosecutors—I looked at General Nikitchenko— had filed a slanderous, arrogant, and unwarranted attack on the Tribunal, a body that would go down to history as the most important court in the world. I did not know what the practice would be in other countries. In mine the author of such an outrage would be cited for contempt. Perhaps in this very extreme case we should send him to prison immediately—there could be no defense.

"What do you think, General? Have you read General Rudenko's petition? What do you propose should be done?"

General Nikitchenko was taken off base. He mumbled that he had read the petition, but rather hurriedly. He had nothing to propose. The French were amused—they guessed what I was up to. The British were surprised—they had not been consulted.

I produced an opinion, which Herbert Wechsler and I had drafted with a good deal of care the night before. With their permission I would read it. It could be read in open court immediately before General Rudenko was arrested.

I read the opinion. It denied the contention that government reports should be accepted as "irrefutable evidence of the facts found"—a contention "unsupported by the Charter and intrinsically unreasonable in itself." The Soviet prosecutor was in gross error in his construction of the Charter.

After a good deal of discussion, it was agreed that the opinion should be filed but not made public—with the Soviet member's dissent. The president would simply announce in court that the petition was dismissed. Nikitchenko no longer argued that German witnesses should not be called. His whole energy was directed to keeping the opinion from the press. He took seriously my suggestion that Rudenko be held in contempt; and as part of the "compromise" it was understood that no such action would be taken. He was pleased with the result. Two hours after we had adjourned I got a pleasant note from him indicating that we understood each other—would I pay his country a visit after the trial? He evidently had grasped the purpose of my tactic after he had time to think a little about it.

The doctors called by the Germans were vigorously (though without damage to their position) cross-examined by the Soviets. But from that day on we heard nothing more about Katyn Woods. The Soviet prosecutor failed to mention these atrocities when he summed up the case against Göring. The evidence before us was inconclusive, and, as I have said, was unrelated to any defendant. Any mention of Katyn Woods was omitted when the judgment was under consideration.

But an investigation conducted by a House committee in 1952 left little doubt that the Soviet N.K.V.D. had been guilty of the killings, as a step in the "extermination of Poland's intellectual leadership . . . to eliminate all Polish leaders who subsequently would have opposed the Soviet's plan for communizing Poland."

The officers, lawyers, doctors, clergymen, government officials, and intellectuals who had been taken prisoner when Russia invaded Poland were separated from the other prisoners and placed in three special camps, 15,000 men in all, where they remained from the fall of 1939 until the following spring. During this period they were exhaustively examined to determine whether they could be converted to communism. A few hundred were. The rest were killed before the Russian evacuation in the spring of 1940, when the Katyn area was still under Soviet control—4143 were "identified in the mass graves of Katyn." Testimony of doctors who had performed autopsies on the bodies indicated that in some cases wounds had been inflicted by bayonets "of the four-bladed type which are used exclusively by the Soviets." The Germans had supported an investigation by an international committee of the Red Cross in 1943, but the Russians had refused to permit one. It was testified that Stalin's son, when asked about the disappearance of the Polish officers, said, "Why those were the intelligentsia, the most dangerous element to us, and they had to be eliminated."

NO. 2 HEBELSTRASSE
AND THE VILLA
CONRADTI

❦ *Chapter Twenty-nine*

The two American judges with their five younger assistants were housed together, at No. 2 Hebelstrasse on the edge of the town, a couple of miles from the courthouse, seven of us, not uncomfortably, with our two drivers and the two guards who had been assigned to look after Parker and me: a skillfully indifferent GI cook, a buxom slattern, Brunhilde, who looked as if she could take care of herself in a pinch; and Hans, a battered German butler, who kept bending at the waist like a mechanical toy that had been wound up too often but went on functioning from force of habit. It was a dreary place, with its bulging sofas under lace covers, antimacassars, draped lamp shades, tobacco-colored walls. Our stenographic help had their own quarters, and the house, wrote my secretary, Mary Johnson, who had been with me in Washington, to my wife, "lacks any character whatsoever, the pieces of furniture are o.k., but since they are very heavy and there is nothing dainty or homelike in the room they do not register favorably." There was something dismally oppressive about the overstuffed German body and the German armchair, the Teutonic temperament taking its creature comforts with a grave, unshakable seriousness.

The bombing, particularly in the old city, had been worse even than in Berlin, and the streets were piles of rubble. When warm weather came, and Parker and I wandered down into the ancient walled town, there was a whiff of rotting flesh on the light, warm spring breeze, where an SS regiment had dug in under the ruins piled up by the bombing, and American artillery had to be brought in to finish the job.

There had recently been discovered in a catacomb a group of immense carvings, eight feet high, a golden Virgin with a chubby child sucking its thumb, half a dozen saints with long, thin, sensitive hands, each carved out of a single log. Veit Stoss, a pupil of Albrecht Dürer and a famous sculptor, who had carved them, was a German from Nürnberg. When Poland was invaded the conquerors pulled them from the high altar in Marienkirche in Cracow, where they had been for centuries, and brought them to Nürnberg.

The winter, settling over the desolate caverns and rubble heaps of the bombed and gutted city, was damp and desolate "with zero at the bone." It was the thousand year old city of Hans Sachs and the Meistersingers, of Dürer and the Iron Maiden, of the Nazi stadium that held half a million spectators. Faceless ghosts poked about the ruins, looking for refuse that could be eaten. The Germans appeared to be completely crushed, and I wondered whether they would ever again recover their vitality and ambition: that was hardly eighteen years ago. . . .

The dreariness that so often seems to haunt men when they are separated from their women permeated the colorless house, and we became irritable or morose. The two older men, who had been a little overaffable to their younger companions, withdrew into themselves, while the others squabbled over their gin rummy.

And it was in an alien land, tense under the suspicion of the conqueror and of the conquered. As Katherine wrote (*Love Poem in an Occupied Country,* later published in *The Saturday Review of Literature*):

More alone than survivors on a storm-wracked island,
Everywhere surrounded by alien sounds and faces,
Alien earth and bread,

Heart looks into heart to find its recognition,
Weighted with meaning are the touch, the glances,
Weighted the words said.

But when she came—late in March—it was

No longer alien or lost; Your breast is all
That I ask of home, and your need of it
My arms hold . . .

But the work—all day in the courthouse until late in the afternoon, so that at night one had little energy except to write a
letter or hungrily scan old copies of *Time,* or *The New Republic,*
or the *Saturday Review,* which we exchanged, seeking some
feeling, some smell or sight of what was American behind the
news—the work filled most of our active time, and it wasn't too
bad. Everyone in Nürnberg was bored—the MPs, lounging
around the Villa Conradti, where the American member and his
friend Wechsler had established themselves in expectation of
the arrival of their wives; the court guards with their side arms,
and white spats and cotton gloves, and belts, standing at attention for two hours at a time; the defendants, yawning in the face
of their deferred doom; the members of the Tribunal, longing to
be home, trying to remember that they must behave like judges.

Time kept shortening the future . . . The Russian case seemed
endless; and when the American member, usually more impatient than the circumstances called for, suggested that the president cut the witnesses down a bit, his Russian colleague said no,
any attempt to hurry General Rudenko would look like prejudice against the Soviets. . . . The president, sitting behind the
great bench, the personification of eminence and dignity, would
beckon to the British clerk beneath him among the lesser officials,
and hand him a communication to be delivered instantly to the
American secretary, for whom he had conceived an instant liking,
which contained the message: "How are you doing, Pops—
bored as we are?"

And late one long, dreary afternoon Birkett, who was to dine
with me that night, wrote:

At half-past four my spirits sink
  My mind a perfect trance is:
But oh! the joy it is to think
  Of half-past seven with Francis.

There was a good deal of going out, at first a bit solemn and
official, then smaller dinners, often with music and singing afterward. Major Thomas Hodges, who was under Brigadier General
Le Roy Hugh Watson, in charge of the Nürnberg enclave, sang
ballads in several languages with gusto and feeling; and Elwyn
Jones, a Labour M.P., with whom I became pleasantly intimate,
rendered fervent Welsh hymns. Telford Taylor, one of Jackson's
assistants, who afterward, with the rank of brigadier general, was
Chief of Counsel for War Crimes in the subsequent trials in
Germany by American tribunals, would play Mozart and Bach,
with occasional bits of Schubert and Debussy. Nicholas Nabokov, his gaiety and sense of fun unhampered by a broad culture, sang Russian gypsy songs . . .

And there were dances.

It was a curious social life, with a fairly compact group of
conquerors to draw from, half a thousand or more Americans,
and a few hundred French and British. Outside of the wives of
members and alternates, who were received and fêted like brides
when they arrived, the women were chiefly stenographers and
typists, and girls working on the translating and interpreting.
They danced well, with the gaiety of an adventure that had begun and would end, like the adventure of being on a boat together or lost on an island, or on war leave in a long weekend. I
remember two particularly, a dark striking-looking girl from
Prague, Leba Barbanova, who afterward married General Watson. We spoke French. "Mademoiselle," I ventured, "vous dansez
comme une ange." She smiled. "But monsieur, would that be fun?
I am reliably informed that angels do not have bodies . . ."
Thérèse Champétier de Ribes, daughter of the chief prosecutor
for the French, seemed out of another century, a girl touching
eighteen, exquisitely bred, serious from the war years, vivid yet
modest, a new excitement stirring her now that the war was over

and one could begin to lead a personal life again . . . Her father had succeeded François de Menthon, who during the trial was taken into the Cabinet as Minister of Justice. Champétier de Ribes had lost an arm in the First World War, and was imprisoned in the Second World War after the German occupation for eighteen months with Leon Blum and Edouard Herriot. He became president of the first post-war Council of the Republic, and died shortly afterward. His ill health prevented him from taking an active part in the courtroom. He had courage, rare distinction, and uncompromising patriotism. I discovered several years later, when I began to write my reminiscences, that his uncle, Dr. de Ribes, had helped my mother bring me into the world, on an unbelievably beautiful spring day in Paris, Sunday, May 9, 1886, while M. Godard was making a balloon ascent in the gardens of the Tuileries![1]

Nürnberg was colonial, we had taken the country after this wretched war, and were living in it, had to be there for a while. We weren't sure how the natives would act, whether they would lie down and lick our boots, or slit our throats on too dark a night, yet we were determined to dine out on occasion and have as much fun as we could. It was like Kipling's Simla, pointed to a different setting in a very different time.

The Russian parties were always the best, after we got over the inevitable national toasts: Biddle might drink to the U.S.S.R.: Volchkov would respond with President Truman; Falco with mild enthusiasm, as if with a shrug, to his Britannic Majesty; and finally Parker, in his most correct man-of-the-great-world-manner: "La Belle France!" The battered frightened German servants first passed Coca-Cola, to Volchkov's annoyance, who too could be a man of the world, if Nikitchenko *had* ordered the silly stuff, and banged on the table with his fist, loudly demanding *visky!* while the harried, trembling maids scurried about, and Volchkov laughed, and pointed at them, and shouted again . . . and as the evening wore on the Russian secretary, a mild little man when not in his cups, Major A. Poltorak, full of vodka, kept beaming at Judge Parker's stenographer, a shy, rigid, strongly corseted spinster, and repeating slowly, "Really, I love you. This

[1] *A Casual Past* (New York: Doubleday & Company, Inc., 1961).

house is your home. Have more vodka." The Russians, when due homage had been paid to the tepid orange and gin cocktails that they considered an ordered part of American civilization, brought forth an inky red wine and sweet champagne, both, I think, from the Caucasus, and endless vodka—before, during, and after.

One particular evening is still fresh in my memory when Parker and I dined with Nikitchenko, who had at that time a pretty, gentle secretary-interpreter, Miss Ninna Orlova. Volchkov, whose frothy geniality bubbled up rapidly when he was drinking, took me aside when I had refused a glass of vodka that followed the cocktails, to explain, as if to an inexperienced Freshman, that the secret of healthful refreshment was to line your stomach with oil before arriving—that was the way his English put it—or at least to eat plenty of sardines, and then your capacity was practically unlimited . . . It grew late, and he expostulated as we rose to go, quoting a Russian proverb, "It is midnight—time for the children to go to bed—then the grownups stay for breakfast." He insisted on taking me home, rather high, for he had found no way of lining his head as well as his stomach; and when we got out of the car stood for a moment at attention, then embraced me like some affectionate bear cub, sprang back into the car, and I heard him burst into song as it careened sympathetically around the corner. He was less restrained than his chief, less reliable I should think from the Party point of view, more impulsive. But like all of them he was compartmentalized, and there were some things touching the U.S.S.R. that you didn't joke about, the Red Revolution particularly.

This I learned the night we were celebrating another revolution, our own. It was a hot, damp evening, and there was little life in any of the innumerable speeches. Parker was running the show, and I hoped he would leave me out; but just before the end his roving eye picked me up on the edge of the crowd, and he introduced me. A girl standing next to my secretary whispered, "My God! Not your boss, too!" . . . I told them it was refreshing to hear judges celebrating a revolution. The British were the oldest hands at it, then the Americans, with the French hot on our heels. But the Russians were new to it, babies, tyros. If they wanted to know how to do it right they ought to come to us, we'd show them . . . Volchkov took me aside. "You are not afraid of our Revolution, Mr. Biddle, are you?"

I smiled. "What, your little revolution? Good Lord— No! Is there anything to be afraid of in the Russian Revolution?" But irony is not a strong point in the contemporary Soviet, and Volchkov's face remained innocent of understanding.

Nikitchenko was not impulsive. One evening he dined with us and stayed for a few minutes after our other guests had gone. He was very sober, as usual. Miss Orlova asked me if I had heard about the general and the little parakeet that had come to visit him. I confessed that I had not. It was very beautiful, she said, but very sad (such is life, was the accent) for the little bird had flown in one morning through the open window and lighted on the general's shoulder while the general was shaving with his safety razor, and had watched him shave—the bird was of a brilliant blue, and spring had come; and from then on the general and his little companion were inseparable; until, just last night, the little bird flew with all its strength against a mirror, and then it was dead, and ever since the general has been deeply melancholy and depressed, which accounted for the fact that tonight he had not been quite himself. She talked to us in English, and the general would grunt now and then, and she would explain to him in Russian what she was telling us, and he smiled sheepishly, his hard little mouth breaking at the corners, the smile hovering, not leaving him altogether until the story was over and at last he could go home to the big house without the little bird.

Everyone visited Nürnberg sooner or later. Lord Jowitt, the Lord Chancellor, came out to see how we were progressing, and brought his wife, who spoke French with hardly a touch of accent, and when I complimented her said it was because she was Scotch. Leslie Hore-Belisha, who had been Secretary for War from 1937 to 1940, an agreeable Jew who might have been an American, told us that Pierre Lorillard, of Tuxedo, New York, after his horse won the Derby, dined with King Edward, and "sold" him the idea of the "tuxedo," as it came to be called. There was Lord Wright, chairman of the British War Crimes Commission, who had been instrumental in persuading the government to join in the plan for an international trial—Lady Wright had been the world's amateur champion horse jumper, leaping her horse to some incredible height; Lord Maugham, who was also a Law Lord, Somerset Maugham's brother; Harold Nicolson, who wrote of Nürnberg in the *Spectator*, "[that] the inhuman is being confronted with the humane, ruthlessness with equity, lawlessness with patient justice, and barbarism with civilization"; Walter Lippmann, who went even further—"the most important event in modern times"; Joseph Alsop; Tony Biddle, at the time political adviser to General Eisenhower, with his new, pretty third wife, a distant cousin of Mackenzie King; Fiorello La Guardia, who looked at Göring with unveiled admiration— "what an actor," he was thinking; Jim Farley, who knew everyone, and wanted to be remembered to everyone's wife, or whoever it happened to be; Robert Patterson, then Secretary of War; Tom Clark; Willis Smith, president of the American Bar Association, and later Senator from North Carolina, defeating Frank Graham, an infinitely better man, in the primaries; Anne O'Hare McCormick; Janet Flanner, Paris correspondent of *The New Yorker;* John Wheeler-Bennett; A. Y. Vishinski; Rebecca West; the Belgian Minister of Justice and the Danish Minister of Justice; *bâtonniers* from Paris and Lyons; generals and admirals —they were all there.

Rebecca West, who stayed with us at the Villa Conradti, did pieces for *The New Yorker*, and reported the trial for one of the London dailies. She was a robust companion. She had a way of translating the inner meaning of the objective world. The Baroque, she would say, as we looked into the little churches, was essentially a secular movement that invaded the places of worship, so that they became ornate palaces, with ballrooms, and gilt and marble, and mirror spaces—you could imagine an orchestra in the organ loft. She had a layer of insecurity and shyness. She could be very funny.

When we parted on the *Queen Elizabeth* Mackenzie King had promised me he would visit Nürnberg. He was the only head of a state to be entertained and Madame Conradti was thrilled that the great man should dine at the Villa. Rushing down the steps that led up to the front door she precipitated herself before the first figure to descend from the cortege, knelt in front of him, and kissed the hand—of a highly embarrassed sergeant, much to the delight of the detail of GIs who guarded the establishment, and of her own domestics. They all hated her.

There were four servants, not many to run such a vast house, and I was padded with comfort. Madame Conradti kept house for us. I would say to her at breakfast that there would be sixteen for dinner, would she speak to my secretary, Mrs. Mary Johnson, who would order what we needed from the PX. But in addition to standard rations Madame Conradti supplied fruit and fresh vegetables and honey from the place—there was a vast, dreary tract of sand and straggling bushes, and pines—and the factory manager brought in brook trout. We gave Madame Conradti and the staff cigarettes and chocolate each week. Food was my only expense, and for thirty or forty dollars a month we lived well. Madame hinted to Rebecca West that a large percentage of her blood was French, and noble—there were crests on the sheets; but her servile attitude to me and her harrying the GI guards who ate and slept on the place in small mean ways indicated that the greater fraction was Teutonic.

She was equally nasty to the servants. Anni, who spoke English, having worked at the German Embassy in London, hated her with an intense, documented zeal, and always referred to her as "double-faced." Madame, she said, sometimes called me a "snake" . . . Anni would bring my breakfast up on Sunday mornings—for years I had been in the habit of having breakfast in bed on Sundays—and tell me about what went on at the Villa while I ate. Had her husband been a Nazi? Of course, Judge Biddle, if you did not join the Party you could not get a job.

The little waitress, Sieglinde, was very pretty, seventeen, eager to be seduced; but the GIs had formed a gentlemen's agreement —"she's only a kid"—and her dreams went unsatisfied. Walter Gilkyson, my old friend, whom I had appointed American Secretary in July of 1946, was living with me at the Villa. One night late in September he and I heard faint sounds of music drifting from one of the sitting rooms—there must have been a dozen. Sieglinde was playing a fiddle, to the accompaniment of which she and Anni sang German songs about joining your lover ten thousand miles away in the blue sky—that sort of thing. Madame was out. We danced with the two girls rather awkwardly. The day before I left, the four maids wrote out a petition, printed in ink and decorated with flowers in water color, begging me to take them to America.

The Villa dated from 1895, and was equipped for two families who dwelt in it until the Army took it over for a VIP house. It contained a strange medley of incredibly vulgar and strikingly beautiful acquisitions: great embossed Japanese bronzes, a painting of two nude damsels fencing under a moon while a silent man watched and waited; over the huge, curling, coiling guestroom bed an oil that depicted a Nordic male as Nature showed him kissing his mate, who was clothed like Melisande in her long tresses (Rebecca called it "Sauckel's dream"); a marble family bust of a Herr Conradti in his prime, with realistic curling moustache; orange and purple stained-glass windows. But there were Aubusson rugs, two or three rather fine Greek torsos, several Lehmbrucks. The house overflowed with flowers—violets, petunias, nasturtiums, calendula, poppies.

One of the two Conradti brothers died while we were living in the Villa, and his funeral cortege moved as if to Valhalla, progressing slowly down the long avenue from the hospital to the church, to the factory, to the house, the body lying in state at each stop—finally to the grave. At the high iron gate and all along the road, fifteen-foot white columns had been erected, twined about with wreaths of evergreen, a flame blowing on top of each column. Two or three thousand persons followed, a voluptuous sorrow on their faces. . . .

Jackson gave Andrei Vishinsky, the Soviet delegate to the UN, a large dinner at the Grand Hotel with the usual flow of speeches and liquor. I sat next to a smart-looking general in his party, obviously eager to please. Like most representatives of his country he spoke not a word of French or English. Through an interpreter we discussed Mark Twain—the Russians had recently discovered him—and the general particularly liked *Life on the Mississippi*. The subject was soon exhausted and, experimentally, I asked him what he thought of the Dardanelles—could not the conflict of interests be worked out? The Soviet claim in the Straits might be recognized to some extent; the difficulty was by no means insoluble. He shrugged, smiled faintly, and answered, "We are not permitted to discuss political problems . . ." Vishinsky rose to his feet, genial, faintly bibulous, expansive. Vodka, he said, was the enemy of man, and should therefore be consumed . . . He wanted to propose a toast. He raised his glass, and we got up; and now he was speaking very fast, so that it was hard to follow the interpreter. "To the German prisoners, may they all be hanged!" The judges, not quite taking in what he said, touched their lips to the champagne. But it did not take long for them to realize what they had done.

Parker came to my room that night to talk about it. It was "awful" he thought. He hadn't understood. He would not be able to sleep, thinking about it.

I tried to brush it off, saying that no one had noticed what we did, it was a triviality that would be forgotten tomorrow—the essential was our approach to the prisoners. So far that had been fair.

"Supposing Drew Pearson gets hold of it? Can't you see the heading: American judges drink to the death sentence of the men whom they are trying . . ."

"Anyway, we're both in the same boat, John," I ventured.

"But you don't seem to care," he ended, shaking his head, looking at me mournfully . . .

Discussion of political issues was not the only taboo in Soviet officialdom. Familiarity with French to the Russian official of the new world seemed also to be considered inappropriate, a mark of bourgeois weakness. Admiral Alan G. Kirk was at the time ambassador to Belgium, and he and his wife—old friends of ours —asked me to spend weekends with them whenever I could get away; the flight to Brussels was only an hour and a half from Nürnberg. What, I asked Mrs. Kirk, comparing notes, was the Russian ambassador like? An awkward, dull man, with disagreeable hands, she said. At a dinner party at the American Embassy he sat next to a Belgian lady, an elderly and conventional aristocrat, who had no idea what to talk to him about. She tried, a little nervously,

"May I ask you, *Monsieur l'Ambassadeur*, what has happened

—*qu' est-ce—qui est devenus*—to all those Russians who spoke French so beautifully in the old days."

He looked at her sternly. *"Ils sont tous morts, Madame!"*

Parker flew home for a brief ten-days holiday at Christmas, but I thought one of us should stay, as the returning plane might be late, and I expected Katherine to be over before long. I spent the holiday with Birkett at his house at Chalfont St. Giles in Buckinghamshire not far from London. Lady Birkett could not have been more hospitable, and I was happy with them. Linnéa was the elder of the two children, tall and handsome, prevented by the war years from the normal fun of coming out, eager for life, companionable. She married her father's attaché at the trial a year or two afterward, Major Gavin Cliffe-Hogdes, a good-looking young officer who adored Birkett. Linnéa's younger brother, Michael, was then about sixteen, a talented boy, with unusual promise. Lady Birkett, who was Swedish, had a rare subtlety, as unconscious as it was instinctive. It was not intellectual, but touched an understanding of life not given to most of us. She did not care about self-expression, but her slow smile suggested an inner serenity and acceptance of life as it came to her. To all animals she belonged, and they would walk toward her across a field as if they had always known her.

The weather at Chalfont St. Giles was all mud and rain and low heavy fogs; but it would break for a bit, not quite come through, but with a touch of hope, while Linnéa and I slogged together for walks before a rewarding tea. We spent our evenings reading poetry aloud—Norman was a passionate poetry lover, like so many Englishmen; or lying round the library fire playing records. We went to a pantomime on Boxing Day, the day after Christmas. On Christmas morning Norman had arranged, without telling me beforehand, for a long-distance call to Katherine in Washington—he had that kind of thoughtfulness. Two days after Christmas he and I were in London, and dropped in to Westminster Abbey to hear the singing, Christmas carols, and old ballads:

Past three o'clock,
And a cold frosty morning:
Past three o'clock;
Good morrow, masters all!

Birkett gave a lunch in my honor at Claridge's, a pleasant and representative group that included Viscount Greenwood, the Canadian industrialist and chairman of the Pilgrims; Sir Gerald Dodson, the Recorder of London; Wilson Harris, M.P., the editor of the *Spectator*; Viscount Simon, former Foreign Secretary and Lord Chancellor; Lawrence Cadbury, owner of the *News-Chronicle*; Sir Patrick Hastings, England's foremost barrister, who in the past had so often been on the other side of a case from Birkett; A. P. Herbert, M.P., the novelist, who gave me a copy of his *Uncommon Law*, a collection of sixty-six "Misleading Cases," with a friendly inscription under which Jowitt scribbled —"Don't be misled by anything that Herbert says." There were half a dozen friendly little informal "speeches," bonds were renewed, fellowship exchanged, the sense of comradeship lingered. Once you are accepted by a Britisher there is nothing he will not do for you.

We came home by train, crossing the Channel and spending two nights with the Duff Coopers at the British Embassy in Paris, in the beautiful eighteenth-century house which the Duke of Wellington had bought before Waterloo, and where Thackeray had been married. Lady Diana showed me a water color of her mother, the daughter of the Duke of Rutland, made by Queen Victoria at Balmoral.

Two of my young associates, Jim Rowe and Bob Stewart, persuaded me to join them for a Saturday and Sunday at Garmisch, on the Austrian border—they had found a comfortable villa, which the Army had requisitioned, and had persuaded (without very much difficulty) three pleasant young ladies to come along. The hotel, where I stayed and which also belonged to the Army, contained signs in almost every room warning visitors against what Don Parker would have called fraternizing. "No male guest allowed in this section of the building," one *verboten* sternly announced; and again "Female visitors are not allowed above the ground floor," doubtless based on the accepted belief that love was always made under the roof—"can you believe it, under my very roof!"—and finally: "Guests will not entertain persons of the opposite sex in their rooms." No one seemed to pay any attention to the signs. "Good old army," said Bob Stewart.

We dined well, and danced late, and I said good night to the others, and went to my room. Across the bed trailed a nylon stocking, a lace-collared nightgown had been thrown negligently on the sofa, and a yellow satin mule peeped from under a chair. They must have had a lark fixing it. I went to bed and my dreams were not unpleasant.

There was a passable opera in Nürnberg, in full swing, and an excellent symphony orchestra, playing constantly amid the ruins. Parker and I, planning an evening "reception," arranged a concert at No. 2 "Hebel street"—as the program put it; first and second violins, viola, cello, bass, and piano. They played beautifully: Mozart, Haydn, Schubert, Beethoven, Percy Grainger; and, of course, inevitably *The Blue Danube* at the end.

We had listened all day to the dreadful accounts of the tortures. The contrast struck me. Could these be the same people? And I said something like that to the wife of Charles Dubost, one of the two French deputy chief prosecutors. Her husband had been a magistrate, had performed his public functions with meticulous precision during the occupation, while at night he was a leader of the underground, particularly adept, so it was rumored, at blowing up trains and bridges. Mme. Dubost was a short plain little French woman, restrained, intelligent, talking quietly.

"*Oui*," she said, "*c'est étrange, les Allemands. On me dit qu'ils sont des excellents maris, frères, parents, fils.*" She paused, and her face was harder. "*Mais ils ne sont pas de très bons voisins.*"

Not very good neighbors, but full of sentiment, the Germans. On Christmas Eve of 1944 twelve of the defendants sang Christmas carols: *Silent Night, Holy Night; Oh, How Joyfully;* an old children's song, *Behold a Branch Is Growing,* grouped around the prison chaplain, Göring holding his head high, tears in his eyes . . .

ATROCITIES, THIEVING, SCANDAL, AND BLACKMAIL

❧❧ *Chapter Thirty*

There was no end to the horrors of the testimony. The mind shrank from them, grew tired, rejected the imaginative and systematic cruelties. Or one tried to feel, to share the heroism of the victims. Auschwitz, a witness related, had a separate camp for extermination, called Monowitz. The bodies of Jews who had been shot were taken to a former ghetto and burned. "The Polish population immediately covered with flowers the blood spots which had been left on the ground." Special rules for Hungarian Jews were adopted. "Children up to the age of twelve or fourteen, older people over fifty, as well as the sick, or people with criminal records [who were transported in specially marked wagons] were taken immediately upon their arrival to the gas chambers. The others passed before an SS doctor who, on sight, indicated who was fit for work and who was not. Those unfit were sent to the gas chambers, while the others were distributed in various labor camps." The commandant at Auschwitz testified that "we knew when the people were dead because their screaming stopped." . . . The SS men carried dog whips. "Without screaming or weeping, these people undressed, stood around in family groups, kissed each other, said farewells, and waited for a sign from another SS man, who stood near the pit, also with a whip in his hand."

Bits of lyrical courage would emerge out of the savagery. M. Dumenil saw the killing of thirteen hostages who were among those shot in a reprisal at Châteaubriant. Two of the youngest, Gloux and Grolleau, students, encouraged the others, saying that it was better to die in this way than to perish uselessly in an accident. The priest was not allowed to accompany them to the place of execution. Gloux and Grolleau made a gesture of farewell to him, smiling and waving their hands, which were chained together. "Une fois montés dans le camion, Gloux et Grolleau, ont fait encore un geste d'adieu en souriant et an agitant leurs deux mains enchaînées ensemble" (Once mounted in the truck, Gloux and Grolleau made one more gesture of farewell, smiling and waving both hands which had been chained together).

The Germans relish hierarchical distinctions, best conveyed in long handles to their names; and they like to record their doings and catalogue their possessions. At the notorious Mathausen camp in Austria they carefully registered the killings—and even recorded the fictitious causes to which they were attributed—five thousand from 1939 to 1945; 203 on a single day from heart trouble. Rosenberg's title and the meticulous manner in which he chronicled his activities were typical of those two Teutonic impulses. He was known officially as Delegate to the Führer for the Total Supervision of Intellectual and Ideological Training and Education of the Party. Under his careful direction the Einsatzstab Rosenberg, organized to collect, arrange, and distribute plundered art objects, drew up a catalogue of sixty-eight volumes, beautifully illustrated, handsomely bound. On April 16, 1943, writing to his Führer on the occasion of the great man's birthday, he reported in a brief "preliminary" manner the art-seizure action. He enclosed three volumes of "the provisional picture catalogues," and ventured to hope "that this short occupation with the beautiful things of art, which are so near to your heart, will send a ray of beauty and joy into your care-laden and revered life."

We find the same note of beauty and joy expressed in another even more famous document entitled: The Warsaw Ghetto Is No More.

The destruction of the Warsaw Ghetto was the subject of a report made by Major General Stroop, in April, 1943, to Berlin. The report went into some detail—it covered seventy-five pages —relish for the subject matter shown in the ornate German craftsmanship, the leather binding, the profuse photographs, the exact typing on the heavy bond paper, tokens of the pride of accomplishment of the Waffen-SS, the police, and the Wehrmacht, who shared the glory of shooting and burning the inhabitants of the Ghetto, and who—so the account ran—"fulfilled their duty indefatigably in faithful comradeship and stood together as models and examples of soldiers." Their "duty" was "to destroy the entire Jewish residential area by setting every block on fire." Stroop spoke of a "proved total of 56,065 people" killed. This did not include the number exterminated by blasting and fire, which, he reported, "cannot be counted."

We sat there, for nine months out of the year, listening to the evidence. Seventeen of the smaller countries had joined in the Charter, and three or four of them asked that atrocities against their people should also be spread on the record.

Hitler's ghost haunted the courtroom, we could all see its outline, standing contemptuously at Göring's elbow; frowning at Schacht as he spoke of the Führer's enormous reading, of his juggling with his knowledge, in certain respects a man of genius, a mass psychologist of really diabolical genius, who finally fell victim to the spell he cast over the masses, for whoever seduces them is finally led and seduced by them. Streicher, who had been thoroughly under his spell, described Hitler after speaking for three hours in the Munich beer cellar in 1921, as "drenched in perspiration, radiant." General Keitel was impressed with the great man's knowledge of tactics, of operations, of strategy, of organization, of the details of armament, of the equipment of all the armies, of the classic authorities on the science of war— Clausewitz, Moltke, Schlieffer. But Jodl, summarizing his views in a last speech, said that the "Wehrmacht was confronted with the impossible task of conducting a war they did not want, under a commander they did not trust, to fight with troops and police forces not under their command"—by no means an inaccurate description.

We watched the defendants day after day, these drab men once great, most of them now turning on the Führer who had led them to their brief spasm of violent triumph. A few were still "loyal." Some felt that it was not "correct" to attack a dead man who had been head of the State. Others transferred their guilt to the man who, they said, was alone responsible, from whom, they pleaded, orders came to them that had to be obeyed: theirs but to do or die, they argued; how could there be a conspiracy, a meeting of the minds, when one man's mind commanded all the others? . . . It was not clear, as Genêt pointed out in one of her articles in *The New Yorker* (and how she could put her finger on the touchstones of the case) whether the defendants sought to prove that they did not wish to conquer the world, or that they were right in trying to do so.

Before long there developed, among the twenty-one, two groups under different leaders. The majority, particularly at first before the worst of the testimony came out, followed Göring, from whom still emanated something of the old charm, the compelling ruffianly power. He sustained the vanishing romance of the Reich, the intoxicating overwhelming dream of a superior race that in the early days had clouded their minds and swollen their hearts with the excitement of the primitive, the barbaric romance of free (lawless) men. It was curious to see how these men, basically conditioned to accept authority and law, rebelled so enthusiastically against the restrictions which their overorganized society had imposed, and finally surrendered to a more compelling need again to be mastered. The Nazi experiment soon became the degeneracy of the Romantic movement, so deeply German, as Thomas Mann has somewhere noted. "We now realize," wrote Rosenberg in his *Myth of the Twentieth Century*, "that the central supreme values of the Roman and the Protestant Churches being a negative Christianity do not respond to our soul, that they hinder the organic powers of the people designated as a Nordic race, that they must give way to them, that they have to be remodelled to conform to a Germanic Christianity." Nonsense, of course, but dangerous nonsense. The revolt against convention and the heavy hand of the past moved before long into a reaction against law itself, and the German people stood about with their arms crossed watching the Brown Shirts pillage the shops of Jews in Nürnberg. For law must not be called on to hamper the primordial urge of the superman, who before long was crawling on his belly to lick the hand and kiss the boots of his new master.

Dr. Gilbert describes the two rival groups.[1] He was with the prisoners constantly, talking to them between sessions of the Tribunal and in the evening. Dignity and stoicism was Göring's line, or at least a part of it, for he was a many-sided actor: Renaissance man, bully, hunter of big game, buffoon, hero, mountebank; brilliant, eloquent, funny; tough, realistic (particularly in the eyes of the weak men), his vision even in his last days playing with the great future of a New Germany; preaching nationalism: the German people must accept their inevitable fate, die like martyrs, remain loyal to their memories, and to the great men they served. If he backed down now after the way he supported the Führer the German people would have nothing but contempt for him. "I'd rather be called a murderer than a hypocrite. Don't forget that the great conquerors of history are not seen as murderers—Genghis Khan, Peter the Great, Frederick the Great . . ." He knew what was in store for him, but since the age of twelve he had not been afraid of death. It was not a question of his dying, but his reputation in history. This was no trial; he could say, like Mary Stuart, that he could be tried only by a court of his peers.

He detested, he asserted, anything that was undignified; but wished they all had the courage to confine their defense to the three simple words which Götz von Berlichingen used in Goethe's play—*lick my arse!* . . . And the others would laugh when he talked like that, or when he said, "You can take your morality and your repentance and your democracy and stick it up . . . Aggressive war? Ach! Fiddle-sticks! What about the grabbing of California and Texas by the Americans? That was plain aggressive warfare for territorial expansion. When it is a

[1] *Nuremberg Diary.* Farrar, Straus and Company, 1947. I have drawn freely on this interesting day-to-day account of the defendants.

question of the interests of the nation morality stops . . ." And his audience would nod, and smile; and their sense of guilt seemed less hard to bear in this comforting assumption that all nations were alike.

It must have been uphill work, often distasteful, for he knew how many of the other defendants despised him. He had been successful in aiding Hitler to subject the Army to the will of the Party, particularly after the von Blomberg and von Fritsch scandals, and the military feared and detested him. General Jodl pictured Göring in the last two or three years of the war as simply disappearing from time to time, hunting, collecting his art treasures, living his soft life at various castles. Grand Admiral Raeder, in a statement made while a prisoner of the Russians, said that "the person Göring had a disastrous effect on the fate of the German Reich"; that his vanity was unimaginable, his ambition immeasurable. He was always showing off, running after popularity—untruthful, selfish, greedy, jealous.

The old-line diplomats, von Neurath and von Papen, considered Göring a bully and an upstart, and referred to him as "the fat one." Frank thought him brutal and corrupt. Speer spoke of him as a lazy, selfish coward, an "irresponsible dope addict." But for over a year Göring had been without his drugs. "We took him off his dope and made a man of him," boasted Colonel Andrus, who was in charge of the prisoners, and spoke of them as "my boys," relating how their health had improved under the prison regime, as one might speak of turkeys being made ready for Thanksgiving.

Göring liked to play one defendant against another, intriguing with these forlorn shadows as he had intrigued when they were great with power. When Ribbentrop had finished testifying, Göring whispered to Raeder, "He's all washed up." But when the Tribunal recessed, he congratulated Ribbentrop on how well he was doing. He would make nasty remarks about the prison psychologist to the psychiatrist, about the Catholic chaplain to the Protestant chaplain. He liked to talk to Gilbert; but when he felt that Gilbert was against him he was overheard to announce from his corner that they had better not talk to that Gilbert any more—Americans did not have the breeding to understand the German point of view. . . .

He could threaten his companions as well as encourage them, and most of them were afraid of him. When Speer testified that, in April 1945, Hitler had told him that he had known for some time that Göring had failed, known that he was corrupt, known that he was a drug addict; and yet, cynically caring nothing for what might happen to the German people, had said that he was willing to let Göring negotiate the capitulation, Göring was furious. In a manner calculated to have Speer overhear him, he told some of the defendants during an intermission, that even if Speer came out of the trial alive the Feme would assassinate him for treason, meaning the Femegerichte, the secret and brutal kangaroo courts, which had been suppressed in the sixteenth century, and revived a few years after the First World War to punish persons suspected of informing on those working for the secret rearmament of the Reich. Speer laughed a little nervously when he repeated this in his cell to Gilbert.

Testifying, Göring was at his very best, twenty-one hours on the stand, opening for the defense, speaking without notes; touching lightly but effectively on his own youth—his father had been an intimate friend of Cecil Rhodes in South Africa; he had been the top ace in the First World War after von Richthofen was killed. He described in detail the Germany that he and his comrades faced when the war ended. Germans had never had experience of a democracy, they did not want one; and the Allies deserted the Weimar Republic after it had been foisted on the country. Then the years of inflation, the profiteers, seven million children, not all orphans, running the streets, the country without order, without discipline. The German principle had always been authority from above downward, and responsibility from below upward. Was it not natural that, looking about for patterns to follow, they should select the two outstanding models? He paused, and let his eye travel over the bench. "The Roman Catholic Church," he continued, "and the U.S.S.R."

The most damaging witness against Göring was Hans Gisevius, a member of the Secret State Police, which Göring considered his special preserve, and which he finally placed under his personal direction. Gisevius was called as a witness for Frick, and Göring must have at once known that he was in for trouble.

The Secret State Police, Gisevius testified, employed one Artur Nebe, a famous Prussian criminologist, who later was hanged for his activity in the plot of July 20, 1944, to assassinate Hitler. In 1933 Göring ordered Nebe to murder Gregor Strasser, a leading member of the National Socialist Party. Nebe, horrified, refused; and Göring to silence him had him promoted. Gisevius went on to describe the Roehm Putsch the following year, which he "followed up" in the Ministry of the Interior. A radiogram from Göring and Himmler, both of whom had engineered the Putsch with Heydrich in consultation with the Führer, fell into Gisevius's hands. It directed that all documents relating to June 30, the day of the Putsch should be destroyed immediately— an unusual direction for a German. Gisevius "took the liberty" of putting these papers into his safe, and hoped some day to recover them. The man was too facile a witness—fluent, detailed, oversure of himself, much too pat, but in the main truthful—he had published most of his testimony in a book, *Bis zum bittern Ende,* which had just appeared. The situation, he continued, verged on civil war: on one side the SA, headed by Roehm; on the other Göring, Himmler, and the SS. Gisevius had, he said, intentionally mentioned Field Marshal Werner von Blomberg's name, because of a little incident that had happened that morning in court. Dr. Otto Stahmer, Göring's lawyer, was talking to Dr. Rudolph Dix, who represented Schacht, in the room allotted to defendants' counsel, and the witness had overheard . . . Stahmer was on his feet instantly.

"May I ask whether a personal conversation which I had with Dr. Dix has anything to do with the taking of evidence?"

A ripple of excitement ran through the court. Göring watched us intently, a monstrous cat, poised to spring. During Gisevius's testimony he saw Parker slip me a note to watch Göring's reaction to this very damning testimony. He began at once to shake his head, shrug, suggest to the defendants who were nearest him— Schacht and Dönitz—his disgust with the witness. Hints of Göring's attempt to silence Gisevius had already got around. Justice Jackson also was on his feet—it was important that the Tribunal should know what happened, he told us, threats were made to the witness as he was standing in the courthouse, waiting to testify. Gisevius was allowed to finish.

Göring had said to his lawyer that Gisevius could attack him as much as he wanted; but if he attacked the dead von Blomberg, then Göring would disclose everything about Schacht, which might not be pleasant for Schacht . . . of course he cared nothing about himself, Göring repeated, but he would protect the name of a lady from the hot breath of scandal. . . . That was the way that Dr. Stahmer had conveyed Göring's threat to Schacht's lawyer.

We let the witness go into *l'affaire* von Blomberg, in detail. It was quite a story, "the most corrupt thing," Gisevius believed, "that Göring ever did."[2]

On January 12, 1938, Field Marshal von Blomberg had married for the second time. No details about his wife or photographs of her were published until a few days later when a single picture appeared of the marshal and his bride in front of the monkey cage at the Leipzig Zoo, whereupon a file was handed the commissioner of police in Berlin, which contained the information that the lady had been previously convicted of prostitution, and had been registered as a prostitute in seven cities. The Frau Field Marshal had also been sentenced for distributing indecent pictures. The witness had seen the file.

The commissioner of police, Count Helldorf, under ordinary circumstances would have submitted the report to his superior, Chief of Police Himmler. But this would have placed the Wehrmacht "in a very embarrassing position." Helldorf took the file to General Keitel, who was related to von Blomberg through the recent marriage of their children. Keitel demanded that the file be suppressed, and told Helldorf to take it to Göring. That gentleman had known all about it from the beginning, for von Blomberg had consulted him confidentially before the marriage. Was it permissible for a field marshal to have an affair with a woman of low birth? Would Göring help him obtain a dispensation to marry this "lady with a past," as he put it? And finally, she had another lover—would Göring help him get rid of the lover? Göring disposed of the lover by sending him to South

---

[2] John W. Wheeler-Bennett gives a lively description of this unsavory episode in his brilliant study of the German army in politics, *The Nemesis of Power* (New York: Macmillan & Co., 1953).

America. It was understandable that Göring should turn up at the wedding, which immediately followed, to serve as witness. He would not have been averse to being appointed minister of war if anything happened to his friend the field marshal.

By this time the president of the Tribunal thought we had heard enough, and asked Dr. Dix whether "these matters, which appear to be personal, are relevant to the charges." Dr. Dix thought they were, and so did Justice Jackson, and much to everyone's relief the witness was allowed to proceed with a warning from Lawrence to confine himself as much as possible "to the political aspects of the matter."

Göring, as one might expect, felt compelled to give the file to Hitler, who in a rage dismissed von Blomberg, would not consider Göring in his place, and was of the opinion that he should appoint General Werner von Fritsch, who was popular with the Army and throughout the country. Göring realized that something pretty drastic had to be done to block the appointment.

Göring and Himmler worked out a plan. They reported to their Führer that as far back as 1935 von Fritsch had been a homosexual. In 1934 the Gestapo had conceived the useful idea, according to Gisevius, of prosecuting homosexuals among other enemies of the State—it was such an easy way to "get" your opponent—and had visited penitentiaries and asked convicted inmates who had engaged in the blackmail of homosexuals for the names of their victims, and the evidence against them. In 1935 the Gestapo turned over the material to Hitler, who was indignant, and ordered the files burned. But they were not burned. Heydrich had simply brought them up to date through further extensive investigations. One of the alleged homosexuals was a certain Herr von Fritsch or Frische. Göring, reporting to Hitler, offered to bring a convict who would identify the general, from his prison to the Reich Chancellery, so that Hitler could see him personally and judge. Göring had already threatened this convict with death if he did not stick to his story. Hitler sent for General von Fritsch—and for the convict.

What a scene it must have been, and what an episode it might make, as I suggested to two representatives of Hollywood producers who came to Nürnberg on the chance of picking up

material; what an episode for *The Rise and Fall of Adolf Hitler.*
In the early days the camera plays away from the little frenzied
man, down to and over the crowds that press about him, small
groups at first, then overflowing as far as one could see, gaping,
worshiping, silent, reverent—then, as he ends in a half scream, his
arm stretched above them, shrieking out the hatred he had
whipped into flame, they begin to march, and to sing, and to
slay and torture, following him . . . there would be the Hoz-
back conference, where he so coolly outlined to the generals and
admirals and diplomats his plans for conquering the world, step
by step, if they could but be persuaded to follow him . . . And
now Hitler tells General von Fritsch of the charges, in the presence of Göring and a group of top-ranking generals. Von Fritsch
gives Hitler his word of honor that the accusations are false.
Hitler scowls at him, goes to the nearest door, opens it, the
convict slouches in, "a shambling, degenerate figure"—to quote
Wheeler-Bennett—looks over the generals as they stand at attention, raises his arm, points to von Fritsch. "That's him!" Von
Fritsch is too frozen with anger to speak. Again Hitler is near a
breakdown in the storm of his fury. Von Fritsch must resign
instantly.

Colonel General Ludwig Beck, Chief of the General Staff,
intervened with Hitler, and demanded an investigation. The
matter hung fire for ten days. Hitler appointed General von
Brauchitsch commander in chief. After a further delay, an investigation was ordered, and Göring became president of the
general court-martial. It was established that there had been
originally a mistake in identity—a retired Captain von Frisch was
the man in question. This fact was known to the Gestapo on
January 15, and therefore to Göring, who had brought the convict to the Reich Chancellery on January 24. Proof of "blackmail, bribery, forgery, and threats of every kind, including
death," writes Wheeler-Bennett, "had been employed by Göring,
Himmler, and Heydrich in the fabrication of the dossier against
the General." Witnesses had to be kept under armed guard to
protect them against the SS. The reaction that all this would
provoke when it was made public might open the long-awaited
opportunity to unseat the regime. Heydrich said to a friend of
Gisevius that the court-martial would be the end of his career.

The court-martial convened on March 11. But history interrupted the meeting, for that was the day chosen for the German armies to march into Austria. There must be an adjournment; and when a week later the court-martial reconvened, the Anschluss had taken place, unopposed by Austria, and Hitler returned stronger than ever, the hero of greater Germany. Gisevius believed that Göring had persuaded Hitler to advance the march into Austria by two days in order to achieve these results, but other evidence is lacking to establish this neat assumption.

Von Fritsch was acquitted and forgotten. Hitler congratulated him on "his recovery of health" without a word of regret. In a last desperate effort to seize the now lost opportunity, von Fritsch challenged Himmler to a duel, formally, in good military tradition. But Himmler simply ignored him. The anticlimax was complete. Hitler had outmaneuvered and humiliated the German Army. Any possibility of the Army's turning in revolt against the Führer had now vanished. "From that time on," Gisevius testified, "we took the steep downward path to radicalism." And Hitler no longer feared his generals.

If Göring was the prime exhibit of the trial, Albert Speer was the most humane and decent of the defendants. His straightforwardness and honesty, his calm and reasonable bearing, his awareness of the moral issues involved, impressed the members of tho Tribunal. Spoor, who wao forty ono whon ho was tried, must have been a highly impressionable young German, idealistic and prone to hero-worship, when he joined the Party in 1932. Soon he became Hitler's architect and personal confidant, lavishing a passionate admiration on his chief if one can judge by the depth and bitterness of his ultimate disillusion, which proved to be the basis of his outlook and testimony at the trial. A man of striking ability, in ten years he was in charge of all war production, with immense powers, trusted by Hitler, who was so suspicious of most of the men he raised about him.

It was not until the last days that Speer began to question the character of his leader. Doubts had of course begun to cross his mind; but, working continually at his immense production job, aloof from the chicaneries and plots that eddied around the seat of power, he seemed like so many other idealists to have been unwilling to face a reality which was bound to destroy the faith that had meant everything to him. He was very German. Unlike the other men in the dock, he cared about Hitler primarily because he believed that Hitler had led the German people out of their despair and impotence, and placed their feet on the path to recovery of national greatness. Speer was serious, deeply thoughtful, without humor, patient, his shoulders bowed under the shame of his people and the moral degradation to which he had helped to lead them. "I have no illusions about my own life," he told Dr. Gilbert. "It is the German people I care about." It was no wonder that hatred burned between him and Göring, for to Speer Göring stood for all the vain and brutal ambitions that had brought the Fatherland to its present misery.

In the prison and in the dock at luncheon and when the defendants exercised, the moral struggle was dominant, the duel between two conceptions. Göring wanted the Nazi myth to persist. Even if they were to be found guilty they could go down to posterity as heroic *übermensch*. He cornered poor, cowardly little Walter Funk in the exercise yard and told him he must reconcile himself to his fate, must stand by Göring and die a martyr's death. He need not worry because someday—even if it took fifty years—"the German people would rise again and recognize them as heroes, and even move their bones to marble caskets, in a national shrine."

But little Funk was not the martyr type, and cared little about what might happen to his bones. He blubbered a good deal. "I assure you," he confided to Dr. Gilbert, "I don't have the stuff for heroism. I didn't then and I don't now. Maybe that is the trouble." "I always came up to the door," he testified wistfully, "but was never allowed to enter." He was an unimportant little man. As president of the Reichsbank he had made an agreement with Himmler to receive for deposit and handle the gold and jewels and currency that the SS brought in. "I was never told about gold teeth placed in my vaults," he whined on the stand. The personal belongings of the Jews who had been burned in the concentration camps amounted to a good deal when you added it up, great carloads bringing it in to the bank from Auschwitz and Mathausen; and there it was neatly sorted and arranged: the jewels and watches sent to the Municipal Pawn Shop; the gold that had been extracted by a special detachment of SS men from the teeth of the corpses before they were cremated at Auschwitz, and the gold spectacle frames to the Prussian mint, where they were melted into bars and returned to the Reichsbank. The notes and coin stayed in the bank. A systematic banker, little Funk. . . .

At first the ranks wavered, Göring was persuasive, the others were afraid of him, had for so many years looked to his pervasive authority. But gradually his followers deserted. The showing of the documentary films of concentration camps, taken by Allied photographers as American troops entered the areas where they were situated, with the bulldozers piling up the huge stacks of naked, unidentifiable bodies, had unmanned most of the prisoners.

Then there was the film, *The Nazi Plan*, all of it shot by the Germans themselves under Dr. Goebbels' personal supervision, depicting the actual trials of the men charged with the plot to assassinate Hitler by placing a bomb in his headquarters on July 20, 1944. The trials were held before Judge Freisler in Berlin from August to the following February. The film was not released to the public, but was used as a confidential report to the Führer, who had it run off for his own satisfaction many times, and ordered it exhibited to every officer above the rank of colonel—many of the defendants implicated in the July 20 plot had been high-ranking officers in the Wehrmacht. The defendants, who had apparently been subjected to torture, cringed as the judge shouted at them. Some of them were hanged by slow strangulation . . . The judge was killed in an air raid, sitting with a defendant's papers in his hands.

Day after day the horrors accumulated—tortures by the Gestapo in France, scientific "experiments" on prisoners who died in agony, the gas chambers, the carefully planned liquidation of the Jews. Hour on hour the twenty-one men in the dock listened, and the shame spread, and steadily washed to the rocks of their loyalty to the man who was responsible for it all. After one day's evidence Hans Fritzsche was physically ill in his cell. And when Hans Frank, the notorious Governor General of Po-

land, made his cheap, dramatic confession—"a thousand years
will pass and still this guilt of Germany will not have been
erased"—Schacht observed to Gilbert that Göring's united front
of loyalty and defiance seemed to have collapsed. After Gisevius had testified, the legend was warped and tarnished. Speer
tried in his testimony to destroy it forever. The Führer principle,
he had at last realized, the authoritarian system, was fundamentally wrong. In 1945 when the situation had become hopeless Hitler "attributed the outcome of the war in an increasing
degree to the failure of the German people, but he never
blamed himself . . . The German people remained faithful to
Adolf Hitler to the end. He knowingly betrayed them."

Speer repeated this in the statement which each defendant
was allowed to make immediately before sentences were imposed. He prophesied that after the trial the people of Germany
would despise and condemn Hitler as the proven author of her
misery. The totalitarian system in the period of modern technical
development can dispense with all subordinate leaders, and
mechanize them into uncritical recipients of orders. "The nightmare of many a man that one day nations could be dominated
by technical means was all but realized in Hitler's system . . .
The more technical the world becomes, the more necessary is
the promotion of individual freedom and the individual's awareness of himself as a counter-balance . . . This war ended with
remote-controlled rockets, aircraft traveling at the speed of
sound, new types of submarines, torpedoes which find their own
target, with atom bombs, and with the prospect of a horrible
kind of chemical warfare . . . In five or ten years the technique
of warfare will be able to destroy one million people in the center
of New York in a matter of seconds with a rocket operated by
only ten men, invisible, without previous warning, faster than
sound, by day and by night . . . Science can spread pestilence
among human beings and animals and destroy crops by insect
warfare . . ."

Speer had finished. He looked at us, and beyond us. Then
very quietly he said, as if to prevent himself from sobbing, "May
God protect Germany and the culture of the West." There was a
long silence in the courtroom.

The defendants were an assorted lot, hardly perhaps typical of the German people, most of them small men, who had once strutted in great places; men whose weaknesses may have attracted them to Hitler. There were ruffians like Kaltenbrunner —"a bony and vicious horse" Rebecca West called him—who had succeeded Heydrich after his assassination as chief of the Security Police, and who knew, as he said, that the hatred of the world was directed against him now that Himmler was no longer alive. A descendant of farmers and scythemakers, he stood six feet four, with the deep purple welt of a sword cut across his face from ear to chin, which seemed to swell and glow as he lied under Colonel John Harlan Amen's cross-examination. He denied his signature when he was confronted with it, and lied so palpably that his associates in the dock turned away from him the next day when they filed in.

At one end sat Schacht in his tall collar and impeccable glow of self-righteous conceit, at the other Julius Streicher, round-shouldered and moth-eaten, chewing gum, mumbling to himself, mean and sullen, with whom none of the other defendants would talk, lewd, sadistic, mouthing his neurotic obsession about the Jews, "a dirty old man," to quote Rebecca West again, "of the sort that gives trouble in parks." In his paper, *der Stürmer,* which was devoted to anti-Semitism, he had advocated "castration for race polluters." For Streicher, his trial was a "triumph of world Jewry." He believed himself to be a man whom destiny had placed in a position to enlighten the world on the Jewish question. He was certain three of the judges were Jews, and practically the whole of the prosecution—they got uncomfortable when he looked at them, he claimed, for he could always recognize the blood. He would harp on circumcision, which was, he said, a rite calculated to preserve the racial consciousness. He wasn't ashamed of circulating the story about Göring, which resulted in Streicher's losing his position as Gauleiter in 1940, the story that Göring had never consummated his marriage and that his child was a test-tube baby.

There was Hess, who once had been the Number Three man, his eyes sunk deep into the sallow cavern of his face, his reading ranging from Edgar Wallace to Goethe, to Jerome's *Three Men in a Boat,* a bony scarecrow, wearing the same black field boots

that he had worn on his famous "mission for humanity," his flight
to England, when he proposed to the startled Duke of Hamilton
what seemed to him such a reasonable solution of the war—
Great Britain should hand back the German colonies and
evacuate Iran, or else the Nazis would set up concentration
camps and starve the population to death if the British attempted to carry on war from the Empire after the German invasion of England.

Franz von Papen, the fox, the "Devil in a High Hat," was
nearing seventy. His son sat with his lawyer, Dr. Egon Kuber-
schok. Von Papen was a vain and crafty intriguer. He had,
during the First World War, been expelled as military attaché
to the German Embassy in Washington. He was a fervent
Catholic, a conservative, and a gentleman jockey and steeple-
chaser.

One June 17, 1934, von Papen, who had become deeply
troubled over the excesses of the Nazis, delivered an address
at the University of Marburg demanding the regeneration of
public life, denouncing the dangers of an approaching dictatorship, and emphasizing the terrible extremes to which certain
Nazi leaders had gone. The speech, which had been written by
von Papen's assistant, Edgar Jung, was an exceptionally courageous attack on the Party chieftains around Hitler, particularly
Goebbels. A fortnight later the Roehm Putsch broke out in Berlin
and Munich. On the night of June 30—"the night of the long
knives"—the leaders of the SA were killed by SS squads. Jung
was arrested and shot. Von Papen was picked up by the SS the
day before the Putsch.

According to his own account Heydrich and Himmler had
wanted him shot, but he had been saved from death by Göring's intervention.

Von Papen's speech had been promptly censored by Goebbels, and only a few extracts appeared in the Frankfurter
Zeitung. Wheeler-Bennett told me that he was at the time in
Berlin busy with his life of Hindenberg, and managed to
smuggle out a copy of the speech to Great Britain. He had
probably been under surveillance by the Secret Police for some
time. A day or two before the speech had been delivered, Jung
persuaded Wheeler-Bennett to meet him in the country, away

from Dictaphones and spies, told him of the proposed speech, and recounted in a good deal of detail the corruption and plotting that had been going on. Jung knew he would be killed after the speech was made, and wanted someone whom he could trust to hear these things . . . When he got back to his hotel Wheeler-Bennett had a message from a very old friend in Geneva, whose wife was dying. Could he come at once? He went at once. The next morning Gestapo agents with drawn revolvers walked into his bedroom. His name was found on one of the Putsch lists.

The defendants Keitel and Jodl were both connected with the O.K.W., the High Command of the Armed Forces, an interservice organization directly responsible to Hitler as supreme commander. Keitel was the chief of the O.K.W., with Jodl immediately subordinate to him. Their loyalty to Hitler was automatic. But Alfred Jodl, who came from a family of intellectuals, was an individual of high intelligence and vigorous personality, who deliberately subordinated his will to the Führer's caprices, and became one of his most idolatrous admirers. Jodl, in a green coat and light blue trousers with red stripes, gave one the impression of strength and of self-control. Like so many of the defendants his attitude toward Hitler fluctuated between adulation and contempt.

Keitel looked like a cross between a battered but respectable coachman and one of the milder Anglican bishops. Obsequious in his cell, he would bow and scrape to a lieutenant. In court he sat upright and apparently composed, in his shabby green uniform, stripped of decorations, always looking "correct." "Sure," Schacht said about him to Dr. Gilbert, "an honest man, but not a man at all." General Keitel kept repeating on the stand in his defense that he had absolutely no "command functions," as if he considered that this description of his duties would absolve him from faithfully carrying out Hitler's orders to murder and to torture.

Of the two admirals, Karl Dönitz, who had succeeded Erich Raeder as head of the Navy, was the modern, highly-trained technician. Grand Admiral Raeder, a little man of an older generation, was born in 1876, entered the Navy at eighteen, and received the commendation of the Kaiser in 1910 when he was navigation officer of the Imperial Yacht *Hohenzollern.* Before retiring in 1943 he had been active in building up the German Navy, and in submarine warfare; but what particularly moved the Tribunal to impose on him a sentence of life imprisonment was his successful pressure on Hitler to invade Norway, in spite of Hitler's desire to keep Scandinavia neutral, one of the clearest acts of aggressive war in the record. He was skeptical about what would happen to him, he hoped he would be shot, at his age he had no desire to serve a prison sentence. He had already attempted suicide when in the hands of the Russians.

Dönitz was proud and stiff, with, I suspect, a violent temper, which he found hard to control. He had the ablest lawyer in the group, a young judge advocate in the Navy who was allowed to appear in court in his uniform during the early stages of the trial since a part of the German Navy was being kept in uniform while it was helping to sweep up the mines in the Baltic and North Seas. Flottenrichter Otto Kranzbuehler, of Düsseldorf, was cool, polite but never obsequious, extraordinarily skillful, handsome. Dönitz's wife acted as his lawyer's secretary. On one occasion, in an intermission after her husband's preliminary cross-examination, she persuaded one of the guards to put a tiny bunch of flowers at his place in the dock, with a few words scribbled on an accompanying slip of paper: "We are proud of you. You are doing splendidly, but don't lose your temper."

Typical of Kranzbuehler's skill was his handling of the interrogatories which he had asked the court to issue to Admiral Chester W. Nimitz, aimed at bringing to the Tribunal's attention the way submarines were used by the United States after she entered the war. The chief charge against his client was that he had been guilty of unrestricted U-boat warfare in violation of the Treaty of London, which provided that warning should be given a merchantman before she was torpedoed, and that wherever possible the survivors should be picked up. The interrogatories were directed to discover whether Admiral Nimitz had complied with these provisions of the treaty.

Jackson opposed the request with his usual vigor. What happened in the Pacific, he insisted, could have no relation to the German uncurbed submarine warfare in the Atlantic. The one was simply not relevant to the other. What the Americans may

have done had no bearing on what the Germans did. Even if
the Americans had committed a breach of the London Agreement—which was not admitted—this gave no excuse to the German Navy. If you get into that kind of thing, comparing how
each country had fought the war, you'd simply never get anywhere. Sir David with great earnestness backed his American
associate. I was not certain as to how much Jackson knew of
the orders which had been issued to Nimitz. It seems hardly
open to doubt that Maxwell Fyfe knew exactly what the British
Admiralty had done in the Skagerrak. They did not relish going
into this. If the Americans opened a path of inquiry, the British
could hardly block the way that led to them—and they didn't
like it. I had good reason to believe that our Navy had no objection to such a line of examination.

Kranzbuehler answered the prosecution's objections deftly,
quietly, persuasively, with a cool reasonableness that must have
irritated his opponents. The prosecution, he suggested, evidently
did not understand his conception of why the interrogations
should be permitted. He was not asking for evidence of what
the Americans did to prove what the Germans had done.
Obviously there was no *factual* relationship. Nor did he suggest that the Navy of the United States in its U-boat warfare
against Japan had committed any breach of international law—
far from it. On the contrary, he would prove that the United
States had behaved strictly in accordance with the law. The
London Agreement of 1930 had been signed by both the
United States and Japan. His position was that where merchantmen had been ordered to offer armed resistance to submarines
the London Agreement no longer applied, because the ships
were no longer merchantmen. He was offering to show that in
practice the American Admiralty interpreted the London Agreement in the same way as the German Admiralty.

It was recognized, he continued, that international law derives not only from treaties, but from acts of governments interpreting treaties. Mr. Jackson had himself made this clear in his
first report to President Truman when he said that international
law was developed by acts of government. What Jackson said in
the report was: "Innovations and revisions in international law
are brought about by the actions of government designed to meet

a change in circumstances. It grows, as did the common law, through decisions reached from time to time in adapting settled principles to new situations." The attitude taken by the United States, one of the great sea powers, should be almost decisive as to the proper interpretation of the London Agreement and the naval warfare in question.

It was a masterly argument, convincing and from the large view, unanswerable. Aside from the law the force of the moral appeal was compelling—if Dönitz had fought in the Atlantic precisely as Nimitz had fought in the Pacific, and the British Admiralty in the Skagerrak, how could we convict his client?

All of which I argued as persuasively as I could to my associates when we met the same afternoon to pass on Kranzbuehler's motion. I said we would look like fools if we refused and it later appeared that Nimitz had torpedoed without warning. The Russians thought that we were wasting time, everyone knew what went on in war, but why grant the German dogs anything more? We'd been leaning over backward—refuse the motion. The French looked at the English, shrugged, they would leave it to the maritime powers to decide. Parker was doubtful. Lawrence didn't relish opening it up. He didn't know how his Admiralty felt about it, whether they preferred not to get into it, though he didn't put it that way. Whereupon I pleaded personal privilege: it was an American question. We had nothing to conceal. I insisted that the others should yield to me, just as I would have yielded to them where some matter of their national policy might be involved. This appeal convinced Lawrence, who was invariably fair and considerate; and we unanimously voted to grant the motion.

There was not involved, in this instance, a conflict between policy and judgment. Had we refused to permit Admiral Nimitz's interrogatories because they might reveal that the United States had acted illegally, we would have been behaving like politicians and not like judges. But to say that judges in our position should never act like politicians oversimplifies an issue that cannot be resolved in such simple terms. We were an international body, viewing our legal and political obligations from different angles. The sense of negotiation was intermingled with judging. In some decisions that sense necessarily played a part in reaching the common judgment.

Admiral Nimitz's answers to the interrogatories, read in court four months later, justified our judgment and sustained Kranzbuehler's position. Nimitz was commander in chief of the United States Pacific Fleet. The Pacific Ocean areas were declared a theater of operations as soon as war broke out.

> Q: Was it customary in such areas for submarines to attack merchantmen without warning, with the exception of her own and those of her allies?
> A: Yes, except hospital and safe-conduct ships.
> Q: Were you under orders to do so?
> A: The Chief of Naval operations on December 7, 1941, ordered unrestricted naval warfare against Japan.

The practice existed since December 7, Admiral Nimitz continued, in declared zones of operation, and corresponded to the issued orders. The Japanese merchantmen reported by radio information regarding the sighting of United States submarines. They were usually armed, and always attacked by any available means—ramming, gunfire, and depth charges. On general principles a United States submarine did not rescue enemy survivors if undue additional hazard to the submarine resulted, or the submarine would be prevented from accomplishing her further mission. The desperate and suicidal character of the enemy was known. It was unsafe to pick up survivors. They were frequently given rubber boats and provisions. The survivors usually did not board the submarine voluntarily, it was necessary to take them prisoners by force. All types of ships that were not combatant ships were classed as merchantmen. The order was fully justified by the Japanese attacks on December 7 on armed and unarmed ships without warning or a declaration of war.

Kranzbuehler issued interrogatories along the same line to the British Admiralty, with the same result.

When it came to our making the final judgment on the guilt of Dönitz, Parker and I were in sharp disagreement. There was little in the record, except the unrestricted submarine warfare, on which a finding of guilt could be predicated. Parker's position was that Dönitz had clearly violated the London Agree-

ment; that merchantmen were merchantmen whether armed or
not; conditions of modern war could not change a treaty. It
was just as imperative to warn a merchantman that you were
going to torpedo her, if she did not stop and surrender, in the
forties as it was in the thirties, when the London Agreement
was signed. He admitted that today that might mean the almost
instant bombing of the submarine, in answer to a radio call by
the merchantman for help. But the law was the law.

There was evidence of shooting down the survivors of one
torpedoed merchantman, the *Peleus,* by a German submarine
commander; and the prosecution tried hard to tie Dönitz into
this, but, in the opinion of all of us, without success. But I
think it had got under Parker's skin, this ruthless machine gun-
ning of sailors clinging to the wreck of their torpedoed ship,
adrift in the vast waste of waters, and to him it was all part of
this horrible business. We must not pass it up, or seem to con-
done it.

Parker hated evil. Sometimes I suspected that he did not
believe in it. The atrocities, to his emotions at least, were incredible, even if his mind could accept them. I am sure that
even now, after that long cruel page of history was spread out
for all to read, based almost entirely on records of the Germans themselves and on the evidence of German witnesses—I am
certain that to many the whole business seems "grossly exaggerated."

I was convinced Parker was wrong, and told him so, from
every angle and several times, as I wanted to persuade him
before we went into conference with the others. I thought we
would look like fools if we condemned Admiral Dönitz for doing,
toward the end of the war, what Admiral Nimitz had begun
when the United States entered it. Finally we agreed to refer
the matter to Lawrence, who after having Major Phipps, one of
his assistants, brief the point carefully, concluded that my position was sound.

Eventually I voted not guilty; but my three other colleagues
thought that there was enough evidence of Dönitz's participation
in certain atrocities to warrant some punishment, and he was
given ten years.

Phipps adored his chief, and would brook no trifling with

the great man's exalted position. On a particular occasion he was hurrying through the long, narrow corridor that finally led into the courtroom, immediately before the Tribunal convened, bearing in his arms a stack of papers and books reaching to his chin. He was stopped by the American lieutenant whose duty it was to check everything that was taken into court—one of the many army precautions to prevent an "incident." The lieutenant indicated to a GI that he should look over the papers. Major Phipps protested—they belonged to His Lordship. The lieutenant gave him a long, cool, skeptical stare. It was almost ten o'clock. "I demand passage," cried Phipps, "in the name of His Britannic Majesty!" The lieutenant turned back to the GI. "Look 'em over, Bill; look 'em over extra careful," he said.

The Charter provided that the judgment "as to the guilt or innocence of any defendant shall give the reasons on which it is based," and it fell to my lot to deal with Dönitz, and the charges of violating the London Agreement. I said candidly that the evidence showed that the rescue provisions were not carried out, and that the defendant ordered that they should not be carried out. The defendant's argument that the development of aircraft had made rescue impossible might be true; but the Protocol of 1936, to which Germany had acceded, and which reaffirmed the rules of submarine warfare laid down in the London Naval Agreement of 1930, was explicit. If the commander cannot rescue, he cannot sink a merchant vessel, and should allow it to pass unharmed before his periscope. Dönitz was guilty of a violation of the Protocol. I continued that in view of the order of the British Admiralty that all vessels should be sunk at night in the Skagerrak, and that unrestricted submarine warfare was carried on in the Pacific Ocean by the United States, the sentence of Dönitz was not "assessed on the ground of his breaches of the international law of submarine warfare."

It may be argued that my stand was inconsistent; that if I objected to punishing the Germans for breaches of international law that both British and Americans had committed, how could I approve of condemning Germans for acts of which the Russians had also been guilty—aggressive war against Finland and Poland, and ruthless brutality in carrying on that war, particularly in Poland? The answer lies not alone in logic or consistency, but in a balance of practical and ideal values. Because the Russians had also done these things it did follow that guilt should not have been borne home to the Germans. Obviously one could not punish both. Yet to insist that aggressive warfare was criminal and should be punished, even if this involved only Germany, was better than to abandon any effort to outlaw it. Germany had set out to conquer the world by force of arms. Inherent in that ambition were the seeds of a ruthlessness which became conscious sadism, planted in the concentration camps of Mathausen, Dachau, Lublin, Sachsenhausen, Oranienberg, Auschwitz, Belzek, Flossenberg, Wolzek, Treblinka . . .

SPRING COMES TO
NÜRNBERG—THE
SECRET TREATY

Chapter Thirty-one

Spring came with an unexpected suddenness, and
vanished into summer. Along the *autobahns* the broom was thick
and insistent; and then lupine, miles of lupine, very tall and all
in full bloom at a single moment. Down the Pegnitz River the
crocuses spread a carpet; and before long men and women, who
had been wheeling about their great vats of liquid manure, were
sweeping down the yellow wheat and russet barley with hand
scythes, along the edge using sickles, bending to the earth, moving with a slow, continuous rhythm. But the oats were still green
and the hops twining up their tall poles. A thousand years
settled in the valley of the old river, and there was time to stretch
again under the warmth of the ancient summer sun.

Our guards changed from time to time as they were relieved
from duty to go home. One, Don Parker, was with me for six or
seven months, and we became friends. He came from Northville, a little town on one of the lakes that dot northern New
York, was an excellent shot, very quick on his feet. He was
fond of the open air, and we formed the habit after the Tribunal
had adjourned for the day of walking along the flat green and

fertile valley of the Pegnitz River, where the peasants with their
oxcarts were growing truck. There was a current saying that it
was "like throwing water into the Pegnitz," about the equivalent
of "carrying coals to Newcastle"; and on one occasion when
some German defense witness had been particularly long-
winded and repetitive and tiresome in proving some irrelevant
and readily accepted fact, I suggested to Lawrence that he tell
the witness that enough was enough, that more would be like
throwing water into the Pegnitz. The London *Times* would love
it—British Judge Shows Remarkable Knowledge of Local Say-
ings . . . Don Parker and I walked in the river bed; and the
wild ducks began to fly north. One day we saw a fox kill a small
fawn, no bigger than a hare; and when the next afternoon we
visited the spot, the fox had cleaned it neatly, leaving but the
head and hoofs and hide.

The language of the GI is ever fresh and wonderful. The Army
was not, as one GI put it, particularly interested in bringing out
six hundred men (the reputed size of Jackson's organization) to
sit around the Grand Hotel and drink and crap all day—to kill
two dozen Germans. Don's talk was no exception. There was
excitement in the *Stars and Stripes* about some order restricting
or broadening the "fraternization" rule, I forget which. Our
policy on this delicate subject, like so much of our policy in
Germany, kept swinging between stern prohibition of any dealings with the female enemy, and a relaxed realization that our
poor boys were lonely and probably would take their fun where
they found it, which of course they did, policy or no policy. I
asked Don just what "fraternization" meant, how would you define it to a man from Mars, parachuting into Nürnberg to look
things over. "What I mean is, Don, has it a technical meaning?
If you took a girl out walking one evening—nothing more—would
that be fraternizing?"

He considered me with a careful eye, searching for words
to convey the exact implication, yet would not offend the dignified ears of a judge, and then, "Yes, I think you'd call it technical,
Judge. I know what you mean, and I don't think taking a walk
would come in under the order. But suppose some of these
officer guys are going out one night, and we'd see them stuffing
their pockets with chocolate and cigarettes, then you'd say—got

your fraternizing tools with you tonight, ain't you? See what I mean, Judge?" I saw. Don liked the "Krauts" well enough, they were clean, not like the "Eyetalians," and they did what you told them. His approach, to quote once more from Rebecca West, was with a friendly "pardon my iron glove."

Don would get long letters from his wife in Northville now and then, and he liked me to know it, rustling a letter, or letting it lie around a bit, as if to indicate that his domestic harmony continued in this sea of "fraternizing." On one occasion I asked him if the news had been good.

"Not altogether, Judge," he answered. "She's had another operation."

I expressed sympathy. "I didn't know your wife had been operated on before, you never told me."

"Oh yes, female stuff," said Don; and added, "the second operation was not serious, just to take out any air pockets they'd left in her after the first operation."

My driver was a heavy, not ill-looking Italian boy from Brooklyn, awkward and half-baked, who turned to Don for advice when he couldn't make up his own mind. He was, as circumstances were to indicate, given to fraternizing. When spring came he confided to me that he was going to be married, a young Polish C.P., a blonde, very sad life, no parents, maybe I had noticed her around now and then, would I come to the wedding, maybe I would give her away, no date was fixed, he'd have to talk to the father again. . . . The date kept moving into the future, and when I asked him about it Tony seemed troubled. Finally Don explained. Tony had got her in a family way. He did want to marry her, but they kept putting it off, until if they fixed a day who could tell, you couldn't be sure, she'd probably have the baby just when the priest was ready, and he'd have to put it off again. Make him look kind of foolish. Don had advised Tony to take me into his confidence. "I told him you were an understanding sort of gentleman," Don concluded, "but Tony couldn't see it that way. I guess Tony thought you thought he was a different kind of guy from what he is, if you see what I mean, Judge."

The Negro soldiers had their own roving imagination, and now and then displayed the courtly dignity so characteristic of their race. They had been injected—so they told the admiring *fräuleins,* with whom they were immensely popular—just before sailing from the other side, with a wonder drug, top secret, which made them invisible at night, for special night fighting, you could see how effective that would be; but of course since the war was over they'd be fixed up soon so as to be white again. . . . One young colored boy, very proud of his stripes, picked up a pretty young German girl, still a child, and to her terrified surprise delivered her to her father's threshold with the admonition, "She's all right this time, but you better not let her get into the hands of any of them poor white trash!"

We took expeditions on Saturday afternoons and Sundays to the little neighboring towns—Lauf, only three or four miles from the Villa Conradti, Rothenberg, content in its walls, with the gaunt primitives in the Lutheran Church; Dinkelsbuhl, and Nordlingen, Donauwörth on the Danube; Doss, with its lemon and crimson and olive and gray houses, high eaves and petunias hanging vinelike from the window boxes. At Rotenberg there was a pretty wooden Virgin smiling down at her suckling child . . .

We spent an enchanted weekend at Salzburg, its cool river running through the warm town, for the musical festival, already revived, where Nicole Heriot played Berlioz and Ravel. Nicole and Nicholas Nabokov and I toiled up the hill to see the Schloss. She had aquamarine eyes and blond hair and bare, brown legs, which showed, she said, the scars that had been left by the Gestapo. She was twenty-three. She had been three years with the underground. She played the *klavier* with the sureness and strength of a man. Nicholas said she had a skeptical mind and a tender heart . . . He took us to see Max Reinhardt's house, and his widow, who had once been a famous German actress, showed us a quilted patchwork altar piece, on one patch a bit of Polish folk melody, which Nicholas hummed for us. On each side of the boat landing stood plaster figures with the heads of horses, and curling fish tails. "Mermares," said Virgil Thomson, the composer and music critic of the *Herald Tribune,* who was along with us. A mountain behind the house lay in the lilac dusk of the afternoon like a tired cloud. . . .

We were lodged with becoming grandeur at Schloss Klessheim, which had been built in 1709 by the Archbishop Count Harrach as a palace of pleasure, which he called Favorita. When the Nazis took it over in 1938—so the brochure informed us— the interior was given a complete change with the installing of "beautiful baths and all type of electrical compliances . . ." We saw the Konigssee and Berchtesgaden, with its sense of violent power. Hitler would look out of the vast plate-glass window, made by Libby-Owens of Toledo, Ohio, to the splendid smoky mountains circling his eagle's nest, waiting for the foreign diplomats who received their credentials below before taking the elevator up to drink a glass of orange juice with him. Now it was in ruins.

The defendants confided to Dr. Gilbert what they thought of the members of the Tribunal. At the beginning, for the first six or seven weeks of the trial, their attitude was skeptical. They believed that they were destined to be condemned. They would be shot, after the form of a trial had been gone through. Gradually that attitude of hopelessness and despair changed. Lawrence was surprisingly fair, they noted, he even reprimanded the prosecution now and then. On January 10, for instance, he had occasion to suggest to a member of the American prosecution, who was reading into the record extracts from a very long report from Frank to Hitler describing conditions in Poland, that counsel should "make sure that no extracts which they were reading" would "make a misleading impression upon the mind of the Tribunal." I had added, a little more bluntly, "Well, what is not satisfactory to the Tribunal is that you did not give us the real purport of the documents." Frank was impressed, and told Gilbert that it was wonderful how the judges pointed out that one quotation was taken out of context—"So fair! So upright! It restores my faith in human nature." There was a general agreement that one could not fool the judges. Respect for them was growing, even if Göring occasionally made wisecracks about them—he told his lawyer that he thought Lawrence was getting tired and wanted to go back to drink whiskey in London. He thought Parker was a "reasonable gentleman," and had given him a friendly look as he left court that morning. . . . After Göring had been on the stand for the second day, Dönitz said to

Gilbert, "Biddle is really paying attention. You can see that he
wants to hear the other side of the story. I wish I could meet
him after the trial."

Two weeks later Ribbentrop's former secretary, Fräulein Mar-
garete Blank, was testifying on his behalf. She said that his
peaceable intentions regarding Russia were shown by the Non-
aggression Pact of August 1939 and the Trade Agreement of
September 1939. Did she know, Dr. Horn, counsel for Ribbentrop, asked her, whether in addition to these treaties a further
agreement was concluded in Moscow—meaning of course the
famous secret arrangement between Germany and Russia to
split and swallow Poland between them. An attempt had already been made through another witness to introduce evidence
of its contents—apparently no copies were available. General
Rudenko sprang to his feet, instantly objecting to the question:
the evidence was irrelevant, its introduction could not shed a
true light on the events, and could be looked upon only as an
act of provocation.

With that unveiled threat we retired. The matter had already
been discussed in great detail before, and on the part of our
Russian colleague with substantial warmth. For some time it
had been obvious that Moscow would make every effort to keep
the secret agreement out of the trial. We listened to Nikitchenko
for two hours. He insisted that the secret treaty was not only
irrelevant, but the attempt to introduce it was propaganda. We
finally overruled him, returned to our bench, and Lawrence announced to a highly interested audience that the witness might
be questioned about the matter. Then came the anticlimax.
Fräulein Blank knew about the treaty, having seen a special
sealed envelope, which, according to instructions, was filed
separately and bore an inscription "German-Russian Secret or
Additional Agreement." But she did not know its contents! Gilbert notes that the defendants were amused. Fritzsche said,
"What a letdown for the whole court! You ought to have seen
Biddle's face"; and Dönitz added, "You can see that Biddle
wanted that thing brought out, and he was disappointed when
it didn't come out . . . But he has a sense of humor . . . Did you
notice that when Miss Blank said her chief never approached
her he gave Parker a nudge."

Von Papen noted his impressions of the members of the Tribunal in his memoirs. Often critical of the trial he was favorably impressed by the judges. Lawrence he thought had great dignity and authority, although he seldom intervened in the proceedings. He considered the American member "the most intelligent" of the judges, particularly where their "colleague" Jackson was concerned. It was impossible for him to reach any conclusion about the French member: "He never addressed a single question to anyone. All he did was to write, for days, weeks and months on end. His notes must have filled countless volumes." The defendants were not interested in the Russian judge. They knew what his verdict would be—with or without a trial. "The only time any expression crossed his youthful face was when the Russian prosecutor, General Rudenko, got into difficulty . . . when the defense attempted to submit in evidence the agreement providing for the joint partition of Poland . . . Both Nikitchenko and Rudenko seemed to regard this 'bourgeois' procedure as a completely superfluous form of Western comedy."

Nikitchenko distrusted kindness. At the request of Anni Neftrich, our little housemaid at the Villa Conradti, whose husband had been taken prisoner by the Russians, I asked him to inquire when she might expect his return. After eight or nine weeks, the reply, which he had repeated to me exactly, in oral quotes, came back from that other world. "He will be returned when he has finished the work assigned to him." That was all. He shrugged when I asked for some more exact news I could give her, any trace of human feeling sponged from the smooth indifference of his face.

One of the mechanical arrangements permitted members of the Tribunal to cut off their conferences on the bench from the public listening system so that they could confer through interpreters going from one judge to the other, without being overheard. More often than not a question of admissibility of evidence or the like could be settled immediately on the spot without our retiring to discuss it in chambers. A little switch in front of each member controlled this mechanism. If it was down—its usual position—our communications were confidential; if up, they could be heard over the earphones all through the room. On a particular occasion in August, Georg Konrad Morgen was testifying on behalf of the SS, of which he was a member. Herr Horst Pelckmann, who represented the SS, asked him about concentration camps. All this talk about the horrors that went on there was, the witness asserted, grossly exaggerated. "I must say that my first visit to a concentration camp—Buchenwald—was a great surprise to me. The camp was situated on wooded heights, with a wonderful view. The installations were clean and freshly painted. There was much lawn and flowers. The prisoners were healthy, normally fed, sun-tanned, working." There was something singularly unpleasant in hearing this description of one of the cruelest of the camps. The witness said that the camp commander aimed at providing the prisoners with an existence "worthy of human beings." "They had regular mail service. They had a large camp library, even books in foreign languages. They had variety shows, motion pictures, sporting contests. They even had a bordello."

The president of the Tribunal had dozed quietly and unobtrusively, through the flowers and libraries and sporting contests. It was just after lunch. The weather was warm, the testimony droned along monotonously. But when the horrid word was spoken he woke instantly, as telegraphers are known to awake when a particular signal is called.

"What was it they even had?" he asked the witness.

I nudged Lawrence, and as he leaned toward me murmured in his ear, "Brothels, Geoffrey, brothels." But I did not at once realize that in straightening up in my seat one of my waistcoat buttons had caught and pushed up the little lever, so that from that moment on my talk with my learned brother was in the public domain. He had not heard me distinctly. "What?" he asked. "Bordello, brothel, whorehouse," I informed him, raising my voice a little. I was aware of a rising murmur of amusement, half suppressed, flowing to us from all over the room.

"I see," said the president with great dignity. "The witness may proceed."

THE JUDGMENT OF THE TRIBUNAL

❦ Chapter Thirty-two

The British and Americans were worried about the judgment, how it should be written, what it should cover, and particularly who should write it. A disturbing suggestion came from the Russians, and the French at first were not unsympathetic to the idea, that the writing should be equally divided, and each member should take a quarter, dealing as far as possible with the crimes committed against his particular country. How to meet this? Fortunately, after a little investigation of the methods of international courts, we turned up with the useful precedent that it was customary for the presiding judge to draft the opinion and pass it around for comment by his associates. The Russians, who a little defensively and consciously were at times great sticklers for the traditional and the correct, agreed at once.

So theoretically Lawrence wrote the judgment. Actually he farmed it out among a number of us. Birkett wrote the historical portions; and I was responsible for the statement of the law, and for the discussion of the guilt or innocence of the individual defendants.

It was a longish document, over 50,000 words. We were able to do much of the preliminary work in the late spring since by that time nearly all the evidence was in, and my assistants had summarized it as we went along, not only under the names of the defendants to whom it related, but under specific subject topics, such as "The General Conspiracy," "Economic Planning and Mobilization for Aggressive War," "Slave Labor Program," and "War Crimes." There were also summaries of the evidence against the six organizations claimed to be criminal. All of these proved invaluable when we began to prepare the drafts of the judgment —there must have been half a dozen, on the average, of each portion, before they were finally approved by the whole Tribunal. We held our first meeting to consider the judgment on June 27, and continued through September 26, sitting twenty-one times in all. We began discussing the evidence of guilt at the first meeting in June.

Mr. Justice Holmes once said that the brethren (in conferences of his court) occasionally descended to the vernacular. We had become friends over the long months of the trial, and were consequently less reluctant to criticize each other than in those early days in Berlin when, eyeing our opposite numbers politely, yet with a certain national distrust, we had solemnly discussed what we should wear in court. Now we were franker over vital issues. We could and did finally agree, the one recorded dissent being from the Russians, who wrote, in accordance with their instructions, that all of the defendants should have been found guilty.

The extent of these differences was clearest in our discussion over the counts charging conspiracy. From the beginning Donnedieu de Vabres argued with a great deal of force that these counts should be thrown out. Conspiracy, he said, was a crime unknown to international law. Aggressive war could be recognized as a crime though not specifically embedded in a statute; but you couldn't go much beyond that and create a new crime of conspiracy, not recognized by continental law. Conspiracy violated a fundamental principle of French criminal law, that a crime must be precisely defined. Your English crimes, he continued, are more elastic, flowing from precedent and often clothed with no statute. To the French it was a shocking idea that under the wide range of the English law of conspiracy an individual could be punished. The substantive crime, they insisted, absorbs the conspiracy, which becomes useless once the substantive crime is committed, and we have no need to resort to a theory which involves psychological as well as moral difficulties. The Hitlerian crimes have roots deep in the people, that we should not dim their sense of responsibility by shifting the blame to the secret plots of a small group. He moved to strike out count one, the conspiracy charge—to which Falco added that conspiracy was hard to define and difficult to apply. It had neither time nor space. Were there many small conspiracies or one great one? Planning and preparation of a war of aggression were expressly defined as a crime by the Charter, as well as initiating and waging such a war. Was conspiracy to wage war really any different from planning it? Perhaps there was a kind of "chameleon" conspiracy, the generals like Keitel taking on color from Hitler, but surely not sitting down with him as fellow plotters, for they but reflected his announced will. We should abandon our respective national ideas of criminal law and place ourselves squarely on the facts. This "collective tendency" violates every rule of individual right. As for you others the choice was a matter of slight technical interest; but of enormous moral value for us.

Nikitchenko, who had become impatient with what he must have considered all this hairsplitting, and who was inclined to consider the French unrealistic theoreticians who wasted the time of men who had a plain job to do, said, rather tartly, that we were a practical group, not a discussion club. You cannot, he kept repeating, regard this abstractly. Fritzsche, for instance, could not be got if we abandoned the conspiracy count, for his acts in themselves, such as speaking over the radio, were not criminal; and Schacht—Schacht did not wage aggressive war, he joined with the others in conspiring to wage it. Why should we object to this particular innovation? We have allowed others. The Tribunal was not an institution to protect old law and shield old principles from violation. He argued for two hours . . .

But the real difficulty on which we had to focus was not so much any fundamental difference between Anglo-Saxon and continental law, as a determination of where to draw the line. Our law punished conspirators, the French, accomplices: but the result was largely the same. Yet Jackson's theory of the con-

spiracy here involved, dating, as he argued, from the formation
of the Nazi Party, and drawing into the net almost anyone who
was a German, went too far from any reasonable point of view.
The decision must rest on a basic sense of justice in determining
the line that divided those who should be held accountable, and
those who should not. I was therefore sympathetic to the view of
the French, and said so. I would not at present vote any defendant's guilt on the conspiracy charge. I had learned to distrust
conspiracy indictments, which in our country were used too often
by the government to catch anyone however remotely connected
with the substantive crime. I had seen them resorted to, particularly when I was an Assistant U. S. Attorney in Philadelphia,
far too casually and without any clear sense of responsibility. I
remembered criticism of the abuses of the charge of conspiracy
made by the Supreme Court. "So many prosecutors," said Judge
Learned Hand in 1940, "seek to sweep within the dragnet of conspiracy all those who have been associated in any degree whatever with the main offenders."

Parker thought that the conspiracy had been proved "beyond
all peradventure"—he liked such old-fashioned phrases, which,
when he used them, sounded like the crack of a long whip,
tearing the other arguments to shreds. The British were upset by
my stand—it was as if I had deserted them. The heart would
be taken out, Birkett believed, if we rejected conspiracy. From
the beginning the Nazis had planned and worked for war.

My tentative opposition had been somewhat dictated by a
sense of the need for compromise, and finally a compromise was
reached, and I was assigned the task of putting into words our
rather vague agreement. Herbert Wechsler, who knew far more
about the subject than any of us, produced a satisfactory statement, which we used in the judgment. We held that the conspiracy must be "clearly outlined in its criminal purpose" and
not "too far removed from the time of decision and action"; and
concluded that it definitely existed on November 5, 1937, the
date of the famous Hossbach meeting, when Hitler, with Göring,
von Neurath, Admiral Raeder, Field Marshal von Blomberg, and
General von Fritsch made plans for the aggressive invasion of
Europe. The decision to seize Austria and Czechoslovakia was
discussed in some detail; and it was decided to take action as

soon as a favorable opportunity presented itself. "The question for Germany," Hitler said in concluding his remarks, "is where the greatest possible conquest could be made at the lowest cost."

It was curious that the French, usually so consistent and logical, were not much bothered about declaring certain of the organizations criminal. The attribution of the intentions of one person to another, a purely legalistic theory, was basic to both doctrines of conspiracy and of mass crime. But they were fundamentally different. Both the French conception of complicity and the English and American theory of conspiracy involved individual responsibility, even if the scope of conspiracy had been stretched. But mass crime held the individual responsible not for any personal action on his part, but for his membership in a group of which other members had been guilty.

The Charter permitted the Tribunal to declare criminal certain groups or organizations of which a defendant was a member; and provided that, where this declaration had been made, any of the four signatory powers might try an individual for such membership, and in that trial the criminal nature of the organization could not be questioned. Parker and I were exceedingly worried about this provision. The only fact that need be proved was the naked fact of membership. After that had been established any defense was automatically ruled out. Millions of members in the Gestapo, the SA, the SS, and the political organizations could be handled, after our trial was over, by this neat device. It was a startling application of the doctrine of guilt by association (a phrase not yet current) on an international level.

Justice Jackson pointed out in his preface to the record of the international negotiations which led up to the Nürnberg trial, published by the State Department in 1947, under the title of *International Conference on Military Trials*, that this procedure was proposed "as a basis for reaching the members in later trials . . . at which the Tribunal's findings as to the criminal character of the organizations would be conclusive on that question." He added: "No other plan had been devised for reaching the multitudes who, as members of such organizations as the Gestapo and SS, promoted and executed the Nazi criminal program."

Analyzed, this is a startling proposal to anyone taking for granted our principles of justice. You have neither the time, the patience, nor the evidence to prove the guilt of several million Nazis. You therefore prove that a group is criminal, and catch all of the members that way. To establish the criminality of the group you show that certain of its members committed crimes. Then you say once this group crime is established every member of the group can be tried for membership in a criminal body, but when he is tried he will not be allowed to prove that the body was in fact not criminal, or that he was ignorant of its purposes.

Jackson said that this was one of the essential features of the Yalta proposal "put forth" by Secretary of War Stimson, Secretary of State Stettinius, and myself as Attorney General. But the proposal, as I have said, was never discussed at Yalta. It had been submitted to the President on January 22, 1945, two weeks before Yalta, and at that time seemed to us justified in the light of events. It suggested that "in view of the nature of the charges and the representative character of the defendants . . . the findings . . . should justly be taken to constitute a general adjudication of the criminal character of groups and organizations . . . binding upon all the members thereof in their subsequent trials in occupation courts." What chiefly influenced our judgment—I remember that Assistant Secretary of War John J. McCloy had worked the plan up for Secretary Stimson—was the shooting of American officers and soldiers after their surrender at Malmédy by an SS regiment, acting under orders. Proof of individual guilt in such a case would have been extremely difficult. It seemed just to hold the SS guilty. But you can't punish a regiment, you can punish only a man. The recommendation, I became convinced when I began to study it again, was wrong.

The question of complicity was no longer theoretical, as it had been when I discussed it with my American associates coming over on the *Queen Elizabeth*. For the Control Council of Germany, made up of representatives of the four occupying powers, had adopted a law providing that membership in an organization determined by our Tribunal to be criminal was a crime, punishable, in the discretion of the occupation court of any of the four powers, by penalties ranging from deprivation of civil

rights to imposition of the death sentence. The crime of the
organization was imputed to him. He could defend only against
the naked fact of membership.

The prosecution defended its position by arguing to the Tribunal that a provision in the Charter required that notice of the
"indictment" of the organizations should be published, so that
members would have a chance to defend, and would have their
day in court. This notice was published in the four zones of
occupation. It was distributed and posted in internment camps,
printed in newspapers, and announced over the radio. Individuals were given the opportunity to file affidavits denying the
alleged guilt of the group to which they belonged. Soon these
began to pour in by the thousand. Lieutenant Colonel Neave
was appointed a special commissioner by the Tribunal to receive
and process the affidavits and arrange for witnesses, many of
whom were selected by counsel for the organizations from the
internment camps. The flow of work was so large that a special
building had to be set apart to house the translators and clerks.
Most of the affidavits denied that the member making the
affidavit had committed any crime. When the time limit for receiving them expired on August 5 the total number submitted
was 313,213! Of these it is interesting that the greatest amount,
155,000, were filed by members of the Leadership Corps, 136,213
by members of the SS, while only 2000 came from the Gestapo.
They were summarized and the summaries submitted to the
Tribunal in addition to the oral evidence of twenty-two witnesses.

The evidence indicated the impossible problems of classification that would be presented when the powers attempted to
make use of any declaration of group criminality that we might
declare. Was a janitor in a building operated by the Gestapo, a
former clerk of the SA, every soldier in the thirty-five divisions
of the SS—were they all to be condemned for membership
alone?

I moved to drop the charges against the organizations. It was
shocking, I argued, somewhat as the French had argued with
reference to the conspiracy charges, to convict men without trial,
which was exactly what we would be doing. The French saw the
point, but thought that public opinion in France would never

understand our refusing to declare the Gestapo and the SS to be criminal. The British did not seem to have any particular qualms —Lawrence indeed believed the matter to be basically one of procedure.

I suggested a formula which I had worked out with my assistants, and which the Tribunal finally adopted: each organization declared criminal was defined to include persons "who became or remained members of the organization with knowledge that it was being used for the commissions of acts declared criminal by . . . the Charter." This in effect took the teeth out of the finding, and in substance restored the necessity of proving individual guilt. I would have much preferred to chuck out the whole business. The Gestapo and the SS, under this formula, were found to be criminal organizations, and the charges against the other three groups were dropped.

The judgment reflected our doubts. "This is a far-reaching and novel procedure," we said. "Its application, unless properly safeguarded, may produce great injustice." We even went a little farther than a strict interpretation of our powers might have warranted, and recommended, largely on the insistence of the French, that the four occupation zones establish uniformity of sentencing. My French colleague wanted the Tribunal to fix the penalties that could be applied by the occupation courts. But the rest of us thought that we had no right to "legislate," and that "recommendation" was as far as our powers could be stretched.

All of this talk the Russians considered a waste of time. They were not the least interested in what we said about international law or future trials. They wanted us to declare criminal all six groups, which the prosecution had requested should be so branded. And one felt, particularly in those closing days as they approached the kill, how little distinction was drawn by the Soviet members between prosecution and court. They were but complementary arms of the state, with the same common end. A conviction was the logical, the essential result of an indictment. Differences between political and legal functions disappeared; between political and judicial; and, finally between political and moral.

The Soviet point of view was well illustrated by General Nikitchenko's original reaction, when he was acting as the Soviet representative at the negotiations which led up to the execution of the Charter, to the suggestion that certain organizations might be declared criminal. He was opposed to it—such organizations as the SS and the Gestapo "had already been declared criminal by authorities higher than the Tribunal"—the Allies had spoken in the Moscow and Crimea declarations, and the criminality established. He could not imagine a situation in which the Tribunal could hold them innocent when they had been labeled criminal by the Allied governments. Finally he agreed to the proposal, although the "automatic provision that because one has been convicted all other members are thereby pronounced guilty" was not familiar to Soviet criminal law. When it came to the judgment he construed the provision of the Charter, which required a vote of three to one for a conviction, to mean that where there was a tie it did not result in an acquittal (as in the case of Schacht), but was inconclusive, leaving the guilt or innocence undetermined, in effect an invitation to a further trial. Nikitchenko's motion to that effect was voted down; and he requested that his motion and dissent be noted on our "secret record."

Given this point of view, Soviet irritation at what appeared to be irrelevant to the central theme was understandable. When Professor Donnedieu de Vabres introduced, and reintroduced at the drop of any hat, his theory of the appropriate classification of the prison sentences which we should impose—different treatment should be accorded those we considered "political" prisoners—Nikitchenko was irritated. "Don't let us get into such ridiculous trifles!" he exclaimed; and added that hanging should be the rule, shooting the rare exception.

Our judgment in all cases, strive as we might to base it solely on the weight of the evidence, was inevitably conditioned by conflicting currents of prejudice and policy. We were a jury as well as a court; and we could not altogether exclude from our consideration the effects of our decision on popular opinion. Largely unconscious with the British and Americans, these mental processes were recognized and spoken of frankly by the French, who thought, for instance, that it would be "unwise" not to sentence every defendant, even if some of the sentences of those whose acquittal had been urged were very light. The enormity of the crimes, Donnedieu de Vabres continued, was impressive irrespective of their personal guilt. But since the law was new we must proceed with prudence and moderation (Nikitchenko's face at that remark, shriveled and hardened). He did not like to acquit von Papen, continued the French member, even if he had not been successfully tied into the crimes, the way the others had, for was he not a "corrupting creature"? Schacht's impulse, he thought, partook less of nobility than of his jealousy of Göring, who, although a high-class brigand, had "a certain nobility."

I tried several times to write out a definition of aggressive war, and found it an impossible task. An act of self-defense might be "aggressive," striking first to prevent the enemy's act of invasion, for instance, but not in the sense we meant. Germany's planning and waging a war of conquest was so clear that definition, except as guidance for future decisions, was unnecessary, and might be dangerous by going too far or not giving enough latitude for unforeseen occasions. Geoffrey Lawrence, who like me was bred on the common law, shared this empirical point of view, and agreed to abandon any attempt to set up a definition. To my surprise the French, who, with their passion for precise codifying, might have been expected to press for a definition, were of the same opinion.

On a point of style the French, particularly Falco, and I felt alike. I thought that the way we expressed ourselves was of importance, and objected to some of the clichés that had crept into the earlier drafts—"an event of the highest possible significance," "it shocked the conscience of the world." Avoid emotional expressions, I urged the others; let the facts speak for themselves. The facts said so much more than anything we could say about them. The Russians on the contrary liked extreme language and raw details, and Volchkov wanted us to underscore such gruesome items of evidence as the use of human skin from backs and chests, chemically treated and placed in the sun to dry, before it was "cut into various sizes for use as saddles, riding breeches, gloves, house slippers, and ladies' handbags." As far as style went, Nikitchenko insisted that whenever the word "honorary" was used in relation to a defendant—and the defendants bristled with honorary Party titles—it must be stricken out. The Germans were not and could not be honorary, our repeated explanations of the difference between the meaning of that word and of "honorable" to the contrary notwithstanding. Lawrence wanted the word "labor" spelled "labour" throughout; and we at once concluded a gentlemen's agreement on the point, to which he seemed to attach a minor emotional value.

Nikitchenko could not understand his French associate's humane approach, his uncertainties, his reluctances, as when he pleaded that Schacht was an old man, and if we imposed any sentence it should be a light one. The British were for an acquittal—Schacht's defense had been impressive. He had been sent to a concentration camp by Hitler for eighteen months, and had been a member of the rather ineffectual group whose conspiracy to kill Hitler had failed in 1944. Schacht was not charged with any crime involving atrocities. To the English he was a respectable man, a banker, not like these other ruffians; and they finally persuaded Donnedieu de Vabres to go along with them, against the Russian view, which I shared, that Schacht had been active in the preparation for aggressive war, a powerful and necessary link in the chain which he helped Hitler forge, and that he should receive a severe sentence. It was then agreed, the British still holding out for an acquittal, that Schacht should receive a term of eight years.

But the next day Donnedieu de Vabres announced that he had changed his mind. Obviously the British had persuaded him. The vote being a tie, Schacht was acquitted. Jim Rowe urged me to file a dissenting opinion, to keep the record straight. The assumption that I had gone along with the British might come up to plague me later. But I do not believe in dissents, any more than resignations, simply to make one's position clear, particularly in this case where international team-play was important —my dissent could not influence the decision. On the other hand if Dönitz had been sentenced on the basis of his submarine activities I would have dissented with all possible vigor—unity or no unity! One cannot always go along.

As the end drew near and the time for the delivery of the judgment and sentences approached, even Göring's factitious gaiety grew thin and forced, and finally deserted him. Schacht looked tired and old, but his *sang-froid* never left him, and his back was like a ramrod. The tragedy of Germany had settled deep in the soul of Speer. Little Funk cried more, and Streicher kept on howling at night. The fear of death turned Ribbentrop to parchment, drawn and sallow between the points of chin and cheeks.

The reading of the judgment, a part of it in turn by each member, was finished on October 1, 1946, by the time to recess for lunch. Three men had been acquitted—Schacht, Fritsche, and the wily old diplomat, Franz von Papen—and were moved to cells on the third tier. The others were waiting to hear their sentences. Fritsche, Gilbert records, was overwhelmed. "Free . . . and not even sent back to Russia" (the Russians had captured him).

The defendants who had been convicted were called after the recess to be sentenced. Standing there before us they behaved like men. I felt sick and miserable. We had seen them day-in day-out for a year. What right had I . . . I knew they deserved it. Göring, who was the first to be sentenced, saluted when Lawrence pronounced his fate: "Defendant Hermann Wilhelm Göring, on the counts of the indictment on which you have been convicted, the International Military Tribunal sentences you to death by hanging." Göring was glad that he had not got a life sentence, he said to Dr. Gilbert—those who were sentenced to life never went down to history as martyrs. How soon he would cheat the law, his thumb to his nose, pulling the phial of cyanide of potassium from some secret crevice in the folds of his vast flesh! The slave labor chief, Fritz Sauckel, when he got to his cell, said to Gilbert, "Death! I have never been cruel myself. But I am a man—and I can take it"—and burst into tears. Speer thought his sentence of twenty years was fair enough, he was glad Fritsche had been acquitted . . . Kaltenbrunner, sentenced to death, tried to kiss his mistress and mother of his two children through the grille of the visitors' room.

Grand Admiral Raeder, who had been sentenced to life imprisonment, petitioned the Allied Control Council to change his sentence to death by shooting—the resistance of his body was low, he said, and his imprisonment would not last very long. The Control Council had the power only to decrease sentences; and

Raeder added that he would regard such a change as "an act of mercy." At Spandau he acted as librarian, fussy and meticulous, liking to repeat the German saying: "A disorderly ship reflects incapability." He was fond of gardening. He was recently released, and is still living at eighty as I write this.

Eleven defendants were condemned to death by hanging. Julius Streicher, a moment before he died, heiled Hitler, and from the gallows screamed, "Purim, 1946!" Haman, too, the cruel Persian minister, had planned to kill the Jews living in his country, 2500 years ago. But when the Emperor Xerxes heard of his intentions, Haman and his ten sons were put to death on the gallows that had been erected for their victims.

Immediately after returning to the United States I saw President Truman and, at his request, submitted a written report on the trial. It seemed to me essential to emphasize that aggressive war—war to conquer territory and subdue populations—necessarily results in the kind of savagery in which the German leaders indulged, the torture rooms of the Gestapo and the concentration camps. The unity of action for which the President had hoped a year ago, when he had appointed us, had been realized, and the fundamental principles of international law stated unanimously in the judgment, as a result of a mutual confidence between the members, which had been achieved only slowly. We were not interrupted by other engagements. We stayed in Nürnberg for a year, until the job was done, sitting six hours a day in court, holding private sessions three or four times a week to iron out differences and keep the work current. From the beginning we established a rule which was rigidly adhered to that no member should talk to the press or give interviews. In my opinion these rather simple practices accounted for the confidence and co-operation that resulted.

Nor was the unity affected by the dissent of the U.S.S.R. It expressed no disagreement with the fundamental principles of international law, in which General Nikitchenko joined. The dissent was over the inference that should be drawn from conflicting evidence—a healthy difference.

What did Nürnberg accomplish? Within a year and a half after the end of the war the major war criminals were tried and punished. The trial was fair and stayed the hand of vengeance. Some said the trial was too long, yet the trial of Warren Hastings ran from 1788 to 1795.

The law of nations, I suggested, which had been the base and background of the judgment, in its practical application had become sterile and academic. The judgment formulated judicially for the first time the proposition that aggressive war was criminal, and should be so treated. It would be naïve to think that because of such pronouncement war would be outlawed. But at least aggressive war, which was once so romantic, was now a crime. "Nations have come to realize," I wrote, "that it means the death not only of individual human beings, but of whole nations, not only with defeat, but in the slow degradation and decay of civilized life that follows that defeat."

I concluded by recommending that the United Nations affirm the principles of the Nürnberg Charter and Judgment, and that the time had come to set about drafting—most cautiously—a code of international criminal law.

President Truman, in a generous and appreciative letter, expressed his hope that the governments of the United Nations might undertake such a code. He ended by saying that to my work I had "brought experience, great learning, a judicial temperament and a prodigious capacity for work. You have earned my thanks and the thanks of the Nation for this great service." This tribute pleased me, and I do not think it was *pro forma*. Yet I had no experience in this field, and nothing that could by any friendly stretch be called learning. Whether my temperament is judicial I do not know. The capacity to work I admit.

Charles Fahy, who was then counsel for the State Department and a member of the United States delegation to UN, introduced an appropriate resolution in that body, which affirmed "the principles of international law recognized by the Charter of the Nürnberg Tribunal and the judgment of the Tribunal," and directed its Committee of International Law to proceed with the codification of an International Criminal Code embodying the principles recognized in the Charter. No international code has ever been adopted, although considerable progress has been made on a code setting up a permanent court to try international offenses, and defining its powers and jurisdiction. *Ad hoc* tribunals obviously suffer from the fact that they must be hastily fashioned to fit particular occasions. A permanent court, whose members might be called upon from time to time when the occasion arose, would be preferable. Definition, moreover, of the adjective and procedural law governing such a tribunal is a much easier undertaking than any attempt to define the substance of international criminal law—an undertaking about which Justice Jackson was rightly skeptical. I am inclined to think that the most fruitful approach would be to push the procedural codification, and to allow substantive law, already largely defined and accepted in the scope of the Nürnberg judgment, to grow empirically, from case to case. Even though nothing can be formulated in the present state of mutual international distrust, there is nothing to prevent the professors and experts having a whack at it, to clear the way for the political statesmen when they are ready, rather cautiously, to begin to act.

The Charter defined as a crime against peace the "planning, preparation, initiation or *waging* of a war of aggression." Those who framed it had in mind, it may be supposed, the punishment of the men who were responsible for unleashing war against a world at peace. They obviously did not mean to authorize the indictment of everyone who had taken part in that war. Such a construction would have been absurd, and yet the words "waging a war of aggression" taken literally would have permitted the trial of any soldier who under the compulsion of patriotism or law fought in the armed services. I believe the essence of the crime should be *starting* war. This in effect the Tribunal determined when it came to consider Speer's guilt. He became head of the armament industry, the judgment pointed out, well after the aggressive wars had begun, and his activities were carried on in the same way as other efforts in the waging of war. The Tribunal refused to find that such activities involved "engaging in the common plan to wage aggressive war as charged." We had a good deal of difficulty with this, and determined to hold down so far as possible the scope of this very broad language, bearing in mind its possible future application.

The attacks on the trial from lawyers as well as laymen came chiefly from ignorance of the law on which it was based. This was an *ad hoc* military trial, in substance a court-martial; and, although the Tribunal was far more judicial than most courts-martial, we were not judges of a court in the strict sense, but members of a tribunal appointed by the heads of states. The President in selecting Parker and me acted in his capacity as Commander in Chief of the Armed Forces. Recognition of this fact largely disposes of one of the most commonly repeated objections to the makeup of the Tribunal—that it was composed of victors instead of neutrals. Courts-martial are always composed of members of the victorious nation, and I have never heard it suggested that Major André or the German saboteurs should have been tried by other than Americans; or that the subsequent trials of Germans by English, French, and American tribunals in Germany were improper because outside "judges" were not brought in to try them.

Another common misunderstanding was that the trial involved the principle that soldiers might be executed for obeying orders. The generals Keitel and Jodl were executed not for obeying orders, but for giving them. The defendants were the leaders of Nazi Germany carrying out by personal orders the ruthless and barbarous program of their Führer. Others had objected and were permitted to retire. Moral choice was not impossible. There was no evidence that they ever exercised the kind of resistance that might have been expected from decent men. Superior orders were never recognized as a complete defense in civil courts. Military manuals in Great Britain and the United States usually stated that they were an excuse, unless manifestly illegal. But in European law they have been and should be construed only as a mitigating factor in imposing sentence. So the judgment held.

The *ex post facto* argument, so current at the time in the mouths of the misinformed, likewise issued from a lack of understanding of the theory of *ex post facto*, or of existing international law. The rubric *nullum crimen et nulla poena sine lege* did not mean that a crime had to be defined and its punishment fixed by statute before the offender could be tried. It meant that some law must exist before it could be said to have been violated. Otherwise the English common law of crimes could never have developed. Murder and treason were punished by courts in the

Middle Ages long before they were incorporated into statute. As Mr. Justice Cardozo wrote in 1934: "International law has at times, like the common law within states, a twilight existence during which it is ; ardly distinguishable from morality or justice, till at length the imprimatur of a court attests its jural quality." The condition of international criminal law—the law of war, as it has often been called—was in 1946 not unlike English criminal law in its formative period. The only real question was whether aggressive war was considered criminal.

On that point there has been a good deal of informed discussion. Without referring in detail to the statutes and international resolutions which expressed the general recognition that aggressive war was a crime, it may once again be emphasized that the Hague Convention of 1907 outlawed certain acts of war, without stating that they were crimes; and that thereafter they were recognized as criminal and punished accordingly: poisoning wells, shooting prisoners, improper use of a white flag. No penalties were fixed, no court existed. That, generally speaking, has been true of all crimes resulting from the conduct of war.

Among the Allies after Germany was beaten there were those who advocated "political action," as they called it—that is shooting a number of selected Germans without trying them. But for what reason? Would it have been more just to dispose of them by this simple expedient, without even connecting them with the atrocities that had been committed? Such a suggestion smacks of Nazi technique, and would have been in violation of the American articles of war, which specify that prisoners when captured shall not be executed without court-martial. A drumhead court-martial then: and the objection to the trial boils down to saying that the defendants were condemned after too long a consideration of their guilt, and with too much deliberation. Careful deliberation may offend taste, but can hardly be said to violate justice. A "political" execution would have served as a punishment, but not for the three other chief purposes of the Nürnberg proceeding: to enforce the rules of international law; to make them a reality through the co-operation of the Allies; and to leave a record of the horrors that this last and greatest of all wars had brought in its wake.

When I got home Walter Lippmann wrote me: "Welcome back after your long labors. I am sure that you know that the result has been accepted as complete vindication of the whole idea and effort. I am one of many who are very proud indeed of you."

On the other hand Senator Robert Taft's reaction was strangely violent for such a moderate conservative. He declared that the verdicts constituted vengeance and were a blot on American justice. I suspect that Mr. Taft was moved into this sincere intemperance by a growing resentment that the world was moving from the age of nationalism to the age of internationalism, and from isolationism to universal law. That struck to the depths of his being.

Two years later, when I was delivering a course of lectures at the invitation of the Walgreen Foundation at the University of Chicago, Julius Klein asked me to discuss the Nürnberg trial at a luncheon given in my honor. Among those whom he invited was Robert R. McCormick, editor and publisher of the Chicago *Tribune*. Mr. McCormick's secretary wrote to Mr. Klein declining; and added that Mr. McCormick asked her to say that "he would not dine with a murderer . . . " Sewell L. Avery, chairman of the board and president of Montgomery Ward, was more polite. He could not come, alas, as he would have liked to see Mr. Biddle again, since Mr. Biddle in 1943 had done more than anyone else to put and keep Mr. Avery on the map!

Another distinguished Republican and conservative, Henry L. Stimson, of very different outlook and quality from Senator Taft, looking to the future saw in the "great undertaking at Nürnberg" a long step ahead on the only upward road. "The central moral problem," he wrote, "is war and not its methods. A continuance of war will in all probability end with the destruction of our civilization." And Mr. Stimson himself had been twice Secretary of War of the United States.

Curiously enough, little attention was paid to what was perhaps the Tribunal's most important pronouncement. I refer to the finding that individuals and not merely nations should be held responsible. Responsibility of the individual for piracy and for violations of the laws of war has long been established. Once it is found that aggressive war is a crime it follows that heads of a state may be punished for their share in starting such a war.

In making responsibility an individual matter, as it must be made if the substance is to be achieved and not merely the rhetoric of law, the Tribunal rejected the fiction of national irresponsibility.

This is no new discovery, but once more the lesson that emerges—if we are to find a simple meaning and above all a moral one—is that what is humane and individual in human beings must be nourished to prevent the sources of violence from engulfing the world. The resort to aggressive war which we punished at Nürnberg was that betrayal of human decency which follows the surrender of the individual to the external and mechanical power of the police state. It is for that reason that the preservation of individual freedom, of personal integrity, alone can keep alive the human spirit. For when that spirit is extinguished there follows the inevitable resort to power for power's sake. The machine state moves in to take the place of men and women and children. The machine does not live and breathe. It cannot know pity or love. Reverence is gone. The machine has no heart, no blood, no flesh, no bowels of compassion. But the machine can kill, it can torture, and can clean out ghettos "with merciless tenacity." As William Butler Yeats has written:

> Mere anarchy is loosed upon the world,
> The blood-dimmed tide is loosed, and everywhere
> The ceremony of innocence is drowned. . . .

· · · ·

The Nürnberg trial was the last of my public jobs—unless I count my rather leisurely and extended chairmanship of the Franklin Delano Roosevelt Memorial Commission, to which President Eisenhower appointed me on November 9, 1955, at the suggestion of Lyndon B. Johnson, who was then leader of the Senate, and Sam Rayburn, the Speaker of the House. Just before I left Nürnberg, President Truman cabled me:

> I wonder whether you would be interested in accepting the position of Secretary General of UNESCO. I understand headquarters are to be in Paris and that your appointment would be looked upon with favor by the British and French governments as well as the people of this country. I would appreciate your early advice. Regards.

I answered that I was interested, and that I would talk to him immediately after my return. I went to see the temporary UNESCO offices that had been set up in London and Paris. My guide from the Foreign Office seemed rather cool to the project as he took me about, in a maddeningly British way, and I heard as soon as I got home that the British would not back me. They had their own candidate, Sir Julian Huxley, the English biologist and educator. The President had been misinformed by the State Department, while the English went quietly about picking up votes for their man. When I arrived in Washington late in October the State Department, still sublimely ignorant of what was going on, urged me to join Archibald MacLeish, the acting chairman of the American delegation to UNESCO and Assistant Secretary of State William Benton, when they went to Paris for the organization meeting, which was to elect the director general. I was told that it was all lined up, and that the Americans had a substantial majority of the votes of the forty-four member nations. But I declined to get on a boat before I had been elected.

Meanwhile a good deal of behind-the-scene jockeying went on. The British argued that I knew nothing about education, to which my backers replied that I certainly did—witness my former membership on the Philadelphia Board of Education! A British delegate remarked, "You cannot educate the world with Bob Hope and Mickey Mouse." The Americans insisted that Huxley was far too much to the left—was he not a professed atheist, who favored birth control and eugenic mating? The Europeans laughed, and suggested that the election of Huxley was one way of bringing in a reluctant Russia.

When Archie MacLeish and Bill Benton had taken a look at the situation after their arrival in Paris, the State Department arranged for me to have a teletype conference with them. The French, Benton said, were tapping all telephone conversations, and he had refused to take any telephone calls. My chances were about fifty-fifty, and they would not now advise me to make reservations. The British were convinced they had the votes, "and we have no evidence that we have them." The opposition to Huxley was rising among the religious groups and the scientists. But also there was a growing fear of "American cultural imperialism—Hollywood, etc."

James F. Byrnes, who was then Secretary of State, thought that my name should not be presented formally unless there was a prior understanding that I would be elected. This could not be given, my name was withdrawn, and Julian Huxley was elected on the understanding that he would resign after two years (the term was seven). Archie MacLeish, who had served as first American member of the council was popular and would have been acceptable to the delegates, but he would not agree to being nominated.

I was soon destined for another disappointment. President Truman, a few weeks after the UNESCO fiasco, appointed me, subject to confirmation by the Senate, to be United States representative on the United Nations Economic and Social Council, to succeed Ambassador John G. Winant, who had just resigned. Senator Austin Warren, a Republican from Vermont, and an old friend who had constantly supported my recommendations as Attorney General to the Judiciary Committee, of which he was a member, had recently been confirmed as our delegate on the Security Council; and under the act of Congress would be the senior representative to whom the rest would report. But he apparently had little influence with the chairman of the Foreign Relations Committee, Senator Arthur H. Vandenberg. The Republicans had come into power on the Hill in the 1946 election. David F. Lilienthal's nomination for chairman of the Atomic Energy Commission was pending, and was violently opposed—Vandenberg got him through the committee and supported him in the Senate. Having stuck his head out to back one ardent New Dealer it was not unnatural that he should be less enthusiastic about another. William L. Clayton, who was then Under Secretary of State, and with whom I had worked closely at the end of the war in connection with postwar policies, wrote to the Senator urging confirmation. Vandenberg replied at some length giving the reasons for his opposition. "Mr. Biddle is looked upon by many important Republican Senators as a veritable symbol of the New Deal; and they consider they have a mandate from last November's election against the perpetuation of these symbols. You have ample evidence of this fact in the Lilienthal case

. . . I have enough of the Administration's problems on my hands without making myself responsible for the high irritation which this controversy would involve." Lilienthal was confirmed and I was not. If a choice had to be made it was fortunate that it fell that way. I never resented Senator Vandenberg's opposition, as I understood his reasons, and admired his responsible leadership in foreign affairs that followed his famous speech in the Senate in 1945 in which he renounced his isolationism, and became a supporter of bipartisanship in foreign policy. It was generally believed in Washington that James ("Scotty") Reston of the New York *Times* had much to do in convincing the Senator to change, and helped him write the speech. This took courage, since Vandenberg might have been ruined politically.

Harry Truman stuck to his friends—and apparently I had become one of them. He offered to appoint me ambassador to South Africa, but I could not see it, and neither Katherine nor I would have been happy in a country where apartheid was practiced.

I considered accepting one of the more interesting offers to go back to practice, this time in Washington. But I had lost touch with the law, after an absence of ten years, and the daily routine of office work did not tempt me at sixty-one. My new "freedom" was not easy to endure for the first few years. Writing and lecturing kept me moderately busy, and I have had leisure to do the pleasant, casual things for which there is not much space or time in the tight schedule of ordinary American life. At first one misses the harness; but not after the new experience becomes sustained as a more suitable way of life as the years advance—a busy, occupied leisure.

We live in Washington half the year, and spend the other half on the lower end of Cape Cod. I never grow tired of the beauty and relaxed ease of Georgetown, and like the funny things that happen there. When I came back from Nürnberg children had stopped writing To Hell With Hitler on the walls of houses, and were announcing solemnly Kilroy Was Here. Later some small fry ventured: I Don't Like Mrs. Smith (a teacher of mathematics, lower grades); and when the supporters of that lady rubbed out this insult, the chalk lettering that took its place was less restrained—Mrs. Smith Stinks!

We spend long summers on Bound Brook Island in Wellfleet, the most contained, remote, and charming spot on Cape Cod. Where we live the land is untamed, with sandy roads that for the most part do not lead anywhere. Our walks bring us through tangled locust and scrub oak and swamp alder between the little dunes down to the bay. We own an old house, with Indian shutters inside the window frames; and arrowheads on rare occasions turn up in the beds of September lilies, and once we found a pair of steel-rimmed spectacles, almost intact, like those that Benjamin Franklin wore. Around the house, quail, fat and unhurried, call to us from their cover; now and then a red fox lopes across the island road; and last summer a young doe jumped in front of our car at night on our way back from dinner with my brother George at Truro.

There are, I suppose, as many cocktail parties on the Cape as in Washington, although the people who go to them are of a different kind—in the District of Columbia diplomats and columnists, representatives of the governments in exile (just now Republicans), the best newspapermen in the world, those who have yielded to the temptation of public service as a career, and others who are taking it as a temporary adventure. At our end of the Cape one rubs elbows with musicians and painters and writers: Xavier Gonzales, Gardner Jencks, Edward Dickinson, Ed O'Connor, Edmund Wilson, Waldo Frank, and Arthur Schlesinger, Jr., relaxed and smiling in spite of the strain of Washington—and a long-haired pretty beatnik now and then, with overalls and dirty feet, whose mission is to remind us older birds not to be too Goddamn fussy . . .

The law creating a park on the lower Cape was adopted a year ago, and our house is included. Perhaps the dunes with their delicate lines and tracery can be preserved from the careless tramp of the vacation crowd. Perhaps we can teach our children reverence toward the world of nature, yielding to her natural rights. I do not wish to see the lower Cape turned into a suburb of Boston. The long problem of the future is the relation of swarming mankind to this little planet that they have overrun and despoiled.

INDEX

70
71
72
74
75
76
77
79
81
83
85

WILLIAM BIDDLE (1630-1712)
m. Sarah Kemp. They came to America in 1681.

|

WILLIAM BIDDLE (1669-1743)

|

JOHN BIDDLE (1707-1789)

|

CLEMENT BIDDLE (1740 - 1814)
"The Quaker Soldier," m. Rebekah Cornell.
Clement's grandmother, Lydia Wardell, was the grand-
daughter of Samuel Wardell, who was burned
as a wizard in Salem in 1692.

|

CLEMENT CORNELL BIDDLE (1784-1855)

|

GEORGE WASHINGTON BIDDLE (1818-1897)
my grandfather, m. Maria Coxe McMurtrie

|

GEORGE BIDDLE (1843-1886)
m. Mary Hosack Rodgers ("Aunt Minnie")

MONCURE BIDDLE (1882-1956)   GEORGE BIDDLE
(1885-)